**Soldiers
West**

SOLDIERS WEST

Biographies
from the
Military
Frontier

Edited by

Paul Andrew Hutton

Introduction by

Robert M. Utley

University of Nebraska Press
Lincoln and London

The paper in this book meets
the minimum requirements of American
National Standard for Information
Sciences—Permanence of Paper
for Printed Library Materials,
ANSI z39.48–1984.

Library of Congress Cataloging-in-Publication Data
Soldiers West.
    Includes index.
    1. Soldiers—West (U.S.)—Biography.
2. Generals—West (U.S.)—Biography.
3. United States. Army—Biography.
4. Frontier and pioneer life—West (U.S.)
5. West (U.S.)—Biography.
6. West (U.S.)—History, Military.
I. Hutton, Paul A. (Paul Andrew), 1949–
F591.S668 1987   978'.02'0922 [B]   86–19283
ISBN 0-8032-2334-X (alk. paper)
ISBN 0-8032-7225-1 (pbk.)

Contents

Maps

Preface

by Paul Andrew Hutton

Few topics in frontier history have generated as much popular and scholarly interest as the military conquest of the trans-Mississippi West. It is an important story, replete with heroes and villains, glory and infamy, triumph and tragedy. Elements of American popular culture — the novels of Charles King, the paintings of Remington and Schreyvogel, the movies of John Ford — have imprinted an enduring image of rugged men in dusty blue manning far-flung outposts that formed a picket line of civilization. In recent times that heroic image has been sullied by charges of genocide and military brutality. Both popular images, of course, have elements of truth in them, but neither is correct. The story of the military frontier of the American West is far more complex.

It is the intent of this book to investigate the nature of the military role in the trans-Mississippi West by exploring the lives of key military figures. The following chapters vividly portray the wide diversity in style, temperament, activity, and occupation that marked the careers of officers on the military frontier. The subjects for essays were chosen because of their significance in frontier military history; their usefulness as an example of an occupational type; and their place within chronological and regional frontier development. The scope has been limited to the trans-Mississippi frontier, with an emphasis on the post–Civil War period because military activity was more intense there after 1865.

An effort was made to include army officers whose biographies represent the diversity of roles performed by the military on the frontier. There are, of course, many other prominent and important officers who could have been included. Nevertheless, I hope that this collection will serve to give a good overview of the soldier as explorer, topographer, engineer, administrator, writer, scientist, combat officer, policy maker, and subaltern. The biographies cover the period from 1800 to 1900, and run from the most important early miltary explorer to cross the Mississippi River to the officer who investigated the military role at Wounded Knee in 1890, and from the officer who first created the popular vision of a "Great American Desert" to the soldier-chronicler who fashioned a lasting image of knightly, self-sacrificing frontier soldiers in his novels.

Robert M. Utley opens this anthology with a provocative essay on the nature of the military frontier and its contribution to the American military tradition. He contends that this military tradition—policy, doctrine, thought, and institutions—has been profoundly influenced by what the frontier has contributed and also by what it has failed to contribute.

William Clark, as presented in the essay by Jerome O. Steffen, is, of course, a fine example of the soldier as explorer. But more important, according to Steffen, was Clark's role as an imperial soldier who performed as a politician, Indian agent, militia general, and ardent expansionist. As such, Clark is a transitional figure between the civilian-oriented army officers of the cis-Mississippi frontier, such as William Henry Harrison and Andrew Jackson, and the professional soldiers of the ante-bellum era. Although he resigned from the regular army in 1807, just after the completion of the Lewis and Clark expedition, Clark promptly accepted a commission as brigadier general of militia for Louisiana (later Missouri) Territory. During the War of 1812 General Clark was responsible for protecting the nation's western territories. After the war he devoted most of his time to Indian affairs and to promoting the western fur trade. Throughout his long career Clark acted as an agent of expansion for the republic, although he eventually found himself out of step with national policy.

Stephen H. Long's major contribution to the development of the ante-bellum military frontier was as an explorer. He spent his military career almost entirely in the topographical engineers, a branch of the service he came to command just before his retirement in 1863. In 1817 he explored the upper Mississippi River; in 1820 he led an expedition along the Platte River to the front range of the Rockies, exploring the Arkansas River country on his way back east; and in 1823 he explored the Minnesota River and the northern national boundary to the Great Lakes. He was actively involved in the construction of eastern railroads in the 1830s and 1840s, publishing several tracts on railroad bridges and grades. As Roger L. Nichols points out in his essay, this straying between the public and private sector was not an unfamiliar pattern for military officers.

William S. Harney best represents the ante-bellum frontier combat officer, acting as the nation's chief Indian fighter in the years before the Civil War. Harney was almost continually on frontier service after distinguishing himself in the Seminole Indian war. As a leader of dragoons during the Mexican War he further enhanced his reputation, although, as Richmond L. Clow asserts in his essay, Harney's penchant for controversy tarnished his career. Harney's brutal 1855 campaign against the Sioux was one of the most effective ever undertaken against the plains tribes, and secured nearly a decade of peace on the northern plains. Harney's southern birth made him suspect to Union politicians and so he retired from the army in 1863. After the war, however, he was recalled to become superintendent of Indian affairs for the northern tribes.

As Arrell M. Gibson makes clear in his essay, no soldier better represents the role played by the army in the trans-Mississippi West during the Civil War than flinty James H. Carleton. Far from being a period when the army withdrew from the frontier to fight on eastern battlefields, the Civil War was a period of intense military activity in the West, although volunteer regiments replaced the regulars. Carleton was the most powerful, and controversial, soldier in the West during this period. His genius for military defense and logistics thwarted rebel moves into New Mexico. His direction of a series of brutal campaigns and his concentration of Apaches and Navajos at Bosque Redondo pacified the Southwest. Under the cloak of military necessity he suspended civil process in New Mexico Territory and essentially ruled that vast region as a military satrapy. Although excluded from high rank in the postwar army reorganization, Carlton nevertheless played a pivotal role in defeating Indians and Confederates alike, and in promoting the development of the Southwest.

Philip H. Sheridan was the nation's premier frontier soldier, commanding the vast Division of the Missouri from 1869 until 1883 and then the entire army until his death in 1888. It was Sheridan who planned and executed the major campaigns against the western tribes after the Civil War, developing an effective strategy of Indian warfare that was continually employed by the army from 1868 until the Wounded Knee affair. Despite his identification with the infamous remark that "the only good Indian is a dead Indian," Sheridan was not an advocate of genocide. Rather, he was a disciple of total war, viewing enemy populations as fair game along with enemy soldiers. His strategy of displacing and threatening noncombatants in order to force a quick surrender marked him as a truly modern warrior.

No frontier soldier is as well known, or as controversial, as George Armstrong Custer. Brian W. Dippie's chapter explores the complexity of Custer's personality and attempts to place his frontier exploits, and his 1876 last stand, in perspective. Custer's participation in the 1867 Hancock campaign, Sheridan's 1868–69 winter campaign, and the Great Sioux War mark him as an important Indian fighter. His part in the 1873 Yellowstone expedition and the 1874 Black Hills exploration are representative of the military role in late-nineteenth-century western expansion. Nevertheless, Custer's fame is far out of proportion to his accomplishments. To explain just why that happened, Dippie adeptly explores the Custer legend that grew out of the disaster on the Little Bighorn. Ultimately, defeat won a lasting fame for Custer that victory failed to win for other, more important army officers.

Jerome A. Greene presents George Crook as an enlightened warrior who, although relentless in campaigning against the Indians in time of war, was also a tireless defender of the defeated tribes during peacetime. Although best known as an innovative campaigner, especially in his application of mobile mule-pack trains to Apache warfare, Crook actually spent three-quarters of his career in positions related to the military administration of Indian affairs. Crook's views on Indians differed sharply from those of most of his army contemporaries and ultimately cost him his southwestern command in 1886. Crook's seniority established him briefly as commander of the Division of the Missouri and he used that position to assist the defeated Indians. Few figures of such prominence have been as neglected by historians as Crook. Greene's essay offers a major reinterpretation of Crook's career that finally places the general in proper historical context.

While Captain John G. Bourke never achieved the high rank or national reputation of a Sheridan or Custer, in many ways his legacy to the future was more substantial. As aide-de-camp to General Crook from 1872 to 1886, Bourke was an eyewitness to several important Indian campaigns. He recorded his observations in detailed diaries that have proven invaluable to researchers, and in numerous books and articles, most notably *An Apache Campaign* (1886) and *On the Border with Crook* (1891). As Joseph C. Porter states in his chapter, Bourke's enthnological studies on southwestern Indians are even more important than his military memoirs. His valuable observations of the Navajo, Pueblo, and Apache tribes mark him as a classic example of the military officer as humanist and scientist.

Benjamin H. Grierson, as Bruce J. Dinges makes clear in his chapter, was a decidedly unconventional cavalryman. A former music teacher, he had won quick promotion in the volunteer ranks during the Civil War, leading a famous cavalry raid in April 1863 that made him a national hero. In 1866 Grierson became colonel of the Tenth Cavalry, a black regiment, which he organized and trained. An early adherent of the Republican party, Grierson was a crusader for civil rights and waged a constant battle against the military establishment in order to secure a measure of equality for his men. His liberalism extended to the Indian question as well, for he was a determined advocate for Indian rights. This won him the enmity of his superiors and his career was marked by repeated controversy. His views reflect the wide diversity of opinions held by frontier officers and of the politicization of the post–Civil War military establishment.

Ranald S. Mackenzie was the leading combat officer of the post–Civil War era. The young colonel of the Fourth Cavalry waged brilliant campaigns against the Comanches and finally brought peace to the frontier of northern Texas. His 1873 incursion into Mexico to destroy a Kickapoo village was a notorious violation of international law, but it settled with one decisive strike a long-festering border problem. Sheridan called him north in 1876 to battle the Sioux and Cheyennes after Custer's defeat, and Mackenzie enhanced his reputation with the destruction of Dull Knife's Powder River village in November 1876. Promoted to brigadier general in 1882, Mackenzie commanded the Department of Texas until insanity cut short his career in 1884. Regarded by both Grant and Sheridan as the finest young officer in the postwar army, Mackenzie has never achieved the historical reputation he deserves. J'Nell Pate attempts to correct that lack of recognition in her chapter.

The image of the frontier army as a monolithic organization operating with one heart and hand is firmly put to rest by Marvin E. Kroeker's study of the life of General William B. Hazen. Few officers were so involved in political and professional controversy. A distinguished Civil War record won Hazen appointment as colonel of the Sixth Infantry, although he rarely served with his regiment. In 1868 he was placed in charge of the southern Indian superintendency and promptly infuriated Sheridan and Custer by restraining them from attacking the Fort Cobb Kiowas. His friendship with General William T. Sherman, however, saved him from Sheridan's wrath. Further controversy surrounded his exposure of the exaggerated claims of Great Plains land promoters and their army friends. His attack on Secretary of War William W. Belknap's corrupt administration of the post-trader system led to the secretary's impeachment but further angered Hazen's military enemies. He was banished to Fort Buford, North Dakota, to keep him out of politics, but was rescued by his friend President James Garfield, in 1880, with an appointment as chief signal officer. Controversy continued to surround Hazen, most notably over the Greely polar expedition and rescue of 1883–84, until his death in 1888.

"A Brave Peacock" was how President Theodore Roosevelt characterized Nelson Miles and it was, according to Robert M. Utley, an accurate description. For in Miles vanity and ambition powered a fierce competitiveness that drove him to revel tastelessly in his own genuine abilities while minimizing or denying those of others. He was the brightest "mustang," or non–West Point graduate, in the postwar military establishment and he blamed the clique of academy men for blocking his rise in rank. Few others would have complained had they been so fortunate as to obtain such quick promotion. But Miles adhered throughout his life to Oscar Wilde's observation "'Tis not enough that I succeed, my friends must also fail.'' Despite his conceit and bravado Miles was a splendid combat officer. He first achieved recognition as an Indian fighter in the Red River War and then went on to win more laurels in the Great Sioux War. It was Miles, in fact, who succeeded against the Sioux when others failed.

His part in the Nez Perce War of 1877 and the final Apache Wars in 1886 was more controversial, though successful. He presided over the final tragic act of the Indian Wars drama at Wounded Knee in 1890. In 1895 Miles achieved his ambition by becoming commanding general of the army—the last officer to hold that post—but it proved an empty honor as a result of his quarrels with the Roosevelt administration.

Frank D. Baldwin was one of the best-known young officers in the post–Civil War trans-Mississippi West. His experiences as leader of the scouting detachment in the Red River War and as a pursuer of Sitting Bull in the Great Sioux War were well known and appreciated by his fellow officers. To the ordinary homesteader, town builder, and itinerant frontiersman of the 1870s and 1880s he was a hero of unmatched proportions. Robert C. Carriker presents Baldwin as a unique individual who was present at an unusually large number of landmark frontier events and a deserving winner of his two Medals of Honor. He is also a fine example of the career officer whose association with a major figure—Nelson A. Miles in this case—caused his own promotions in rank to fluctuate with the political tenor of the times. Baldwin retired from the army in 1906 as a major general, and is representative of the experience of numerous subalterns during the final Indian Wars.

The frontier soldier as chronicler is best represented by the life and work of Charles King. In sixty-nine books, most of them novels based on army life, King created a lasting stereotype of the frontier army that was later carefully brought to the screen by such film directors as John Ford. Graduated from West Point in 1866, King was soon assigned to the Fifth Cavalry. At Sunset Pass, Arizona, in 1874 he was seriously wounded by Apaches. This troublesome injury eventually forced King out of the army in 1879, but not before he participated in the 1876–77 Great Sioux War, which he later chronicled in the classic *Campaigning with Crook*. Before his death in 1933 King became a popular novelist. His fiction has not sustained an audience, but it nevertheless was instrumental in creating the modern image of the Indian-fighting army. Today these novels still prove useful as a source for social history. To understand the modern image of the Indian-fighting army of the trans-Mississippi West we must look at the life and writings of Charles King, which Paul Hedren provides an excellent introduction to.

There were, of course, many other officers of importance in both the antebellum and post–Civil War eras. But this sampling of significant military careers will give the reader an overview of the multifaceted and diverse roles performed by the military on the frontier. Military officers, and the men under their command, made major contributions to national expansion that went far beyond the romantic image of snapping guidons, thundering charges, and bugles in the afternoon.

It is a pleasure to acknowledge the assistance of others with this project. The contributors to this book were not only talented but also cooperative and patient. R. David Edmunds, whose anthology on Indian leaders inspired this volume, played Cassandra, offering sound and solemn warnings on the dangers inherent in such an enterprise. Although I ignored his prophetic warnings, he was nevertheless quick to give timely and helpful assistance. The department of history, United States Air Force Academy, kindly granted permission to publish Robert M. Utley's "The Contribution of the Frontier to the American Military Tradition," which was delivered, in a different form, as the 1976 Harmon Memorial Lecture at the academy. David Holtby, of the University of New Mexico Press, secured permission for the use of three of the maps in this book. I am delighted to gratefully acknowledge also the assistance of Lynn Brittner, George Chalou, Stephen Cox, Theodore Crackel, Ray DeMallie, Peter Hassrick, Thomas Pew, Brian Pohanka, Martin Ridge, David Weber, and Paul Wilderson. All of these people contributed to the completion of this book.

Introduction:
The Frontier and the American Military Tradition

by Robert M. Utley

America's military tradition owes a large debt to her frontier experience. From the earliest colonial times until the close of the nineteenth century, the frontier loomed large in military affairs. The American military tradition is in part a record—a record as we perceive it today, not necessarily as it was in fact—of those people and events of the past that we have singled out to provide us with inspiration, edification, guidance, and even self-reproach. The American military tradition is also in part the accumulated body of military usage, belief, custom, and practice that has descended to us from the past. Finally, the American military tradition is in part policy, doctrine, thought, and institutions as they have evolved by selection, rejection, and modification through past generations to the present. Each of these aspects of the national military tradition has been profoundly influenced by what the frontier contributed, or what it failed to contribute.

Today's selective record of our frontier military experience may well be the frontier's most enduring contribution. From this heritage we have drawn a congeries of vignettes that loom conspicuously in the national memory and thus in the national military tradition. "Mad Anthony" Wayne's Legion sweeps with fixed bayonets through the forest debris of Fallen Timbers, routing the Indian defenders and planting the roots of the fledgling regular army. Andrew Jackson's infantry storms the fortifications at Horseshoe Bend, slaughtering more than 500 Red Sticks and crushing a Creek uprising that threatens the Old Southwest in the War of 1812. Edward Canby dies by assassination during a peace conference in California's lava beds, the only regular army general to lose his life in Indian warfare. The golden-haired Custer falls with every man of his immediate command in the best-known and most controversial of all frontier encounters. To Nelson A. Miles, Chief Joseph utters the moving words: "From where the sun now stands, I will fight no more, forever." This part of our tradition is one that arouses pride, or at least the thrill of adventure. Its symbols are battle and campaign streamers gracing the army's colors, the military art of Frederic Remington, Charles Schreyvogel, and Rufus Zogbaum, and the motion picture depiction of the frontier army.

Especially the motion pictures. It is difficult to exaggerate their influence. John Ford was the master. In the climactic scene of *Fort Apache,* for example, cavalry officer John Wayne philosophizes on the courage, stamina, skill, and jocular nature of the regular army troopers who opened the American West. A cavalry column with banners flying marches in silhouette against a desert sunrise as swelling music proclaims the majesty of their part in the epic of America. With such stirring scenes Ford shaped a whole generation's conception of the frontier army. In a television tribute, John Wayne conceded that Ford was not above perpetuating legends, consoling himself that if this was not exactly the way it happened, it was the way it ought to have happened.

Darker images form part of the picture too. General Winfield Scott's troops uproot Cherokees and herd them, suffering and dying, over the "Trail of Tears" to new homes in the West. General James Carleton's volunteers conduct Navajos on an eastward "Long March," replete with similar tragic scenes, to new homes in the sterile bottoms of the Pecos River. Colonel John Chivington's "hundred-dazers" slaughter Black Kettle's Cheyennes at Sand Creek. Exploding artillery shells shatter Big Foot's Sioux at Wounded Knee. Such scenes, likewise reinforced and distorted by novels, motion pictures, and television, take their place beside the stirring and the heroic in the mosaic of the national military tradition.

What we choose to remember and the way we choose to remember it may unduly flatter or unfairly condemn our military forebears, may indeed be more legend than history. Legends thus form a conspicuous part of our military tradition and are often far more influential in shaping our attitudes and beliefs than the complex, contradictory, and ambiguous truth. Our reading of truth, or at least the meaning of truth, changes from generation to generation. What is uplifting to one may be shameful to the next. We select and portray our heroes and villains to meet the needs of the present, just as we formulate doctrine, policy, practice, and other aspects of military tradition to meet the conditions of the present. The U.S. Army's frontier heritage, its stereotypes and legends as well as its genuine historical substance, has furnished a galaxy of heroes and villains.

In the people and events of the military frontier we have found a major source of inspiration, guidance, pride, institutional continuity, and, not least, self-deprecation. But several centuries of Indian warfare should have contributed more to the national military tradition than a kaleidoscope of images.

The regular army was almost wholly a creature of the frontier. Frontier needs prompted creation of the regular army. Except for two foreign wars and one civil war, frontier needs fixed the principal mission and employment of the regular army for a century. Frontier needs dictated the periodic enlargements of the regular army in the nineteenth century.[1] Frontier needs underlay Secretary of War John C. Calhoun's "expansible army" plan of 1820, which, though never adopted, contained assumptions that shaped U.S. military policy until 1917.[2] For a century the regulars worked the frontier West. They explored and mapped it. They laid out roads and telegraph lines, and aided significantly in the advance of the railroads. They campaigned against Indians. They guarded travel routes and protected settlers. By offering security or the appearance of it, together with a market for labor and produce, they encouraged further settlement. As enlistments expired, some stayed to help people the frontier themselves.

Citizen soldiers also contributed, though less significantly. From King Philip's War to the Ghost Dance, colonial and state militia, territorial and national volunteers, rangers, "minute companies," spontaneously formed home guards, and other less admirable aggregations of fighting men supplemented or altogether supplanted the regulars on the frontier. Often, indeed, the two worked at dramatic cross-purposes.

The contribution of the frontier to American military history was of paramount significance, but its contribution to the American military tradition was not of comparable significance. Inviting particular attention is the influence of the special conditions and requirements of the frontier on military organization, composition, strategy, and especially doctrine. A century of Indian warfare, extending a record of such conflict that reached well back into colonial times, should have taught us much about dealing with people who did not fight in conventional ways, and our military tradition might reasonably have been expected to reflect the lessons thus learned. Some were not without relevance in Vietnam.

In examining the role of the frontier in nineteenth-century military history, however, we encounter a paradox. It is that the army's frontier employment unfitted it for orthodox war at the same time that its preoccupation with orthodox war unfitted it for its frontier mission. In this paradox we find the theories of Emory Upton and Samuel P. Huntington contradicting what seem to be fairly evident realities. Emory Upton first stated the proposition that the army had never been ready for a real war because it had been maintained chiefly to fight Indians.[3] More recently, Samuel P. Huntington has enlarged on Upton's thesis and concluded that "the requirements of the frontier shaped the strategy and structure of the Army."[4] Organization, composition, command and staff, tactics, weapons, and the system of military education were all, in the Upton-Huntington view, decisively influenced if not altogether dictated by the frontier mission.

If so, all these features of military policy proved singularly unresponsive to frontier conditions. A commanding general was supposedly needed for the operational direction of an active force on the frontier, yet he commanded scarcely more than his personal aides. A staff was needed not to plan for the next war but to support the ones currently underway on the frontier, yet the staff system contained flaws that severely impeded its logistical function. The organization of companies and regiments seems wholly conventional in nineteenth-century terms; it is difficult to see how they would have been differently organized for conventional war—and in fact they were not basically changed when conventional war came. The cavalry arm traced its beginnings to frontier needs, but the Mexican War or Civil War would surely have prompted the formation of mounted units anyway. The "rough and unsavory" rank and file that Huntington sees as well fitted for Indian fighting and road building were not well fitted for much of any duty, and the record of federalized volunteer units in the West during the Civil War plainly established the superiority of this class of troops over the typical peacetime regulars. Nor, with the possible exception of the revolving pistol—a response to the frontier only insofar as mounted troops found a repeating handgun of great utility—can the evolution of military weaponry be linked to frontier needs.

To the extent that a system of border outposts constituted strategy, it was of course shaped by the frontier. But these forts represented less a deliberate plan than erratic responses to the demands of pioneer communities for security and local markets. The forts, incidentally, encouraged settlers to move beyond the range of military protection, stirred up the Indians, and led to still more forts—many beyond effective logistical support. Secretary of War Peter B. Porter lamented this trend toward overextension as early as the 1820s, but it continued for the balance of the century.[5]

On the operational level, strategy and tactics were clearly not a product of frontier conditions. Most army officers recognized their foe as a master of guerrilla warfare. Their writings abound in admiring descriptions of his cunning, stealth, horsemanship, agility and endurance, skill with weapons, mobility, and exploitation of the natural habitat for military advantage. Yet the army as an institution never acted on this recognition. No military school or training program, no tactics manual, and very little professional literature provided guidance on how to fight or treat with Indians, although it should be noted in minor qualification that Dennis Hart Mahan apparently included in one of his courses at West Point a brief discussion of Indian-fighting tactics.[6]

Lacking a formal body of doctrine for unconventional war, the army waged conventional war against the Indians. Heavy columns of infantry and cavalry, locked to slow-moving supply trains, crawled about the vast western distances in search of Indians who could scatter and vanish almost instantly. The conventional tactics of the Scott, Casey, and Upton manuals sometimes worked, by routing an adversary that had foolishly decided to stand and fight on the white man's terms, by smashing a village whose inhabitants had grown careless, or by wearing out a quarry with persistent campaigning that made surrender preferable to constant fatigue and insecurity. But most such offensives merely broke down the grain-fed cavalry horses and ended with the troops devoting as much effort to keeping themselves supplied as to chasing Indians. The campaign of 1876 following the Custer disaster is a classic example.

The fact is, military leaders looked upon Indian warfare as a fleeting bother. Today's conflict or tomorrow's would be the last, and to develop a special system for it seemed hardly worthwhile. Lieutenant Henry W. Halleck implied as much in his *Elements of Military Art and Science,* published in 1846, and the thought lay at the heart of Emory Upton's attempted redefinition of the army's role in the late 1870s.[7] In 1876 General Winfield S. Hancock informed a congressional committee that the army's Indian mission merited no consideration at all in determining its proper strength, organization, and composition.[8] In part, the generals were motivated by a desire to place the army on a more enduring basis than that afforded by Indian warfare. But in part, too, they were genuinely concerned about national defense. Therefore, although the staff was not organized to plan for conventional war, or any other kind for that matter, the generals were preoccupied with it, and the army they fashioned was designed for the next conventional war rather than the present unconventional one.

However orthodox the conduct of Indian wars, the frontier not only failed as a training ground for orthodox wars; it positively unfitted the army for them, as became painfully evident in 1812, 1846, 1861, and 1898. Scattered across the continent in little border forts, units rarely operated or assembled for practice and instruction in more than battalion strength. The company was the basic unit, and it defined the social and professional horizons of most line officers. Growing old in grade, with energies and ambitions dulled by boredom and isolation, the officer corps could well subscribe to General Richard S. Ewell's observation that on the frontier an officer "learned all there was to know about commanding forty dragoons, and forgot everything else."[9]

That the army as an institution never elaborated a doctrine of Indian warfare does not mean that it contained no officers capable of breaking free of conventional thought. The most original thinker was General George Crook, who advocated reliance on mule trains as the means of achieving mobility and who saw the conquest of the Indian as dependent upon pitting Indian against Indian. Army organization provided for Indian scouts, but Crook's concept went considerably beyond their use as guides and trailers. "To polish a diamond there is nothing like its own dust," he explained to a reporter in 1886:

> It is the same with these fellows. Nothing breaks them up like turning their own people against them. They don't fear the white soldiers, whom they easily surpass in the peculiar style of warfare which they force upon us, but put upon their trail an enemy of their own blood, an enemy as tireless, as foxy, and as stealthy and familiar with the country as they themselves, and it breaks them all up. It is not merely a question of catching them better with Indians, but of a broader and more enduring aim—their disintegration.[10]

Had the nation's leaders understood the lessons of Crook's experience, they would have recognized that the frontier army was a conventional military force trying to control, by conventional military methods, a people that did not behave like conventional enemies and who, indeed, quite often were not enemies at all. They would have recognized that the situation usually called not for warfare but merely for policing; that is, offending individuals needed to be separated from the innocent and punished. They would have recognized that the conventional force was unable to do this and that as a result punishment often fell, when it fell at all, on guilty and innocent alike.

Had the nation's leaders acted on such understandings, the army might have played a more significant role in the westward movement—and one less vulnerable to criticism. An Indian auxiliary force might have been developed that could differentiate between guilty and innocent and, using the Indian's own fighting style, contend with the guilty. Indian units were indeed developed, but never on a scale and with a continuity that permitted the full effect to be demonstrated. Such an Indian force would have differed from the reservation police—who in fact did remarkably well, considering their limitations.[11] It would have been larger, better equipped, and less influenced by the vagaries of the patronage politics that afflicted the Indian Bureau. Above all, it would have been led by a cadre of carefully chosen officers imbued with a sense of mission and experienced in Indian relations—the kind of officers artist Frederic Remington said were not so much "Indian fighters" as "Indian thinkers."[12] How different might have been the history of the westward movement had such a force been created and employed in place of the regular army line. How vastly more substantial might have been the contribution of the frontier to our traditions of unconventional warfare.

By contrast, a major aspect of twentieth-century practice owes a large debt to the frontier. Total war—warring on whole enemy populations—finds ample precedent in the frontier experience. Russell Weigley has pointed out how different the colonial Indian wars were from the formal and not very destructive warfare of the European pattern. In King Philip's War of 1675–76, for example, the Indians almost wiped out the New England settlements, and the colonists in response all but wiped out the Indians. "The logic of a contest for survival was always implicit in the Indian wars," Weigley writes, "as it never was in the eighteenth century wars wherein European powers competed for possession of fortresses and countries, but always shared an awareness of their common participation in one civilization, Voltaire's 'Republic of Europe.' "[13]

Examples of total war may be found through subsequent centuries of Indian conflict, notably in the Seminole Wars, but it remained for Generals William T. Sherman and Philip H. Sheridan to sanctify it as deliberate doctrine. With the march across Georgia and the wasting of the Shenandoah Valley as models, they set forth in the two decades after the Civil War to find the enemy in their winter camps, kill or drive them from their lodges, destroy their ponies, food, and shelter, and hound them mercilessly across a frigid landscape until they gave up. If women and children fell victim to such methods, it was regrettable, but justified because it resolved the issue quickly and decisively and thus more humanely. Although prosecuted along conventional lines and thus usually an exercise in logistical futility, this approach yielded an occasional triumph, such as the Washita and Dull Knife fights, that saved if from serious challenge. Scarcely a direct inspiration for the leveling of whole cities in World War II and Vietnam, frontier precedents of total war may nevertheless be viewed as part of the historical foundation on which this feature of our military tradition rests.[14]

Another area that might be usefully probed is the relationship of the frontier to the militia tradition, whose modern expression, after generations of modification, is the mass citizen army. Though not exclusively a product of the frontier, the militia owed a great debt to the recurring Indian hostilities that brought pioneers together for common defense, and it figured prominently enough in the American Revolution for Walter Millis to see it as the principal factor in the "democratization" of war that prompted the collapse of the setpiece warfare of the eighteenth century.[15] So firmly implanted was the militia tradition in the thinking of the revolutionary generation, together with abhorrence of standing armies, that the architects of the nation conceived it as the foundation of the military system, the chief reliance for national defense as well as frontier employment. Frontier experience demonstrated how wrong they were. The Indian rout of Josiah Harmer in 1790 and Arthur St. Clair in 1791 so dramatically exposed the inadequacies of militia as to give birth to the regular army, a contribution of the militia to U.S. military history of no small significance, however negative. The organized militia fell apart after 1820, as foreign threats receded, but the militia tradition, nourished in part by the Indian frontier, evolved through various mutations into the twentieth century.

A clear and undeniable contribution of the frontier to the national military tradition is its large role in the rise of professionalism in the army. Albert Gallatin wrote in 1802: "The distribution of our little army to distant garrisons where hardly any other inhabitant is to be found is the most eligible arrangement of that perhaps necessary evil that can be contrived. But I never want to see the face of one in our cities and intermixed with the people."[16] And rarely for a century, except in the Mexican and Civil Wars, were the soldiers intermixed with the people. Physically, socially, and at last in attitudes, interests, and spirit, the regulars on the frontier remained isolated from the rest of the population. This separation, so costly in terms of public and governmental support, had one enduring benefit. Turning inward, the army laid the groundwork for a professionalism that was to prove indispensable in the great world wars of the twentieth century. The postgraduate military school system, original thought about the nature and theory of warfare, and professional associations and publications find their origins in this time of rejection of the soldiers by their countrymen.[17]

A final feature of our military tradition with strong frontier roots is the prominent role of minorities. The regular army's black regiments served on the frontier for three decades following their organization in 1866 and wrote some stirring chapters of achievement. They saw harder service than the white regiments and, because they afforded continuous and honorable employment in a time when blacks found few other opportunities, boasted lower desertion rates and higher reenlistment rates.[18] Immigrants, too, found a congenial home in the army, as well as a means of learning the English language and reaching beyond the teeming port cities of the East where so many of their countrymen suffered in poverty and despair. And not to be overlooked are the Indians themselves, who loyally served the white troops as scouts, auxiliaries, and finally—for a brief time in the 1890s—in units integral to the regimental organization.[19]

Today the American military tradition must be responsive to the imperatives of nuclear warfare, and that warfare discloses few parallels with the small-unit Indian combats of forest, plains, and desert. But the tradition must also be responsive to the "limited wars" that the nuclear specter has spawned, and these do disclose parallels with frontier warfare. It is a measure of the failure of the Indian-fighting generations to understand their task that today's doctrine does not reflect the lessons of that experience. And yet the American military tradition owes a debt of noteworthy magnitude to the frontier experience.

Notes

1. The First and Second Dragoons were established in 1832 and 1836, the Regiment of Mounted Riflemen in 1846, the First and Second Cavalry and Ninth and Tenth Infantry in 1855. The Army Act of 1866 expanded the regular army to meet both frontier and Reconstruction duty; the subsequent reduction in 1869, as Reconstruction needs diminished, left a net gain of four cavalry regiments and six infantry regiments that may be

attributed to frontier needs. (All mounted regiments had been restyled "cavalry" in 1861 and a Sixth Cavalry added in response to Civil War needs.)

2. Walter Millis, *Arms and Men: A Study in American Military History* (New York: Mentor Books, 1956), 73. John C. Calhoun's plan was an attempt to reconcile the differing needs of war and peace. The frontier, of course, made a peacetime army necessary. See also Russell F. Weigley, *Towards an American Army: Military Thought from Washington to Marshall* (New York: Columbia University Press, 1962), 30–37.

3. Stephen E. Ambrose, *Upton and the Army* (Baton Rouge: Louisiana State University Press, 1964), 106.

4. Samuel P. Huntington, "Equilibrium and Disequilibrium in American Military Policy," *Political Science Quarterly* 76 (December 1961): 490.

5. Russell F. Weigley, *The American Way of War: A History of United States Military Strategy and Policy* (New York: Macmillan, 1976), 69.

6. Had Emory Upton responded to General Sherman's belief that the British experience in India held lessons for the American frontier, Upton's *The Armies of Asia and Europe* (New York: Appleton, 1878) might have ventured into the doctrine of unconventional war. In fact, Upton did see some parallels between India and the American frontier. He admired the organization, discipline, and record of native troops led by British officers. He likened the native peoples with whom the British dealt to the American Indians in their disposition to fight one another more than their colonial rulers, and he attributed British success to a policy of mingling in their quarrels and playing off one group against another. He declared that the British Indian army was worthy of imitation. But except for rotation of officers between staff and line (scarcely a reform of special frontier application), he failed to spell out particulars (pp. 75–80). Upton forgot about India in his enchantment with the Prussian war machine, and he finally concluded (p. 97) that the United States must look to the armies of Europe for its models. See also in this connection Weigley, *Towards an American Army,* 105–6. Captain Arthur L. Wagner's *The Service of Security and Information,* first published in 1893, contained a short chapter on Indian scouting, but it seems almost an afterthought to the substance of the book.

Mahan's West Point lecture on Indian warfare is noted in William B. Skelton, "Army Officers' Attitudes toward Indians, 1830–1860," *Pacific Northwest Quarterly* 67 (1976): 114, 121, citing Thomas E. Griess, "Dennis Hart Mahan: West Point Professor and Advocate of Military Professionalism," (Ph.D. diss., Duke University, 1968), 306–7. In 1881, Edward S. Farrow, a West Point instructor, published *Mountain Scouting: A Hand-Book for Officers and Soldiers on the Frontiers.* Together with much material applicable to service anywhere, it contained useful information on Indian and frontier campaigning. The extent of its use at West Point and on the frontier is not apparent.

7. Weigley, *American Way of War,* pp. 84–85. Ambrose, *Upton and the Army,* pp. 106–7.

8. *House Misc. Docs.,* 45th Cong., 2d sess., no. 56, p. 5.

9. Quoted in Huntington, "Equilibrium and Disequilibrium," 499.

10. Charles F. Lummis, *General Crook and the Apache Wars* (Flagstaff, Ariz.: Northland, 1966), 17. This is a series of articles that correspondent Lummis wrote for the Los Angeles *Times* during the Geronimo campaign of 1886.

11. See William T. Hagan, *Indian Police and Judges* (New Haven, Conn.: Yale University Press, 1966).

12. Frederic Remington, "How an Apache War Was Won," in Harold McCracken,

ed., *Frederic Remington's Own West* (New York: Promontory Press, 1961), 49.

13. Weigley, *American Way of War,* 19.

14. The role of Sherman and Sheridan is discussed in Robert M. Utley, *Frontier Regulars: The United States Army and the Indian, 1866–1891* (New York: Macmillan, 1973), 144–46. Also see Paul Andrew Hutton, *Phil Sheridan and His Army* (Lincoln: University of Nebraska Press, 1985); and Robert G. Athearn, *William Tecumseh Sherman and the Settlement of the West* (Norman: University of Oklahoma Press, 1956).

15. Millis, *Arms and Men,* 19–20, 34. Also see John K. Mahon, *History of the Militia and the National Guard* (New York: Macmillan, 1983).

16. Quoted in Leonard D. White, *The Jeffersonians: A Study in Administrative History, 1809–1829* (New York: Macmillan, 1959), 214.

17. Samuel P. Huntington, *The Soldier and the State: The Theory and Politics of Civil-Military Relations* (Cambridge, Mass.: Harvard University Press, 1957), ch. 9; Utley, *Frontier Regulars,* 59–68. This thesis has been thoughtfully challenged by John M. Gates, ''The Alleged Isolation of US Army Officers in the Late 19th Century,'' *Parameters: Journal of the US Army War College* 10 (1980): 32–45.

18. For the role of black soldiers on the frontier, see William H. Leckie, *The Buffalo Soldiers: A Narrative of the Negro Cavalry in the West* (Norman: University of Oklahoma Press, 1967); and Arlen L. Fowler, *The Black Infantry in the West, 1869–1891* (Westport, Conn.: Greenwood Press, 1971).

19. Thomas W. Dunlay, *Wolves for the Blue Soldiers: Indian Scouts and Auxiliaries with the United States Army, 1860–90* (Lincoln: University of Nebraska Press, 1982).

William Clark

by Jerome O. Steffen

William Clark is known primarily for his participation in the Lewis and Clark expedition. This was, however, but one of Clark's many functions in his more encompassing role as an imperial soldier and diplomatic figure who—much like his English, Spanish, and French counterparts—explored and secured national colonial possessions. Clark's life can be clearly understood only when it is considered in the same mercantilistic context as the lives of earlier explorers and entrepreneurs in the New World.

Mercantilism correlated national strength with self-sufficiency and with economic growth regulated by the central government. Since an essential element was a network of colonial possessions to provide the mother country with goods that otherwise would have to be purchased from competing nations, a key figure in the implementation of this policy was the mercantile capitalist or trader. The trader, while pursuing personal profit in distant lands, also served the interests of his nation-state through exploration and colonization. With the purchase of the Louisiana Territory in 1803, the United States had acquired a "colony" that was administered under a policy very much inspired by mercantilism.[1] A major part of Clark's adult life was concerned with seeking security for this American territory; he was, therefore, a soldier in the imperial struggle between the United States and Great Britian for the trans-Mississippi West.

To his death, Clark feared and distrusted the British because of the threat that he imagined they posed to his nation's security and prosperity; this fear manifested itself in a continuing crisis mentality. Born in 1770 to a family that sent five sons to the colonial struggle for independence, William was old enough to appreciate the importance of that event. Of his older brothers who participated in the conflict, George Rogers Clark made the most distinguished contribution. He was recognized with distinction as the individual responsible for winning the Ohio Valley for the struggling colonies and thus acquiring for the young country its first colonial possession.[2] Benjamin Franklin said of his efforts, "Young man, you have given an empire to the Republic."[3]

After the war, in 1784, the Clark family moved from Virginia to Kentucky, then part of the "empire" that George Rogers had won for the republic.[4] During the next decade, William Clark's life became deeply embroiled in the Indian campaigns of the Ohio Valley. These conflicts resulted from the intrusion of white settlers on Indian lands and from the British success in convincing the natives that the security of their tribal lands lay in their becoming British allies. An ill-conceived American Indian policy also contributed to the problem. The United States as victor in the Revolutionary War assumed that it could determine boundaries at will in the frontier areas because they were conquered territories; treaties negotiated in 1784 with the Indians of the Ohio Valley utilized the conquered-territory doctrine to establish American dominion over the native inhabitants of the region, including the total cession of their tribal lands. Unfortunately, these treaties were never uniformly accepted by the affected tribes. Thus, when encouraged by the British, the beleaguered tribes began a persistent campaign against newly established white settlements in the region—which, in turn, felt isolated with little expectation of help from the federal government. As a result, beginning in 1784, a number of locally organized expeditions were carried on against the raiding Indians. William Clark began his military career in these unofficial campaigns: in 1786 he joined a local militia led by his brother George Rogers, and again in 1789 he joined an expedition led by Major John Hardin.[5]

The first formal campaign against the Indians of the Ohio Valley was launched in 1790 when President George Washington ordered Kentucky, Virginia, and Pennsylvania to contribute troops to an army under the command of Colonel Josiah Harmer. Harmer's expedition against the Indians, like the one led by Major General Arthur St. Clair one year later, was totally unsuccessful; his hastily drawn battle plans did not include adequate supply lines, satisfactory fortifications, or enough time to train the soldiers properly.

American efforts to subdue the Ohio Valley Indians were not successful until President Washington appointed Major General Anthony Wayne to head the campaign. Wayne, unlike his predecessors, took the necessary time to prepare his army and to devise a feasible battle strategy that provided proper security for his troops and for the territory that he occupied. After organizing the Legion of the United States in the fall of 1793, Wayne chose to winter it in the relative safety of newly constructed Fort Greenville. During this period, Wayne diligently prepared his troops for the spring campaign. When the army finally did march the next spring, it assumed a deliberate, almost plodding pace. For example, Wayne paused to construct Fort Recovery on the site of St. Clair's defeat when some thought he should have aggressively pursued the troublesome Indians. His strategy was vindicated when the Indians took the offensive with an all-out attack, and Wayne's troops were able to inflict heavy losses among the Indian forces because of their superior fortifications.

Following that attack, Wayne moved against the natives at their chosen defensive position at Fallen Timbers, near the Maumee River, where the Indians were confident of British assistance from nearby Fort Miami. The expected participation of the British did not materialize, however; the result was a total Indian defeat after only two hours of battle.

As a first lieutenant in Wayne's army, under the direct command of Major General James Wilkinson, William Clark was primarily responsible for maintaining supply lines and constructing fortifications. The young lieutenant was among those impatient with Wayne's deliberate pace. At times, it appeared to Clark that the general had let Indians escape when the situation called for attack.[6] Wayne's success notwithstanding, Clark was restless and frustrated. "My merit for my dispositions and Officer like conduct . . . has not been sufficiently rewarded," he complained.[7]

In 1796, Clark received the most important assignment of his young military career when General Wayne sent him to investigate the illegal construction of a Spanish fort on the Mississippi River south of St. Louis. Clark met with the Spanish and was successful in settling the matter without incident. His report to Wayne indicated that while the fort's location was technically in violation of treaty agreements between Spain and the United States, it was of little military value. Most important, he was able to gather valuable information concerning Spanish military strength and placement. Wayne was so impressed with Clark's report that he dispatched it to Washington with his own.[8]

Nevertheless, Clark continued to be dissatisfied. As early as 1794, he had written to his brother Jonathan: "I wuld bid adieu to this unthankful unpolish[ed] service. I [am] determined to resign and seek for some more honorable imployment for my youthful days."[9] Clark did resign from this first phase of his military life in 1796, leaving behind a career of little soldierly distinction but one that gave early indication of his ability to organize and manage people and his skill as a diplomat.

It was in the Ohio Valley Indian campaigns that Clark came to realize the importance of commerce. He saw that it not only could provide wealth for the astute private trader but also could serve as a powerful diplomatic weapon in dealing with Native Americans. From Clark's perspective, British success among the Indians was due to their strong trade relations with them, and he eventually came to view commerce as more important than the military in securing American colonial possessions. His intention of entering the business world after resigning from the military, however, was delayed when he received a request from Meriwether Lewis—whom he had met during the Wayne campaign—to join in a government-sponsored expedition to the Far Northwest.

The Americans had an interest in that region long before it became their possession. As early as 1783, Thomas Jefferson noted his concern over British domination in that territory: ''They pretend it is only to promote knowledge, I am afraid they have thoughts of colonization into that quarter. Some of us have been talking here in a feeble way of making the attempt to search that country but doubt whether we have enough of that kind of spirit to raise the money.''[10] A British expedition, led by Alexander Mackenzie in 1794, was successful in locating a feasible route across Canada and thus linking the important trade center of Montreal with the Pacific Coast. The published results of this expedition, which included plans for future trade with western regions, were viewed with alarm in the American Congress, affording Jefferson an opportunity to request and receive the federal funds he needed to outfit a similar American expedition.

The two principle objectives of the Lewis and Clark journey were to find a usable water route to the Pacific and to record scientific data along the way—objectives similar to those of the British under Mackenzie. American western outlets to the sea were precarious at best. Spain had been a passive western neighbor, allowing American shipping to use the Mississippi and the port of New Orleans; however, when the French acquired the Louisiana Territory in 1800, American officials feared that this outlet might be closed to them in the future. Fortunately for American interests, Napoleon, then engaged in a war with Great Britain, decided to divest his holdings in the New World in order to procure desperately needed funds for his war chest.[11] The Americans eagerly purchased Louisiana in 1803 because of its potential source of furs and because it would link American trade with the valuable commodities of the Orient.

Although Louisiana belonged to the United States, its western sectors were controlled by British traders through a network of commercial alliances with the local tribes. Thus American trade in the Far Northwest was considered vital, especially because no immediate agricultural settlement was expected in the region. In fact, after the Louisiana Purchase, Congress debated whether to allow any settlement within the newly acquired territory for fear that citizens so far removed from American seats of government might succumb to foreign influence.

Jefferson clearly understood the importance of trade as a diplomatic tool. In 1803 he wrote to Meriwether Lewis: "The commerce which may be carried on with the people inhabiting the line you will pursue, renders a knolege [*sic*] of these people important." Jefferson advised Lewis and Clark to become thoroughly acquainted with the tribes they would encounter in order to determine what "articles of commerce they may need or furnish, & to what extent."[12] This thinking was further reinforced in a letter from Lewis to Clark that same year:

> You will readily conceive the importance of an early and friendly and intimate acquaintance with the tribes that inhabit that country, that they should be early impressed with a just idea of the rising importance of the U. States and of her friendly dispositions toward them; as also her desire to become useful to them by furnishing them thrugh [*sic*] her citizens with such articles by way of barter as may be desired by them or useful to them.[13]

Clark shared Jefferson's belief that if America was ever to secure this portion of its imperial domain, and thus realize the region's commercial potential as a link to the Orient, it would have to be the fur traders through their relations with the Indians of the West who would accomplish this feat. In 1806, after his return from the Pacific, he wrote:

> I consider this tract across the continent of immense advantage to the fur trade, as all the furs collected in 9/10 parts of the most valuable fur country in America may be conveyed to the mouth of the Columbia and shipped thence to the East Indies by the 1 of August in each year and will of course reach Canton earlier than the furs which are annually exported from Montreal in Great Britian.[14]

The scientific aspects of the mission were no less important and in fact were closely linked to its commercial goals. Jefferson's Enlightenment philosophy saw the world as a mechanistic creation of God. If human beings could discover and understand God-made natural laws, then it would be possible to construct institutions that would conform to them; and since all elements on earth were linked, an understanding of these natural laws could be derived most clearly from studying all forms of natural phenomena. The Far Northwest was a great natural laboratory in which these natural laws could be more clearly understood because they had not yet been disturbed by man's artificial conventions.[15] Lewis and Clark were to study

> The soil & face of the country, it's growth & vegetable productions; especially those not of the U.S.
>
> The animals of the country generally, & especially those not known in the U.S.
>
> The remains and accounts of any which may be deemed rare or extinct.
>
> The mineral productions of every kind; but more particularly metals, limestone, pit coal & saltpetre; salines & mineral waters, noting the

temperature of the last, & such circumstances as may indicate their character.

Volcanic appearances.

Climate as characterized by the thermometer, by the proportion of rainy, cloudy & clear days, by lightening, hail, snow, ice, by the access & recess of frost, by the winds prevailing at different seasons, the dates at which particular plants put forth or lose their flowers, or leaf, times of appearance of particular birds, reptiles or insects.[16]

From Jefferson's perspective, it was necessary to understand these things because they led to an understanding of higher truths and because they were linked to the duty that every nation had in "extending & strengthening the authority & justice among the people around them."[17]

Meriwether Lewis and William Clark shared Jefferson's intellectual point of view. Since Lewis was specially trained to carry out the scientific goals of the expedition and Clark was not, it has been commonly but mistakenly thought that his contributions to this aspect of the mission were negligible. In fact, Clark had a keen interest in geography and natural history, instilled in him by his brother George Rogers.[18] He was the principal cartographer of the mission, and to this day the accuracy of his maps is still viewed with amazement. He also made significant contributions to the ethnographic study of the tribes the mission encountered. Clark's ability to describe, in a detached and objective manner, behavior patterns contrary to those of the Western Christian world is still striking to readers of the expedition's journals.[19] There is also strong evidence that he made significant linguistic contributions. A recent study concluded that he was "responsible for several natural history terms applied to the animals of the west. . . . There are many good examples."[20]

Clark's value as a scientific observer was clearly understood by Jefferson; in 1807 the President dispatched him to Big Bone Lick, Kentucky, to excavate the fossils of Pleistocene mammals.[21] Clark's continuing interest in natural history was reflected in his patronage of the museum of natural history at the University of Virginia and the museum of considerable size that he maintained in St. Louis. After his death in 1838, Clark was eulogized by the Academy of Natural Science for his scientific merits; as a token of their loss, the members wore black crepe armbands for 30 days.[22]

The Lewis and Clark expedition also reaffirmed Clark's skills as a diplomat and his ability to manage people. After the expedition returned, Jefferson appointed Clark brigadier general of the Louisiana territorial militia and Indian agent for the tribes within its boundary. American policy in the western territories involved both economic and military objectives, and Clark became a key figure in both aspects.

The primary military goal was to maintain a strong militia, but when Clark arrived in St. Louis, he was shocked at its condition and wrote to the secretary of war:

The Militia (when organized) was so scattered that they will afford but a feeble defence to extensive frontiers of this Territory against the Indians. Their numbers, I believe to be about Two thousand four hundred effective men. To prevent the probability of an Indian [attack] (Which can only be effected by Spanish or British influence and intreague) it will in my opinion be necessary to have some establishments of troops in the Indian Country; as well to watch the embisarys of those Nations; as to inforce the laws regulating the intercourse with the Indian tribes & c.[23]

Clark's concern was prompted not only by his fear of British "intreague" but also by fear of the internal dissension that had resulted from the alleged Aaron Burr conspiracy. Burr reportedly had attempted to organize western settlers into an independent nation with New Orleans as its capital. Since military personnel, including such highly placed officials as Major General James Wilkinson (under whom Clark had served in Wayne's campaign), were involved in the alleged scheme, Clark completely reorganized the militia with people he deemed loyal to national interests.

The economic portion of Jefferson's program for the West was even more critical than the military. In 1808 he wrote, "Commerce is the great engine by which we are to coerce [the Indians], and not war."[24] He was fearful, however, of the disruptive influence that intense competition would have on the natives. American traders were engaged in competition not only with British traders but also among themselves. In response, Jefferson—rather than granting monopolies, as in the classic mercantilistic tradition—planned to regulate private traders and to increase the number of government trading posts known as "factories." Jefferson reasoned that if a network of factories, which he eventually hoped to extend all the way to the Pacific Coast, could provide better goods at lower prices, private trader would be driven into other pursuits less harmful to national interests.[25]

Clark shared Jefferson's opinion of the harmful effects that private traders had on American relations with the Indians:

The maney abuses which has crept into the habits of the Indian Trade, and the unfair practices of the white hunters, on the Indians hunting Lands has been a just cause of complaint; and induced me to establish certain regulations to be observed [which] . . . I flatter myself correct these abuses, and bring more friendship sistem and order, and the Indian of that quarter will be more under the eye of the U State Agents.[26]

It was no doubt because of these views that Jefferson charged Clark with supervising the government factory system and also with administering trade regulations west of the Mississippi.

In addition to carrying on his duties as a commercial and military government agent, Clark entered the world of private commerce. In 1809 he became one of the organizing members of the Missouri Fur Company, which hoped to penetrate the British-dominated trade in the Far Northwest. If successful, the venture would increase the fortunes of its members and at the same time serve American national interests by gaining the allegiance of those Indian tribes that had been traditional British allies.[27]

Clark's participation in the Missouri Fur Company may appear at first glance to be hypocritical, given his negative statements concerning private traders and their harmful influence on the Indians. It may also appear that Clark was guilty of a conflict of interest in joining a segment of the economy that he was charged with regulating. Closer investigation of the circumstances, however, reveals a different picture. When Lewis and Clark returned from their historic journey to the Far Northwest, they advised Jefferson that he should either establish a large government-operated fur company to compete with the British on the upper Missouri or else remove all regulations governing private traders in that region. Jefferson chose the latter course; thus the Missouri Fur Company was not subject to those regulations that Clark had to enforce. Moreover, the Missouri Fur Company, undercapitalized from the start, never posed a serious threat to British domination on the upper Missouri River. When hostilities between Great Britain and the United States erupted in the War of 1812, the company, which had experienced only moderate returns, was dissolved.[28]

In the public arena of Clark's life, the years immediately preceding the War of 1812 were especially perplexing. In addition to regulating the fur trade, he had to keep peace between the tribes indigenous to the territory and those that were encroaching from the East. To complicate matters, the western territories lived in constant fear of British-instigated Indian attacks. In addition to his other duties, therefore, Clark was forced to keep a close watch on the movement of suspicious Indian tribes, using a spy network that comprised government agents, military personnel, and friendly Indians.

In April 1813, Benjamin Howard was commissioned brigadier general in the regular army and resigned as governor of the Louisiana Territory. At the same time, Congress established Missouri as a separate territory and appointed William Clark as its governor. Clark held several positions simultaneously at this juncture in his career: in addition to being governor he was also superintendent of Indian affairs, brigadier general of the Louisiana militia, and inspector general of the same force. His routine changed little, however, because conditions in the West at this time were such that military, political, and diplomatic functions became blurred in a common concern for frontier defense.

From the perspective of the western settlers, the War of 1812 actually began on November 16, 1811. On that date, William Henry Harrison attacked an encampment of Indians assembled at Tippecanoe Creek in Indiana Territory, where Tenskwatawa (the "Shawnee Prophet") and his brother Tecumseh had attempted to organize a collective resistance against the increasing white menace. Following Harrison's attack, white settlements throughout the western territories suffered increased and persistent reprisals; therefore, it was paramount for Clark to draw a proper defense plan for Missouri.[29] To do so, he felt it necessary to determine accurately the extent of Indian hostility. Since newspaper reports of actual and impending attacks were often unreliable, Clark polled his agents and factors on the disposition of the Indians within their jurisdictions. He also asked for a list of the injured and the amount of property loss resulting from Indian assaults. Next, he set out to move friendly tribes farther from British influence by transplanting the more northerly groups south into Osage Territory. The tribes involved were compensated with newly established government factories. Clark also commissioned the purchase of four armed barges, which patrolled the Mississippi and Illinois rivers to watch for suspicious Indian movements.[30]

Clark persistently tried to persuade Washington to provide more soldiers for the defense of the West. His sense of urgency was prompted by his belief that the British were assembling at Prairie du Chien, on the upper Mississippi, for an attack on St. Louis. The British were indeed using this site to assemble their forces, but their efforts were directed toward the Great Lakes region, not southward. Clark's battle plan, based on his mistaken assumption, was to use a large military force to push as far north as Green Bay and there draw a defensive line to assure the safety of white settlements in Illinois and Missouri. Unfortunately, the only available regular army regiment was reassigned to the eastern theater of the war, leaving the West virtually defenseless.

Lacking sufficient military strength to establish fortifications to the north, then, Clark decided to use the gunboats in a hit-and-run campaign along the Mississippi River. The unexpected arrival of Major Zachary Taylor and a company of 61 regulars in 1814, however, prompted him to attempt an attack on Prairie du Chien, with the intention of establishing a defensive position there. On June 2, to their surprise, Clark's forces occupied Prairie du Chien with ease: the main British force had left for the Great Lakes 20 days earlier. Clark had Fort Shelby constructed on the site, confident that the areas to the south were now secure. But two weeks later, an Indian army numbering between 1,200 and 1,500 recaptured the newly constructed fortification after only two days of battle.[31]

The humiliation of losing Fort Shelby was compounded by the fact that the normally friendly tribes on the lower Missouri were showing signs of increased hostility toward Americans. Consequently, the settlers in Missouri were increasingly critical of Clark for not using more force against these tribes. Despite these criticisms, Clark continued to rely on diplomacy in his Indian relations. In June 1814, for example, he appointed Manuel Lisa, the founder of the Missouri Fur Company and a skilled Indian negotiator, to go among the lower Missouri tribes in order to convince them of American friendship and to persuade them to make war on Britain's Indian allies on the upper Mississippi. Before this diplomatic maneuver could be fully implemented, however, the Treaty of Ghent was signed on December 25, 1814.[32]

The end of the War of 1812, however, did not remove the fears of the citizens in the western territories. A formal peace conference with the warring tribes was set for July 1815, but during the intervening six months the northern tribes were still technically at war with the United States, and the spring of 1815 saw an increase in raids on Missouri settlements. Thus, the atmosphere was tense when the appointed commissioners—William Clark, Ninian Edwards, and Auguste Chouteau—finally met with the Indian representatives.[33] The commissioners were fully aware that British traders still exerted a strong influence over the tribes.[34] The conference lasted over three months, with the final peace treaty signed on September 16, 1815.

Because of Clark's lingering fear of British traders, he was never satisfied with American fur-trading policy as it related to Indian diplomacy. He had come to believe that the fur trade should be carried on by government-sponsored ventures large enough to be able to compete successfully with British counterparts, such as the Hudson's Bay Company and the North West Company. Late in life, Clark even advocated a government monopoly in the fur trade at a time when most Americans were clamoring for more individual freedom in the economy. Nevertheless, Clark persisted in his earlier view that "the great variety of interests conceived in the Indian Trade of this country and the irregular method [with] which they have carried it on, is calculated to give the Indians an unfavorable opinion of the American regulations."[35] Contrary to American practice, the British had only one trading company in operation in the Far Northwest; clearly, Clark was attempting to establish a similar policy. Although he feared and distrusted the British, he believed that their methods were effective because they took "the most rigorous Measures against . . . improper conduct toward, the Indians."[36]

Unfortunately, Clark's views on securing the western territories and on Indian relations during the last two decades of his life were out of touch with prevailing sentiment. It was therefore inevitable that Clark as governor would sharply clash with the confident and strongly individualistic agrarian settlers who flocked to the Missouri Territory after 1815. As the territory matured, a political power struggle ensued between the new agricultural settlers and the old commercial and trading elements identified with the region's earlier history. Clark's colonial view of the West naturally placed him on the side of the commercial elements, thus jeopardizing whatever political career he might have anticipated. While the agrarian elements were clamoring for more local control, Clark continued to stress government regulation and control over territorial affairs, including such economic activities as the fur trade, mining, and the disposition of public lands. Consequently, his image as a colonial governor rather than a direct representative of Missouri citizens caused him to be soundly defeated in the territory's first statehood election in 1820.

After that political defeat, Clark began the last phase of his public career. In 1822 a special act of Congress appointed him superintendent of Indian affairs in

St. Louis, his jurisdiction vaguely defined as including ''all the tribes that frequent that place.''[37] The Indian situation was as perplexing as ever. The termination of the government factory system in 1821 had resulted in the need to renegotiate treaties with all the tribes who had been connected with those trading facilities; this arduous process was finally completed in 1822. The next two decades were made especially difficult by the tribulations of Indian removal, a concept first introduced in an 1818 treaty with the Delaware Indians of Ohio and Indiana. From then on the process accelerated until by 1840 virtually all Indians had been removed from land east of the Mississippi.

Early in Clark's career as an Indian agent, American policy east of the Mississippi had stressed Indian assimilation rather than removal. Jefferson's and Madison's policy, inspired by the Enlightenment, was based on the assumption that human behavior was dictated by environment; therefore, Native Americans must be exposed to Euro-American social-environmental conditions. These would have their effect in gradually assimilating these people, but the process must unfold free from the harmful influences of white settlers encroaching on Indian lands and also free from the harmful influences of private traders. By 1816, however, it was apparent to President James Monroe that white settlement had spread westward too rapidly to allow Indian assimilation to take place in the manner intended. This rationale provided the basis for early removal thinking.[38]

By the third decade of the nineteenth century, the nation's ideological outlook had changed dramatically. The hopes and expectations for assimilation had been replaced by the then commonly held Jacksonian philosophy, which viewed the Indian as incapable of improvement. Thus it was inevitable to most Americans that the Indians should be removed to some distant territory where they could live, as President Andrew Jackson put it, ''under their own rude institutions.''[39] In 1833, Jackson expressed the feelings of most of the nation: ''That those tribes cannot exist surrounded by our settlements and in continual contact with our citizens is certain. They have neither the intelligence, the industry, the moral habits, nor the desire of improvement which are essential to any favorable change in their condition.''[40]

Nevertheless, Clark naively clung to his old views. He believed that the whites would accept the Indians into their midst once they had become assimilated but that assimilation would require 30 years of uninterrupted interaction between the newly created agrarian environment and the Indians. Clark therefore supported Indian removal policies for reasons different from those commonly held during the Jacksonian era: he thought removal to the Indian territory would provide that necessary time. In 1826 he described how the process would unfold:

> The period of danger to him [the Indian] is that in which he ceases to be a
> hunter, from the extinction of game, and before he gets the means of living

from the produce of flocks and agriculture. In this transit from the hunter to the farming state, he degenerates from a proud and independent savage to the condition of a beggar, drunkard and thief; neglecting his family, suffering for food and clothes, and living the life of a mere animal.

Clark felt that at this stage it would be critical to supply the Indians with large, lump-sum annuities that could be used to make the transition process less painful. In addition, the affected Indians should be assisted

in planting orchards, and instructed in raising cotton, and in spinning and weaving it into cloth, and making it up into garments. Small mills should be built, and a miller provided, to save the women from the labor of pounding corn; useful mechanics employed to make their ploughs, carts, wheels, hoes, axes, & c., and for the purpose of teaching the young Indians how to use and make them.[41]

During the tragic years of Indian removal, Clark continued to plead for more regulation of Indian trade and more humane treatment of Native Americans. He and a few other Indian officials did manage to influence the passage in 1834 of the Indian Intercourse and Indian Reorganization Acts, which tightened trade regulations and helped to curb the abusive use of liquor in trade practices.[42] But the history of Indian affairs in the last half of the nineteenth century clearly indicates that these measures fell far short. Clark died on September 1, 1838; he did not have to witness that tragic chapter in American Indian history.

Missourians afforded Clark a hero's burial partially because his support of Indian removal had created a favorable image. The real Clark, however, was not known to them, because his vision was not of their age. The hope for an ordered, pastoral society, red and white, respectful of its laws and leaders, was anachronistic in an age when change and growth were bywords for progress. Clark remained popular in the last years of life only because his vision of an eventual Indian pastoral community alongside white settlements never materialized, and because the most obtuse could recognize that the Indian was gone.[43]

Notes

1. Jerome O. Steffen, *Comparative Frontiers: A Proposal For Studying the American West* (Norman: University of Oklahoma Press, 1981), 29–32.

2. Francis B. Heitman, *Historical Register of Officers of the Continental Army during the War of the Revolution, April 1775 to December 1783*, 2 vols. (Washington, D.C.: Government Printing Office, 1903), 1:157; William Hayden English, *Conquest of the Country Northwest of the River Ohio, 1778–1783; Life of Gen. George Rogers Clark*, 2 vols. (Indianapolis, Ind.: n.p., 1895), 1:38; William Clark Kennerly, as told to Elizabeth Russell, *Persimmon Hill: A Narrative of Old St. Louis and the Far West* (Norman: University of Oklahoma Press, 1948), 8.

3. Kennerly, *Persimmon Hill*, 8.

4. Ludie Kinkead, "How the Parents of George Rogers Clark Came to Kentucky in 1784–1785," *Filson Club History Quarterly* (October 1928): 1–4; Reuben G. Thwaites, "William Clark: Soldier, Explorer, Statesman," *Missouri Historical Society Collections* 2 (October 1906): 6.

5. William Clark, "Journal of Hardin's Campaign August 2, 1789–March 18, 1790," William Clark Papers, Missouri Historical Society, Jefferson Memorial, St. Louis, Missouri.

6. Jerome O. Steffen, *William Clark, Jeffersonian Man on the Frontier* (Norman: University of Oklahoma Press, 1977), 23–24. For Anthony Wayne's campaign, see Richard C. Knopf, ed., *Anthony Wayne: A Name in Arms* (Pittsburgh, Pa.: University of Pittsburgh Press, 1960); James Ripley Jacobs, *The Beginning of the U.S. Army, 1783–1812* (Princeton, N.J.: Princeton University Press, 1947), 124–88; Francis Paul Prucha, *The Sword of the Republic: The United States Army on the Frontier, 1783–1846* (New York: Macmillan, 1969), 17–38; Harrison Bird, *War for the West, 1790–1813* (New York: Oxford University Press, 1971), 40–64; Reginald McGrane, ed., "William Clark's Journal of General Wayne's Campaign," *Mississippi Valley Historical Review* 1 (December 1914): 418–44; Paul A. Hutton, "William Wells: Frontier Scout and Indian Agent," *Indiana Magazine of History* 74 (September 1978): 183–222.

7. William Clark to Jonathan Clark, May 25, 1794, Jonathan Clark Papers, Draper Collection 2L33, State Historical Society of Wisconsin, Madison.

8. Anthony Wayne to Secretary of War, August 14, 1794, *American State Papers: Military Affairs*, 7 vols. (Washington, D.C.: Gales and Seaton, 1860), 4: 490; William Clark, Report to Major Wayne, November 4, 1795, William Clark Papers (Missouri).

9. William Clark to Jonathan Clark, November 25, 1794, Draper Collection 1L37.

10. Thomas Jefferson to George Rogers Clark, December 4, 1783, William Clark Papers (Missouri).

11. Steffen, *William Clark*, 35.

12. Jefferson's instructions to Meriwether Lewis, June 20, 1803, in Donald Jackson, ed., *Letters of the Lewis and Clark Expedition: With Related Documents, 1783–1854* (Urbana: University of Illinois Press, 1962), 61–66.

13. Meriwether Lewis to William Clark, June 19, 1803, William Clark Papers (Missouri).

14. Reuben G. Thwaites, ed., *Original Journals of the Lewis and Clark Expeditions, 1804–1806*, 8 vols. (New York: Dodd, Mead, 1904–5), 7:338–39.

15. Steffen, *William Clark*, 3–6.

16. Jackson, *Letters of the Lewis and Clark Expedition*, 61–66.

17. Ibid.

18. "Donald Robertson's School, King and Queen County Virginia, 1758–1769," *Virginia Magazine of History* 33 (April 1925): 194–98; 33 (July 1925): 288–92; 34 (April 1926): 141–48; 34 (July 1926): 232–36.

19. Steffen, *William Clark*, 46–47.

20. Elijah Harry Criswell, *Lewis and Clark: Linguistic Pioneers* (Columbia: University of Missouri Press, 1940), xv–xxiv. For Clark's cartographic contribution, see Gary E. Moulton, *Atlas of the Lewis and Clark Expedition* (Lincoln: University of Nebraska Press, 1983).

21. Steffen, *William Clark,* 47.

22. *Missouri Republican,* September 11, 1838.

23. William Clark to Secretary of War, June 1, 1807, in Clarence Edward Carter, *The Territorial Papers of the United States* (Washington, D.C.: Government Printing Office, 1951), 14:126. (Clark's spelling seemed less unusual in his day than in ours.)

24. Thomas Jefferson to Meriwether Lewis, August 21, 1808, in Carter, *Territorial Papers,* 14:220.

25. Steffen, *William Clark,* 55–56.

26. William Clark to Secretary of War, September 23, 1808, in Carter, *Territorial Papers,* 14:226.

27. Steffen, *William Clark,* 75–85.

28. Ibid.

29. Ibid., 87–88.

30. Ibid.

31. Ibid.

32. William Clark to Secretary of War, December 11, 1814, William Clark Papers (Missouri).

33. Steffen, *William Clark,* 96–99.

34. Joint Letter, William Clark, Ninian Edwards, Auguste Chouteau to Secretary of War, September 18, 1815, *American State Papers: Indian Affairs,* 2 vols. (Washington, D.C.: Government Printing Office, 1836), 2:9.

35. William Clark to Secretary of War, May 18, 1807, William Clark Papers (Missouri).

36. William Clark to Secretary of War, November 20, 1831, William Clark Papers, Kansas State Historical Society, Topeka, Kansas.

37. Secretary of War to William Clark, April 2, 1821, in Carter, *Territorial Papers,* 14:712.

38. Steffen, *William Clark,* 58–61.

39. James D. Richardson, ed., *A Compilation of the Messages and Papers of the Presidents,* 10 vols. (Washington, D.C.: Government Printing Office, 1898), 3:1083.

40. Ibid., 1252.

41. William Clark to Secretary of War, March 1, 1826, *American State Papers: Indian Affairs,* 2:653–54.

42. Francis Paul Prucha, *American Indian Policy in the Formative Years: The Indian Trade and Intercourse Acts, 1790–1834* (Cambridge, Mass.: Harvard University Press, 1962), 250–73.

43. Steffen, *William Clark,* 156–57.

Stephen H. Long

by Roger L. Nichols

*Portrait by Charles Willson Peale, courtesy
Independence National Historical Park*

At Buffalo, New York, on June 14, 1863, Colonel Stephen H. Long received
news of his retirement from the United States Army. His military career
stretched back to December 1814, when a letter appointing him second lieutenant in the Corps of Engineers went into the mail. During the intervening five
decades he served in many parts of the country, his duties taking him from the
Rocky Mountains east to the Atlantic coast, and from the Canadian border south
to New Orleans. Never a battlefield commander, he is not remembered for stirring charges or bloody forays against the nation's enemies. Rather, as a member
of the Engineers during the first half of the nineteenth century, his activities
helped shape American ideas about the West and contributed in important ways
to travel and settlement there. Working as an explorer, railroad surveyor and
planner, and longtime supervisor of army efforts to rid midwestern and western
rivers of navigational obstacles, he helped gather knowledge and develop tech-
nology that benefited the pioneers then pushing across the continent.

Born on December 30, 1784, Stephen was one of 13 children in the family of
Moses and Lucy Long of Hopkinton, New Hampshire. His father had served
during the War for Independence, and in the years that followed he worked as a
farmer, cooper, and local politician. Little is known about Stephen Long's boy-

hood. It is likely that he attended whatever public school operated in Hopkinton, and perhaps he had some local tutor in addition; whatever the case, by 1806 he was enrolled as a student at Dartmouth College. In August 1809, at the age of 25, he graduated from that institution with no definite career prospects. For a couple of years he was employed as a teacher and then as the principal of a public school in Germantown, Pennsylvania, where he met leaders of nearby Philadelphia's educational and scientific community, members of the American Philosophical Society, and others who played important roles later in his career as a frontier army officer.[1]

During the few years between his college graduation and his entry into the army, Long's interests varied widely. He corresponded with friends about agricultural issues: the quality of soil in Pennsylvania and the varieties of crops that might prosper there. He participated in local musical and theatrical groups and became interested in medicine. At one point a local physician offered to train him as a medical student, but Long declined. Of more immediate significance to his military career, the young teacher worked as an occasional surveyor and tinkered with several varieties of hydraulic machinery. In the process he developed a modest local name for himself as a mechanic and mathematician. His local reputation and social activities brought him to the attention of Major Isaac Roberdeau of the Army Topographical Engineers, and through him Long came to meet General Joseph Swift, then chief of engineers of the army. Swift took an immediate interest in Long and his mechanical inventions, and that interest eventually led the general to suggest that Stephen abandon schoolteaching for a career as a military engineer.[2]

Apparently, the army failed to attract Long, because he declined Swift's help in obtaining a commission. Instead, he accepted employment as a civilian engineer working for the army to strengthen the harbor defenses at Brooklyn. After a few months, however, General Swift persuaded him that an army career offered more promise than anything else he had tried, so in late 1814, Stephen Long applied for a commission in the Corps of Engineers. The support of the general in command undoubtedly helped, and in December 1814 the War Department commissioned Long a second lieutenant of engineers. Because there was some confusion about where the commission should be sent, he did not receive it for several months; when it finally arrived, however, he accepted it promptly.[3]

Long's commission provides a clear example of the many peculiarities related to army appointments, transfers, or promotions at the time. The War of 1812 had just ended, and thousands of officers and enlisted men were returning to civilian life. Yet while veteran, battlewise officers lost their positions, the untested 30-year-old former schoolteacher began his climb through the officers' ranks. Only a month or so after Long entered the army, apparently fearing that the new lieutenant might be dropped from the rolls, General Swift arranged to get him assigned to the faculty of the Military Academy at West Point, where Long put his teaching skills to use as an assistant professor of mathematics. In late 1815 he requested a transfer to the Topographical Engineers, then a small group within the larger corps. To strengthen his case, he included recommendations from both General Swift and his friend Major Roberdeau. With their support he succeeded, and in May 1816 the War Department notified him of his transfer to the Topographical Engineers and of his unexpected promotion to the rank of captain and then of brevet major, which meant that he could perform the duties and receive the pay of a major if the circumstances demanded such action.[4] Clearly, he had persuasive friends within the army.

For much of the next decade Long served on the frontier or worked on assignments that focused directly on American territorial expansion. His transfer to the Topographical Engineers came at a time when the federal government was moving to reassert its control over the Indian peoples then living in the Mississippi and Missouri river valleys. The War of 1812 had reduced American influence and even presence among some of those tribes, while British influence had grown. With the war over, the United States was determined to reverse that trend. For the new engineer this focus on the frontier meant frequent duty in the wilderness as a cartographer, observer of the Indians, or surveyor and locator of army garrisons.

Long's first minor assignments exposed him to the challenges of wilderness travel, alone or in small groups, and gave him experience with many of the tasks he would be called upon to carry out as an explorer only a few years later. In 1816, Secretary of War William Crawford dispatched him west to St. Louis, where he was to report for local assignments in the Mississippi Valley. By August his superiors had directed him up the Illinois River to inspect the crumbling remains of Fort Clark, built years before as part of the frontier defenses against the Indians. His instructions also noted that his efforts "should yield . . . acquisition of general knowledge" about the region.[5] Along with other educated Americans of that day, his army superiors assumed that anyone with college training in natural history, chemistry, or geology was competent to make scientific judgments about the countryside. After this brief trip, Long returned to St. Louis, but soon new orders sent him back to the Illinois and Indiana frontier regions and then to Washington to report directly to the War Department. There his findings received careful attention, and a copy of his report appeared in a local newspaper only a few weeks after he had left again for the West.[6]

During his brief stay in Washington, Long forwarded to President-elect James Monroe an ambitious plan for exploring the Great Lakes and the major western streams by steamboat, but he got no response.[7] In sending the proposal directly to Monroe—going around rather than through the usual military channels—Long demonstrated the disregard for army protocol that would repeatedly affect his career. His recommendations also indicated the lure that frontier assignments held for him. His early travels on the midwestern frontier actually detracted from his later contributions as an explorer, however. Because much of his early work focused on military objectives, he became accustomed to traveling long distances with a few men in a short time. Obviously, that method of travel could inhibit the gathering of thorough scientific data. Nevertheless, by the time Stephen Long returned to St. Louis, his work had gained considerable attention, and he looked forward to other frontier assignments enthusiastically.

During the spring of 1817, President James Monroe assumed office, and he appointed John C. Calhoun the new secretary of war. A strong nationalist and avid expansionist, Calhoun used his cabinet position to focus much army activity in the West, thus extending American influence. For the Corps of Engineers this meant an increase in frontier assignments. The intense anti-British feelings engendered by the War of 1812 helped stimulate such actions, as American fur traders, officials, and speculators alike denounced the continuing British influence among the frontier Indians. Many tribes south of the Great Lakes and along the upper Mississippi and Missouri valleys had in fact sided with the British or at best retained a sullen neutrality during and immediately after the war, and official misgivings about growing competition from British and Canadian fur traders had a direct impact on Stephen Long's military career as the War Department labored to reestablish or strengthen American control in the border regions.

In 1817, General Thomas Smith, Long's immediate superior in the West, ordered him "to proceed on a military and topographical reconnaissance of the upper Mississippi." He was to visit each army post near the river as far north as Prairie du Chien in present Wisconsin; then he was to head northeast up the Wisconsin River Valley to the portage between that stream and the Fox River, which flowed east into Green Bay. Along the way he was to seek out potential sites for new forts and to learn the attitudes of the nearby Indians toward the United States. After meeting with tribal leaders, he was to proceed on up the Mississippi to survey more sites for later army posts.[8]

In addition, Long was to record any other information that would add to the "general knowledge" of the region. In that sense, the instructions resembled those issued more than a decade earlier to Lewis and Clark before they set out up the Missouri River, and to Thomas Freeman and Peter Custis in their expedition up the Red River. Clearly, Long's primary duties were mapping the area and planning frontier fortifications; nevertheless, on each assignment his superiors made it known they wished him to gather additional data about the people and environment. In this way these minor expeditions gave him experience with the basic issues of frontier exploration within the context of army needs and the country's gradually developing policy of territorial expansion that some of his later work helped encourage.

The explorers left Fort Belle Fontaine near the mouth of the Missouri River on June 1, 1817, and proceeded up the Mississippi. Two and a half months later they completed their jaunt, but even before he had a chance to begin his report, Long got new orders. They directed him to join Major William Bradford, then leading troops south to the Arkansas River; Long was to travel up that stream ahead of the troops to choose a good location for a new fort. This task resulted from federal efforts to move the southeastern Indians beyond the Mississippi. In 1809, President Thomas Jefferson had set the stage for later conflict when he encouraged some Cherokees to begin moving west into Arkansas. By 1814 nearly 2,000 Cherokees had migrated, and soon their hunting parties roamed far to the west, intruding on hunting lands claimed by the Osage tribe. Because of the intermittent raiding that ensued between the two Indian groups, the Indian Office asked that the army place a fort between the warring tribes. In October 1817 the major chose the site of future Fort Smith, designed the facility quickly, and then returned north to Belle Fontaine.[9]

During that autumn Long had reiterated his earlier recommendation to President Monroe that he be authorized to explore parts of the West by steamboat. Later, in February 1818, the major repeated his plea for such an expedition to General Thomas Smith, his immediate superior, who agreed that the plan was useful and forwarded his subordinate's proposal to Washington.[10]

Stephen Long had become an experienced engineer and frontier observer. His reports outlined the resources, agricultural potential, and possible liabilities of each area. They also discussed Indian affairs, which he knew less about. Apparently, Long accepted the views of frontier citizens and fur traders because he seemed to see British agents lurking behind every bush. Perhaps he decided that this was the perception of his superiors. Whatever the case, Long added his voice to the chorus then denouncing British interference with the Indians. In fact, he went beyond some in predicting that in any future war between the United States and Great Britain, "strenuous attempts would be made to wrest a portion of [the Northwest] from our possession." To avoid this, he proposed that the army add several new forts to inhibit British meddling and impress the Indians with American authority.[11]

In the early summer of 1818, Long headed east to Washington to discuss his travels and recommendations with War Department officials. Some of the major's suggestions for new forts seem to have reached willing ears, because within the next year Secretary of War John Calhoun ordered troops to the region on the Missouri known as the Council Bluffs, just above present Omaha, and to the confluence of the Mississippi and St. Peter's rivers—both sites that Long had recommended. In addition, Calhoun agreed that soldiers should ascend far up the Missouri River valley to seize control of that region from the British and to convince the resident Indians of American determination and strength. Although not playing an important role in that troop movement, Stephen Long would accompany it part of the time as a government-sponsored explorer.

The increasing War Department enthusiasm for sending troops to the frontier persuaded Long to submit once again his proposals for scientific exploration of the West. He offered to design a steamboat of modest size with which he could traverse both western streams and the Great Lakes. With what became typical overoptimism, he again claimed that at a modest cost and with a small crew he could explore much of the West in the next four years. Long was apparently more persuasive in person than on paper; this time, Secretary of War Calhoun approved the plan the same day he received it. He authorized the would-be explorer to superintend construction of the steamboat and ordered him to Pittsburgh to begin the project. An eager Stephen Long set out at once.[12]

While the major toiled through the winter of 1818–19 to get the steamboat *Western Engineer* built, Secretary Calhoun accepted the idea that the expedition should serve both military and civilian needs. Originally, he had assumed that Long's activities would focus on mapping, surveying, and fort site selection, and only after repeated urgings from other administration officials as well as from members of Congress did he approve using civilian scientists to help gather data. Once Calhoun's initial reluctance had been overcome, Long was able to recruit a group of competent scientists to accompany him. These included Dr. William Baldwin as botanist, Augustus E. Jessup as geologist, Thomas Say as zoologist, Samuel Seymour as artist, and Titian Peale as assistant naturalist. In addition to the "scientific gentlemen," the major completed his party with Captain Thomas Biddle, Jr.; Lieutenant James D. Graham, a recent West Point graduate; and 19-year-old West Point cadet William Swift, the younger brother of General Joseph Swift.[13]

On the whole, these men were as prepared for scientific exploration of the West as any similar group might have been. By twentieth-century standards their experience and training appear weak or at least questionable, but by early nineteenth-century standards Long had assembled an able set of colleagues. Few Americans had more than a rudimentary education or much travel experience; these men were the exception. Of the nine, only one had no higher education, and four had college degrees. Six of the party had substantial travel experience; four had taken part in other scientific or topographical expeditions. All but one were in their twenties or thirties and so may be assumed to have had the energy and stamina to carry out their tasks.[14]

At 4:00 P.M. on May 3, 1819, the new steamboat headed downstream, and the scientific expedition began. From Pittsburgh the explorers steamed down the Ohio River to the Mississippi and turned north to St. Louis. Unfortunately, the *Western Engineer* experienced numerous difficulties: the new engine broke down repeatedly, and even when it functioned smoothly, it lacked adequate power; the cabin leaked, threatening the safety of specimens, notes, and sketches; and once the craft reached the Mississippi, Long found that mud and sand from the turgid water clogged the boiler continually. If these difficulties were not enough, on June 5 the vessel struck a submerged log; repairs took two days. Despite these problems, on June 9, 1819, the *Western Engineer* steamed up to the St. Louis docks, where the local citizens welcomed the travelers with a noisy and enthusiastic reception.[15]

On June 21, 1819, the *Western Engineer* left St. Louis and the next day entered the mouth of the Missouri River. Within a few days, the explorers had encountered all of the problems that would bedevil them for the rest of the summer. Sandbars, floating debris, and underwater obstacles slowed progress. The wood they burned gave so little heat that the engine lacked enough steam pressure for the craft to overcome the strong current. The silt-laden water clogged the boiler with mud so badly that it had to be cleaned almost daily. The party pushed on, but not without tension and disappointment. The crew complained about having to scrape mud out of the boiler every day or two. The scientists grumbled that the slow pace would limit their explorations. Major Thomas Biddle, second in command, refused to take orders, claiming that he outranked Long. Unlike Lewis and Clark, who had worked well together, these two men argued repeatedly; the friction between them soon became so heated that they refused to speak to each other, and Biddle demanded a duel to settle matters. Long rejected the challenge, and at the end of the summer Major Biddle left the expedition. Both officers seem to have been at fault: at times Long's manner was brusque, and his associates found him a difficult commander; on the other hand, Major Biddle possessed a large ego and a short temper (these brought about his death in a duel a decade later).[16]

With the *Western Engineer* performing undependably, some of the explorers went ashore to carry out their research. Although they escaped the frustrations of those who remained aboard the ill-fated steamer, their cross-country hike proved equally difficult and accident-ridden. They suffered from a shortage of food and water, excessive heat, and clouds of voracious insects. Their pack horse ran off, scattering notes and equipment across the countryside, and they retrieved it only after hours of hot, dusty tracking. A few days later the uncooperative beast ran off again. Even the pioneer settlers along their route proved inhospitable. One refused to give them water for a time.[17]

On August 6, 1819, most of the scientists and officers, with a small escort of soldiers, left Fort Osage in western Missouri and hiked west along the Kansas River; on August 20 they reached the main Kansa Indian village. There the footsore travelers received a noisy welcome, and the usual council meeting and ceremonial meal. For the next couple of days the whites poked into every corner of the village, questioning the inhabitants about their diet, agriculture, government, alliances, marriage practices, and religious beliefs.

On August 24 the shore party set out for the Platte River, where they were to meet the *Western Engineer* and the rest of the expedition. They had ridden only a few miles from the Kansa village when a party of nearly 140 Pawnee warriors rode up to their camp. As the explorers prepared to defend themselves, the Pawnees showed the peace sign, but soon the Indians began pawing through their supplies, while others drove off three pack animals. At that point John Dougherty, who had signed on as interpreter, rode into view with a companion, apparently surprising the Pawnees, who rode away in disorder. Nevertheless, the whites sent back to the Kansa village for aid, and frightened by this incident, they abandoned their plan of traveling to the Platte and instead headed directly back to the Missouri. Two weeks later the *Western Engineer* halted for the winter, and the explorers constructed shelter along the river bank in southeastern Nebraska.[18]

Despite the meager results of the 1819 scientific expedition, Stephen Long traveled east to report its findings and to urge support for the next year. If the expedition were to continue, he also had to replace three members who left it: Dr. Baldwin, Major Biddle, and geologist Augustus Jessup. Seymour, Peale, and Dougherty remained at the Council Bluffs for the winter to assist Thomas Say, the last remaining scientist. These men made some of the most solid contributions of the expedition during the winter of 1819–20 while Long was in Washington and Philadelphia. They sketched and interviewed Indians, translated texts of speeches, recorded word lists and grammar, and witnessed meetings held at the nearby Council Bluffs; their findings, published three years later, included a wealth of ethnographic data about the tribes of the Missouri Valley. In addition, Say and Peale gathered, sketched, described, and named many varieties of insects and plants, and even a few animals of the region.[19]

When Long reached Washington, he became aware of the criticism of War Department expenditures and his expedition was mounting. Recognizing the need for good publicity, he gave lengthy interviews and prepared statements that stressed positive accomplishments. He also submitted a preliminary report to the War Department, recounting the explorers' activities and noting that they would continue to gather data during the winter. In early January 1820 he met with John Calhoun to consider the expedition's status. Clearly, in their discussions Long minimized the obstacles to further exploration; nevertheless, the panic of 1819 and the resulting financial crash and depression forced Calhoun to urge caution. The War Department faced a sharply reduced budget for the next year, and he acceded to Long's request for continued exploration with obvious reluctance. It is difficult to understand why he considered any of the major's suggestions, given the evidence that the 1819 expedition had failed to achieve most of its stated goals, but perhaps Calhoun hoped for spectacular discoveries or at least solid accomplishments to help deflect congressional criticism of his department.

More likely the successful negotiations that led to the 1819 Adams-Onís Treaty between the United States and Spain affected his decision. That agreement set the boundary separating Louisiana from Spanish territory in Texas and beyond, using portions of the Red and Arkansas rivers to mark the line. Calhoun's orders to Long called for him to lead his men west along the Platte, then south to the Arkansas and Red rivers, returning along the latter streams to Fort Smith. While exploring the headwaters of each of these three rivers and portions of the central and southern plains, the 1820 expedition would serve to map the nation's new border as well as pursue the military and scientific goals that Long had proposed.[20]

Once Calhoun approved Long's journey, the major set out quickly to recruit new personnel and to rejoin his command. To replace Baldwin and Jessup he chose Dr. Edwin James, who had studied botany, geology, and medicine. With this background James could serve as physician as well as carrying out the duties of the two other men. Long's inability to sign on more scientists appears to have been the result of financial difficulties in the War Department; however, he was allowed to accept Captain John R. Bell as expedition journalist. Bell, an experienced officer, asked for a chance to exchange the "dull rounds of garrison duty" for what he hoped would be the excitement of travel and exploration. Having gotten a commitment of funds by late March 1820, Long and his two companions headed west.[21]

When they arrived at St. Louis, the promised funds had not yet arrived. Calhoun had warned Long that he should submit no bills for supplies or equipment before Congress approved the new budget, and it was not until April 28 that the War Department finally sent him a $2,000 draft. Unfortunately, it arrived in St. Louis weeks after the explorers had gone on, so they began the year without money and without the needed supplies it could have purchased.[22]

Because of these budgetary restraints, the 1820 expedition across the central plains lacked almost everything necessary to ensure success. The participants had a mere handful of instruments for survey and mapping work and some small boxes for carrying skins, plant samples, rock specimens, and the like. The 21-man expedition had only six extra horses to use during their four-month journey, and a food supply designed to last only one month. True, they took some goods that could be exchanged for food, but they expected to meet few Indians with whom to trade, and their supply proved far too small to sustain them all that summer. Whether Long was overoptimistic about being able to feed his men by hunting and trading, blind to the potential danger of starvation, or just plain foolhardy and willing to risk disaster remains unclear. Certainly, he thought he had little choice but to proceed, ill-equipped as he was. His orders directed him to lead the expedition west that summer; there was no time to write Calhoun in Washington asking for a delay. In fact, it seems likely that had they not set out when they did, the expedition would have been canceled, and after years of hoping for this opportunity, he refused to take that chance.

Despite their incomplete supplies, then, on the morning of June 6, 1820, Long and his companions set out from the Council Bluffs. They traveled west to the Pawnee villages in present east central Nebraska, halting briefly to hire guides from among the French traders living there, then headed west again along the Platte River. Shortages plagued them almost from the start; occasionally, the hunters succeeded in killing large animals, but within a few days each man's daily diet was reduced to a single pint of cornmeal, supplemented by a watery soup made with tiny scraps of salted or dried meat.[23]

For the next several weeks the explorers moved rapidly across Nebraska and eastern Colorado. Each morning and late afternoon the naturalists were able to do some work, but they spent most of the day riding rather than gathering scientific data. On Sundays they halted to rest the horses, clean equipment, and make astronomical observations. These breaks in the routine helped keep morale high; more important, they gave the scientists extra time. Traveling steadily, the group reached the Sand Hills in western Nebraska on June 19, and in early July they rode up to the foothills of the Rocky Mountains. On July 14 some of the explorers climbed Pike's Peak. While this might seem to have been a waste of time for men already pressed by a food shortage, in reality it allowed the expedition to learn about the headwaters of the Platte without having to follow that stream into the mountains. From Pike's Peak they traveled south to the Arkansas River.[24]

Long's orders from Calhoun called for the men to explore the headwaters of this stream, as well as those of the Platte and the Red, but noted that "the farther you can extend your route to the West *with safety*" (emphasis added), the better it would be. Clearly, Calhoun hoped for extensive probing into new areas, but he left the details to Long.[25] When the explorers reached the Arkansas River, Long dispatched a detachment upstream. These men rode west only through Royal Gorge before turning back to rejoin their companions; for the second time the party had failed to continue its explorations as far west as Calhoun had anticipated. Long's decision not to complete his assigned task to trace the Arkansas had more significance than not following the Platte, for the new border between American and Spanish territory ran along the south bank of the Arkansas River to its source. Since existing maps lacked the river course west of the Rockies, the expedition's failure to provide that information was its most significant omission of the 1820 summer.

Rather than continue west along the Arkansas, Long decided that the shortage of food for the men and forage for the animals had weakened the party so much that he needed to hurry the return trip to Fort Smith. He therefore divided the expedition, sending half, under Captain Bell, back east along the Arkansas and leading the others on southward to search for the Red River. Just how his superiors expected him to recognize which of the many streams flowing across the southern plains was the Red is unclear. In his 1806–7 expedition through that region, Zebulon Pike had encountered the same difficulty, and Stephen Long's party had no more information in 1820 about that illusive stream than had their predecessor. After enduring not only short rations but buffalo stampedes and violent thunderstorms, the explorers found the Red. Or at least they thought they had. Turning downstream, they headed east as fast as their tired mounts could carry them. On September 9, 1820, Long's astronomical observations indicated that they were farther north than expected, and several of the party voiced their "unpleasant fears" that this stream was a tributary of the Arkansas rather than the Red. Their fears proved correct: the river they followed was the Canadian.[26] After weeks of toil, danger, and near starvation, the disappointed explorers realized that once again they had failed to reach their objectives: during that summer they had not explored the sources of the Platte, the Arkansas, or the Red. It was with a sense of deep disappointment that the exhausted men struggled east to meet their comrades at Fort Smith, where the expedition ended in September.

During the return from the Rockies several of the soldiers in the escort detail deserted, taking horses and packs loaded with many of the scientists' notes and specimens and thus greatly reducing the scientific achievements made that summer.[27] Nevertheless the explorers reunited in Philadelphia during the 1820–21 winter, and there they began preparing maps and compiling Indian vocabularies, plant and animal descriptions, astronomical tables, and reports of their findings. The work went slowly, as several of the men suffered from malaria acquired on the expedition, but finally, in 1823, their report appeared under the title *Account of an Expedition from Pittsburgh to the Rocky Mountains . . . ,* essentially Edwin James's travel narrative with the scientists' findings woven into the discussion. The book offered scholars much new information about trans-Mississippi flora, fauna, geology, Indians, and agricultural potential. Soon the men were publishing scholarly articles and papers as well, and this outpouring of data and ideas about the West proved to be Long's most significant contribution to nineteenth-century science and knowledge.[28] One less positive contribution came from his labeling the area between the Platte and Arkansas rivers as the "Great American Desert" on one of his topographical maps. The idea of the plains as desert was nothing new — as far as the government was concerned, it merely echoed earlier descriptions by Lewis and Clark and Zebulon Pike — but Long's map was the first to incorporate the term.

Once the results of his 1819–20 expedition were published, Major Long appears to have tired of office work. On February 1, 1823, he proposed a national survey to map all the major towns, rivers, and other points of significance, offering to gather an "account of the Topography, soil and productions of the country."[29] Whether his letter nudged the War Department into renewed attention to frontier exploration is uncertain, but only a month later Colonel Alexander Macomb, then chief of engineers, asked Long to undertake another expedition. This one would focus on the upper Mississippi and Minnesota rivers and the Red River of the North, plus the region between the Red and the western tip of Lake Superior; Macomb asked "whether such duty at this time would be agreeable."[30]

Long hesitated for some weeks. Disappointed at the muted response to his earlier expedition, he appears to have considered declining the invitation. He had a growing but sickly family that needed attention, and he had thought of leaving the army to accept a civilian engineering position with the State of Virginia.

Once he decided to undertake the trip, however, he lost little time in recruiting scientists and gathering instruments and maps for the coming summer. Thomas Say and Samuel Seymour, both veterans of the 1819 and 1820 expeditions, agreed to participate; in addition, Long enlisted William Keating, described as "perhaps the nation's one and only professional mining engineer" at the time. James Colhoun, a cousin of the secretary of war, also joined the group to help with cartographic and astronomical duties. Long wrote asking Edwin James to join, too, but slow mail delivery prevented the doctor from learning of the expedition until it was to late to take part. On April 30, 1823, the explorers left Philadelphia for the frontier.[31] At Fort Crawford in Wisconsin they hired interpreters and added their escort of soldiers for the trip before heading up the Mississippi. On July 9 they left Fort St. Anthony at present Minneapolis and started up the Minnesota River west and north toward Canada.

This expedition proved less dangerous than that of 1820 but less productive as well. The party moved northwest to the Red River of the North and then to the Canadian border. From there they proceeded to Lake Winnipeg and east to Lake Superior. They explored its north shore and returned south to Detroit in early October. Eventually, William Keating published an account of this journey, but the 1823 expedition yielded far less of cartographic, military, and scientific value than had the movement across the plains.[32] It also brought to a close Stephen Long's career as an army explorer. For the next 40 years he labored as an officer in the Corps of Engineers, but never again did he get a frontier assignment. The excitement, danger, and attention that came to more successful explorers passed him by; the honors went to others.

In the meantime his orders called him to tasks perhaps equally significant for the settlement of the West but usually far less glamorous than exploring. As national interest in western explorations declined in favor of support for improved transportation, the Topographical Engineers lost no time assigning officers to transportation projects; in 1827, Long's superiors assigned him and another officer to help survey and plan construction of the Baltimore & Ohio Railroad. Long had experience with steam engines and locomotives, so the duty allowed him to focus his inventive skills where they might prove beneficial. In late 1827, Long suggested four potential routes, and the next spring he and a colleague submitted a full report to the railroad's board of directors. They also continued their survey work through the mountains. As a result of this experience Long published a railroad manual for surveyors and people directing construction. It included detailed tables for grades and curves, information about cuts and fills, and even computations of anticipated wind resistance to locomotives of varied shapes. Often copied, this manual offered competent guidance to other engineers.[33]

With that assignment completed, Long continued to perform railroad survey and design work for most of the 1830s. He invented or perfected and patented several new ways to build locomotive wheels and steam boilers. In addition, he surveyed the route for another railroad from Memphis to Cumberland, Maryland, with the idea of meeting the Baltimore & Ohio line there. Always optimistic, he proposed other routes throughout the Southeast but had neither time nor energy to survey them. For the next few years he designed parts of steam engines, carried out survey work for several New England states, and developed and patented a plan for bridge design that was first used by the B & O Railroad. He later published a bridge-building manual based on his calculations and experiences with that structure.[34]

Despite this heavy involvement in railroad issues, for most of the rest of his career Stephen Long concentrated on the problems of river transportation. Even before his railroad work began, he had struggled with the difficulties of improving navigational channels on the Ohio River. Then in 1830 his superiors assigned him temporarily to assist in the survey for the Pennsylvania Portage Canal.[35] He also helped design and build the system of inclined planes and stationary engines needed to complete the system.

From 1838 to the end of his career, with just a few short interruptions, Long spent most of his time and effort striving to improve navigation on the Ohio, Mississippi, Arkansas, Red, and lower Missouri rivers. In most cases snags and sandbars constituted the major dangers for shipping on these inland waterways. Working with Henry Shreve, Long supervised the development and use of snagboats to winch water-soaked trees and sunken logs out of the water. The army's attack on sandbars proved less successful; one could remove the old logs from the streambed, but the sand and silt merely shifted positions. Dredging proved laborious, expensive, and frequently ineffective. The engineers tried constructing small wing dams to divert the water, hoping to scour silted-in parts of the channel by using the power of the rushing water itself. Occasionally this worked for a time, but often it merely moved the sandbar downstream a few hundred yards. During the early 1840s Stephen Long superintended these efforts from his headquarters in Cincinnati.[36] Although his crews rarely got more than 100 miles beyond the Mississippi, these actions did improve transportation for people moving west and for merchants wanting to supply the pioneers.

During the Mexican War most of the army moved to the Southwest or the lower Mississippi Valley. To get men and supplies into the battle theater the army needed boats, so Long was temporarily assigned to the Quartermaster Department. With that move came orders to build two steamboats for use in supplying the troops. By February 1847 he had them ready for use and then received orders to build two more, which were completed by June. Later that year Long supervised construction of yet another pair of steamers for the army.[37]

Through the late summer and into the winter of 1847, Long served as a member of the court-martial that tried John C. Frémont for mutiny and insubordination, which arose out of the confusion of command in California. More the result of contradictory orders and the personal idiosyncrasies of Frémont and General Stephen Watts Kearney than of any particular crime or dereliction of duty, this trial attracted widespread national attention for months. Because Frémont had married Jessie Benton, daughter of Senator Thomas Hart Benton of Missouri, the trial took on political connotations and attracted far more attention than it probably deserved. When the posturing ended, the court found Frémont guilty on all counts, with the recommendation that he be dismissed from the service. President James Polk restored Frémont to duty a short time later, but the aggrieved officer soon resigned.[38]

When the Mexican war ended in 1848, Long received new orders, this time to supervise the construction of marine hospitals meant to provide care for boat crews on the Ohio and Mississippi rivers. He had begun work on one of these prior to the war and now returned to an enlarged assignment. The hospitals were to be built at Louisville and Paducah, Kentucky; Natchez, Mississippi; and Napoleon, Arkansas. For the next several years the Topographical Corps labored to complete the structures. Floods, varying appropriations, what Long described as excessive costs, and other assignments that called him away from the task all slowed the work. The hospitals took years to complete, cost tens of thousands of dollars, and yet rarely cared for many boatmen for the river crews. In 1868 the one at Napoleon, Arkansas, fell prey to the floodwaters of the Arkansas River.[39]

In 1853 the War Department appointed Long superintendent of western rivers, a term that seems to have encompassed all streams beyond the Appalachians.[40] Working out of headquarters in Louisville, Long was responsible for keeping the rivers open to navigation. Again he dispatched snagboat crews, dam builders, and surveyors throughout the summer and autumn months. Major projects attempted by his crews during the 1850s included blasting a channel around the Rock Island Rapids on the Mississippi, removing snags from the major streams, and opening the Red River by digging a channel through and around the Great Raft (a buildup of floating timber). These duties occupied most of Long's attention during the 1850s, although he received frequent orders to travel east to serve on a variety of boards and commissions. In some years the Topographical Corps received such a small appropriation from

Congress that it made little progress in achieving its goal of clearing the river channels. Nevertheless, its engineers worked steadily throughout the decade with such men and money as their budget allowed.[41]

When the Civil War broke out in April 1861, Long applied for promotion to the rank of colonel. After a hearing by a board of officers held that he was still capable of service, the aging engineer received his long-awaited promotion. Because of personnel changes throughout the army, Long became chief of the Topographical Engineers during the spring of that same year. In that capacity he supervised the work of the corps and strove to have his office prepare and distribute the thousands of maps that army commanders demanded. In early 1863 the Corps of Engineers absorbed the smaller Topographical Engineers, thus ending Long's independent command. Some months later, after several minor assignments around Buffalo, New York, Long received the news that his army career was over. On June 24, 1863, he replied that he would happily "take my place on the Retired list." Just a little over a year later, on September 4, 1864, he died at age seventy-nine at his home in Alton, Illinois.[42]

A competent though not particularly colorful man, Stephen Long served his country during its decades of rapid territorial growth and development. His career spanned the years 1815 to 1863, and during that time the Republic grew rapidly from a small, technologically underdeveloped society into a large industrial one. In several ways his experience typified that of many career officers of the era who spent decades carrying out routine tasks with only an occasional dangerous or exciting assignment. He did not fight Indians or Mexicans or even Confederates; rather, he worked to help the government establish its presence and control in frontier and western regions. His explorations brought scientific knowledge, new military installations, and increased geographic awareness of the West. His work as a railroad planner and engineer obviously made it easier for the United States and its citizens to move into the West during the last half of the nineteenth century. Finally, his efforts to improve and maintain safe transportation facilities on midwestern rivers promoted economic development and encouraged population movement throughout the central portions of the country and into the West.

Notes

1. Roger L. Nichols and Patrick Halley, *Stephen Long and American Frontier Exploration* (Newark: University of Delaware Press, 1980), 21–24; Richard G. Wood, *Stephen Harriman Long, 1784–1864* (Glendale, Calif.: Arthur H. Clark, 1966), 27–37.

2. Nichols, *Stephen Long*, 24–26; Wood, *Stephen Harriman Long*, 36–37.

3. Nichols, *Stephen Long*, 26; Joseph G. Swift, *Memoirs of General Joseph Gardner Swift* (Worcester, Mass: Press of F. S. Blanchard, 1890), 128, 204; Stephen Long to

James Monroe, February 20, 1815, Letters Received, Office of the Adjutant General (hereafter AG), Record Group (hereafter RG) 94, National Archives (hereafter NA).

4. John Livingston, "Colonel Stephen H. Long of the United States Army," in *Portraits of Eminent Americans Now Living: With Biographical and Historical Memoirs of their Lives and Actions,* 4 vols. (New York: Cornish, Lamport, 1853–54), 4:477; Swift, *Memoirs,* 142, 177. The recommendations from Swift and Roberdeau accompanied Long to the Secretary of War, Letters Received, AG, RG 94, NA.

5. Nichols, *Stephen Long,* 28–37; William Crawford to Long, July 2, 1816, Letters Sent, Office of the Secretary of War (hereafter SW), RG 107, NA.

6. *National Register,* March 29, 1817.

7. Long to James Monroe, March 15, 1817, Letters Received, SW, RG 107, NA.

8. Nichols, *Stephen Long,* 41–43; Smith to Long, May 1, 1817, Miscellaneous Treasury Accounts, Records of the General Accounting Office, RG 217, NA; Livingston, "Colonel Stephen H. Long," 479–80.

9. Stephen Long, "Voyage in a Six-Oared Skiff to the Falls of Saint Anthony in 1817," in *Collections of the Minnesota Historical Society* (St. Paul: Minnesota Historical Society, 1860–67), 2:8–88; Nichols, *Stephen Long,* 43–58; Wood, *Stephen Harriman Long,* 47–53.

10. Long to Joseph Swift, October 15, 1817, Letters Received, Office of the Chief of Engineers (hereafter CE), RG 77, NA; Long to Smith, February 12, 1818, Letters Received, SW, RG 107, NA.

11. Stephen Long, "Report of the Country composing the 9th Military Department," May 12, 1818, Engineers' Bulky File, CE, RG 77, NA.

12. Long to John Calhoun, August 31, 1818, Letters Received, SW, RG 107, NA; Calhoun to Joseph Swift, September 1, 1818, Letters Received, Engineers' Misc., RG 77, NA.

13. Nichols, *Stephen Long,* 65–76; Wood, *Stephen Harriman Long,* 61–76.

14. Nichols, *Stephen Long,* 70–71.

15. *Niles' Weekly Register,* May 22, 1819; Nichols, *Stephen Long,* 80–87; Wood, *Stephen Harriman Long,* 77–79.

16. Nichols, *Stephen Long,* 87–89; Edwin James, *Account of an Expedition from Pittsburgh to the Rocky Mountains,* vols. 14–17 of Reuben G. Thwaites, ed., *Early Western Travels,* 32 vols. (Cleveland, Ohio: Arthur Clark, 1904–7), 14:121–24.

17. Nichols, *Stephen Long,* 89–92; James, *Account,* 14:126–42.

18. Nichols, *Stephen Long,* 95–99; James, *Account,* 14:171–221; John Gale, *The Missouri Expedition, 1818–1820,* ed. Roger L. Nichols (Norman: University of Oklahoma Press, 1969), 62–63, 75.

19. Nichols, *Stephen Long,* 101–7; James, *Account,* 14:221–22, 229–30, 248–49, 251–52, 256–58, 263–64, 270–71.

20. Nichols, *Stephen Long,* 108–10; Long to Calhoun, January 22, 1820, Letters Received, SW, RG 107, NA; Calhoun to Long, February 22, 1820, Letters Sent, SW, RG 107, NA.

21. Nichols, *Stephen Long,* 111–12; Maxine Benson, "Edwin James: Scientist, Linguist, Humanitarian" (Ph.D. diss., University of Colorado, 1968), 6–24; John R. Bell to Calhoun, February 29, 1820, Letters Received, AG, RG 94, NA; Long to Calhoun, February 8, 1820, Letters Received, SW, RG 107, NA.

22. Nichols, *Stephen Long,* 112–13.

23. Wood, Stephen Harriman Long, 94–101; Nichols, *Stephen Long,* 117–29.

24. Wood, *Stephen Harriman Long,* 102–4; Nichols, *Stephen Long,* 130–33.

25. Calhoun to Long, February 29, 1820, Letters Sent, SW, RG 107, NA.

26. Nichols, *Stephen Long,* 136–48; James, *Account,* 16:180–81.

27. John R. Bell, *The Journal of Captain John R. Bell,* in Harlin M. Fuller and LeRoy R. Hafen, eds., *The Far West and Rockies Historical Series,* 15 vols. (Glendale, Calif.: Arthur H. Clark, 1957), 6:256–58.

28. Nichols, *Stephen Long,* 159–80.

29. Long to Christopher Vandeventer, February 1, 1823, in Robert L. Meriwether and W. Edwin Hemphill, eds., *The Papers of John C. Calhoun,* 9 vols. (Columbia: University of South Carolina Press, 1959–76), 7:452–55.

30. Alexander Macomb to Long, March 8, 1823, Letters Sent, CE, RG 77, NA.

31. Wyndham D. Miles, ''A Versatile Explorer: A Sketch of William H. Keating,'' *Minnesota History* 36 (December 1959): 297; Nichols, *Stephen Long,* 183–86.

32. Wood, *Stephen Harriman Long,* 121–31; Nichols, *Stephen Long,* 186–216. William H. Keating, *Narrative of an Expedition to the Source of St. Peter's River . . . Performed in the Year 1823,* 2 vols. (London: Geo. B. Whittaker, 1825; rpt., Minneapolis, Minn.: Ross and Haines, 1959), gives the expedition narrative and includes its scientific findings.

33. Wood, *Stephen Harriman Long,* 155–59; Livingston, ''Col. Stephen H. Long,'' 493–94; Stephen H. Long, *Railroad Manual, or a Brief Exposition of Principles and Deductions Applicable in Tracing the Route of a Railroad* (Baltimore, Md.: W. Wooddy, 1829).

34. Wood, *Stephen Harriman Long,* 161, 166–67.

35. Ibid., 150–51.

36. Louis H. Hunter, *Steamboats on the Western Rivers: An Economic and Technological History* (Cambridge, Mass: Harvard University Press, 1949), 181–86; Wood, *Stephen Harriman Long,* 201–10.

37. Wood, *Stephen Harriman Long,* 211–14.

38. Ibid., 214–16.

39. Ibid., 219–32.

40. John L. Abert to Long, April 27, 1853, Letters Sent, Topographical Engineers, RG 77, NA.

41. Wood, *Stephen Harriman Long,* 238–50.

42. Ibid., 253–63.

William S. Harney

by Richmond L. Clow

In 1861, after the Confederate attack on Fort Sumter, Brigadier General William Selby Harney waited at his St. Louis home for orders. The general was 61 years old and a veteran of numerous military campaigns in the American West; with northern politicians searching for capable military leaders, his exclusion from a Civil War command was too conspicuous to be an oversight. Rather, it was the result of the War Department's decades of conflict with the troublesome, strong-willed general, who had lost the trust of his superiors when he entered into an agreement with a Missouri secessionist.[1]

William S. Harney was born on August 27, 1800, in Haysboro, Tennessee, and received his commission as a second lieutenant in the First Infantry in 1818. During these early years, while stationed at Fort Warren, near Boston, Harney demonstrated a proclivity to get into trouble when, in the absence of his commanding officer, he assumed command of the military post. His commander believed Harney's actions were improper and ordered the young man court-martialed. He was acquitted, but this incident demonstrated a willingness to take matters into his own hands. It was the first of several such incidents: Harney was prone to speak out, take action, and worry about the results later.[2]

In August 1824, Harney, by then a first lieutenant, was assigned to Jefferson Barracks outside St. Louis, Missouri, and that city became his home. From this outpost he went with Major Benjamin O'Fallon and General Henry Atkinson on their treaty-making excursion to the tribes of the upper Missouri in the spring of 1825. After the expedition returned in the fall, William Ashley, the enterprising St. Louis fur trader, offered the newly promoted captain a position in his company, but Harney declined the offer, preferring to remain a soldier.[3]

His next military assignment was to accompany General Atkinson on a military expedition against Red Bird, a Winnebago leader who led an attack against several settlements in southern Wisconsin in June 1827. After a brief and unglamorous campaign, the Winnebagos were defeated, and Harney returned to life at the military post.[4] This short foray was his first military engagement against the Indians.

Harney next saw action against the Sauk and Fox Indians of Illinois who, pressured by whites, had ceded their lands east of the Mississippi River and moved into Iowa following the signing of the Treaty of St. Louis on November 3, 1804. Ignoring the treaty provision requiring them to remain west of the river, Black Hawk and his Sauk and Fox followers later returned to Illinois. Recognizing that he was considered a troublemaker and facing the threat of military hostilities, Black Hawk signed an agreement with Illinois Governor John Reynolds on June 30, 1831, agreeing never to return to the state without official permission.[5] Nevertheless, Sauk and Fox people under the leadership of Black Hawk crossed the Mississippi River again in the spring of 1832. When the Black Hawk War against these Indians began in Illinois, Harney served as General Zachary Taylor's assistant inspector and participated in the battle of Bad Axe.[6]

Although this war was never a source of pride for the army, Harney defended it, pointing out that the Sauk and Fox had violated the treaty by crossing the river without permission.[7] Unbending in his demand that the letter of the law be upheld by all parties, Harney never considered that laws and treaties might sometimes be broken because they were unjust. Throughout his professional life he employed the same reasoning, citing the letter of the law against any individual who disagreed with him. In an army composed of officers jealous and distrustful of each other, Harney was not above using the court-martial as a means of revenge against his professional adversaries.

Harney's next opportunity to uphold his vision of the law occurred in Florida during the Second Seminole War, a conflict that lasted eight years. According to Harney's strict understanding of Indian-white relations, because the Seminoles had signed the Treaty of Paynes Landing in 1832 that required them to leave Florida for the Indian Territory (present Oklahoma) after three years, those who refused to depart were guilty of breaking a treaty with the United States.[8] When many of the Seminoles decided to stay in Florida, Congress responded on May 23, 1836, by creating the Second Dragoons. In contrast to the First Dragoons, an older and steadier organization, the Second Dragoons were bold and dashing, always trying to surpass their predecessors in splendor.[9]

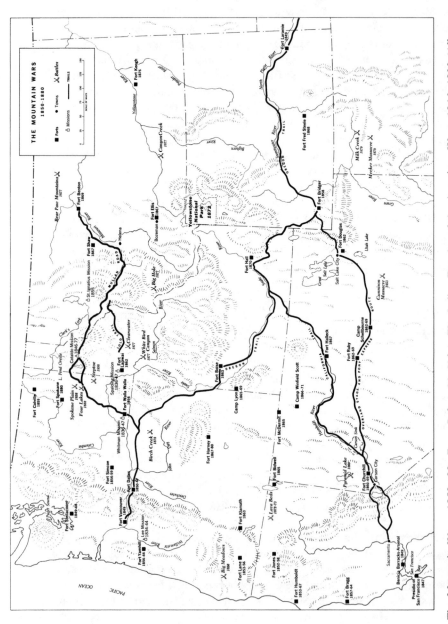

The Mountain Wars, 1850–80. *From Robert M. Utley,* The Indian Frontier of the American West, 1846–1890 *(Albuquerque: University of New Mexico Press, 1984). Reprinted by permission of the University of New Mexico Press.*

Harney, at this time a major and paymaster of the army, wanted to serve in the new regiment because of its potential for action. Neither he nor Wheaton Rector, who was appointed lieutenant colonel of the Second Dragoons, was happy with his assignment, so Harney—a Tennessee Democrat who understood the importance of political connections—pressed his old friend President Andrew Jackson for help; like other officers in the nineteenth-century American army, he often sought and used political favors. Subsequently, Jackson ordered the men to exchange positions; this action made Harney a lieutenant colonel and the second ranking officer of the Second Dragoons.[10] The young officer quickly became the ideal of a mounted soldier: tall, physically fit, a good judge of horse and rider. He possessed that added dash of flamboyance and confidence that helped make the Second Dragoons a proud unit.

Soon after its organization, the regiment was sent to Florida for duty in the Second Seminole War. Departing from Charleston, South Carolina, the raw recruits and their officers arrived at Fort Mellon, Florida, on February 6, 1837. Two days later, Wild Cat, also known as Coachoochee, attacked the fortification. Lieutenant Colonel Alexander Fanning stated that in his first Florida battle Harney "displayed the greatest boldness and vigor."[11]

William Harney gained valuable field experience in Florida which he did not forget in later years. In addition, his actions against the Seminoles earned him a reputation for daring, even to the point of rashness, as he pushed himself and his men into dangerous situations. In describing Harney's actions in Florida, Stephen Watts Kearny of the First Dragoons wrote in 1841: "You know the opinion I have of Col Harney, that he has no more brains than a Greyhound. Yet I consider that by his stupidity and repair in action, he has done more to inject the Indians with a fear of us and the desperate state of their cause, than all the other commanders."[12]

Kearny did not hide his dislike, but he realized that Harney's often ruthless and bold actions against the Seminoles brought some degree of success in a decidedly unglamorous war. In July 1839, Harney opened a trading post on the Caloosahatchee River in southwest Florida. Soon after his arrival, Seminoles attacked his party, killing 11 dragoons, but Harney escaped with his black slave and eight soldiers. Almost two years later, he avenged this attack when he and 35 soldiers surprised a party of Seminoles. They killed four men who were involved in the post raid and hanged five others as an example to the other Indians. Harney spared the life of one man only on the condition that the captive guide the soldiers to the Everglades camp of the Seminole chief known as Sam Jones.[13] Despite the many dishonorable aspects of the Second Seminole War, Harney emerged as a brevet colonel, honored for gallant and meritorious conduct in the Everglades campaigns. His reputation as an Indian fighter was growing.[14]

Duty in Florida ended for Harney in 1841 when he took an extended leave. By the time he returned to active duty late in 1842, the war in Florida was nearly over, and he was assigned to Baton Rouge Barracks, Louisiana. In 1843, he became post commander at Fort Washita, Indian Territory.[15]

After the Republic of Texas was annexed by the the United States in 1845, the Second Dragoons went to the Texas frontier, where they were assigned the difficult task of stopping Comanche and Lipan Apache raids against the frontier settlements. In October 1845, Lieutenant Colonel Harney rejoined the dragoons stationed at Camp Olmus near San Antonio de Bexar, Texas.[16] His first winter in Texas was uneventful, despite the growing tensions between Mexico and the United States, but in April 1846 a scouting party of dragoons approaching the north side of the Rio Grande was fired upon by Mexican troops. Harney was not with this detachment.

Once hostilities began, Zachary Taylor, commander of the forces in Texas, prepared to invade northern Mexico. The commander charged Harney with the protection of the Texas frontier from Indian raids and reluctantly gave him wide discretionary powers, including authority to ask the governor of Texas for volunteer troops for the defense of the remote settlements. Taylor allowed Harney these broad powers only because of the great distance between the general's headquarters at Matamoros, on the Rio Grande, and the West Texas frontier where troops were needed for defense.[18]

Harney, who was said to be as strong and determined as a lion but just as impossible to tame, boasted that he would take Mexico. In his attempt to do so, he disobeyed Taylor's orders and raised seven volunteer units of Texans, along with one company of Delaware Indians, as an invasion force to supplement the three companies of the Second Dragoons already at his disposal. Harney's confident, bold manner even convinced some civilians in Texas that he would make good his boast. In midsummer the recently promoted colonel marched south toward his destination, the Presidio de Rio Grande, and this unauthorized expedition crossed the river, encountering no hostilities at the town of Presidio. Meanwhile, General John E. Wool became the new commander of Texas, and he promptly ordered Colonel Harney to return to San Antonio. Harney waited five days; then he obeyed Wool's command but left three companies of Texas volunteers on the north bank of the Rio Grande.[19]

Harney claimed that this expedition to the river was designed only to obtain supplies, and Wool, though not satisfied with this explanation, did not arrest him. To make matters worse, Mexican soldiers eventually fired upon the Texas volunteers that Harney left behind, and these undisciplined Texans hastily retreated, burning the supplies that they were guarding. Harney's unauthorized campaign thus ended in complete failure.[20]

Harney's recruitment of an Indian company violated military regulations; Indians were to be used only as ''guides or spies.'' He also misused the volunteer troops, and his short foray to the south delayed Wool's departure from Texas to join the larger force preparing to invade Mexico.[21] This excursion to the Rio Grande was viewed by some as the act of an overzealous patriot; others saw it as the glory hunting of a vain, self-centered officer. Whatever the reasons, Colonel Harney's actions made him particularly vulnerable in the political battles that were fought in the officer corps during the Mexican War.

Because of Harney's disastrous expedition to the Rio Grande, General Winfield Scott ordered him to turn over seven companies of the Second Dragoons to a junior officer, Major Edwin Sumner. Harney, retaining command of only two companies, was ordered to stay with Taylor at Monterrey. This would prevent him from participating in the expedition against Mexico City. Scott wanted a more reliable officer to lead the dragoons, but he could not find a replacement with Harney's daring or his readiness to accept any dangerous assignment.[22] Harney wanted to accompany Scott in his invasion of Mexico; he protested loudly, and his complaint was heard in Washington. He believed that he had been slighted and that this order was an insult to his honor; in protest, he refused to obey it.[23]

Harney's defiance resulted in a court-martial. When the court convened, the accused pleaded guilty to all charges but also argued that an officer could not be separated from his command in such a manner. The judges, impressed by his desire for combat, were lenient and ordered him reprimanded by general orders. As a result, Harney remained as commander of the Second Dragoons and stayed with Scott for the duration of the land invasion. Because of Sumner's role in this affair, Harney did whatever he could to belittle him thereafter.[24]

Finally, in January 1847, the expeditionary force moved to the mouth of the Rio Grande and departed by oceangoing vessels to the Mexican coastal settlement of Veracruz. On March 21, Harney was scouting the region near Veracruz for Mexican guerillas. Against orders, he routed a force of Mexican nationals at the small village of Medelin. The incident was initially not reported, since Harney entered combat without orders or adequate support, not to mention danger to himself, but later he received distinction for the Medelin engagement. As the American army marched west from Veracruz, Harney and his dragoons drove the enemy from the small village of Plan del Rio on April 11, 1847. The retreating Mexican forces then took possession of Cerro Gordo and waited for the Americans.[25]

Cerro Gordo was a conical hill on the national road that led to Mexico City. At the top of the hill, the Mexican forces had established an artillery post. Two American officers, Ulysses S. Grant and Robert E. Lee, described the terrain as impossible to climb, but the summit had to be taken before the Americans could move on to Mexico City.[26] To a man like Harney who enjoyed overcoming adversity, Cerro Gordo presented a challenge he could not refuse.

On the clear Sunday morning of April 17, the battle for Cerro Gordo began. Both sides first exchanged artillery fire. As grapeshot peppered the ground,

Harney and his mounted troops charged, taking the small hill in front of Cerro Gordo. He held that position through the night, and another fight began the next day. Against destructive fire and ground obstacles, Harney and his dragoons charged to the summit of Cerro Gordo; his soldiers captured the guns at the top and turned the weapons upon the retreating Mexican soldiers. His pleased superiors promoted him to the rank of brevet brigadier general "for gallant and meritorious conduct in the Battle of Cerro Gordo." [27]

General Scott's forces slowed their westward march after the fall of Cerro Gordo. When the expedition resumed, Harney and the Second Dragoons were in front of the main body of infantry, performing scouting duty. At the same time, the dragoons drove away any stragglers from the retreating Mexican army, thus decreasing sniper activity. Late in August, Harney was involved in several minor skirmishes, but as the Americans entered the Valley of Mexico, lava rocks and the rugged terrain decreased the efficiency of the mounted soldiers. On August 20, however, Harney's dragoons routed the defenders and charged to the very gates of Mexico City, cutting the enemy down with saber blows. [28]

During the remaining days of the siege of Mexico City, Harney did not play a prominent role because the dragoons were ill-suited for street fighting. Instead, he worked at various camp duties and hunted for deserters. After a general court-martial, deserters who were captured following the Battle of Churubusco and accused of fighting with the Mexican Army were convicted of their crimes and sentenced to death by hanging. Harney, assigned to carry out the executions, arranged to have their hanging coincide with the fall of the enemy stronghold of Chapultepec. On September 13, 30 deserters stood in wagons with ropes around their necks tied to overhead beams. The prisoners waited in that position for two hours; not until the American flag slowly rose over the castle, signifying the victory, did Harney give the command to execute the men. He had used the full extent of the rules of war to make an example to other soldiers. The commander of the Second Dragoons approved of this brutal punishment for those who broke military law. [29]

Following the surrender of the Mexican army, the dragoons accompanied General Scott on his grand entry into the capital. The Mexican War both provided Harney with a personal victory and promoted his personal vendetta against those officers who were involved in his earlier court-martial. The officer corps of the American army ended the war in internal strife; future political developments only created additional tensions.

After the war, Harney was assigned to Texas, where Indian depredations were increasing. Attempting to prevent a general Indian war, General George Brooke, commander of military forces in Texas, established a line of posts from the Red River to the Rio Grande. This tactic of separating the tribes from the settlers had not worked in the past, and without adequate funding it was doomed to fail in Texas as well. Throughout 1849, Harney inspected these outposts and reported that the fortifications along the line were too far apart, permitting the Indians to slip between the installations and frontier towns. Harney stated that the Indians usually stole only small quantities of corn and rarely ever took any horses, but no matter how minor the infractions, frontiersmen did not tolerate petty theft. To stop a general war, Harney proposed that the main trail used by the Indians should be blocked by new military posts. In October 1849, at his recommendation, Fort Gates was established on the Leon River to prevent the Texas tribes from moving east. The man best known for fighting Indians now sought a nonviolent means to maintain peace by using military posts to prevent hostilities. A more compromising side of Harney was slowly surfacing.[30]

General Brooke died during his tour of duty in Texas, and Harney assumed command of the Eighth Military Department. He continued to rearrange both troops and garrisons in an attempt to protect the frontier by means of a line of forts. When General Persifor Smith took charge of the Eighth Military Department, he commended Harney's performance: "This officer displayed his accustomed activity in arresting incursions of the Indians, and the good effect of the measures adapted by him, are already discernible in the comparative tranquility which that section of the country has, for some time past, enjoyed."[31] When he left Texas in the summer of 1854, Harney had a better understanding of the causes of Indian discontent as well as the problems associated with defending the Great Plains.

Within a year Harney was on the Great Plains again, leading a military expedition against the Brulé Sioux. Open hostilities began on August 18, 1854, when a Mormon traveler reported to the post commander at Fort Laramie that a Sioux had butchered his lame cow. John L. Grattan, a young untried officer, pressed the incident as a perfect opportunity to teach the Sioux a lesson. The following day he took 29 men and one interpreter and marched to the nearby Brulé village under the leadership of Conquering Bear. Grattan bungled the entire operation, however; after the smoke of battle cleared, only one soldier had survived, and he later died. The official reports chastised the army for erring in judgment. The Sioux, in response to Grattan's defeat, increased their raids against travelers on the Overland Trail. Those raids could not be tolerated. A military campaign was ordered, and Harney was placed in command of the forthcoming Sioux expedition.[32]

On Christmas Eve of 1854, Harney returned to the United States from France, where he and his French wife of 20 years had been visiting, and started preparations for the military campaign against the Brulé bands. In the spring of 1855, he began assembling his troops at Fort Leavenworth, Kansas. Additional troops were ordered to Fort Pierre, the old American Fur Company post on the upper Missouri River. Inclement weather, disabled riverboats, and disease delayed the expedition, and summer had nearly passed before Harney was able to move west after the Sioux.[33]

The Brulé had broken the peace, violated the 1851 Treaty of Fort Laramie, and killed American soldiers. Therefore, Harney believed, they must be punished. He located Little Thunder's band at Blue Water Creek only a short distance east of Fort Laramie. On the morning of September 3, he ordered his troops to attack Little Thunder's camp. When the battle began, the infantry fired into the camp, forcing the Sioux to retreat northward up the valley, where the waiting cavalry completely routed them. It was the worst defeat that any Teton group had suffered to that time at the hands of the army.[34]

The Blue Water episode effectively humbled the Sioux. They feared the man who among the Teton people had become known as "Mad Bear." His attack on the village brought about a peace which, although based upon military strength, held for several years.

Harney, not wanting to lose the advantage gained over the Sioux at Blue Water, immediately prepared to march through their lands. Hearing rumors that the Sioux were retreating north toward the Black Hills, he left Fort Laramie and moved northeast to Fort Pierre in hopes of forcing the Indians to fight. Using confiscated Sioux lodges to protect themselves from the cold and wind, the soldiers trekked to the Missouri River. No Sioux warriors challenged them.[35]

Fort Pierre was their intended winter quarters, but its limited space forced many soldiers to winter in temporary camps either north or south of the old fur-trading post. During the winter, Harney rode between the camps, visiting his soldiers and inspecting the condition of the horses. Despite his gruff exterior, Harney was concerned for the welfare of his men and their horses; the health of both man and animal would determine whether that soldier could campaign in the spring. Sioux leaders came to Fort Pierre that winter, however, and told Harney that they wanted peace. Harney ordered a conference at Fort Pierre for March 1856, and articles of peace were ratified in the spring.[36]

Congress did not appropriate funds to implement the Harney treaty because Commissioner of Indian Affairs George Manypenny and Thomas Twiss, Indian agent for the Upper Platte Agency, convinced several members of Congress that it would be too costly to put into operation. The irony was that Harney's treaty stressed farming as a way of life for the Sioux, the same goal that Commissioner Manypenny espoused. The issue was not what the Sioux should do, but who would be in charge of making them change their lifestyle: the Indian Office or the army.

In assuming command of the Sioux expedition, Harney had taken control of Indian affairs in the war zone. He ordered all trading in horses stopped and confined all other business dealings with the Sioux to military posts. Harney defended his actions as a means to prevent the war from spreading; moreover, he believed that Indian Agent Twiss was trading ball and powder to the Indians.

Twiss was angered by Harney's actions and tried to persuade the Sioux not to meet with the colonel in the spring. This initiated a drawn-out conflict between the civilian and military branches of the government over the control of Indian affairs.[37]

The disagreement began at a time when the Department of the Interior had existed for only six years. Harney disliked the transfer of the Indian Bureau to the Interior Department; he believed the War Department should retain control over Indian affairs. He thought that the Indians respected and feared the army and that military officers could more honestly handle the natives, since they had nothing to gain by stealing from them, as tribal leaders complained the agents were doing. Moreover, the colonel claimed, the army with its police powers could hang or shoot whiskey peddlers and deal with violators on the spot. As always, action before words characterized Harney, and events like the slaughter at Blue Water helped to convince the public that the Interior Department should control Indian affairs. The support for civilian control was further reinforced by Harney's continued advocacy of military action as the necessary first step in dealing with the tribes on the plains: after they were subdued, he said, then they could become farmers.[38]

As part of his concept of military control, Harney advocated new equipment and new tactics for men serving on the northern plains during winter. Soldiers had to have better clothes in order to be efficient: Harney wanted hide moccasins to replace traditional footgear, buckskin gloves lined with flannel, buffalo coats, and new hats with ear flaps. Skin lodges obtained from plains tribes completed his requested equipment changes. Once properly outfitted, Harney contended, small units of 100 well-mounted soldiers could contain the northern plains warriors in the winter when the tribesmen were most vulnerable.[39]

From the northern plains of Nebraska Territory, Harney went to Kansas, where he used the army to maintain peace in the state during the general elections of 1857. In the summer of 1858 he was promoted to brigadier general and turned the leadership of the Second Dragoons over to a junior officer. He was then assigned to command the recently created military district in Oregon.[40]

Government officials feared a general uprising by the tribes in the Pacific Northwest, and Harney was sent to end the trouble. Before he arrived in the fall, however, Colonel George Wright had defeated the tribes, leaving to Harney the job of making peace. Harney turned the peacemaking duties over to a Jesuit, Pierre-Jean de Smet, who succeeded in reaching an agreement with the tribes. Meanwhile, Harney continued his battles with the Indian Bureau. When one Indian agent asked for military troops to protect his agency, the general responded by sending him 40 rifles and telling him to protect himself. Harney was never able to hide his dislike for civilian Indian agents.[41]

As the commander in Oregon without an Indian war, Harney occupied himself with administrative duties. He opened the Walla Walla Valley, closed since 1855, to white settlers. He also ordered soldiers to make a reconnaisance of the road from Walla Walla to The Dalles on the Columbia River, and then on to Salt Lake City.[42]

But the general found no satisfaction in mapping military roads; he enjoyed conflict and did not have to look hard to find it. In 1846, American and English negotiators had failed to determine the exact boundary through the Strait of Juan de Fuca, leaving the ownership of San Juan Island in question. Joint occupation of the island continued, with the Hudson's Bay Company maintaining a settlement near several American farmers. The two groups were never friendly, and when an American shot a pig owned by the company because it had damaged the farmer's fence and garden, violence almost erupted on the island. All attempts to reach a favorable settlement failed, and the English threatened to take the American to British Columbia for trial. Harney, taking a dim view of any threat to a U.S. citizen, responded promptly. Never known to be cautious, he ordered soldiers onto the island and sent a naval steamer to cruise its waterways. His actions created an international situation that took President James Buchanan by surprise.[43]

Harney claimed that he was protecting the American population on the island from the English and hostile Indians, but these were only surface issues. The importance of the San Juan affair was that the controversy involved the Hudson's Bay Company and its possessory rights below the forty-ninth parallel. In 1859, when the company's charter expired in British Columbia, Harney and other officials believed that the company had also lost the right to occupy the island below the international boundary. Government officials from both countries were already studying this diplomatic question when Harney moved his soldiers onto the island. Although Harney had acted without orders, his actions were sustained by Secretary of War John Floyd.[44]

After the Americans landed on the island, the English dispatched a warship, and both sides waited. President Buchanan, hoping to avoid a confrontation, ordered General Winfield Scott to Oregon with instructions to settle the issue. Scott negotiated a military compromise whereby the United States would keep one company of infantry on the island and the English were allowed one warship. Scott also replaced the commanding officer of the island with a man whom he considered more reliable.[45] Scott's entry into the San Juan situation only increased the animosity that existed between him and Harney. Harney retaliated against Scott by court-martialing for minor infractions any junior officers who supported his superior—thus maintaining the letter of the law while violating the spirit of the military service. George Ihrei, a disgruntled first lieutenant, wrote the secretary of war that Harney was a rough man who should not be leading soldiers.[46]

Following the San Juan affair, Harney was relieved of duty on the Pacific coast and ordered to assume command of the Department of the West. The eastern boundary of this department was the entire length of the Mississippi River and north to the international line. The western border was the continental divide. The boundary then ran south to the northern edge of New Mexico Territory, east to the Arkansas River, and south to the Gulf of Mexico following the Louisiana-Texas border. This command permitted Harney to return to his home in St. Louis, but what should have been a happy occasion was soured by the impending Civil War. Many of his friends sympathized with the south; officers he had served with resigned their commissions and joined the Confederate army. In this crisis, political position became more important than military ability: the fact that Harney was a good Democrat from a slave state made him an unreliable officer in the eyes of many northern political leaders.

Despite the doubts of others, Harney remained loyal to the Union and prepared to defend the Department of the West. He removed troops from Fort Randall and Fort Kearny, Nebraska Territory, and stationed these soldiers at Fort Leavenworth. It was also his duty to protect the military arsenal at St. Louis, a potential target for Confederate forces, but his methods angered Union leaders. In April, the secession question had not been resolved in Missouri, and to make certain that the arsenal did not fall to the enemy, Union men urged Harney to accept Missouri civilian volunteers to help the regular army guard the installation. The general refused, asking for restraint instead. He hoped to prevent the arming of a mob that might create additional troubles. Union leaders viewed this decision as bordering on treason.

Ordered to Washington, D.C., to confer with northern military leaders, Harney departed on April 21, 1861; four days later Confederate soldiers stopped his train near Harpers Ferry, Virginia, and placed Harney under house arrest at the Confederate governor's home in Richmond. He thus became the first prisoner of war, an inglorious position for such a headstrong and proud officer.[47] While they detained Harney in Virginia, the rebels asked him to defect and join the Southern cause. When the general refused, they released him and permitted him to continue on his way to Washington. Initially, then, both sides had wanted him, but by the end of April 1861, neither the North nor the South trusted Harney.[48] This distrust was understandable during those desperate times when no one on either side tolerated anything less than absolute loyalty.

Returning to St. Louis in early May, Harney was confronted by the ongoing crisis. The mob had grown angrier in his absence, and in order to protect the arsenal, Harney ordered more soldiers and several pieces of artillery into the city; he still maintained his position that civilians should not be armed. As tempers flared, the general urged the people of Missouri to remain in the Union and assured them that the army would not become involved in state affairs. His last act as commander of the Department of the West was to sign an agreement with Major General Sterling Price, civilian commander of the state troops of Missouri, giving Price the authority to make all military decisions in Missouri pertaining to state affairs.[49]

In signing the ill-fated Harney-Price agreement, Harney had hoped to spare

Missouri the hostilities that were imminent in other states by keeping his own federal troops out of a conflict with state militia. His downfall resulted from trusting the secessionist and later Confederate officer Sterling Price. He was guilty of an error in judgment, and zealous unionists demanded his removal. Several students of the period have viewed Harney's action as both honorable and sincere, but the general had trusted the wrong people during those days of despair.[50] Northern critics opposed his nonaction in Missouri and forced him out of his command. On May 30 unionist leader Francis Blair delivered *Special Orders 135,* removing Harney from command of the federal Department of the West and granting him leave of absence until further orders.[51]

With Harney's removal, Missouri became the middle ground as the secessionists and unionists squared off. Characteristically, Harney did not contain his bitterness; he believed that he had been "relieved from the command . . . in a manner that has inflicted unmerited disgrace upon a true and loyal soldier." Surely, he added, "my countrymen will be slow to believe that I have chosen this portion of my career to damn with treason my life."[52]

During the early years of the Civil War, Harney remained in St. Louis and continued to seek a command, requesting assignments on the Pacific coast or in the southwest, where he could be away from the eastern conflict. He never was reassigned, and in 1863 he retired from active service as a major general. Whenever trouble erupted between settlers and western Indian tribes, however, frontiersmen asked government officials to send Harney to their region. Writing about the mood of the people on the plains, General Samuel R. Curtis commented on the extent of Harney's fame: "Since General Harney's attack of the Sioux, many years ago at Ash Hollow [Blue Water Creek], the popular cry of settlers and soldiers on the frontier favors an indiscriminate slaughter, which is difficult to restrain." Curtis went on, "I abhor the style, but so it goes from Minnesota to Texas."[53]

This popular opinion of Harney and his reputation as an Indian fighter reflected only part of his character, since he had also worked for peace between Indians and whites. In later years his greatest asset was not his ability to fight the Indians but his usefulness as a peace negotiator who believed that the plains tribes had been mistreated and who possessed a keen knowledge of Indian peoples and their cultures. In 1865, President Andrew Johnson appointed Harney to the government commission that was to make peace with the Cheyenne, Arapaho, Kiowa, and Commanche tribes. Harney's appointment was a sensible one; his years of experience among the Indian people gave him a perspective tempered by reality.

Truces were completed with the warring southern plains tribes before the peace commission could begin its work. In the fall of 1865 the commission began negotiations at a council site near Wichita, Kansas. The Treaty of the Little Arkansas was signed with the Cheyennes and Arapahos on October 14, 1865, and a subsequent Treaty of the Little Arkansas was made with the Comanches and Kiowas four days later. Generally, the tribes promised to stop their raids on the settlers and withdraw to the lands south of Kansas and east of New Mexico in return for government rations.[54]

These treaties of 1865 did not bring immediate peace to the southern plains, however. In order to end the fighting throughout the Great Plains, Congress established the Indian Peace Commission of 1867. Harney served on this commission, which traveled to the southern plains in 1867, its members hoping to create a lasting peace between the tribes and the United States. When the first council convened, Harney was in his late sixties, with snow white hair and a full white beard. He was the only member of the Peace Commission whom the Indians recognized, and he found old friends as he went from council to council. Indians he had fought before the Civil War now saw him come to make peace; in the end, they had earned his respect, and he had earned theirs. Though not an orator, his practical approach to the Indian people's problems was important to the commission's ultimate success.[55]

During the councils, Harney became the defender of the Indian. He stressed that they needed food and clothing first; then the whites could worry about saving their souls. As the buffalo diminished, the tribes needed government help in order to survive. (Harney's concern for the Indian stopped at the ''wild Indian,'' however; he held acculturated Indians in disfavor. He called them ''tame Indians'' and felt that they were as evil as any white whiskey peddler in the country.)[56] The signing of the Medicine Lodge Treaty of 1867 was due in part to Harney's patience and sympathy for the Indians.

The members of the commission next attempted to bring peace to the northern plains. During the discussions that led to the 1868 Treaty of Fort Laramie, Harney played a similar role. He was later instrumental in the establishment of government facilities on the Great Sioux Reservation. In partial fulfillment of this treaty, Harney was placed in charge of the administrative district known as the Great Sioux Reservation; this included all the land west of the Missouri River in present South Dakota. In the fall of 1868, Harney ordered several Indian agencies built along the Missouri River. One was constructed at the mouth of Whetstone Creek, another at Cheyenne River, and a third at the Grand River; with the agent's help, the Sioux were to become farmers and pursue the path of white civilization. Harney left this temporary assignment in 1869 once these agencies were in operation. It was his last government assignment.[57]

The general had journeyed far since entering the United States Army 51 years before. He had participated fully in the nation's frontier expansion. When the movement west resulted in the displacement of tribes and led to military campaigns, it was Harney's active and successful involvement in these confrontations that earned him an enviable reputation as an Indian fighter, especially after he subdued the Brulés at Blue Water. That engagement became a standard for other officers to follow. The image of a single-minded Indian fighter, however, misrepresents his character, for in addition to his passion for battle, he also understood the need for a humane policy once conflict was over. Few officers ever equaled his success with Indian peoples. By the time he died in Orlando, Florida, on May 9, 1889, William Harney's name was synonomous with the American military frontier.

Notes

1. *The National Cyclopedia of American Biography,* 59 vols. (New York: James White, 1907), 5:288; Dumas Malone, ed. *Dictionary of American Biography,* 20 vols. (New York: Scribner, 1932), 8:280–81.

2. St. Louis *Republic,* May 10, 1889; Logan U. Reavis, *The Life and Military Services of General William Selby Harney* (St. Louis, Mo.: Bryan, Brand, 1878), 45. The latter is a vanity biography but contains some useful information. The best single study of Harney is George Rollie Adams, "General William Selby Harney: Frontier Soldier, 1800–1889" (Ph.D. diss., University of Arizona, 1983).

3. Reavis, *Harney,* 60–68.

4. Ibid., 70.

5. Perry A. Armstrong, *The Sauks and the Black Hawk War with Biographical Sketches* (Springfield, Ill.: H. W. Rokker, 1887; rpt., New York: AMS Press, 1979), 176–77.

6. Holman Hamilton, *Zachary Taylor: Soldier of the Republic* (Indianapolis, Ind.: Bobbs-Merrill, 1941), 91.

7. Reavis, *Harney,* 433.

8. Ibid.

9. Theophilus F. Rodenbough, comp., *From Everglade to Canon with the Second Dragoons* (New York: Van Nostrand, 1875), 18; Albert G. Brackett, *History of the United States Cavalry from the Formation of the Federal Government to the 1st of June, 1863* (New York: Argonaut Press, 1965), 38, 159.

10. Reavis, *Harney,* 91.

11. Quoted in Rodenbough, *From Everglade to Canon,* 24.

12. Stephen W. Kearny to Ethan A. Hitchcock, May 6, 1841, Ethan A. Hitchcock Collection, Missouri Historical Society, St. Louis.

13. Captain Joseph La Motte to Doctor William Beaumont, January 7, 1841, William Beaumont Papers, Missouri Historical Society, St. Louis.

14. Francis B. Heitman, comp. *Historical Register and Dictionary of the U.S. Army,* 2 vols. (Washington, D.C.: Government Printing Office, 1903), 1:502.

15. Adams, "General William Selby Harney," 127–31.

16. Reavis, *Harney,* 154; *Mexican War Correspondence, House Exec. Docs.,* 30th Cong., 1st sess., no. 60, p. 83.

17. *Mexican War Correspondence, House Exec. Doc.* no. 60, pp. 140, 288.

18. Ibid., 304–5, 400.

19. Ibid., 304–5; Justin H. Smith, *The War with Mexico,* 2 vols. (New York: Macmillan, 1919), 1:369.

20. *Mexican War Correspondence, House Exec. Doc.* no. 60, pp. 424–25.

21. Ibid., 400

22. Ibid., 866–70.

23. Ibid., 869.

24. Charles W. Elliott, *Winfield Scott, the Soldier and the Man* (New York: Macmillan, 1937), 449–50.

25. Rodenbough, *From Everglade to Canon,* 135–40.

26. Smith, *War with Mexico,* 2:49.

27. *Mexican War, House Exec. Docs.,* 30th Cong., 1st Sess., no. 8, pp. 274–81; Rodenbough, *From Everglade to Canon,* 436.

28. *Mexican War, House Exec. Doc.* no. 8, pp. 303–4, 307, 318.

29. Charles S. Hamilton, "Memoirs of the Mexican War," *Wisconsin Magazine of History* 14 (September 1930): 82; Smith, *War with Mexico,* 2:385 n.

30. *Annual Report of the Secretary of War* (Washington, D.C.: Government Printing Office, 1849), 138–39, 143–45; Robert A. Trennert, Jr., *Alternative To Extinction: Federal Indian Policy and the Beginning of the Reservation System, 1846–1851* (Philadelphia: Temple University Press, 1975), 90.

31. *Annual Report of the Secretary of War* (Washington, D.C.: Government Printing Office, 1851), 105.

32. Robert M. Utley, *Frontiersmen in Blue: The United States Army and the Indian, 1848–1865* (New York: Macmillan, 1967), 113–15.

33. Richmond L. Clow, "Mad Bear: William S. Harney and the Sioux Expedition of 1855–1856," *Nebraska History* 61 (Summer 1980): 135–37.

34. Utley, *Frontiersmen in Blue,* 116–18.

35. Clow, "Mad Bear," 142.

36. Utley, *Frontiersmen in Blue,* 118–19.

37. Harry S. Anderson, "Harney v. Twiss: Nebraska Territory, 1856," *Westerners Brand Book* 20 (March 1963): 1–3, 7–8.

38. William S. Harney to the Secretary of War, November 10, 1855, Department of the West, Records of the U.S. Continental Commands, Record Group 393, National Archives.

39. William S. Harney to Samuel Cooper, February 21, 22, 1856, ibid.

40. Herbert H. Bancroft, *History of the Pacific States of North America,* 25 vols. (San Francisco: History Company, 1888), 11:461.

41. Bancroft, *Pacific States,* 11:464; Hiram M. Chittenden and Alfred Talbot Richardson, eds. *Life and Letters and Travels of Father Pierre-Jean De Smet, 1801–1873, among the North American Indians,* 4 vols. (New York: Francis P. Harper, 1905), 2:730–32.

42. D. E. Livingston-Little, "An Economic History of North Idaho, 1800–1900," *Journal of the West* 3 (January 1964): 49; Bancroft, *Pacific States,* 11:461–65.

43. *Island of San Juan, Senate Exec. Docs.,* 36th Cong., 1st sess., no. 10, pp. 6–9.

44. *Correspondence with General Harney, House Exec. Docs.,* 36th Cong., 1st sess., no. 98, pp. 2–5.

45. Elliott, *Winfield Scott,* 665–70.

46. *Correspondence with General Harney, House Exec. Doc.* no. 98, pp. 6, 15–17, 21; *General Harney's Administration in Oregon, House Exec. Docs.*, 36th Cong., 2d sess., no. 51, pp. 1–2.

47. *The War of the Rebellion: A Compilation of the Official Records of the Union and Confederate Armies*, 53 vols. (Washington, D.C.: Government Printing Office, 1902), 1:662, 670; 51:350; 51:50, 64–65; 53:482, 487.

48. Ibid., 15:501; 52:152.

49. Ibid., 15:374–75.

50. Albert Castel, *General Sterling Price and the Civil War in the West* (Baton Rouge: Louisiana State University Press, 1968), 16–24; Robert E. Shalhope, *Sterling Price: Portrait of a Southerner* (Columbia: University of Missouri Press, 1971), 160–66.

51. Gerald E. Gannon, "The Harney-Price Agreement," *Civil War Times* 23 (December 1984): 44.

52. *War of the Rebellion,* 3:383.

53. Ibid., 48:503.

54. Utley, *Frontiersmen in Blue,* 337–38; Donald J. Berthrong, *The Southern Cheyennes* (Norman: University of Oklahoma Press, 1963), 241–44.

55. *Army and Navy Journal,* December 7, 1867, p. 251.

56. Douglas C. Jones, *The Treaty of Medicine Lodge: The Story of the Great Treaty Council as Told by Eyewitnesses* (Norman: University of Oklahoma Press, 1966), 18, 42, 100, 120–23.

57. Ray H. Mattison, "The Indian Reservation System on the Upper Missouri, 1865–1890," *Nebraska History* 36 (September 1955): 145–46.

James H. Carleton

by
Arrell Morgan Gibson

Courtesy Museum of New Mexico

At the close of the Civil War, Brigadier General (Brevet Major General) James Henry Carleton was the most powerful military figure in the American West. He ruled the territory between the Pecos and Colorado rivers with an iron hand. Carleton's genius for military defense and logistics had thwarted fulfillment of the Confederacy's western design. His direction of a series of intensive and extended Indian campaigns, and his concentration of the Apaches and Navajos on the military reservation at Bosque Redondo, had pacified the territory. Under a cloak of the necessity of war, he had suspended civil process in the Department of New Mexico and, according to local citizens, administered that jurisdiction as a military satrapy. In March 1865 he was breveted major general in both volunteer and regular ranks for meritorious service during the war. Then on October 6, 1866, at his power summit, Carleton was informed by the secretary of war that he had been reduced in rank to lieutenant colonel and assigned to the Fourth Cavalry at San Antonio, Texas. Postwar army politics prevented Carleton from recouping his military fortunes in rank and assignment. He died in 1873, bitter toward the nation he regarded as having ill-used his talents.

Born at Bangor, Maine, in 1814, Carleton grew up under the care of a widowed mother. As a youth he worked at becoming a writer. His literary correspondents included Charles Dickens, who urged him to pay special heed to the land and its people, particularly the Indians. Carleton's bent for writing surfaced throughout his military career in an imposing list of publications and in the humanistic flavor he imparted to his military correspondence.[1]

In 1838, Maine Governor John Fairfield sent forth a call for militia volunteers to guard the state border in a dispute with Canada. Carleton, then 25, responded and was commissioned lieutenant in a volunteer rifle company. Upon his discharge in 1838, Carleton sought to become an officer in the regular army. Since the War Department reserved commissions for West Point graduates except in those cases where an applicant had strong political support, Governor Fairfield, Hannibal Hamlin (later Vice-President in Lincoln's first administration), and Maine senators and representatives wrote letters to Secretary of War Joel Poinsett, recommending Carleton for a commission. Carleton was soon summoned to Washington, D.C., where he passed the officer's examination. On October 18, 1839, he was commissioned second lieutenant in the First Dragoons and assigned to the United States Cavalry School of Practice, Carlisle Barracks, Pennsylvania. In early 1841, Carleton sailed from Baltimore in charge of a detail of 100 cavalrymen. At New Orleans, he and his men boarded river steamers that transported them, via the Mississippi and Arkansas rivers, to Fort Gibson, situated near the mouth of Grand River in the Indian Territory (present Oklahoma). Thereafter, except for two brief periods, Carleton's entire military career was spent in the American West.[2]

His early assignments at Fort Gibson included leading dragoon patrols along the American border on the Red River, exploring and mapping remote areas, marking new trails and roads, and escorting travelers bound for New Mexico, California, and Oregon. He early learned the construction, supply, and management of frontier military posts and the peculiar problems of maintaining a frontier army.

The most demanding tasks of Carleton's Indian Territory duty were investigating the frontier slave trade and suppressing liquor traffic among the emigrant Indians from the southern states. Comanche and Kiowa raiders carried black slaves from the Texas settlements to remote trading posts in western Indian Territory and bartered them for blankets and guns. The traders then sold the slaves to emigrant Creek and Choctaw planters. Carleton's charge was to seek out the bondsmen and restore them to their erstwhile owners. Small distilleries along the Red River in Texas produced great quantities of raw frontier whiskey, which traders pandered among the Indian nations in violation of the federal Intercourse Law. Carleton's dragoon patrols suppressed this traffic with a vengeance.[3]

Carleton departed Fort Gibson for Fort Leavenworth in 1842. From that Missouri River post he led a party of dragoons to a point near the Council Bluffs, where he supervised the construction of Fort Croghan. The garrison at this post was expected to separate the Sioux from the Potawatomis and other eastern Indians being relocated on the northern margins of the Indian Territory. Carleton's assignments at Fort Leavenworth included maintaining surveillance for contraband liquor cargo stowed among goods being shipped up the Missouri River for traders working among the northern tribes.[4]

Carleton was also a member of Major Clifton Wharton's dragoon expedition to the Pawnee villages in Nebraska, carried out to improve relations between the Pawnees and the Sioux. Expedition members explored and mapped the Platte River and its lower tributaries. During the winter of 1844–45, Carleton was assigned to a dragoon force commanded by Colonel Stephen Watts Kearny. Its mission was to escort an Oregon-bound party to South Pass, Wyoming. There Kearny was to explore south to Bent's Fort on the Arkansas River, then return to Fort Leavenworth.[5]

At the outbreak of the Mexican War in 1846, Carleton was transferred from Fort Leavenworth back to Fort Gibson and then to San Antonio, assigned to the Central Division commanded by Brigadier General John Wool. Carleton rode into Mexico as commander of Company A, First Dragoon Regiment, and special aide to General Wool. He served at Buena Vista and on Wool's orders studied the approaches to Saltillo. During 1847, Carleton was successively advanced in rank to captain and major.[6]

Following the Mexican War, Carleton returned briefly to Carlisle Barracks, then proceeded to Fort Leavenworth. During 1850 he was assigned to the military Department of New Mexico, commanded by his wife's uncle, Colonel John Garland. Carleton and his dragoon unit, Company K, performed escort duty on the Santa Fe Trail until 1851, when he assisted in the construction of Fort Union. The following year he led a dragoon column across eastern New Mexico in search of the Mescalero Apaches. It was on this reconnaissance that he first saw and explored the Bosque Redondo sector of the Pecos valley. Carleton's report of the expedition to the Mescalero country included a recommendation that the War Department authorize construction of a military post at Bosque Redondo. During 1853, Carleton was placed in command of the cavalry station at Albuquerque, which remained his duty post until his assignment to California.[7]

Soon after he reached Albuquerque, Carleton was ordered to explore the Gran Quivira country, examine the ruins of that place, ascertain the suitability of the Abo Pass for a railroad route, and make contact with the Apaches. Carleton led his squadron of cavalry, Companies H and K, First Dragoons, out of Albuquerque on December 14, 1853. He found the Quivira ruins and the Abo Pass (which he strongly recommended for the projected railroad route across south central New Mexico), but no Apaches. The Indians had faded into the mountains ahead of his march.[8]

During the mid-1850s, Navajo and Apache raiders increased their depredations on the settlements of New Mexico. Regular and volunteer troops were in the field much of the time, attempting to search out and destroy the Indian settlements that supported these attacks. Carleton and his dragoon squadron joined with Kit Carson and his company of New Mexico volunteers during 1854 for a campaign against the Jicarilla Apache bands that were desolating the settlements of northern New Mexico. When Pueblo Indian scouts trailed the Jicarilla raiders beyond Taos to the Purgatory River into the Raton Mountains and discovered the Indian encampment, Carleton and Carson moved their men up for a surprise attack. Most of the Apaches escaped but abandoned their large encampment. The troops captured vast quantities of camp equipage, food, weapons, plunder, and a large herd of horses. Relentless pressure by regular and militia troops forced Apache and Navajo leaders to negotiate peace agreements with American officials, which had the effect of bringing temporary order to the Department of New Mexico.[9]

Major Carleton's next assignment was at Philadelphia. In 1855, Secretary of War Jefferson Davis had sent a United States military commission consisting of Captain George B. McClellan, Major Alfred Mordecai, and Major Richard Delafield to Europe to study the continental army tactics applied in the Crimean War. The commission collected its vast files of notes, memoranda, maps, drawings, and reports at Philadelphia, and Carleton was one of the field officers called in to analyze and evaluate the commission's files. His assignment was to study the papers on cavalry tactics, paying special heed to Cossack maneuvers. Carleton also examined the supply, commissary, and ordnance papers containing information on camp equipment and clothing, arms and ammunition, subsistence, transportation of men and animals, freight vehicles, camp hospitals, and construction of fortifications, bridges, and pontoons.[10]

Carleton completed his military commission studies in August 1857; on his return to the West he commanded recruit replacements for the Eighth Infantry in their movement to New Mexico. Ordered back to Washington in 1858, he was directed to command 700 soldiers consigned to California via the Isthmus of Panama. After delivering the men to the officer in charge of the Pacific Department, he was assigned to Fort Tejon on the Butterfield Overland Stage Road.[11]

Fort Tejon remained Carleton's duty station until the outbreak of the Civil War. The principal activity of troops at this post was to guard Tejon Pass and escort mail stages and other traffic through this hazardous crossing. Occasionally, Carleton received orders calling for special assignment away from Fort Tejon. In April 1859 he marched with 80 dragoons for Salt Lake City. His mission was to escort the United States paymaster, and to investigate the bloody 1857 Mountain Meadows Massacre (when 120 emigrants had been murdered by Mormons and their Indian allies) and "bury the bones of the victims." The findings he submitted to the War Department were subsequently published as a congressional document titled *Report on the Mountain Meadows Massacre.*[12]

Upon his return to Fort Tejon, Carleton led dragoon patrols on the Mohave Desert and supervised the construction of camps to accommodate travelers on the Salt Lake route. During May 1861, as the sectional crisis intensified, Carleton and 50 men from Company K, First Dragoons, were transferred from Fort Tejon to Los Angeles. Carleton supervised the organization of home guard companies in the communities of southern California, with Dragoons serving as drill instructors. Since Confederate agents were active in southern California, Carleton's duties included a visit to San Bernardino, dressed as a civilian, to investigate local political sentiment and determine the need for companies of troops there.[13]

In July 1861, Secretary of War Simon Cameron telegraphed California Governor John G. Downey, directing him to muster a regiment of volunteer infantry and five companies of volunteer cavalry to replace those regular troops being drawn from the Pacific coast to bolster Union defenses in the eastern United States. Initially, the California volunteer army was to guard the Overland Mail, which was being moved from the southern to the central route. Cameron recommended that Major Carleton be promoted to colonel in the volunteers and placed in command of this California volunteer army. Upon receiving the appointment, Carleton went to San Francisco to supervise the recruitment of the First California Volunteers, drawn chiefly from the San Francisco–Sacramento area.[14]

The dominant Union community in California was apprehensive about the threat of a Confederate cabal in the state. Southern California, particularly the Los Angeles area, was regarded as a rebel nest; in the minds of state Union leaders, "treason stalked abroad" there. To guard this part of the state against an anticipated Confederate uprising, Colonel Carleton was directed to concentrate his volunteer army in the Los Angeles area. During September 1861 he moved the troops from San Francisco to San Pedro by steamer and scattered the companies in camps across the Los Angeles–San Bernardino sector, where he ordered his company commanders to continue the training of their troops with daily marching and skirmishing practice.[15]

The failure of the rebel cabal to materialize led Carleton to spread his volunteer army in a wider defensive cordon extending from San Diego and Los Angeles east to Fort Yuma on the Colorado River. His zeal for his command assignment and mission manifested itself in his orders to the company commanders. He warned them to be alert for Confederate agents attempting to slip through their lines: "If you use circumspection you can never be surprised. . . . All persons passing into Sonora or to Arizona from California must take the oath of allegiance before they pass; so must all coming into California by the route overland via Yuma. Do not hesitate to hold in confinement any person or persons in that vicinity, or who may attempt to pass to or from California, who are avowed enemies of the Government or who will not submit to the oath of allegiance. Keep an exact record of name, place of residence, age, occupation, and whence he came and whither he is to go, of each person passing the river to or from California." The garrison at Yuma was directed to "seize all the ferryboats, large and small upon the Colorado River. All the crossings of the river must be done at one point under the guns of the fort."[16]

Carleton goaded his officers to stay constantly in the field watching for Confederate agents or leading details into the desert for the purpose of cleaning sand and debris from every well and spring between Camp Wright on the Butterfield Road and Fort Yuma on the Colorado River. For fear the troops might still have idle moments, Carleton directed that each company increase its skirmish practice and that the officers and noncoms "recite their [Hardee] tactics, commencing at the beginning of the first volume and going through seriatim, both volumes. Report at the end of each month the progress you have made."[17]

As the spring of 1862 approached, ominous tidings arrived from New Mexico Territory. During early March a Confederate Texas army under Brigadier General Henry H. Sibley had smashed Union defenses on the Rio Grande and captured Albuquerque and Santa Fe. In addition, it was reported that another Confederate army was organizing in Texas for the purpose of driving through to California. A rebel vanguard under Captain R. S. Hunter had already entered Arizona and occupied Tucson. Carleton received orders from the West Coast high command to move his army east and recover "all of our forts in Arizona and New Mexico, driving the rebel forces out of that country or capturing them."[18]

Colonel Carleton's preparation, planning, and execution of the campaign is a tableau of precision and attention to detail. He directed his officers to prepare their men for the expedition by having them "in fighting order all the time, night or day. Keep me advised of all you do. Much is expected of you . . . drill, drill, drill until your men become perfect as soldiers, as skirmishers, as marksmen. Keep the command in good health. . . . Have a drill at the target, three shots per man a day for ten days, commencing at 100 yards and increasing ten yards each day. Have also two hours' skirmish drill. Make a tabular report of every shot to me."[19]

During the spring of 1862, additional units joining Carleton's First California Infantry and Cavalry included the Fifth California Infantry, the Second California Cavalry, and a light battery from the Third United States Artillery. Carleton now had a fighting force of nearly 2,000 men, which he designated the California Column.

Under Carleton's watchful eye and driving energy, Camp Wright and Fort Yuma bulged with mountains of commissary stores and equipment—flour, sugar, rice, beans, salt, pork, coffee, and beef (over 10,000 pounds of jerked meat plus a 90-day supply of cattle to be driven with the expedition and slaughtered as needed), artillery, rifle and revolver ammunition, riflemen's knives, and 300 water kegs of six-gallon capacity. Each of the 150 wagons distributed to the companies of the California Column was loaded and weighed under the watchful eye of company commanders. By Carleton's order, no wagon was to make the crossing with more than 1,000 pounds of cargo, and to assure maximum space for provisions and ammunition, no officer from Carleton down was permitted baggage to exceed 80 pounds. Since the officers and men were expected to sleep in the open, the only shelters loaded were hospital tents. By March 31, seven companies of the California Column had been equipped and provisioned for the overland march and departed Camp Wright and Fort Yuma for Tucson.[20]

The California Column approached Tucson by companies, spaced a day apart to allow wells and springs to fill along the route. Carleton's army met only light resistance on the approaches to Tucson and occupied the city on May 20, 1862. The previous week, most of Captain Hunter's Confederate force had retreated toward the Rio Grande, and a number of civilian Confederate sympathizers had crossed into Sonora. The United States flag was raised over Tucson with appropriate ceremony, and Carleton, now a brigadier general of volunteers, divided his time between establishing a military government for Arizona Territory and readying his Californians for the long march to the Rio Grande.[21]

Tucson, midway between Fort Yuma and Mesilla, bustled with military activity. Infantry and cavalry companies drilled daily under the scorching Arizona sun, sharpening their combat tactics. Supplies, including grain and beef, were gathered from nearby Pima villages and from settlements in Sonora. When not on the drill field, the troopers were divided into details: some guarded the horse and mule herds as the animals grazed on the sparse Gila grass in the canyons about Tucson; others were assigned to repair the wagons. The grinding march from Camp Wright and Fort Yuma had loosened the wagon beds, and the heat and dryness had shrunk the wheels, which had to be cut and refitted. During June, Carleton learned of Confederate General Sibley's disastrous defeat at Glorieta Pass, between Santa Fe and Fort Union, by combined New Mexico and Colorado Union volunteer forces. Hopeful of intercepting the limping Confederate army before it reached Texas, Carleton ordered Colonel Edward Eyre with 140 men from the First California Cavalry to make a forced reconnaissance to the Rio Grande. This was to be a lightning thrust, and the mounted squadron traveled with only 30 days' rations, ammunition, and weapons.[22]

In late June, the California Column resumed the march, moving in sections. To combat the intense heat, company commanders marched their men at night and interspersed light marches during the day with rest periods. The California Column generally followed the Butterfield Overland Mail Road, a primitive thoroughfare that twisted through mesquite thickets and sand-floored canyons. Powdery alkali dust on the lowland roadbed, stirred by the moving column, spread "out over the country on either hand like a lake," and remained in suspension for some time after the train of mules, horses, wagons, and foot soldiers had passed. The infantry, by preceding the wagons, avoided most of the discomfort from the dust, but the hapless teamsters suffered "greatly with inflamed eyes and with coughs," and at times were so engulfed with the whitish pall that they could not see the lead mules.[23]

In mid-July the forward company of the California Column, under Captain Thomas L. Roberts, reached Apache Pass, a depression in the Chiricahua mountain range four miles long at an elevation of 4,800 feet. The Butterfield Stage Company had constructed a station in the pass near a spring, and there the company's passage was contested by a large force of well-armed Chiricahua and Mimbreño Apaches positioned in the rock-strewn headlands above the spring. Their deadly fire arrested the column's advance until the howitzers were brought up. Then gunners dropped canister into the ramparts with telling effect. Infantrymen charged with fixed bayonets and drove the Apaches from their hiding places.[24]

The column resumed the march after a refreshing rest at the Apache Pass spring and reached the Rio Grande in early August 1862. But Sibley's brigade had retreated into Texas, and there was little likelihood of combat. Carleton expressed his regret in a letter to Brigadier General Edward R. S. Canby, commander of Union forces at Santa Fe: "As the gallantry of the troops under your command has left us nothing to do on the Rio Grande, it would be a sad disappointment to those from California if they should be obliged to retrace their steps without feeling the enemy. . . . Could not a force . . . profitably be thrown into western Texas, where it is reported the Union men are only waiting for a little help to run up the old flag?"[25]

Canby, his reassignment imminent, gave Carleton a free hand in southern New Mexico and western Texas. Reports of fresh Confederate attempts to reconquer New Mexico and drive through Arizona into California caused Carleton to disperse his troops in companies throughout the larger towns and the military posts of southern New Mexico. He extended his defensive perimeter as far downriver as Franklin (El Paso) and nearby Fort Bliss.[26]

Once billets had been assigned, the Californians swarmed in patrols along the river, searching for stragglers from the Sibley brigade, confiscating the property of Confederate sympathizers, checking the passports of travelers, and guarding the roads against spies and small enemy forces that might attempt to infiltrate the towns. Cavalry patrols operating across the river at El Paso (Juarez) captured a large supply of hospital stores and quartermaster supplies cached in public buildings by the Confederates. Infantry patrols gathered up 12 wagonloads of goods, which were delivered to the headquarters depot at Mesilla. The California Column's search of public buildings and private residences in El Paso netted a Confederate surgeon and 25 sick and disabled enemy soldiers. Combing the houses, public buildings, and shops and stores in Franklin, they succeeded in rounding up 93 additional rebel soldiers. By Carleton's order, the prisoners were paroled, issued rations and clothing, and sent to San Antonio; he authorized two wagons to carry those prisoners unable to walk.[27]

During August 1862, Carleton succeeded Canby as commandant of the military Department of New Mexico, a jurisdiction that embraced the present states of New Mexico and Arizona. Carleton regarded the primary mission of the California Column as the defense of the Southwest against a threatened Confederate offensive. Because New Mexico was the most forward base in checking this expected assault, he concluded that there had to be peace and order in New Mexico if the California Column were to carry out its primary function.[28]

He felt compelled to do three things. First, he had to maintain a state of military readiness. To accomplish this, he required his company commanders to keep their men on constant alert. He also increased Union strength by reorganizing the New Mexico volunteer forces under the command of Colonel Kit Carson, issuing them modern weapons, and directing more attention to their military training. He regarded the long and tenuous supply line from the Pacific coast to the Rio Grande, with intermediate supply depots along the Butterfield Road, as too uncertain and vulnerable. Therefore, he turned his attention northeast and worked out a logistics line from his old station at Fort Leavenworth and other Kansas military posts to the Rio Grande, generally coursing over the well-traveled Santa Fe Trail. Because this route was vulnerable to attack by Kiowa, Comanche, Cheyenne, and Arapaho raiders, Carleton placed cavalry squads in base camps along the supply road.[29]

Second, he had to maintain an effective state of military occupation in New Mexico. To accomplish this, he believed it essential to subdue the Apaches and Navajos. Carleton's solution to this problem, focusing on the infamous Bosque Redondo, contributed to his demise as a professional soldier and military administrator.

Third, because of the state of war and because the presence of a cadre of Confederate supporters posed a threat to the internal security of New Mexico, Canby had instituted martial law in this jurisdiction in 1861; Carleton directed that this condition be continued. It produced a tension-filled contest between the general Carleton and local politicians, which also substantially contributed to his professional demise.

In the early months of his regime as commandant of the Department of New Mexico, Carleton gave most of his attention to subduing the Apaches and Navajos. Along the valley of the Rio Grande eastward into the Guadalupe Mountains of western Texas ranged the Mescalero Apaches. Before the Civil

War, the United States, with vigilant military patrols operating from Fort Bliss and Fort Stanton and with rations and gifts issued by Indian agents, had made some progress in subduing these mountain people. In 1861 the Confederates had provoked the Indians to all-out war. The Texans had shown poorly in their Apache campaigns; the Indians had cut off and destroyed entire companies and captured substantial stores of provisions and weapons. Well-armed and more deadly than ever, the Mescalero Apaches were at the peak of their martial power when the California Column arrived in New Mexico. In August 1862 alone, Mescalero war parties killed 46 settlers, carried scores of children into captivity, and ran off great herds of cattle, horses, mules, donkeys, and sheep. These Apache raids caused the Mexicans to abandon their *placitas* and flee to the garrisoned towns for protection.[30]

On October 11, 1862, Carleton sent his army against the Apaches. The troops in the field included five companies of New Mexico volunteers commanded by Colonel Kit Carson. Carleton advised his company commanders: "There will be no council held with the Indians. . . . The men are to be slain whenever and wherever they can be found. Their women and children may be taken prisoner, but of course they are not to be killed . . . much is expected of the California troops. I trust that these . . . demonstrations will give these Indians a wholesome lesson. They have robbed and murdered the people with impunity too long already."[31]

Relentless pressure by California and New Mexico troops during the winter of 1862–63 forced the Mescaleros to abandon their country. Many fled to Mexico, and over 400 members of the tribe surrendered to Carleton's forces. Carleton decided to intern the Indian prisoners on a military reservation, which he planned to establish at Bosque Redondo, a dense cottonwood forest thrusting above the surrounding plains on the lower Pecos River. It was the same area he had explored in 1852, recommending that a military post be established there. Now, Carleton directed that a 40-square-mile area encompassing Bosque Redondo be set aside as a reservation and internment zone, and he ordered the construction of a post, Fort Sumner, on the grounds. The garrison, two companies of cavalry and one company of infantry, was to mount a constant guard and enforce residence once the Indians were brought in. Carleton was optimistic about the future of the Bosque Redondo military reservation as an Indian concentration center, not only because of its isolation from the settlements but because the open plains country for miles in every direction would make it easier for the troops to maintain surveillance over the captives.[32]

The successful relocation of the Mescalero Apache captives on the Pecos led Carleton to decide to concentrate at Bosque Redondo other tribes that he regarded as a menace to peace and order in his jurisdiction, notably the Navajos. Three factors influenced his decision to relocate the Navajos who resided in western New Mexico and eastern Arizona. First, Navajo war parties had broken the peace and raided the local settlements, although not as consistently and devastatingly as the Mescalero Apaches. Second, gold and silver strikes were being made with increasing regularity in western New Mexico and Arizona, and prospectors were roaming the countryside in search of new deposits. News of the mineral discoveries was attracting miners, and settlements were developing in the mining region. Carleton expected the Navajos and other tribes to rise up against this trespass of their territory, and he regarded forced evacuation of their country as the only means of maintaining peace and order. Third, the enlistment term for many of his California volunteer troops would soon end. He felt it essential to use his present strength to mitigate the Indian menace. Once concentrated at Bosque Redondo, the Navajos would be more manageable with the reduced troop strength he would have in his command after 1864.

The Navajo campaign began in the spring of 1863. Colonel Carson and the New Mexico volunteers carried out most of the work. Mexican scouts found Navajo settlements which the troops destroyed. As the invaders captured stored grain, burned crops, destroyed orchards, and scattered flocks of sheep, cattle, and horses, Navajo bands reluctantly surrendered to Carson and were escorted to Bosque Redondo. The removal was completed during 1864; by that time there were nearly 9,000 Indians at the internment center.

The captives were expected to raise their own food in garden plots and fields on the reservation, but drought conditions withered most of the corn and other food crops, and the internees largely subsisted on government rations of flour, corn, salt pork, and beef. They suffered untold misery from the heat, malnutrition, and disease. Stagnant, brackish water standing in the river channel was a breeding area for mosquitoes, so that most were stricken with malaria and dysentery. Troops at Fort Sumner infected many of the Indian women with syphilis and gonorrhea, which in turn were transmitted widely among the interred tribesmen. An estimated one-fourth of the aboriginal residents at Bosque Redondo perished before their release in 1868.[33]

The shame of Bosque Redondo became widespread and brought public denunciation and scorn to General Carleton. Federal Indian agents and inspectors reported the shocking conditions of the Indian relocation center to superiors in Washington. Leaders in Congress, the secretary of war, and even the President showed concern over the fate of the captives. Many citizens of New Mexico, though generally holding the Indians in low esteem, became aroused, and General Carleton and Bosque Redondo became issues in local politics. During 1865 a joint special committee of the Congress traveled to New Mexico to hold hearings at Santa Fe concerning General Carleton's management of Indian affairs in the military Department of New Mexico. Critics of Carleton's concentration policy declared that the Navajo campaign was "brutally harsh" and that the relocation of the Navajos to Bosque Redondo "was carried out with all the feelings of a cattle drive.'' But when the committee recommended that the Department of the Interior make a more thorough investigation of the concentration of tribes, Interior Department agents visited New Mexico, inspected Bosque Redondo, and reported ''that General Carleton's policy was having an 'excellent effect.' ''[34]

Bosque Redondo as an issue in General Carleton's management of the Department of New Mexico was matched in controversy by his exercise of what he regarded as the proper prerogatives of department commander under the aegis of martial law. It was because Carleton believed that a state of war existed in the department, given the Confederate aim to drive from Texas through New Mexico and Arizona to the Pacific shore, that he continued and extended the state of martial law established by Canby during the Confederate invasion. He created military tribunals with jurisdiction over court cases involving violation of the military rules he issued for the governance of his department. His troops, in company with United States marshals, confiscated the property of Confederates and Confederate sympathizers. Carleton set curfews for the civilian population and regularly inspected the towns, commonly becoming distressed at their disordered, unkempt appearance. He directed local leaders to ''repair their buildings and clean up their streets.'' Traveling citizens were subjected to careful search at various checkpoints along the roads.[35]

Probably Carleton's most controversial and despised order concerned passports. His rhetoric for the creation of this security system declared that ''the enemy troops hover along the road from New Mexico to the East. These bands, doubtless, have their emissaries in our midst to give information of the trains of our citizens who carry large funds for the purchase of goods in the States and thus they are exposed to attack. . . . All can comply with this Passport Order without inconvenience or lack of dignity. When vigilance is relaxed, then are we endangered. While no one must give way to causeless and unmanly fear, all must be prepared to guard against traitors in our midst and the lawless bands that infest the roads. In times like these we must know friends and enemies. It is but slight inconvenience to the loyal and may be the means of detecting traitors who are still plotting to bring this beautiful country again under the cloud . . . and attach a curse to every spot of our beloved land over which this cruel and causeless rebellion has had sway.'' Each resident of the department had to carry a passport showing business and point of origin and destination. Nonresidents were required to take an oath of allegiance to the United States, which was entered on their passports, before they could enter the department. The passports were issued by Carleton's officers at the towns and military posts in the department.[36]

The inconstancy of the civilian attitude was manifested in public reaction to military occupation. When Carleton's California troops first reached New Mexico, the people welcomed them as conquering heroes and cherished guardians. The New Mexico legislature passed a joint resolution expressing deep gratitude for "their timely aid and assistance in driving the traitors and rebels" from the Rio Grande and "the utmost confidence" in General Carleton. Public praise and appreciation continued during the early period of Carleton's pacification of the Indian tribes of the department.[37]

Before long, however, the memory of Sibley's Confederate invasion faded in the minds of New Mexicans. The war seemed remote, and they returned to their workaday lives to find General Carleton's martial law oppressive and objectionable. They began to demand that they be freed from Carleton's "iron rule" and the "military despotism" he had installed in their territory. Several newspapers, particularly the Santa Fe *New Mexican,* voiced the growing public demand for an early end to military rule and the restoration of complete civilian control. The *New Mexican* disparaged General Carleton and the California Column with vitriolic editorial references to "Carleton's tyranny" and spoke of "the Civil Nose . . . brought to the Military grindstone."[38]

The martial law issue came to focus on the New Mexico judiciary, where there occurred a regular collision of military and civil courts over jurisdictional questions. Associate Justice J. G. Knapp of the Third Judicial District was General Carleton's principal antagonist. He charged that "this territory is under a military despotism" and that the "civil courts are embarrassed by the military." Knapp's verbal attacks on Carleton led the general, during the January 1863 session of the territorial supreme court, to have Knapp arrested and placed under guard in Santa Fe. Later in the same year Carleton had Knapp arrested again and held in the military guardhouse at Mesilla for three days. In November 1863, Knapp boarded a stage at Mesilla bound for Santa Fe to serve in the regular term of the territorial supreme court. Carleton ordered that he be removed from the stage and returned to his residence until he received permission to leave. In order to travel to Santa Fe, Judge Knapp had to apply for a passport. This he refused to do, and the territorial supreme court did not meet for lack of a quorum. Knapp countered by informing Carleton that he had written to the President, the secretary of war, and the attorney general denouncing the general's tyrannical management of the Department of New Mexico. He added that he had taken the action to "establish the fact that you are unworthy of your present position under the government of the United States, and of the society and companionship of honorable men."[39]

A steady stream of protests and denunciatory statements coursed from enraged local citizens and public officials to the President, secretary of war, attorney general, secretary of the interior, and leaders of Congress. Grand juries in Santa Fe and other towns began during 1864 to hold hearings and investigate local conditions where abuses of martial law by Carleton's troops were alleged; these bodies submitted reports and resolutions denouncing the military occupation and the general.

Carleton seemed vindicated, at least by federal officials, when on March 13, 1865, he was breveted major general in both the regular army and the volunteer army. On July 4, 1865, he issued General Order Seventeen, which ended martial law in all its aspects—including the accursed passport system—for all of his department except Bosque Redondo. The order included a statement that could be regarded as his attempt to make a gracious retreat: "After preserving the life of the nation," the troops "have quietly disbanded and each individual returned to his home and the pursuits of private life. These armies were no Praetorian Guard to overawe the people or to proclaim this or that man as ruler, but armies of intelligent patriots who, having seen their country past its perils, fell back into the ranks of the people, and, as men of the people, with the power of the ballot alone, show their preference in common with their fellow citizens for those they would prefer in official positions."[40]

Nevertheless, invective and demonstrations against Carleton continued. During December 1865 the New Mexico territorial legislature sent a memorandum to the secretary of war demanding an investigation of his regime by a court of inquiry, but no response was made to the demand.[41]

Carleton became an issue in the territory-wide election of 1865 to select a delegate to Congress. The Union party nominated Francisco Perea, who defended Carleton, the troops, military occupation, and Bosque Redondo. Perea's opposition, forming into the Administration Party, claimed that Carleton's defenders were recipients of military government favors, including contracts to supply the Bosque Redondo captives. J. Francisco Chaves, candidate of the Administration Party, campaigned to oust Carleton from the Department of New Mexico. When Chaves triumphed, officials in Washington took this to amount to a territory-wide repudiation of Carleton. On October 6, 1866, the secretary of war informed the general that he had been assigned to the Fourth Cavalry as lieutenant colonel and ordered him to report to his new regiment at San Antonio, Texas.[42]

This action by the secretary of war to all intents and purposes concluded a military career that spanned nearly 30 years' service as a cavalryman on the western frontier. The duty profile that had accumulated on Carleton by the time he was removed as commander of the Department of New Mexico revealed an eminently versatile and successful explorer, writer, strategist, naturalist, logistical expert, and military administrator. It also exposed his consummate failure as a politician, his lack of the skill and patience essential for dealing successfully with those New Mexico politicos who dug his professional grave.

Carleton was a complex person, sensitive, creative, and highly intelligent yet devoid of compassion. He was vain, and his imperious manner—perhaps appropriate for a major general of the 1860s—antagonized many people. "Behold him!" wrote the editor of the Santa Fe *New Mexican*. "His martial cloak thrown gracefully around him like a Roman toga, his military cap worn precisely six inches from the extreme tip of his nose, his chin drawn gracefully in, his teeth set firm, his Jove-like front, his eyes like Mars, that threaten and command as with slow and measured tread, each step exactly twenty-eight inches, he rules the land.''[43]

Carleton was a sort of military automaton compulsively committed to duty and command responsibility. He was hardy and tough, able to stay in the saddle as long as any trooper; he could endure hardship and all manner of personal suffering in the performance of a mission, expecting nothing of his men that he could not perform himself. A martinet, he practiced a harsh discipline. He considered drinking a vile practice and punished drunken troopers by ordering the bugler to sound an early "To Horse!"; those unable to mount were placed in rope harnesses and forced to move on foot, towed by horses in the fast-moving column. During an early morning march across northern New Mexico in the winter of 1851–52, one drunken trooper died from this punishment.[44]

Carleton was a zealot. He saw the Civil War as a holy cause wherein honorable men had the sacred duty to crush treasonous secession and preserve the Union. Likewise he was a puritan. He particularly scorned the prostitutes who collected about the western military posts. On several occasions he led squads of dragoons through the settlement adjacent to Fort Union, whipping the women from the brothels and burning their shanties. He was a pioneer in attempting to introduce prohibition in the West. He had vigorously suppressed the liquor traffic in the Indian Territory and along the Missouri River above Fort Leavenworth as a young dragoon officer; later in New Mexico he regularly drove saloonkeepers from the environs of military posts, confiscated their stock, and burned their houses of business. Yet he was ambivalent to the streams of reform in the antebellum age, for he was a slaveowner and imported into New Mexico Territory two bondsmen whom he sold to local citizens.[45]

Carleton's family life included two marriages. In 1840 he wedded Henrietta Tracy Loring of Boston. She joined him at Fort Gibson and died there the next year, probably of typhoid fever. Eight years later he married Sophia Garland Wolfe, niece of Colonel (Brevet Brigadier General) John Garland, then commandant of the Department of New Mexico. Three children issued from this marriage.

Carleton's versatility and creativity are best illustrated by his work as a naturalist and a writer. His attention to the world of nature was eclectic: he displayed equal interest in western plants, animals, soils, landforms, rocks, and meteorological phenomena. In 1843, while in command of a dragoon column on the Missouri River near the Council Bluffs, he met John J. Audubon and spent several days with the naturalist-artist. Carleton collected mammal, insect, and rock specimens and several meteorites from the western wilds and sent them to Harvard University and the Smithsonian Institution. One item, named the Carleton Meteorite, weighed 632 pounds. He obtained it in Arizona, where it was being used by a Mexican blacksmith as an anvil, and sent it to the Smithsonian Institution.[46]

His early interest in writing continued throughout his military career. Carleton's literary penchant led to his assignment of keeping the journals of expeditions from Fort Gibson, Fort Leavenworth, and Fort Union. At councils between federal officials and tribal leaders on the Platte, Arkansas, and Rio Grande, he frequently was designated official recorder of the proceedings. Carleton's first published work was the "First Log Book," which appeared in the *Spirit of the Times* (New York), on November 9, 1844, and April 12, 1845; the "Second Log Book" followed on December 25, 1845, and May 30, 1846. These articles were later reprinted in the *Missouri Western Democrat* under the title "Occidental Reminiscences." He detailed his Mexican War experiences in *The Battle of Buena Vista, with the Operations of the "Army of Occupation" for One Month,* published by Harper in 1848. In the same year he published "Logbook of the Central Division" in the *Washington Union*. To assist western travelers, Carleton produced a "Table of Distances" for *Stryker's American Register and Magazine* in 1850. Accounts of his western explorations and investigations were published as government documents. These include the Gran Quivira–Abo Pass reconnaissance and the Mountain Meadows Massacre report; the latter was reprinted in 1902 with a run of 5,000 copies. Also, throughout Carleton's military career, he maintained correspondence with such noted authors as Charles Dickens and Henry Wadsworth Longfellow. He collected seeds of the western compass (polar) plant and sent them to Longfellow, who described the plant in *Evangeline:* "This is the compass-flower, that the finger of God has planted/Here in the houseless wild, to direct the traveler's journey."[47]

Of all his accomplishments, however, his mission as commandant of the Department of New Mexico must rate as his greatest. Regardless of his unpopularity, he accomplished many things for the future states of New Mexico and Arizona, including the establishment of a great number of posts in that military department: Fort Barrett near Sacaton, Fort Bowie on the approaches to Apache Pass, Fort Canby near Ganado, Fort Goodwin south of Gila in Tulurosa valley, Fort Lowell in the city of Tucson, Fort Tubac near Tubac, Fort Verde near Prescott, Fort Whipple in the Chine Valley, Fort Bascom on the Canadian River near Tucumcari, Fort Bayard near the base of the Santa Rita Mountains, Fort Cummings near Cook's Springs on the Mesilla-Tucson Road, Fort McRae near Ojo del Muerto, Fort Selden just above Doña Ana, Fort Sumner in the Bosque Redondo, and Fort Wingate at El Gallo. These military stations established Union presence in the southwestern wilderness, in many instances were operational posts in the turbulent post–Civil War period, and provided a basis for urban development on the New Mexico–Arizona frontier, serving as nuclei for later towns.[48]

Despite that contribution to the long-term development of the Southwest, Carleton's immediate actions were clearly repudiated by his government in 1866; he never again rose above his post-war rank of lieutenant colonel. He died of pneumonia at San Antonio, Texas, on January 7, 1873. Finally, in death, James Henry Carleton left the West: his body was removed to Mount Auburn Cemetery in Cambridge, Massachusetts, for burial.

Notes

1. Aurora Hunt, *Major General James Henry Carleton, 1814–1873: Western Frontier Dragoon* (Glendale, Calif.: Arthur H. Clark, 1958), 29–32.

2. Ibid., 37–43.

3. See Grant Foreman, *The Five Civilized Tribes* (Norman: University of Oklahoma Press, 1934), for accounts of frontier traffic in slaves and whiskey.

4. Hunt, *Carleton*, 67.

5. Dwight L. Clarke, *Stephen Watts Kearny: Soldier of the West* (Norman: University of Oklahoma Press, 1961), 87–100. Carleton's account of these two expeditions has recently been reprinted: see J. Henry Carleton, *The Prairie Logbooks: Dragoon Campaigns to the Pawnee Villages in 1844, and to the Rocky Mountains in 1845*, ed. Louis Pelzer (Lincoln: University of Nebraska Press, 1983).

6. Hunt, *Carleton*, 97–112.

7. Frank McNitt, "Fort Sumner: A Study in Origins," *New Mexico Historical Review* 45 (April 1970): 103–5; Chris Emmett, *Fort Union and the Winning of the Southwest* (Norman: University of Oklahoma Press, 1965), 124–53.

8. A. B. Bender, "Government Explorations in the Territory of New Mexico, 1846–1859," *New Mexico Historical Review* 9 (January 1934): 17–20.

9. M. Morgan Estergreen, *Kit Carson: A Portrait in Courage* (Norman: University of Oklahoma Press, 1962), 214–15. Also see Thelma S. Guild and Harvey L. Carter, *Kit Carson: A Pattern for Heroes* (Lincoln: University of Nebraska Press, 1984).

10. Hunt, *Carleton*, 166–70.

11. Ibid., 171.

12. *Senate Exec. Docs.*, 36th Cong., 1st sess., no. 42. Also see *House Exec. Docs.*, 57th Cong., 1st sess., no. 605.

13. Hunt, *Carleton*, 191–93.

14. Arrell M. Gibson, *The Life and Death of Colonel Albert Jennings Fountain* (Norman: University of Oklahoma Press, 1965), 10; Darlis A. Miller, *The California Column in New Mexico* (Albuquerque: University of New Mexico Press, 1982), 3–11.

15. *The War of the Rebellion: A Compilation of the Official Records of the Union and Confederate Armies*, 53 vols. (Washington, D.C.: Government Printing Office, 1902), 50:136–45.

16. Gibson, *Fountain*, 11.

17. *War of the Rebellion*, 50:672.

18. *War of the Rebellion*, 4:91.

19. *War of the Rebellion*, 50:700, 773.

20. Gibson, *Fountain*, 14.

21. *War of the Rebellion*, 9:553.

22. *War of the Rebellion*, 50:98. For an overview of this campaign, see Martin H. Hall, *Sibley's New Mexico Campaign* (Austin: University of Texas Press, 1960); and Ray C. Colton, *The Civil War in the Western Territories: Arizona, Colorado, New Mexico and Utah* (Norman: University of Oklahoma Press, 1959), 13–99.

23. *War of the Rebellion*, 50:99.

24. *Rio Grande Republican*, January 2, 1891.

25. *War of the Rebellion*, 9:559.

26. Gibson, *Fountain*, 21.

27. Ibid., 24.

28. Ibid., 26.

29. Leo E. Oliva, *Soldiers on the Santa Fe Trail* (Norman: University of Oklahoma Press, 1967), 145–66; Robert M. Frazer, *Forts of the West* (Norman: University of Oklahoma Press, 1965), 95.

30. *Report of the Commissioner of Indian Affairs for 1862* (Washington, D.C.: Government Printing Office, 1862), 247–48; C. L. Sonnichsen, *The Mescalero Apaches* (Norman: University of Oklahoma Press, 1958), 99–133.

31. *War of the Rebellion*, 15:580.

32. McNitt, "Fort Sumner," 101–17.

33. See *Condition of the Indian Tribes: Report of the Joint Special Committee, Appointed under Joint Resolution of March 3, 1865* (Washington, D.C.: Government Printing Office, 1867); Lynn R. Bailey, *Bosque Redondo: An American Concentration Camp* (Pasadena, Calif.: Socio-Technical Books, 1970); Gerald Thompson, *The Army and the Navajo: The Bosque Redondo Reservation Experiment, 1863–1868* (Tucson: University of Arizona Press, 1976); Clifford E. Trafzer, *The Kit Carson Campaign: The Last Great Navajo War* (Norman: University of Oklahoma Press, 1982).

34. Bailey, *Bosque Redondo*, 87–91, 130–34. Also see Ruth M. Underhill, *The Navajos* (Norman: University of Oklahoma Press, 1956), 112–43.

35. Gibson, *Fountain*, 21–22; Larry D. Ball, *The United States Marshals of New Mexico and Arizona Territories, 1846–1912* (Albuquerque: University of New Mexico Press, 1978), 33–46.

36. *War of the Rebellion*, 41:168–70.

37. *Laws of the Territory of New Mexico, 1862–63* (Santa Fe, N.M.: Charles Leib, 1868), 106.

38. Santa Fe *New Mexican*, September 23, 1864.

39. Ibid., January 13, 1865.

40. Quoted in Hunt, *Carleton*, 252.

41. Santa Fe *New Mexican*, July 1, 1864; December 30, 1865.

42. Santa Fe *Gazette*, September 30, 1865; Hunt, *Carleton*, 344. Although it was of little solace to Carleton, this was actually a promotion from his regular army rank of major.

43. Santa Fe *New Mexican*, December 16, 1864.

44. Hunt, *Carleton*, 115.

45. Ibid., 120–21.

46. Ibid., 325–34.

47. See *House Misc. Docs.*, 33d Cong., 2d sess., no. 37.; and *Senate Exec. Docs.*, vol. 9, 36th Cong., 1st sess., no. 42.

48. Frazer, *Forts of the West*, 3–15, 95–109.

Philip H. Sheridan

by Paul Andrew Hutton

Courtesy Massachusetts Commandery,
Military Order of the Loyal Legion and the
U.S. Army Military History Institute

Philip Henry Sheridan was the nation's premier frontier soldier, commanding a larger frontier region for a longer period of time than any other officer. From 1867 to 1869 he commanded the Department of the Missouri, and from 1869 to 1883 the vast Division of the Missouri. During that period Sheridan gave overall direction to the final, and greatest, Indian wars in the history of the Republic. Between 1867 and 1884 the troops under his command fought 619 engagements with the Indians so that by the 1880s Sheridan had completed the subjugation of the Native Americans.[1]

Born in Albany, New York, on March 6, 1831, Sheridan was raised in Somerset, Ohio, where his family moved while his father, an Irish immigrant, was working as a laborer on a road construction crew. Despite his Irish-Catholic origins, which normally should have led him to vote Democrat, Sheridan's father had strong Whig political connections, and he used them to get his son an appointment to West Point. Sheridan was never happy at the Military Academy, and a fight with another cadet delayed his graduation by one year. But despite low grades and numerous conduct demerits, he managed to graduate in 1853 and was assigned to the First Infantry.

After a brief stay at Fort Duncan, Texas, on the Rio Grande, Sheridan was transferred to the Fourth Infantry and ordered to Fort Reading, California, at the northern end of the Sacramento Valley. The outbreak of the Yakima War in 1855 gave the young shavetail his first taste of Indian fighting. He distinguished himself in March 1856 when he led 40 dragoons to the rescue of besieged settlers at the Oregon Cascades. The Yakimas, although outnumbering the soldiers, were forced to withdraw, and the young lieutenant was commended in General Orders signed by General Winfield Scott.

After the defeat of the Yakimas, Sheridan was assigned to the Grande Ronde Indian Reservation in western Oregon, where his detachment of troops guarded the Rogue River, Coquille, Klamath, Modoc, and Chinook Indians who lived on the reservation. Sheridan learned the Chinook language, no doubt assisted by Frances, a Rogue River Indian girl who lived with him during his remaining years in the Pacific Northwest.[2]

The attack on Fort Sumter found Sheridan a 30-year-old captain of infantry. In September 1861 he was ordered to join the Thirteenth Infantry and hurried east, optimistic that if the war lasted long enough, he might "have a chance to earn a major's commission."[3]

After commanding a desk as chief quartermaster for General Samuel R. Curtis's Army of the Southwest, headquartered in Missouri, Sheridan gained an appointment as colonel of the Second Michigan Cavalry. He was promoted to brigadier general of volunteers in September 1862 and quickly won a high reputation in army circles for tenacity and courage by his actions at Perryville, Kentucky, and Stones River, Tennessee. His counterattack at Stones River turned seeming defeat into an important but grisly Union victory and earned him a second star in the volunteer army.

It was his bold charge up Missionary Ridge, however, that secured General Ulysses S. Grant's esteem and guaranteed his future. Sheridan had shared in the humiliation of the Army of the Cumberland, first defeated at Chickamauga and then besieged in Chattanooga, Tennessee. When, on November 25, 1863, the men of Sheridan's Second Division were given a chance at redemption, they did not waste it. The Army of the Cumberland, with Sheridan's division leading, swept up the ridge against murderous fire to plant their regimental colors on the crest. Moreover, unlike the other Union commanders, Sheridan did not halt after taking the summit but plunged after the retreating rebels.

General Grant, who had watched the assault, was delighted. "Sheridan showed his genius in that battle," Grant later declared, "and to him I owe the capture of most of the prisoners that were taken. Although commanding a division only, he saw in the crisis of that engagement that it was necessary to advance beyond the point indicated by his orders. He saw what I could not know, on account of my ignorance of the ground, and with the instinct of military genius pushed ahead."[4]

When Grant, then in command of all Union forces, went east in March 1864,

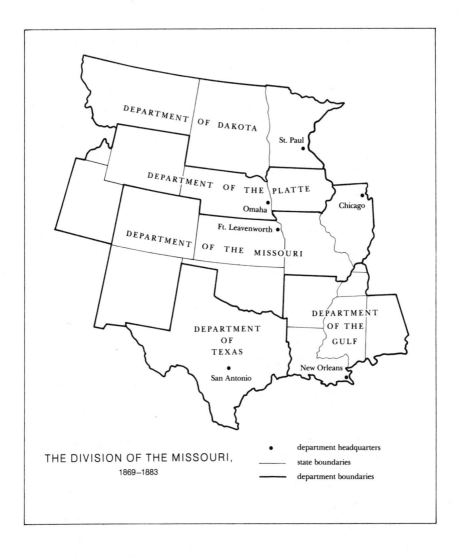

THE DIVISION OF THE MISSOURI,
1869–1883

The Division of the Missouri, 1869–83. *From Paul Andrew Hutton,* Phil Sheridan and His Army *(Lincoln: University of Nebraska Press, 1985).*

he took Sheridan with him to command the Army of the Potomac's cavalry. Sheridan soon led his 10,000 troopers on a bold raid to the very gates of Richmond, brushing aside the vaunted rebel cavalry along the way and killing the Confederate cavalry commander J. E. B. Stuart at Yellow Tavern.

Grant rewarded Sheridan with an independent command in the Shenandoah Valley, with orders to block the advance of General Jubal Early's Confederates and seal off the rebel breadbasket once and for all. In September 1864, Sheridan defeated Early at Winchester and Fisher's Hill, securing a brigadier's star in the regular army as a reward.

His greatest triumph, however, came as the result of a Union defeat. While he was absent at a meeting, his army was taken by surprise at Cedar Creek on October 19, 1864. Sheridan, 14 miles away in Winchester, heard the roar of battle and galloped to the sound of the guns. His appearance electrified his stricken army; they rallied and crushed Early's Confederates. "Sheridan's ride," as it was called, became one of the most memorable episodes of the Civil War, soon celebrated in poem, story, and painting. With the rebel forces destroyed, Sheridan and his "robbers," as his army was thereafter known, ravaged the Shenandoah Valley so that it could never again support an invading army from the South. Sheridan boasted that a crow would be compelled to carry his own rations when crossing the valley.

President Abraham Lincoln, his reelection hopes given a timely boost by the victory at Cedar Creek, appointed Sheridan a major general in the regular army. At 34, Sheridan stood with Grant and Sherman in the front rank of Union heroes. Marching southward, he rejoined Grant in time for the final thrust against General Robert E. Lee's Army of Northern Virginia. At Appomattox it was Sheridan's troops who blocked Lee's final line of retreat and compelled his surrender.[5]

Immediately after Appomattox, Sheridan was ordered to Texas, where he provided moral and material support to the forces of Benito Juarez in their struggle with Maximilian, the puppet of the French emperor, Louis Napoleon. Sheridan relished the prospect of confronting French troops in battle, but as it happened, no battles were necessary; Juarez's troops, supplied by Sheridan, defeated the imperialists.

Sheridan was also in charge of the defeated rebel states of Texas and Louisiana, and in this task he was not as successful. His enthusiastic application of the relatively harsh Reconstruction policies of the congressional Radical Republicans led President Andrew Johnson to dismiss him from this command on July 31, 1867.[6]

Reassigned to command the Department of the Missouri, which included present Kansas, Oklahoma (Indian Territory), New Mexico, and Colorado, Sheridan found the task of Indian fighting far more congenial work. Although the 1867 Treaty of Medicine Lodge had established reservations for the

Cheyennes, Arapahos, Kiowas, Comanches, and Kiowa-Apaches in the Indian Territory, the tribes had for the most part failed to settle on their new lands. Congress, preoccupied with the impeachment of President Johnson, also failed to appropriate funds to fulfill the government promises of food, clothing, doctors, and teachers until July 1868. By then it was too late to prevent hostilities with the disgruntled and still undefeated Indians.

The Cheyennes, in particular, were not interested in peace. With the 1864 Sand Creek Massacre still fresh in their minds, they were naturally hesitant about placing themselves under the government's protection and control. In June 1868 a party of Cheyennes raided their traditional enemies, the Kaws, in Kansas, and two months later a large raiding party attacked the white settlements along the Saline and Solomon Rivers in Kansas, killing 15 men and raping five women. Sheridan sent two of his most trusted scouts, William Comstock and Abner Grover, to meet with the Cheyennes and discuss their grievances. Near a Cheyenne village on the Solomon River, Comstock was killed, and Grover was seriously wounded by a Cheyenne war party.

None of this surprised Sheridan, who felt that the peace had been tenuous at best. To his mind the only way to ensure a lasting peace was to see the Cheyennes "soundly whipped, and the ringleaders in the present trouble hung, their ponies killed, and such destruction of their property as will make them very poor."[7] He ordered the Cheyennes and Arapahos to report to their Indian Territory reservations and to surrender the leaders of the Kansas raids as stipulated in the Medicine Lodge Treaty. This the Indians refused to do, and so all the Cheyennes and Arapahos were branded as hostiles. The Comanches, Kiowas, and Kiowa-Apaches, who had taken no part in the Kansas raids, were considered friendly (even though they often raided the Texas settlements to the south) and were promised sanctuary on their Indian Territory reservations.

Realizing that he had too few soldiers to mount much of a summer offensive, Sheridan concentrated on protecting the line of the Kansas Pacific Railroad, though he did recruit 50 frontiersmen to be used as a ranger detachment against the Indians. Commanded by Sheridan's aide, Major George A. Forsyth, these scouts confronted a large party of Cheyennes under Roman Nose and Tall Bull on Colorado's Arickaree Fork of the Republican River in September 1868. Surprised by hundreds of warriors, the scouts were besieged on a small island in the Arickaree for nine days before a column of the Tenth Cavalry rescued the survivors. They had put up a stiff defense, killing Roman Nose and a large number of his warriors, but Forsyth was shot three times and gravely wounded; his second in command, Lieutenant Fred Beecher, was killed, as was the doctor and five of the scouts; and 19 other scouts were wounded. The Battle of Beecher's Island disabused Sheridan of using such small detachments for offensive operations.[8]

In hopes of pulling the hostiles down out of Kansas, Sheridan next sent

Lieutenant Colonel Alfred Sully, with eight companies of cavalry and another of infantry, south across the Arkansas River to attack the families of the Cheyennes and Arapahos reportedly camped along the Cimarron River in Indian Territory. Although Sully skirmished with the Indians, he moved too slowly to close with them and returned to Fort Dodge on September 18, 1868, in failure.[9]

Within the boundaries of Sheridan's command, since the Kansas raids of early August, 110 civilians had been killed, 13 women raped, and over 1,000 head of stock stolen. Farms, stage buildings, and wagons had been burned and all travel halted on the major roads. Eighteen of Sheridan's troopers had been killed and 45 wounded, with little damage inflicted upon the hostiles. Western political and business interests demanded action. The army, which had emerged from the Civil War with a self-image as one of the world's great modern fighting forces, was humiliated by its inability to handle a few thousand poorly armed nomadic natives.

Sheridan determined on a winter campaign to crush the hostiles. Although campaigning against Indians in winter was not a new idea, Sheridan's plan was universally viewed as bold and innovative. He was convinced that his well-fed and -clothed soldiers could challenge the severe climate long enough to strike a decisive blow, while winter would limit the Indians' mobility, which was their greatest advantage. Their ponies would be weakened by scarce fodder, and the Indians would seek the comfort of their tepees, lulled into a false sense of security by the weather. Distance and climate had always protected them from their enemies in winter, but the railroad had ended that advantage. The fact that supplies could now be shipped to distant depots gave the soldiers greater mobility.

Sheridan planned for several columns to converge on the country of the Cheyennes and Arapahos. Major Andrew W. Evans would lead over 500 men eastward from Fort Bascom, New Mexico, to scour the Canadian River region of the Texas Panhandle. Major Eugene A. Carr was to march south from Fort Lyon, Colorado, with seven companies of his Fifth Cavalry—to be joined on the North Canadian by five more companies of cavalry already in the field under Captain William Penrose—and proceed toward the Antelope Hills. Sheridan did not expect these columns to do much damage to the hostiles but hoped they might drive them toward the Antelope Hills. Then, when Sheridan's main column from Fort Dodge attacked the Indians there, the troops under Carr and Evans would block any escape to the west or north.

The central strike force commanded by Sheridan consisted of 11 companies of the Seventh Cavalry under Lieutenant Colonel George A. Custer; the Nineteenth Kansas Volunteer Cavalry under Colonel Samuel J. Crawford, who had resigned as governor of Kansas to lead the new volunteer regiment; and five companies of infantry under Captain J. H. Page.

First blood was drawn by Custer, who struck Black Kettle's Cheyenne village on the Washita River in Indian Territory on November 27, 1868. Custer claimed to have slain 103 warriors and captured 53 women and children. Among the dead was Black Kettle himself, the leading peace chief among the Cheyennes. Despite his peaceful reputation, Black Kettle's camp contained letters taken from murdered army couriers, army mules, and photographs captured in the Kansas raids. It was, however, a costly victory for the army, with two officers and 19 enlisted men killed, and 14 others wounded.[10]

A month later, on Christmas Day, Major Evans struck a Kiowa and Comanche village on Soldier Spring, due south of the Washita battlefield, and routed the inhabitants. Although he inflicted few casualties, Evans did destroy large quantities of food and camp items. Most of the Kiowas and Comanches who had not already gone to their Indian Territory reservation now did so.[11]

After establishing a major post, Fort Sill, to guard the new Indian reservations, Sheridan sent Custer westward into the Texas Panhandle, with the Seventh and the Nineteenth Kansas, in search of the remaining Cheyennes and Arapahos who had not surrendered. On March 25, 1869, Custer located a large Cheyenne village on Sweetwater Creek, just west of the Texas line. Because the Cheyennes held two white women as captives, Custer chose to negotiate rather than attack. In a parley Custer siezed three Cheyennes as hostages and forced the Indians to turn over the women. He then promised to release the three hostages, as well as his Washita prisoners, if the Cheyennes would surrender. The Indians agreed, and Custer, short on rations, hurried back to his supply base in the Indian Territory.

Most of the Cheyenne and Arapaho bands surrendered in the spring of 1869, but the most belligerent of the Cheyennes, Tall Bull's Dog Soldiers, moved north to join the Sioux. To counter the Dog Soldier threat, Sheridan transferred Carr and the Fifth from Fort Lyon to Fort McPherson, Nebraska. Carr finally surprised Tall Bull's village on July 11, 1869, at Summit Springs in northeastern Colorado. In a fierce engagement the Cheyennes were routed, their 84 lodges and all other property destroyed; 52 Indians were killed and another 17 captured.[12]

The Battle of Summit Springs climaxed Sheridan's 1868–69 campaign and broke the power of the Cheyennes. Although some of the other Dog Soldier bands escaped north into Wyoming, most returned to the Indian Territory to surrender. Sheridan had achieved the three major goals of his campaign: the Indians were removed from the land between the Platte and Arkansas rivers and the security of the railroads and settlers secured; the Indians involved in the Kansas raids had been punished; and the southern plains tribes had been forced onto their reservations. Although a success, the campaign was not decisive. The Red River War of 1874–75 completed the subjugation of the southern plains tribes.[13]

The winter campaign secured Sheridan an enviable reputation as an Indian fighter. The general's pragmatism and elastic ethics made him the perfect frontier soldier for an expansionist republic. He was more than willing to ruthlessly carry out the dictates of his government, never faltering in his conviction that what he did was right. Although he denied ever uttering it and the sentiment certainly did not originate with the general, the infamous epigram that "the only good Indian is a dead Indian" became closely identified with Sheridan's Indian policy. It has the ring of typical Sheridan rhetoric, and he certainly appeared to dedicate much of his career to making that cruel sentiment come true.[14]

In March 1869, President Ulysses S. Grant appointed Sheridan lieutenant general in command of the Division of the Missouri, a vast area extending from Chicago on the east to the western borders of New Mexico, Utah, Wyoming, and Montana on the west, and from the Canadian boundary on the north to the Rio Grande on the south. Some were surprised by the promotion, since Generals Henry Halleck and George Meade outranked Sheridan, but those who recognized Grant's penchant for cronyism expected it. And despite the President's obvious favoritism, Sheridan was well suited to his new command. But now, as the nation's chief Indian fighter, he would be closely watched by the public — especially the humanitarians concerned with the Indians — in order to observe his attitude and treatment of the tribes.

Sheridan agreed with the so-called friends of the Indian that the ultimate goal of the government's Indian policy should be the conversion of the nomadic tribes from their old culture to an agricultural way of life built around mainstream American white culture. He disagreed with them, however, about the means to achieve this end. Sheridan regarded all Indians as savages, with "only one profession, that of arms, and every one of them belongs to it, and they never can resist the natural desire to join in a fight if it happens to be in their vicinity."[15] To curb this "natural inclination" to war, the Indians had to be severely punished after every crime. Sheridan liked to make the point that "an attempt has been made to control the Indians, a wild and savage people, by moral suasion, while we all know that the most stringent laws have to be enacted for the government of civilized white people."[16]

Sheridan agreed with the reservation policy, for he was convinced that contact between the two races should be avoided for the benefit of both, but he disagreed with what he viewed as overly mild treatment accorded the reservation tribes. "I have the interest of the Indian at heart as much as anyone, and sympathize with his fading out race," Sheridan told his superiors, "but many years of experiences have taught me that to civilize and Christianize the wild Indian it is not only necessary to put him on Reservations but it is also necessary to exercise some strong authority over him." Sheridan believed that such firm control could be exercised only by the army. He repeatedly recommended, as did almost all his military colleagues, that control of Indian affairs be transferred back from the Department of the Interior to its pre-1849 status in the War Department. He held the employees of the Department of the Interior's Indian Bureau in contempt, feeling that "the admirable system of civilizing and providing for the wild tribes is constantly being thrown into chaos by the impracticable, unbusinesslike actions of some of the men engaged in carrying it out."[17] He contended that the obvious failings of the Indian Bureau, some caused by corruption and others by an overdose of humanitarian zeal, could be rectified by the use of army officers as Indian agents and by the stationing of military contingents on the reservations.

Sheridan foresaw a golden age of Indian administration, where the tribes would no longer be cheated and the government no longer robbed, if only Congress would authorize transfer of Indian affairs to the army. But in this he would be frustrated. A coalition of politicians who worried about the loss of patronage and humanitarians who worried about ruthless army officers defeated several congressional attempts to pass a transfer bill.[18]

Sheridan's chief concern, however, was not with the treatment of Indians on the reservations but rather with the causes of the Indian wars. He believed that there were two distinct factors leading to conflict. The first was inevitable and would have occurred no matter what policy the government might have adopted: "We took away their country and their means of support," the general commented, "broke up their mode of living, their habits of life, introduced disease and decay among them, and it was for this and against this they made war. Could any one expect less?" Ever the pragmatist, he made no moral judgment on this dispossession but flatly admitted that "we could not deprive these primitive people of their homes, where they had lived in barbarous contentment for centuries, without war."[19]

The responsibility for the second cause of conflict, the failure of the reservation system to adequately feed and clothe the Indians, Sheridan laid squarely on the government. He chided Congress for miserly appropriations, reminding the government that all the country between the Missouri River and the Rocky Mountains had been recently wrested from the Indians and taken over by miners, ranchers, and farmers who reaped millions from the land. It seemed that "such beneficial results as these should induce Congress to furnish the poor people from whom this country has been taken with sufficient food to enable them to live without suffering the pangs of hunger."[20] Such a call for minimal justice was not unusual in late-nineteenth-century America, but it may well have surprised many who regarded Sheridan as an advocate of Indian extermination.

It would be a mistake, however, to view Sheridan as a consistent defender of Indian rights. Like most men, he was moved by the sight of obvious injustice. But the fact that he used his position to aid the oppressed Indian on occasion did not, by any means, make him a friend of the Indian. With most of his fellow citizens, he viewed the Native Americans as members of an inferior race embracing a primitive culture. In war he felt them to be inordinately barbarous, and he attributed this behavior to a natural, ingrained savageness of the race. From his official capacity as division commander he saw the tribes as a Stone Age barrier to an inevitable progress resulting from the expansion of white Christian civilization. Not only did he favor such progress; he proudly saw himself as its instrument.

What bothered Sheridan most about Indian warfare was not the morality or immorality of subjugating the tribes and taking their lands but rather the lack of a firm national consensus on the righteousness of the conquest. During the Civil War his every action had been applauded by a grateful nation, even when he had waged war on civilian populations. But now he found himself sharply criticized for pursuing the same tactics against Indians.

Never able to fathom why so many opposed his methods of Indian campaigning, Sheridan believed he was profiting from the errors of previous campaigns that had employed conventional military methods and failed. He was convinced that the army could not "successfully fight Indians on the principle of high-toned warfare; that is where the mistake has been." "In taking the offensive," he once explained to Commanding General of the Army William T. Sherman in defense of his methods, "I have to select that season when I can catch the fiends; and if a village is attacked and women and children killed, the responsibility is not with the soldiers but with the people whose crimes necessitated the attack. During the war did any one hesitate to attack a village or town occupied by the enemy because women and children were within its limits? Did we cease to throw shells into Vicksburg or Atlanta because women and children were there?"[21]

It was a no-win situation for Sheridan. "We cannot avoid being abused by one side or the other," he mused in 1870. "If we allow the defenseless people on the frontier to be scalped and ravished, we are burnt in effigy and execrated as soulless monsters, insensible to the suffering of humanity. If the Indian is punished to give security to these people, we are the same soulless monsters from the other side."[22] Consciously, even combatively, he made his decision to support the settlers on the extended frontier line encompassed by his military division. Soon after assuming division command he made his position clear to his eastern critics: "My duties are to protect these people [settlers]. I have nothing to do with Indians but in this connection. There is scarcely a day in which I do not receive the most heart rendering appeals to save settlers . . . and I am forced to the alternative of choosing whether I shall regard their appeals or allow them to be butchered in order to save myself from the hue and cry of the people who know not the Indians and whose families have not the fear, morning, noon, and night, of being ravished and scalped by them. The wife of the man at the center of wealth and civilization and refinement is not more dear to him than is the wife of the pioneer of the frontier. I have no hesitation in making my choice. I am going to stand by the people over whom I am placed and give them what protection I can."[23]

Such sentiments endeared Sheridan to the westerners, who soon came to regard him as their special advocate. To them the alternatives were clear: "Shall we Williampennize or Sheridanize the Indians?" asked the Columbus, Nebraska, *Platte Journal* in 1870. An angry Texan's letter in 1870 to the Chicago *Tribune* clearly expressed the position of many western whites: "Give us Phil Sheridan and Send Philanthropy to the devil!"[24] But Indiana Congressman Daniel Voorhees spoke for many in the East when he rose in the House to denounce the "curious spectacle" of President Grant "upon the one hand welcoming his Indian agents in their peaceful garments and broadbrims coming to tell him what they have done as missionaries of a gospel of peace and of a beneficent Government, and upon the other hand welcoming this man, General Sheridan, stained with the blood of innocent women and children!"[25]

Within the boundaries of the four geographic military departments that made up the Division of the Missouri—the Missouri, the Platte, Dakota, and Texas—lived most of the Indian population of the United States. Before he left his frontier post to assume the position of commanding general of the army in 1883, Sheridan planned and directed campaigns against the Sioux, Northern and Southern Cheyennes, Kiowas, Comanches, Arapahos, Utes, Kickapoos, and Apaches.

In the largest of these campaigns, the Red River War of 1874–75 on the southern plains and the Great Sioux War of 1876–77 on the northern plains, Sheridan employed the same overall strategy that had proved so successful in his 1868–69 winter campaign. In each case he attempted to employ winter as an ally (although both campaigns saw summer fighting as well) and to have converging columns trap the hostiles. Recognizing the difficulties of distance and terrain, he never expected these columns to meet or work in concert; rather, they would keep the Indians insecure, off balance, and constantly moving. One column or another would eventually find the natives and strike. In neither of these campaigns did the Indians suffer much loss of life in battle; they were defeated by starvation, exposure, stock and property losses, and constant insecurity. Both campaigns reaffirmed the effectiveness of Sheridan's philosophy of total war, for it was concern over the suffering of their families that brought the warriors in to the reservations to surrender. If Indian women and children had been allowed to find sanctuary on the reservations—which they were not—or if the soldiers had been prohibited from attacking the Indian villages, then Sheridan's strategy could not have been successful. Only by making war on the entire tribe—men, women, and children—could he hope for quick results. Although brutal, his strategy was eminently successful.

Sheridan often proved obstinate in his commitment to the strategy of converging columns in a winter campaign. His unwillingness to consider alternatives, or accept advice from his officers in the field, sometimes led to serious problems, as it did in the Great Sioux War.

Sheridan participated in a White House meeting on November 3, 1875, with President Grant, Secretary of War William W. Belknap, Secretary of the Interior Zachariah Chandler, Commissioner of Indian Affairs Edward Smith, and Brigadier General George Crook in which a plan was formulated to seize the Black Hills of South Dakota and launch a military campaign against the non-reservation Sioux under Sitting Bull. Gold had been discovered in the Black Hills in 1874 by miners accompanying Lieutenant Colonel George A. Custer's exploring expedition. At first Sheridan's troopers were used to prevent the entrance of miners into the Black Hills, which had been guaranteed to the Sioux by the 1868 Fort Laramie Treaty. But after government efforts to purchase the hills proved unsuccessful, it was decided at the November 3 meeting that while the President's order prohibiting white entry into the hills would stand, no further military resistance would be offered to the horde of miners. To break the power of the Sioux further, it was also decided that all the Indians would be ordered to report to their agencies by January 31, 1876, including those Sioux who were legally hunting in unceded lands in the Yellowstone River Valley and near the Big Horn Mountains. If they did not report to their agencies (and the government officials knew they would not), then Sheridan was to launch a campaign to force them there. Sheridan, of course, began planning his campaign as soon as the White House meeting ended.[26]

On February 7, 1876, Sheridan received authorization from the secretary of the interior to proceed against the nonreservation Sioux. The general's plan called for troops to converge on the Sioux hunting lands from three different directions. Lieutenant Colonel Custer was to march westward with the Seventh Cavalry from Fort Abraham Lincoln, on the Missouri River; Colonel John Gibbon would move eastward from Fort Ellis, Montana, with six companies of infantry and four companies of cavalry, to patrol the Yellowstone River; and General Crook would proceed north from Fort Fetterman, Wyoming, with ten companies of cavalry and two of infantry.

Climate, distance, and the unexpected tenacity of the foe all conspired to frustrate Sheridan's plan. Deep snow prevented Custer's column from leaving Fort Lincoln. Sheridan had been unable to convince Congress to appropriate funds for the construction of forts on Montana's Tongue and Bighorn rivers, and now he had no way to resupply his troops in the field during winter. Gibbon's column did manage to establish a supply depot at the junction of the Bighorn and the Yellowstone rivers, but his troops found no Indians. Crook's column found the Indians, but the 300-man strike force commanded by Colonel Joseph Reynolds was defeated by the Cheyennes and Oglala Sioux on Montana's Powder River on March 17, 1876. These failures made a summer campaign essential.[27]

For the summer expedition, Sheridan planned to repeat his winter strategy, with Custer sweeping west from Fort Lincoln to push the Sioux and their allies toward the Bighorn, where Crook, again moving north from Fort Fetterman, would force them back onto Custer. Gibbon, still in the field, would continue to move along the Yellowstone River. To block the hostiles from slipping back to their reservation and to prevent the reservation Sioux from aiding their brethren with supplies and reinforcements, Sheridan requested permission to assume control over the agencies. With the agencies under military authority and with their best hunting grounds swarming with troops, the hostiles would have no choice but unconditional surrender. At least that was the plan.

Sheridan left the actual organization and field strategy of the campaign to his department commanders, Crook and Brigadier General Alfred Terry, allowing them wide discretionary powers. "I have given no instructions to Gens. Crook or Terry," Sheridan explained to General Sherman, "as I think it would be unwise to make any combinations in such a country as they will have to operate in. As hostile Indians, in any great number, cannot keep the field as a body for a week or at most ten days, I therefore consider—and so do Terry and Crook— that each column will be able to take care of itself, and of chastising the Indians should it have the opportunity."[28]

This misapprehension as to Indian strength was the most critical flaw in Sheridan's planning. Throughout the early spring, evidence mounted that Sitting Bull's strength was rapidly increasing. General Terry's scouts on the Little Missouri reported Sitting Bull's village at 1,500 lodges by May. From Fort Laramie came reports that 1,400 warriors had left the Sioux agencies on Nebraska's White River to join the hostiles.

Terry had assumed overall charge of the Dakota column from Fort Lincoln after Custer was stripped of the command by President Grant for testifying against Secretary of War Belknap before Congress. Terry's inexperience in Indian campaigning gave him a healthy sense of caution that others lacked, but with Custer still commanding the column's main strike force, Terry would depart Fort Lincoln on May 17. He ordered Gibbon to push farther east to meet his column and wired Sheridan to speed up Crook's departure from Fort Fetterman.

Terry's worry over the reports of Sioux numbers did not concern Sheridan. "I will hurry up Crook," Sheridan replied, "but you must rely on the ability of your own column for your best success. I believe it to be fully equal to all the Sioux which can be brought against it, and only hope they will hold fast to meet it."[29]

General Crook now reported from Fort Laramie that Red Cloud's reservation Sioux were in a defiant mood and that many of the young men had gone north to join the hostiles. Crook then departed for Fort Fetterman, marching out of the post on May 29, 1876, with over 1,000 men.

Crook's report led Sheridan to transfer Lieutenant Colonel Eugene Carr and eight companies of the crack Fifth Cavalry to Wyoming. The general then journeyed to Fort Laramie to inspect the White River Sioux agencies himself. He visited the agencies for a single day, finding everything quiet; this seemed to confirm his suspicion that the reports of Indians leaving the agencies were exaggerated. After ordering Carr and the Fifth Cavalry to scout along the Powder River trail in order to block the retreat of Indians fleeing toward the agencies and to prevent any agency Sioux from reinforcing the hostiles, Sheridan departed for his Chicago headquarters.[30]

As soon as he reached Chicago, Sheridan learned that Crook's column had found the hostiles on Montana's Rosebud River on June 17. The Indians—well organized, fighting on favorable terrain, and well led by Crazy Horse—had battled Crook for six hours before withdrawing. Crook claimed victory because he had held the field, but his immediate retreat to his supply base on Goose Creek told the true story.[31]

Crazy Horse, having defeated one of Sheridan's three columns, now moved north with his Sioux and Cheyenne followers to join Sitting Bull's people on the Little Bighorn River. General Terry, meanwhile, had unwisely divided his force, sending the brash Custer with the Seventh Cavalry up the Rosebud to approach the suspected hostile concentration from the southeast, while he moved up the Bighorn River with Gibbon's troops. "I hope that one of the two columns will find the Indians," Terry wrote Sheridan on June 21.[32]

On July 4, 1876, an Associated Press wire story originating in Salt Lake City claimed that Custer and every man of five companies of the Seventh had been killed at the Little Bighorn. Sheridan, in Philadelphia for the centennial celebration, labeled the story absurd. The next day, however, he received a confidential report from Terry. Custer had rashly attacked an enormous Indian village on the Little Bighorn on June 25, and the Seventh had been shattered as a result. Custer and 263 men had been killed and another 59 wounded.[33]

Sheridan, stunned by the death of his young protégé and the destruction of one of the best cavalry regiments in the army, moved quickly to counteract the setback. Lieutenant Colonel Elwell S. Otis and Colonel Nelson A. Miles, each with six companies of infantry, were ordered to reinforce Terry; the Fifth Cavalry was ordered to join Crook. "Terry and Crook are all right," Sheridan assured a worried General Sherman. "I will take the campaign fully in hand, and will push it to a successful termination sending every man that can be spared."[34]

Custer's defeat also shocked Congress into action, and Sheridan now received authorization to construct the two forts he wanted on the Yellowstone's tributaries. He was also given permission to take control of all the Sioux agencies.

Changing his mind as to the wisdom of combining the Terry and Crook columns, Sheridan wrote both men in July to suggest that they join forces. They did so, but the battles on the Rosebud and Little Bighorn had so shaken their confidence that there was no hope for success. They blundered ponderously across the Montana prairie with an army so large that they could not supply it for a week. The two groups quickly parted; Terry disbanded his forces, while Crook marched on toward the Black Hills. On September 9, 1876, a detachment of Crook's column struck a Sioux village at Slim Buttes, South Dakota, and defeated the Indians there. The fight boosted morale but was of little significance, since Crook's column was so weak from hunger and exposure that it could not pursue the Indians once it found them.[35]

Sheridan had lost all hope for a decisive battlefield victory over the Sioux. "I have never looked on any decisive battle with these Indians as a settlement of the trouble," Sheridan told Sherman. "Indians do not fight such battles; they only fight boldly when they have the advantage, as in the Custer case, or to cover the movement of their women and children as in the case of Crook on June 17, but Indians have scarcely ever been severely punished unless by their own mode of warfare or tactics and stealing on them."[36]

Sheridan's strategy for the fall and winter moved away from large attack columns. He now planned to place his troops in the favored Sioux hunting grounds, operating out of the two new forts on the Tongue and Bighorn rivers in Montana and another post on the Powder River in Wyoming. In this way the Sioux could be continually harrassed and forced by insecurity and hunger to return to their agencies. With the agencies under Sheridan's control, the Indians would find a severe reception and be disarmed, dismounted, and punished.

Although General Crook did advance north with another vast column of over 2,000 men in November 1876 and destroy a Cheyenne village on the Red Fork of the Powder River on November 25, it was really small detachments operating out of the new forts and the troops occupying the agencies that defeated the Sioux. Colonel Miles, in particular, kept up a determined winter campaign with only 500 men, using the new Tongue River post as a base camp. Miles's troops chased Sitting Bull's band over a good portion of Montana and eventually forced the Sioux into Canada. Miles also defeated Crazy Horse and his followers at Wolf Mountain, Montana, on January 8, 1877. Most of the Sioux and Cheyennes now drifted into the agencies to surrender. With the surrender of Crazy Horse on May 6, 1877, the Great Sioux War ended.

The war had been a dismal affair from the army's perspective. "Surely in Grand Strategy we ought not to allow savages to beat us," Sherman complained, "but in this instance they did."[37] The Great Sioux War was, in fact, the only conventional war the army ever fought against the western Indians. It was the sort of conflict that these Civil War veterans were experienced at. A campaign in which large, massed bodies of troops maneuvered for control of battlefields. Reynolds, Crook, and Custer were outmaneuvered and defeated in quite conventional battles. It was only when Sheridan turned to occupation of the Sioux hunting grounds, harassing tactics, and control of the Sioux agencies that the Indians were defeated by starvation and exhaustion.

Sheridan deserved much of the blame for the failures in the Great Sioux War. He was so wedded to his converging-columns, winter-campaign strategy that he refused to consider alternatives. Blinded by victories on the southern plains in 1868–69 and 1874–75, he put into operation a strategy that overlooked the greater distances and harsher climate to be overcome on the northern plains. Sheridan's most grievous error, however, was his underestimation of the numbers, tenacity, and ability of the Indians. No amount of evidence could dissuade him from his conviction that large numbers of Indians could not combine against his troops. A one-day visit to the Sioux agencies was enough to persuade him that all the scouting reports were false. His worry was that the troops might not find the Indians, not that they could be defeated if they did.[38]

After the Great Sioux War the nature of Indian campaigning changed. No longer would Sheridan send his soldiers marching into strange country against a foe of unknown size. Now his troopers ringed the Indian reservations with their forts, guarding against outbreaks. The Indians were clearly on the defensive and never able to muster much strength.

"Indian troubles that will hereafter occur will be those which arise upon the different Indians reservations," Sheridan declared in 1879, "or from attempts made to reduce the number and size of these reservations, by the concentration of the Indian tribes."[39] He was correct, for the characteristic campaign after 1877 was the pursuit of Indian fugitives over a large expanse of territory. Such was the case with Chief Joseph's Nez Perce band in 1877 and the Northern Cheyennes of Dull Knife and Little Wolf in 1878.

To guard against these outbreaks, Sheridan could muster few troops. In the Departments of the Missouri, the Platte, and Dakota he had but one man for every 75 square miles of territory; in the Department of Texas, one for every 120 square miles. His infantry companies averaged only 40 men, while the cavalry and artillery did just slightly better with 60 and 50 men, respectively. Sheridan complained that three or four of his companies were "expected to hold and guard, against one of the most acute and wary foes in the world, a space of country that in any other land would be held by a brigade."[40]

With his troops scattered across the frontier at small posts, Sheridan found it difficult to prosecute the few Indian campaigns he faced after 1877. The cost of mobilizing forces at any one place was high, and the time lost in concentrating men gave the Indians a brief advantage. These problems were especially telling in the pursuit of Indian fugitives. Rapid expansion of railroads, however, eased these problems, allowing the abandonment of many small posts and the concentration of troops at larger forts.

Keeping the peace on the Indian frontier remained Sheridan's primary duty throughout his years as commander of the Division of the Missouri. Even during periods of Indian unrest, however, troops were quickly pulled from the frontier to meet various other threats to national order. Indian wars were already anachronistic to Gilded Age Americans, and the requirements of frontier expansion were usually subordinated to more pressing political or economic needs in the East. Thus Sheridan and his troopers were called from frontier service to play important roles in Reconstruction, in the election crisis of 1876, and in the labor strife of 1877. Sheridan's duties went far beyond Indian campaigning.

Decisions on the establishment, construction, maintenance, and abandonment of forts within the Division of the Missouri took up much of Sheridan's time. Congress, anxious to cut military expenditures, never appropriated the funds to build new posts and keep established forts in even a modest state of repair. Western communities competed for forts, depots, or headquarters offices, since any government construction meant additional economic growth. Sheridan often confronted irate citizens, congressmen, and even his own officers over the location, construction, and budget of forts and depots.[41]

Sheridan was also active in the exploration and promotion of western lands. He sent numerous expeditions into the Yellowstone region, sponsored several scientific expeditions into the West—most notably those of O. C. Marsh of Yale—and promoted the value of frontier regions such as the Black Hills and the Yellowstone Valley.

Sheridan also aided national expansion by the active assistance he gave to the western railroads. The natural alliance between the railroad capitalists and the army worked to the benefit of both. The greatly increased mobility afforded the army by the railroads spelled doom for the Indians. The steel rails provided not only quicker but cheaper movement of men and supplies and finally overthrew the tyranny of distance that had for so long plagued the soldiers. This allowed Sheridan to abandon posts for additional financial savings and eventually to end the long-standing policy of establishing many small outposts across the frontier.[42]

Sheridan also actively promoted professionalism in the service through his support of the School of Application for Infantry and Cavalry at Fort Leavenworth, the Fort Monroe Artillery School, the Engineering School of Application, and the Fort Riley Cavalry School, and through his sponsorship of the scholarship of Emory Upton, William Philo Clark, and John G. Bourke. He advocated an improved system of regulated target practice and lobbied for the adoption of a European magazine rifle over the single-shot, breechloading Springfield rifle. Despite such efforts, however, Sheridan was hardly about to lead a military renaissance. He was deeply conservative and generally hostile to change. Traditionalism set the tone of his post–Civil War career.

On November 1, 1883, General Sherman retired from the army, and Sheridan moved to Washington to assume the position of commanding general. By law, however, Sherman's four stars retired with him so that Sheridan retained the rank of lieutenant general.

Among Sheridan's first acts in his new position was an attempt to resolve the long-standing dispute between the secretary of war and the commanding general as to who actually controlled the army. The controversy was perennial, and bitterness between the two traditional. General Winfield Scott and General Sherman had both removed army headquarters from Washington to other cities after quarreling with the secretary of war; nevertheless, the adjutant general, acting under the authority of the secretary of war, remained the de facto army commander. Chiefs of staff corps, departments, and bureaus all reported to and acted under the orders of the secretary of war. The fact was that the commanding general had no vital responsibilities in time of peace. When Sheridan attempted to limit the staff bureau chiefs to what he interpreted as their proper prerogative—the fiscal administration of the army—and issued them orders without the prior approval of the secretary's office, he was kindly but firmly reprimanded by Secretary of War Robert T. Lincoln.

At this point Sheridan suddenly declined to press the fight, and the bureau chiefs retained their independence. Sheridan could enjoy the high honor of his sinecure as commanding general, but in essence it was an office devoid of real authority. He remained an advisor to the secretary of war, while the actual administration of the army was performed by the various staff bureau chiefs.[43]

Sheridan's tenure as commanding general was brief and marked by only modest achievements. His health had been slipping for years, and he withdrew from the public limelight to spend more time with his wife, Irene, and their four young children. He spent much of his time working on his memoirs, which he completed in March 1888.

On May 22, 1888, having just returned from Chicago and his inspection of the site for Fort Sheridan, the general collapsed with a severe heart attack. The announcement of his grave condition led Congress to revive the grade of general of the army, and President Grover Cleveland promptly signed the commission. Sheridan now joined Washington, Grant, and Sherman in holding the four-star rank. The promotion briefly buoyed his spirits, and there was some hope for his recovery. But the heart attacks returned with increasing severity, and the general finally succumbed on August 5, 1888.[44]

Sheridan's Civil War achievements were so dramatic and important that they have overshadowed his impressive record as a frontier soldier. In the West, he tended to step aside in order to give his subordinates their chance for glory and not to compromise their independent commands. Thus younger officers like Ranald Mackenzie, Nelson Miles, and George Custer made reputations as frontier soldiers that far overshadowed their impressive Civil War records. Sheridan, even though he took an active part in some Indian campaigns and planned the overall strategy for most of them, never became identified in the public mind as a frontier soldier. Nevertheless, Philip Sheridan was the nation's preeminent western soldier both in subjugating the Native Americans and in the opening of the frontier to an expanding population.

Notes

1. There were several nineteenth-century biographies of Sheridan, the two best being Henry E. Davies, *General Sheridan* (New York: D. Appleton, 1895); and Frank A. Burr and Richard J. Hinton, *The Life of Gen. Philip H. Sheridan: Its Romance and Reality* (Providence, R.I.: J. A. & R. A. Reid, 1888). A good nonscholarly biography is Richard O'Connor, *Sheridan the Inevitable* (Indianapolis, Ind.: Bobbs-Merrill, 1953); a nice pictorial compilation is Lawrence A. Frost, *The Phil Sheridan Album* (Seattle, Wash.: Superior Publishing, 1968). For Sheridan's frontier career, see Paul Andrew Hutton, *Phil Sheridan and His Army* (Lincoln: University of Nebraska Press, 1985).

2. Hutton, *Phil Sheridan*, 6–11.

3. Whitelaw Reid, *Ohio in the War: Her Statesmen, Her Generals, and Soldiers*, 2 vols. (New York: Moore, Wilstach & Baldwin, 1868), 1:500.

4. Quoted in Bruce Catton, *Grant Takes Command* (Boston: Little, Brown, 1968), 90.

5. For Sheridan's Civil War career, see Joseph Hergesheimer, *Sheridan: A Military Narrative* (Boston: Houghton Mifflin, 1931); Edward J. Stackpole, *Sheridan in the Shenandoah: Jubal Early's Nemesis* (Harrisburg, Pa.: Stackpole, 1961); Stephen Z. Starr, *The Union Cavalry in the Civil War: The War in the East from Gettysburg to Appomattox, 1863–1865* (Baton Rouge: Louisiana State University Press, 1981); Robert Thomas Zeimet, "Philip H. Sheridan and the Civil War in the West" (Ph.D. diss., Marquette University, 1981).

6. For Sheridan and Reconstruction, see Joseph G. Dawson III, *Army Generals and Reconstruction: Louisiana, 1862–1877* (Baton Rouge: Louisiana State University Press, 1982); and James E. Sefton, *The United States Army and Reconstruction, 1865–1877* (Baton Rouge: Louisiana State University Press, 1967).

7. Philip H. Sheridan, "Report, In the Field, Fort Hays, Sept. 26, 1868," Box 83, Philip H. Sheridan Papers, Library of Congress.

8. G. A. Forsyth, "A Frontier Fight," *Harper's New Monthly Magazine* 91 (June 1895): 42–62; Lonnie J. White, "The Battle of Beecher Island: The Scouts Hold Fast on the Arickaree," *Journal of the West* 5 (January 1966): 1–24; Robert Lynam, ed., *The Beecher Island Annual: Sixty-second Anniversary of the Battle of Beecher Island, Sept. 17, 18, 1868* (Wray, Colo.: Beecher Island Memorial Association, 1930).

9. E. S. Godfrey, "Some Reminiscences, Including an Account of General Sully's Expedition against the Southern Plains Indians," *Cavalry Journal* 36 (July 1927): 421–23; Lonnie J. White, "General Sully's Expedition to the North Canadian, 1868," *Journal of the West* 11 (January 1972): 75–98; Robert M. Utley, ed., *Life in Custer's Cavalry: Diaries and Letters of Albert and Jennie Barnitz, 1867–1868* (New Haven, Conn.: Yale University Press, 1977), 183–91.

10. "Report of Lieutenant Colonel G. A. Custer," November 28, 1868, Box 83, Sheridan Papers. For Washita, see Stan Hoig, *The Battle of the Washita: The Sheridan-Custer Indian Campaign of 1867–69* (Garden City, N.Y.: Doubleday, 1976); John M. Carroll, ed., *General Custer and the Battle of the Washita: The Federal View* (Bryan, Tex.: Guidon Press, 1978); Charles J. Brill, *Conquest of the Southern Plains: Uncensored Narrative of the Battle of the Washita and Custer's Southern Plains Campaign* (Oklahoma City, Okla.: Golden Saga, 1938); Edward S. Godfrey, "Some Reminiscences, including the Washita Battle, November 27, 1868," *Cavalry Journal* 37 (October 1928): 481–500; Paul Nesbitt, "Battle of the Washita," *Chronicles of Oklahoma* 3 (April 1925): 3–32.

11. Carl C. Rister, "Colonel A. W. Evans' Christmas Day Indian Fight (1868)," *Chronicles of Oklahoma* 16 (September 1938): 281–92.

12. James T. King, *War Eagle: A Life of General Eugene A. Carr* (Lincoln: University of Nebraska Press, 1963), 112–16; George F. Price, *Across the Continent with the Fifth Cavalry* (New York: Antiquarian Press, 1959), 138–41; Richard Weingardt, *Sound the Charge* (Englewood, Colo.: Jacqueline Enterprises, 1978).

13. For general overviews of Sheridan's winter campaign, see Hutton, *Phil Sheridan*, 28–114; William H. Leckie, *The Military Conquest of the Southern Plains* (Norman: University of Oklahoma Press, 1963), 88–132; Carl C. Rister, *Border Command: General Phil Sheridan in the West* (Norman: University of Oklahoma Press, 1944), 71–159; DeB. Randolph Keim, *Sheridan's Troopers on the Borders: A Winter Campaign on the Plains* (Lincoln: University of Nebraska Press, 1985); David L. Spotts, *Campaigning with Custer and the Nineteenth Kansas Volunteer Cavalry on the Washita Campaign, 1868–'69* (Los Angeles: Wetzel, 1928); Lonnie J. White, "Winter Campaigning with Sheridan and Custer: The Expedition of the Nineteenth Kansas Volunteer Cavalry," *Journal of the West* 6 (January 1967): 68–98.

14. Philip Henry Sheridan and Michael V. Sheridan, *Personal Memoirs of Philip Henry Sheridan, General United States Army: New and Enlarged Edition with an Account of His Life from 1871 to his Death, in 1888*, 2 vols. (New York: D. Appleton, 1904), 2:464–65.

15. Philip H. Sheridan to Secretary of War, May 17, 1873, Box 9, Sheridan Papers.

16. Sheridan to J. T. Averill, January 28, 1874, Box 10, Sheridan Papers.

17. Sheridan to War Department, July 11, 1872, Box 7; November 7, 1872, Box 8, Sheridan Papers.

18. For Sheridan's testimony before Congress on transfer, see *Army and Navy Journal*, February 26, 1876, p. 469. For background on the transfer controversy, see Robert Winston Mardock, *The Reformers and the American Indian* (Columbia: University of Missouri Press, 1971), 42–46, 139–41, 159–67; Francis Paul Prucha, *American Indian Policy in Crisis: Christian Reformers and the Indian, 1865–1900* (Norman: University of Oklahoma Press, 1976), 71–102; Robert M. Utley, *Frontier Regulars: The United States Army and the Indian, 1866–1899* (New York: Macmillan, 1973), 188–92; Donald J. D'Elia, "The Argument over Civilian or Military Indian Control, 1865–1880," *Historian* 24 (February 1962): 207–25; Francis Paul Prucha, *The Great Father: The United States Government and the American Indians*, 2 vols. (Lincoln: University of Nebraska Press, 1984), 1:549–61.

19. *Annual Report of the Secretary of War for the Year 1878*, 2 vols. (Washington, D.C.: Government Printing Office, 1878), 1:36.

20. *Annual Report of the Secretary of War for the Year 1879,* 4 vols. (Washington, D.C.: Government Printing Office, 1879), 1:45.

21. Sheridan to William T. Sherman, May 9, 1873, Division of the Missouri, Letters Sent, Records of U.S. Continental Commands, Record Group (hereafter RG) 393, National Archives (hereafter NA); Sheridan to Sherman, March 18, 1870, Box 91, Sheridan Papers.

22. Sheridan to Sherman, March 18, 1870, Box 91, Sheridan Papers.

23. Ibid.

24. Columbus, Nebraska, *Platte Journal,* June 29, 1870; Chicago *Tribune,* April 25, 1870.

25. Prucha, *American Indian Policy in Crisis,* 50.

26. For the government conspiracy to seize the Black Hills, see Sheridan to Alfred Terry, November 9, 1875; Sheridan to William T. Sherman, November 13, 1875; Sherman to Sheridan, November 20, 1875, Box 39, Sheridan Papers.

27. J. W. Vaughn, *The Reynolds Campaign on Powder River* (Norman: University of Oklahoma Press, 1961); John G. Bourke, *On the Border with Crook* (New York: Scribner, 1891), 256–82; James H. Bradley, *The March of the Montana Column: A Prelude to the Custer Disaster,* ed. Edgar I. Stewart (Norman: University of Oklahoma Press, 1961), 7–85.

28. Sheridan to Sherman, May 29, 1876, Box 15, Sheridan Papers.

29. Sheridan to Terry, June 23, 1876, Division of the Missouri, Letters Sent, RG 393, NA.

30. Sheridan to George Crook, May 29, June 18, 20, 1876; Sheridan to Eugene Carr, June 20, 1876, ibid. Also see Paul L. Hedren, *First Scalp for Custer: The Skirmish at Warbonnet Creek, Nebraska, July 17, 1876* (Glendale, Calif.: Arthur H. Clark, 1980), 139–48; Charles King, "The Story of a March," *Journal of the United Stated Cavalry Association* 3 (March 1890): 121–29.

31. For the Battle of the Rosebud, see J. W. Vaughn, *With Crook at the Rosebud* (Harrisburg, Pa.: Stackpole, 1956), 47–171; also consult the Crook essay in this volume.

32. Drum to Sheridan, enclosing Terry to Sheridan, June 21, 1876, Division of the Missouri, Letters Sent, RG 393, NA.

33. The two standard accounts of Custer's defeat are Edgar I. Stewart, *Custer's Luck* (Norman: University of Oklahoma Press, 1955); and John S. Gray, *Centennial Campaign: The Sioux War of 1876* (Fort Collins, Colo.: Old Army Press, 1976). The historical literature on Custer and his last battle is enormous: see the Custer essay in this volume.

34. Sheridan to Sherman, July 7, 1876, Division of the Missouri, Letters Sent, RG 393, NA.

35. For the operations after Custer's defeat, see Jerome A. Greene, *Slim Buttes, 1876: An Episode of the Great Sioux War* (Norman: University of Oklahoma Press, 1982); Paul L. Hedren, *With Crook in the Black Hills: Stanley J. Morrow's 1876 Photographic Legacy* (Boulder, Colo.: Pruett, 1985).

36. Sheridan to Sherman, August 10, 1876, Division of the Missouri, Letters Sent, RG 393, NA.

37. Sherman to Sheridan, February 17, 1877, Box 39, Sheridan Papers.

38. There is no monograph covering the entire Great Sioux War. A good brief account is in Utley, *Frontier Regulars*, 236–95.

39. *Annual Report of the Secretary of War [1879]*, 2 vols. (Washington, D.C.: Government Printing Office, 1879), 1:45.

40. Ibid.

41. Hutton, *Phil Sheridan*, 156–59.

42. Ibid., 170–75.

43. For this dispute, see Russell F. Weigley, *History of the United States Army* (New York: Macmillan, 1967), 192–94, 185–86; William Harding Carter, *The American Army* (Indianapolis, Ind.: Bobbs-Merrill, 1915), 188–92.

44. Hutton, *Phil Sheridan*, 371–72.

George A. Custer

by Brian W. Dippie

Courtesy Mrs. Ethel Yates Gray

The irony of George Armstrong Custer's historical and popular reputation is manifest. He is an American soldier best known for defeat, and because of defeat he is one of America's best-known soldiers—certainly the best-known officer to serve in the post–Civil War Indian-fighting army. And because he is the best known, he has become the most prominent figure of the late nineteenth-century Indian wars—a martyred hero to some, a villain to others. Indeed, the latter role completes the irony: by losing absolutely to the Sioux and Cheyenne on the Little Bighorn in 1876, he has become the ultimate symbol of white conquest of the Indian ("Custer Died for Your Sins . . . Had It Coming . . . Wore an Arrow Shirt," etc.). A loser, Custer now stands for the "winning of the West."

Instead of explaining who he was and what he did, Custer's biographer must account for a fame out of all proportion to his accomplishments. Why is George Armstrong Custer so much better known than his military peers? Or, as a distinguished western historian put the question several years ago, why have so many pages been "wasted" on the last battle of a man who "did less toward hurrying the occupation of western America than the little-known commanders who won engagements with the Indians?"[1] It is not enough to point out that the flamboyant Custer had received more than his share of attention during the Civil War and, after an inauspicious—indeed dismal—introduction to Indian campaigning on the Kansas plains in 1867, through an astute combination of field service and self-promotion had impressed himself upon his contemporaries as America's premier Indian fighter. The Little Bighorn would seem sufficient to have squelched *that* notion. At the time, the Seventh Cavalry's colonel and Custer's superior, Samuel D. Sturgis, doubly embittered over the devastation of the regiment and the loss of his son in the battle, characterized Custer as "a very selfish man . . . insanely ambitious for glory," whose reputation was "to a great extent formed from his writings and newspaper reports."[2] Custer's memoir of his service against the southern tribes, *My Life on the Plains,* published in installments in *Galaxy* magazine and as a book in 1874, had solidified his popular reputation as an Indian fighter. But why did that reputation survive a catastrophe that Colonel Sturgis, for one, thought put the lie to it? Why *have* so many pages been "wasted" on a loser?

From the outset the public accepted Custer's Last Stand as the epitome of self-sacrificing heroism. Death, spectacular death, removed Custer to a realm apart where artists teach us to see the epics that poets sing, novelists and dramatists serve as the historians of myth, and disastrous defeat is transformed into higher victory.[3] The two most influential biographies of Custer have been the work of novelists who found in his life compelling themes. For Frederick Whittaker in 1876, Custer was a peerless cavalier hero betrayed by the envious and destined for a martyr's death.[4] Frederic F. Van de Water in 1934 portrayed him as an overgrown adolescent who craved glory above all else and sacrificed his command to his obsession.[5] More recently, novelist Evan S. Connell's *Son of the Morning Star,* a pointilist portrait juxtaposing details freely drawn from history and myth to explain the Custer enigma, has been hailed as "a new American classic" and the best life of Custer ever written.[6] Popular legends are public property; Custer, in whatever guise, now belongs to us all.

But George Armstrong Custer was a man before he was a legend. Born on December 5, 1839, in the small farm town of New Rumley, Ohio, he grew up in Monroe, Michigan, but was appointed from Ohio to the Military Academy at West Point in 1857. Exemplary in neither his studies nor his behavior, he graduated at the bottom of his class in 1861. Commissioned a second lieutenant in the Second Cavalry, he won distinction in the Civil War as a fighting officer and emerged at the end a captain and brevet brigadier general in the regular army and a major general in the volunteers. With his long blond hair set off by a red tie, a sailor's blouse, and a blue jacket agleam with gold, he cut a dashing figure. Admired by some fellow officers, he was detested by others. The Northern public, however, hungry for a romantic cavalier of the sort that seemed to bloom with the magnolias down south, took him to heart as the Boy General.

After the South's surrender, Custer was assigned to Reconstruction duty in

Texas to pacify the locals and prevent Confederate retrenchment in Mexico. Commanding several regiments of unwilling volunteers, he made an object lesson of two soldiers before setting out from Louisiana: he executed one and subjected the other to a mock execution, nearly precipitating a mutiny in the process. But the mixture of stern justice and mercy with a touch of gallows humor quieted the situation, though not the resentments in his command. During a five-month stay in Texas, which ended when he was mustered out of the volunteer service on February 1, 1866, Custer continued to alienate officers and men by strict enforcement of regulations against foraging and destruction of private property, by the same token winning the gratitude of Texans.[7] Schooled in combat, Custer was not temperamentally suited to peacetime duty. War fostered obedience and loyalty; peace, laxity and disrespect. Custer's command problems in this period presaged those he would encounter in his first year of Indian campaigning as well.

Effective July 28, 1866, Custer was appointed lieutenant colonel of the Seventh Cavalry, then organizing in Kansas, and awarded the brevet rank of major general; when he fell at the Little Bighorn a decade later, he was still Lieutenant Colonel, Brevet Major General, George Armstrong Custer, Seventh Cavalry. For him, as for other officers, the end of the Civil War meant an end to a meteoric rise. The post–Civil War army, a favorite target of economy-minded Democrats sensitive to Reconstruction issues, was under pressure to reduce further throughout the depressed 1870s. Promotion was frustratingly slow, compounding the tensions created by Civil War rank and stymied ambition. Most veteran officers held brevets or had served in elevated capacities in the volunteers, often outranking the regular army officers under whom they served following the war. Custer, for example, as major general of volunteers, commanded Colonel Sturgis in Texas in 1865 but served under him in the Seventh after 1869. Others experienced similar reversals, and tact had to be built into the command structure. Custer, who would never be without loyal friends, had a knack for offending and permanently estranging some of his officers in the Seventh, and Minnie Dubbs Millbrook has advanced a plausible explanation.[8] Custer was almost literally a "boy general" when he commanded brigades and divisions in the Civil War; he was still a young man when his days as major general ended; and he joined the Seventh at Fort Riley, Kansas, in October 1866, shortly before his twenty-seventh birthday. In the past, high command had sheltered him from some of the routine realities of soldiering. He liked his men a great deal in the abstract, but he did not like dealing with them. In Kansas, he struggled with the loss of amenities of rank and the unfamiliar feeling of being on the periphery instead of at the center of events. Far from instantly falling in love with the West's wide open spaces, Custer sank into depression during a listless campaign under Major General Winfield S. Hancock.

Mounted in March 1867, 1,400 men strong, Hancock's expedition was intended to awe the warriors of the southern plains into docility by a substantial show of force. "Our visit may prevent an outbreak," Hancock wrote, but "if one is intended, it may precipitate it."[9] With such muddled objectives, failure was foreordained. Custer, in charge of the Seventh Cavalry under Hancock, despaired. He had begun with the kind of war he was meant to fight, and he would never find another like it. He needed battle lines and brave charges to expose his virtues, his tireless determination and excitable, winning courage. Used to decisive actions, he found Indian campaigning an exercise in futility. With a command plagued by supply problems and depleted by desertions, he covered hundreds of miles over a four-month period, exhausted men and horses chasing after an elusive foe, and never really fought any Indians—though he was involved in Hancock's decision to burn an abandoned Sioux and Cheyenne village on April 19, a provocation that spread Indian unrest on the plains.

It is worth noting that if nine years later Custer badly underestimated the Indians' capacity for resistance at the Little Bighorn, no wonder. His earliest experiences had taught him the lesson, confirmed by subsequent campaigns, that plains warriors normally avoided direct confrontation and specialized in strategic retreat, tempting officers besides Custer, aware though they were of the danger, to fatal miscalculation when the mobile, scattering foe suddenly reformed into an unyielding, aggressive force—which they would do if a village was in peril, or if numerical superiority or command of the terrain made a successful fight possible. An army attack, as Major Marcus Reno discovered at the Little Bighorn, could quickly disintegrate into a panicky retreat when the Indians failed to act as they were supposed to. Custer has been berated for overweening confidence. But if he thought the numerically superior Indian force along the Little Bighorn would flee from the Seventh Cavalry, it was not because he was an arrogant fool but because he was by then a veteran plains campaigner who only twice in nine years had experienced anything different.

Custer's problems on his first Indian campaign in 1867 were summed up on July 21 when he was placed under arrest at Fort Harker, Kansas. His wife, Elizabeth, whom he had married in February 1864, had been his anchor in a period of change. She doted on him, made his new situation bearable. But the spring campaign had separated them, and as the summer dragged on, Custer found himself at Fort Wallace while she waited at Fort Riley, 275 miles to the east. On July 15 he had left his command at Fort Wallace and with an escort of four officers and 72 men had made a punishing ride eastward to be by her side. He justified his unwise foray on military grounds; nevertheless, he was charged with absence without leave from his command and conduct prejudicial to good order and military discipline. A disgruntled officer in the Seventh Cavalry filed additional charges stemming from an incident earlier that month when Custer, incensed by a spate of desertions, ordered 13 troopers who were making off in broad daylight to be ridden down and shot. Three were wounded, one fatally, and Custer made a public display of denying them medical aid when they were brought in. It was the mock execution strategy revisited, and it appalled some officers already disillusioned with their mercurial commander. A court-martial convened at Fort Leavenworth found Custer guilty on all specifications, with no criminality attached to the most serious, and on October 11 ordered him suspended from rank and pay for one year. For Custer, it marked a humiliating end to an inauspicious introduction to Indian campaigning. He saw himself as the scapegoat for Hancock's costly failure and reacted with predictable fury, blaming the general for all his troubles. The fact remains that the man destined to become America's best-known Indian fighter did not, as Mrs. Millbrook has written, take to the plains like a seal to the sea; instead, he foundered.

But things were already beginning to look up for Custer. In September 1867, Major General Philip H. Sheridan replaced Hancock as commander of the Department of the Missouri. Sheridan had an abiding affection for Custer, reaching back to his service against Robert E. Lee in the closing phase of the Civil War. Impulsive, even reckless, Custer nevertheless personified what there was of the "poetry of romance in war" for Sheridan, and he watched over his protégé with a paternal eye.[10] He could do nothing about Custer's court-martial in 1867 but took some of the sting out of it by allowing him the use of his own quarters at Fort Leavenworth over the winter. In March 1868, Sheridan assumed active command of his department. Impatient for results, he decided to mount a winter campaign against the Indians to catch them when they were least mobile and most vulnerable. Success demanded the energy and perseverance of a Custer. If he had not displayed these qualities to advantage under Hancock, he would for his old commander, and on September 24, 1868, Sheridan interceded on his behalf. "Can you come at once?" he wrote. "Eleven companies of your regiment will move about the 1st of October against the hostile Indians."[11]

The import of such an extraordinary dispensation did not escape Custer. He returned to the field and became again the vigorous, energetic cavalryman of Civil War fame. On November 27, on the Washita River in the Indian Territory, he visited destruction upon Black Kettle's village of Cheyennes. A dawn attack caught the Indians by surprise; after fierce fighting they were driven from their camp with losses placed at 103 killed and 53 women and children captured. The Cheyenne ponies were shot, and their property—lodge skins, saddles, robes, weapons, food—destroyed. Sheridan cheered the victory as decisive, and Custer returned to a hero's welcome, despite mounting protest in the East that the Battle of the Washita was a disgraceful massacre of peaceful Indians. Custer was learning another lesson about frontier warfare: victory elicited a mixed response at best, corresponding to deep national divisions over Indian policy. This was indeed not the Civil War.[12]

Custer remained in the field through the spring of 1869, braced by constant evidence of Sheridan's esteem and the growing conviction that he was the foremost Indian-fighting officer of the day. In March 1871 his plains service was interrupted by what proved to be two years of Reconstruction duty in the Department of the South. The Seventh Cavalry served principally in South Carolina and Kentucky, which satisfied Custer's passion for fine horses, although Elizabethtown, where he was stationed, was the "stillest, dullest place."[13] Assisting state and federal officials in carrying out court orders, breaking up illegal distilleries and combatting the spread of the Ku Klux Klan struck Custer as "political" duty, uncongenial to a Democrat like himself out of sympathy with Republican postwar policies and unworthy of a regiment like the Seventh Cavalry that was born on the plains. He chafed at the inactivity and was delighted to receive orders, in February 1873, reassigning the Seventh to the Department of Dakota for service against the Sioux. Steamboats transported the scattered components of the regiment up the Mississippi to Cairo, Illinois, where they assembled for a train ride to the end of track at Yankton, Dakota Territory. The last 350 miles to Fort Rice were on horseback, proof that the regiment had left civilization behind.

The troops arrived at Fort Rice on June 10; ten days later they were off, with 11 companies of infantry and artillery and a wagon train, on the Yellowstone Expedition under the command of Colonel David S. Stanley, Twenty-second Infantry. Its task was to protect the survey crews of the Northern Pacific Railway and serve notice on the Indians that the white man's road would be built despite their opposition. All did not go smoothly. Custer clashed with Stanley. Demanding of those under him—a lieutenant with the expedition characterized Custer as "selfishly indifferent to others, and ruthlessly determined to make himself conspicuous at all hazards"[14]—he was himself a reluctant subordinate, given to chasing after game with his pack of hounds or scouting ahead of the main column. An abstemious man, he regarded Stanley as an incompetent inebriate; Stanley in turn resented Custer's insolent assumption that he had an independent command and could come and go as he pleased. But they sorted out their differences, and Custer found the action he wanted in two dangerous brushes with the Sioux. One foreshadowed 1876. On August 4, 1873, Custer bivouacked with a squadron of 90 men at the campsite chosen for the main column, which, as usual, was trailing far behind. Six Sioux rode up, stampeded the grazing cavalry horses, and—acting as decoys—nearly led the small pursuit party mounted by Custer into a trap. It was good luck rather than good management that averted disaster; even then, Custer had to ride for his life, rejoining his men for a hot fight that might still have ended in catastrophe had reinforcements not arrived. Adopting racetrack parlance, Custer wrote with his usual insouciance, "I was up, the Indians were up, and for a little while, I thought it was 'all up' with me. It was a dash race. I'm glad it wasn't heats. I won the dash, but might have lost the second heat."[15] The Sioux would get their rematch three years later at the Little Bighorn.

The Yellowstone Expedition ended for Custer's command on September 21 when they reached winter quarters, newly constructed Fort Abraham Lincoln on the Missouri just downriver from Bismarck. Thereafter, while companies of the Seventh would be stationed at Forts Rice and Totten and regimental head-quarters would remain at Fort Snelling in Minnesota, Fort Lincoln would be Custer's home. From there a major expedition, the only one Custer would per-sonally lead into Sioux country, departed on July 2, 1874. Though it proved uneventful from the standpoint of Indian fighting, the Black Hills Expedition was of primary importance to future Sioux-white relations. Simply, it was in direct violation of the Treaty of 1868, which established the Sioux reservation (embracing present-day South Dakota west of the Missouri, including the Black Hills) and designated the area west of the reservation "unceded Indian territory," closed to white occupation or even passage without Indian consent "so long as the buffalo may range thereon in such numbers as to justify the chase." The army charged that the Sioux were using the Black Hills as a sanc-tuary for raiding parties, thereby violating the treaty and forfeiting their rights under it. An army post in the Hills might be necessary to remedy the situation, and thus an exploration was mandatory.[16]

Compounding matters were long-standing rumors that the Hills were rich in gold. When a correspondent for the Chicago *Inter-Ocean* reported the discov-ery of gold "from the grassroots down" on August 7, the news created wild excitement in a country mired in depression.[17] The western press demanded the opening of an area presently occupied by "a few miserable savages";[18] some eastern journals spoke up for Sioux rights; the War Department as usual was caught in the middle. The army kept the Black Hills relatively clear of miners through the summer of 1875, but that September, yielding to public pressure, Congress sent a commission to negotiate with the Sioux for purchase of the Hills. Their refusal to sell apparently justified the government in its refusal to continue protecting the reservation's boundaries against white incursion. Over the fall and winter of 1875–76 the Black Hills gold rush was on. Further, the government decided to crack down on Sioux who still hunted in the unceded Indian territory. On December 3 the secretary of the interior directed the com-missioner of Indian affairs to notify all Sioux to be on the reservation by Janu-ary 31, 1876. Noncompliance meant they would be deemed hostile and, under the terms of President Grant's peace policy, turned over to the War Department for punitive action.[19]

Meanwhile, Custer had passed an unexpectedly quiet year in 1875. The Seventh got a respite from extended field service, and he spent part of the spring and most of the fall visiting in the East. Photographs from the 1870s showing Custer in his buckskin outfit, bronzed (or, in his case, since he was fair-skinned, probably sunburnt) and confident, suggest that the transformation from Civil War Boy General to mature western Indian fighter was complete. In fact, while Custer had pets and hobbies enough to keep him busy — including a writing career that played heavily on the romance of frontier life—like most officers stationed out west, he sought frequent leaves stateside. The West might be the place to visit in Grant's America and perhaps shoot a buffalo or two, but the industrializing East was where things were happening.[20] Caught up in Custer's spectacular finale and his fluctuating reputation, we have judged him primarily as an Indian campaigner and framed our questions about him in the light of present concerns. Was Custer, we have asked, an Indian hater or a compassionate foe of those whom circumstances forced him to fight? We might better ask, what *were* his own primary concerns in the 1870s?

Because Custer's affiliation with the Democratic Party, inherited from his father, would play a part in the events of 1876, it is commonly assumed that he was out of harmony with Republican values and was a victim of the spoils system, or "Grantism," as the Democrats labeled it. But this ignores Custer's own eagerness for an invitation to the Great Barbecue. He was a man of his times, after all, involved in investment schemes and promotional activities. Put aside the photographs of Custer in his buckskin hunting suit for those showing him in his thirties in civilian apparel, and a different impression emerges: this is a small-time businessman, comfortably nondescript, dreaming of making it big. His posting in the West afforded him an exceptional opportunity to be in on the ground floor of a speculator's paradise. Indian title was being extinguished, while mining concerns, cattlemen, railroad barons, land agents, town planners, and a host of others moved in to stake their claims. Custer operated as a stock jobber for a Colorado silver mine, enlisted his pen in the service of the Kansas Pacific and Northern Pacific railroads in exchange for "courtesies," and may have participated in an elaborate scheme involving railroads, stage lines, land speculators, and manufacturing concerns in the Black Hills in 1875. Even his love of fine horseflesh had a speculative side to it. Besides the thoroughbreds he purchased for personal use, Custer acquired a racehorse of his own in 1872, though its on-track performance fell short of expectation, and he ruefully concluded that the sport of kings was too rich for a lieutenant colonel's pay. Indians represented to Custer a colorful, passing phase of America's development, dangerous enough from a soldier's point of view but doomed by the law of civilized advance—a temporary impediment to a prime entrepreneurial opportunity that probably engaged him more than they ever did. The doomed cavalier-hero might well be recast as a recognizable, post-Civil War type: the aspiring capitalist.[21] In 1876, however, the Sioux were Custer's preoccupation.

On February 1, the ultimatum ordering all Sioux onto their reservation having expired, the secretary of the interior notified the War Department that it was now free to compel the "hostiles" to obey.[22] Three military columns took the field. One, under Brigadier General George Crook, set out from Fort Fetterman in Wyoming; a second, under Colonel John Gibbon, from Forts Shaw and Ellis in Montana; and a third, under Brigadier General Alfred H. Terry, from Fort

Lincoln in Dakota Territory. By working in concert, the three columns would converge on the Sioux and thrash them into submission.

Custer, with Terry's Dakota Column as commander of the Seventh Cavalry, was fortunate to be along at all. That March and April he had testified in Washington before a House committee investigating charges of corruption in the War Department, offering what a fellow officer characterized as "nothing but hearsay . . . largely made up of frontier gossip and stories," in which he managed to implicate both W. W. Belknap, the secretary of war (who subsequently resigned to avoid impeachment), and Orvil Grant, the President's brother.[23] Furious, Grant removed Custer from command of the Dakota Column, then detained him in Chicago awaiting further orders while the Seventh Cavalry prepared to take the field. Humbled, Custer begged the President to spare him the humiliation of seeing his regiment "march to meet the enemy and I not to share its dangers." With Custer's superiors, including Sheridan, rallying to him, Grant relented.[24]

Crook's column, after an abortive campaign in March, set out again on May 29. Gibbon's Montana Column had been in the field since early April. The Dakota Column, plagued by delays, did not leave Fort Lincoln until May 17. One month later Crook met the Sioux on the Rosebud, was fought to a standstill, and withdrew to his base camp in northern Wyoming. The other two columns were unaware of Crook's setback when they rendezvoused at the junction of the Rosebud and Yellowstone Rivers on June 21. They knew the approximate location of the Indians, however, and devised a strategy designed to prevent their escape, despite scouting intelligence that young men had been streaming out from the reservations to join the hostiles since early spring. Instead of the 1,000 or so Sioux warriors expected, the Indian force, augmented by Cheyennes and a few Arapahos, would be double that size. Nevertheless, the army proceeded on the assumption that the Indians would flee, probably to the south. The strategy, then, was to send one column up the Rosebud, west to the source of the Little Bighorn, then down that river—in whose valley, it was correctly assumed, the hostiles would be found. Meanwhile, the second column, having followed the Yellowstone west to the confluence of the Bighorn, was to ascend it and then its tributary, the Little Bighorn, thereby precluding escape to the north. Trapped between the columns, the Indians would have no choice but to fight or surrender.

Because speed was imperative, General Terry decided to send Custer up the Rosebud with the Seventh Cavalry—the coveted independent command—while he accompanied Colonel Gibbon's mixed column of cavalry and infantry. Though Custer's critics have charged that once he was on his own he rushed to meet the Indians, thereby upsetting Terry's plan of coordinated attack, there is ample evidence that Terry expected Custer to "strike the blow" and drive the hostiles north into his advancing column. Certainly Terry's written orders of

June 22 left much to Custer's discretion while outlining a preferred course of action. The Seventh Cavalry was to follow an Indian trail that Terry assumed would cut over to the Little Bighorn; he was so concerned about the Indians escaping to the south, however, that even if the trail turned west sooner, he wanted Custer to press on up the Rosebud to the headwaters of the Tongue before descending the Little Bighorn. But he also said that it was "impossible" to give any "definite instructions," and he placed "too much confidence" in Custer's "zeal, energy and ability" to impose "precise orders" upon him anyway. Custer could decide for himself, in short, but the responsibility for any departure from Terry's instructions would clearly be his.[25]

After receiving his orders, Custer dashed off a short letter to his wife. "Do not be anxious about me," he wrote. "A success will start us all toward [Fort] Lincoln."[26] That noon, Custer headed up the Rosebud with 12 companies of the Seventh Cavalry—nearly 600 officers and men—and another 50 Crow, Arikara, and civilian employees. The early morning hours of June 25 found the Seventh marching in inky blackness. When a halt was ordered at 2:30 A.M., exhausted troopers flopped down to sleep where they could, unaware that for almost half of them the day ahead would be their last. For Custer had decided to ignore Terry's instructions and follow the Indian trail west toward the Little Bighorn. The alternative, he had informed his officers, was to let the Indians scatter and escape. While the weary troopers rested, scouts reported that they had located the village some 15 miles away on the Little Bighorn. The command was in the saddle again by 8 A.M. as Custer hurried to meet the foe.

Interpretations of what followed that day have been, as much as anything else, attempts to penetrate the mind of George Armstrong Custer. The Seventh crossed the divide between the Rosebud and Little Bighorn about noon and advanced on the Indian village. Custer, certain that his force had been discovered and more convinced than ever that the Indians would run, had decided to attack at once. He split the regiment into four battalions. One, under Captain Frederick W. Benteen, was sent to the south to prevent an Indian escape in that direction. A second, consisting of the pack train, followed Benteen. After a two-hour march Custer ordered the third, under Major Marcus A. Reno, to charge the village across the river with a promise of full support. The fourth, his personal command of five companies, then turned north to attack the camp at a vulnerable point downstream. After his charge stalled, Reno retreated back across the Little Bighorn and—with more than half of his battalion dead, wounded, or missing—assumed a defensive posture on the bluffs above the river. There Benteen and the pack train joined him and dug in for a two-day siege that was lifted on June 27 with the arrival of Terry and Gibbon's men.

Meanwhile, about four miles away on the afternoon of June 25, the Indians utterly destroyed Custer's battalion of 210 men in a battle that lasted perhaps an hour. With Custer died two brothers, a nephew, and a brother-in-law, suggesting how much he had made the Seventh Cavalry *his* regiment. Every scrap of evidence about what happened that day has been closely scrutinized; theories, some ingenious, abound. But the fact remains that after nearly 110 years the battle of the Little Bighorn—Custer's Last Stand—is still shrouded in mystery.[27]

News of the disaster reached the East just two days after the country celebrated its centennial. "Shall This Be the Beginning of the End?" a Bismarck paper asked.[28] Indeed it was—for the Indians who had dealt the United States such a stunning rebuke in the midst of its gala hundredth birthday party. The top army brass first heard the news in Philadelphia, where they were attending an exposition dedicated to the theme "A Century of Progress." Custer's Last Stand was a rude reminder that a nation preoccupied with the future had still not wrapped up the old business of securing its frontiers. That would be done in short order: by fall, one-third of the country's military strength was concentrated in the theater of the Sioux war; by the spring of 1877, most of the warriors who had whipped Custer were confined to reservations.

The practical consequences of the Custer disaster were never really in doubt, but responsibility for it was. Charges flew back and forth, inaugurating a rancorous, bitterly partisan controversy that still has the power to stir passions.[29] For the second time in a presidential election year, Custer was embroiled in party politics. Did he die trying to prove himself to President Grant and his Republican detractors? Was his final charge a calculated risk intended to propel him into the White House? The Democratic press knew the answer to the first question—"Grant, the Murderer of Custer," an Atlanta weekly headlined a typically balanced account[30]—and students since have loved to debate the second. The army, which initially dismissed the reports of a disaster to Custer's command, was further embarrassed by fumbled attempts to present a unified front once the reports were confirmed. Officers stepped forward to offer their personal opinions, adding heat to the public debate over responsibility. Some said that Custer had disobeyed orders in attacking the village without waiting for Terry and Gibbon, thereby wrecking the battle plan and dooming his command; others, that the blame lay with the senior officers who had underestimated the size and determination of the Indian force in mapping campaign strategy, and with Reno and Benteen, who had failed to support a man Reno disliked and Benteen despised. Reno was accused of cowardice, Benteen of indifference, while Custer became a hero in spite of himself. An officer who knew him believed he had "sacrificed the Seventh cavalry to ambition and wounded vanity" but added that his "glorious death and the valor of his men will become a legend in our history."[31] Reckless, impetuous, even foolish as he might have been, Custer had ended well "the splendid fever" of his deeds, as Walt Whitman observed in a typical tribute:

There in the far northwest, in struggle, charge, and
    sabre-smite,

> Desperate and glorious—aye, in defeat most desperate,
>   most glorious,
> After thy many battles, in which, never yielding up a gun or a
>   color,
> Leaving behind thee a memory sweet to soldiers,
> Thou yieldest up thyself.[32]

Such also was the message that informed three volumes of reminiscences written out of an undying devotion to Custer's memory by his widow. Elizabeth had married her beloved Autie (or ''the General'') at 21, and she lived on for almost 57 years after his death, the watchful guardian of an American legend she had helped create. Her books pictured the general as a loving son and husband, a loyal friend and perfect gentleman; as cool and courageous on the battlefield, gentle and studious at home, with a fondness for sentimental poetry, military history, animals of all stripes, and practical jokes. His playful side preserved the boy in the Boy General and made their life together a breathless romance, as enduring as it was brief. Criticisms of Custer's actions at the Little Bighorn had circulated freely in the press in 1876, but Mrs. Custer outlasted the critics. In 1931, Frederic Van de Water mused on ''how much of true historical importance has been omitted,'' by those who wrote of Custer, ''out of consideration for his widow.''[33] Not until 1934, the year after her death, did he bring out his own iconoclastic biography, *Glory-Hunter*.

The revised Custer image has proved as acceptable to Americans since the 1930s as the heroic image was to earlier generations. By the 1960s Custer had come to symbolize a whole range of contemporary concerns—racism, militarism, Vietnam, indifference to ecology. Arthur Penn's 1970 film *Little Big Man* (based on the Thomas Berger novel) summed up this tendency, portraying Custer as a pompous egotist, a belligerent incompetent, and finally a raving lunatic.[34] There is a man behind the myth—something less than Elizabeth Custer's flawless cavalier, something more than *Little Big Man*'s bombastic caricature. But the ongoing Custer battle is still a clash of extremes. Custer's modern champions, out to resurrect his heroic reputation, insist that the Last Stand has been viewed out of context; they have directed particular attention to his impressive Civil War record.[35]

But it is the Last Stand that still holds our attention. Move away from it, and one discovers what those impervious to his appeal have all along maintained: Custer was not a very significant historical figure. He did not win the Civil War singlehandedly, but he *may* have been solely responsible for his defeat on the Little Bighorn. And so the debate goes on. Victory that day on the Little Bighorn would have made Custer the historical equivalent of a Nelson A. Miles: an important frontier officer, certainly, but not a figure to command the popular imagination. Defeat brought immortality. Custer's Last Stand: the very words still conjure up an unforgettable image of a soldier at bay, surrounded and doomed, winning lasting fame by failing to win a battle.

Notes

1. Ray Allen Billington, "The New Western Social Order and the Synthesis of Western Scholarship," in Robert G. Ferris, ed., *The American West: An Appraisal. Papers from the Denver Conference on the History of Western America* (Santa Fe: Museum of New Mexico Press, 1963), 12.

2. "Sturgis on Custer," *New York Times,* July 21, 1876; "Gen. Custer's Death," *New York Times,* July 17–18, 1876.

3. See Bruce A. Rosenberg, *Custer and the Epic of Defeat* (University Park: Pennsylvania State University Press, 1974); and Brian W. Dippie, *Custer's Last Stand: The Anatomy of an American Myth* (Missoula: University of Montana Publications in History, 1976).

4. Frederick Whittaker, *A Complete Life of Gen. George A. Custer* (New York: Sheldon, 1876).

5. Frederic F. Van de Water, *Glory-Hunter: A Life of General Custer* (Indianapolis, Ind.: Bobbs-Merrill, 1934).

6. "Yellow Hair's Final Ride," *Time,* November 5, 1984, p. 104; Evan S. Connell, *Son of the Morning Star* (San Francisco: North Point Press, 1984). For a chronological bibliography of Custer biographies, see Dippie, *Custer's Last Stand,* 181–84.

7. See Minnie Dubbs Millbrook, "The Boy General and How He Grew: George Custer after Appomattox," *Montana, the Magazine of Western History* 23 (April 1973): 34–43, and "Custer's March to Texas" in *The Prairie Scout* (Abilene: Kansas Corral of the Westerners, 1973), 1:31–69; John M. Carroll, comp., *Custer in Texas: An Interrupted Narrative* (New York: Sol Lewis/Liveright, 1975).

8. See Minnie Dubbs Millbrook, "The West Breaks in General Custer," *Kansas Historical Quarterly* 36 (Summer 1970): 113–48, and "Custer's First Scout in the West," ibid. 39 (Spring 1973): 75–95. See also Robert M. Utley, ed., *Life in Custer's Cavalry: Diaries and Letters of Albert and Jennie Barnitz, 1867–1868* (New Haven, Conn.: Yale University Press, 1977); and Brian W. Dippie, ed., *Nomad: George A. Custer in Turf, Field and Farm* (Austin: University of Texas Press, 1980).

9. Hancock to Theodore R. Davis, March 10, 1867, in Robert Taft, *Artists and Illustrators of the Old West, 1850–1900* (New York: Scribner, 1953), 300 n. 48.

10. Quoted in Paul A. Hutton, *Phil Sheridan and His Army* (Lincoln: University of Nebraska Press, 1985), 32.

11. Quoted in G. A. Custer, *My Life on the Plains; or, Personal Experiences with Indians* (New York: Sheldon, 1874), 125.

12. See Stan Hoig, *The Battle of the Washita: The Sheridan-Custer Indian Campaign of 1867–69* (Garden City, N.Y.: Doubleday, 1976). For documents presenting the army's perspective, see John M. Carroll, ed., *General Custer and the Battle of the Washita: The Federal View* (Bryan, Tex.: Guidon Press, 1978).

13. Elizabeth Custer to Mrs. Sabin, 1871, in Marguerite Merington, ed., *The Custer Story: The Life and Intimate Letters of General George A. Custer and His Wife Elizabeth* (New York: Devin-Adair, 1950), 241. See also Theodore J. Crackel, "Custer's Kentucky: General George Armstrong Custer and Elizabethtown, Kentucky, 1871–1873," *Filson Club Historical Quarterly* 48 (April 1974): 144–55; and Dippie, *Nomad,* 73–101.

14. Charles W. Larned to his mother, April 30, 1873, in George Frederick Howe, ed., "Expedition to the Yellowstone River in 1873: Letters of a Young Cavalry Officer," *Mississippi Valley Historical Review* 39 (December, 1952): 524.

15. "Letter from 'Nomad,'" *Turf, Field and Farm,* October 17, 1873, in Dippie, *Nomad,* 105. For a full account of the expedition by Custer's brother-in-law, James Calhoun, see Lawrence A. Frost, ed., *Some Observations on the Yellowstone Expedition of 1873* (Glendale, Calif.: Arthur H. Clark, 1980).

16. See Donald Jackson, *Custer's Gold: The United States Cavalry Expedition of 1874* (New Haven, Conn.: Yale University Press, 1966); the 1868 treaty appears as an appendix.

17. Chicago *Inter-Ocean,* August 27, 1874, in Herbert Krause and Gary D. Olson, *Prelude to Glory: A Newspaper Accounting of Custer's 1874 Expedition to the Black Hills* (Sioux Falls, S.D.: Brevet Press, 1974), 126. The reporter was William E. Curtis; his story was datelined "Custer's Black Hills Expedition, in Camp at Custer's Park, Dakota Territory, Aug. 7, 1874."

18. Letter from John E. Maxwell, March 20, 1875, *Faribault Republican,* April 7, 1875, in Arthur J. Larsen, ed., "The Black Hills Gold Rush: Letters from Men Who Participated," *North Dakota Historical Quarterly* 6 (July 1932): 305.

19. *House Exec. Docs.,* 44th Cong., 1st sess., no. 184, p. 10.

20. Custer's jaunty buckskin poses and self-assured air had less to do with Indian fighting than his perception of himself as a masterful plains hunter adept at bringing down the bounding deer or lumbering buffalo in midstride. He doted on his pack of hounds, fancied himself an expert marksman, tallied up his scores with pride, and relished retelling his exploits for the sportsman's weekly, *Turf, Field and Farm.*

21. Sources for this are cited in Dippie, *Nomad,* 142–43 n. 1, 147 n. 14. Especially pertinent is Richard Slotkin, "'. . . & *Then* the Mare Will Go!': An 1875 Black Hills Scheme by Custer, Holladay and Buford," *Journal of the West* 15 (July 1976): 60–77.

22. *House Exec. Doc.,* 44th Cong., 1st sess., no. 184, pp. 19–20.

23. J. W. Forsyth to W. W. Belknap, April 15, 1876, in Earl K. Brigham, "Custer's Meeting with Secretary of War Belknap at Fort Abraham Lincoln," *North Dakota History* 19 (April 1952): 131. See also Hutton, *Phil Sheridan,* 305–11, 328.

24. Custer to the President, May 6, 1876, in Whittaker, *Complete Life,* 559. The bibliography for the Sioux war of 1876 is simply enormous, most of it focused on Custer and the Little Bighorn. For a critical selection, see Tal Luther, *Custer High Spots* (Fort Collins, Colo.: Old Army Press, 1972); for the most recent attempt at a comprehensive listing, see James Patrick Dowd, *Custer Lives!* (Fairfield, Wash.: Ye Galleon Press, 1982). The best overviews of the campaign are Edgar I. Stewart, *Custer's Luck* (Norman: University of Oklahoma Press, 1955); and John S. Gray, *Centennial Campaign: The Sioux War of 1876* (Fort Collins, Colo.: Old Army Press, 1976), which is noteworthy for its coverage of events after Custer's defeat.

25. The question of whether or not Custer disobeyed Terry's orders has produced a literature all its own. The orders can be found in *House Exec. Docs.,* 44th Cong., 2d sess., no. 1, pt. 2, p. 462. Recently, the debate has heated up again over an affidavit said to prove that Terry verbally augmented Custer's orders, giving him even wider latitude to do as he pleased once in the field: see John S. Manion, *Last Statement to Custer* (Monroe, Mich.: Monroe County Library System, 1983). See also *Little Big Horn Associates*

Newsletter 18 (January 1984): 5–6; 18 (February 1984): 3. In fact, the affidavit remains an uncorroborated recollection of a conversation two years after the fact by an individual who can fairly be described as intensely loyal to Custer.

26. Custer to Elizabeth Custer, June 22, 1876, in Merington, *The Custer Story,* 307.

27. For an example of the thoroughness with which the evidence has been examined, see James Willert, *Little Big Horn Diary: Chronicle of the 1876 Indian War* (La Mirada, Calif.: James Willert, 1977); for the most influential theory, see Charles Kuhlman, *Legend into History: The Custer Mystery* (Harrisburg, Pa.: Stackpole, 1951). Otherwise, consult the bibliographies cited in n. 24—and take the plunge!

28. Bismarck, D.T., *Tribune Extra,* July 6, 1876.

29. See Robert M. Utley, *Custer and the Great Controversy: The Origin and Development of a Legend* (Los Angeles: Westernlore Press, 1962); and Brian W. Dippie, " 'What Will Congress Do About It?': The Congressional Reaction to the Little Big Horn Disaster," *North Dakota History* 37 (Summer 1970): 160–89.

30. Atlanta *Weekly Commonwealth,* July 18, 1876.

31. New York *Herald,* July 7, 1876. The officer, interviewed in Philadelphia, asked not to be identified.

32. "A Death-Sonnet for Custer," New York *Tribune,* July 10, 1876. See Brian W. Dippie, with John M. Carroll, comps., *Bards of the Little Big Horn* (Bryan, Tex.: Guidon Press, 1978), 17–75.

33. Van de Water to Edward S. Godfrey, May 26, 1931, William J. Ghent Papers, container 22, folder 4, Library of Congress, Washington, D.C.

34. See Brian W. Dippie, "Popcorn and Indians: Custer on the Screen," *Cultures* 2 (1974): 139–68; Paul A. Hutton, "The Celluloid Custer," *Red River Valley Historical Review* 4 (Fall 1979): 20–43, and "From Little Bighorn to Little Big Man: The Changing Image of a Western Hero in Popular Culture," *Western Historical Quarterly* 7 (January 1976): 19–45.

35. See John M. Carroll, comp., *Custer in the Civil War: His Unfinished Memoirs* (San Rafael, Calif.: Presidio Press, 1977); and Gregory J. W. Urwin, *Custer Victorious: The Civil War Battles of General George Armstrong Custer* (Rutherford, N.J.: Fairleigh Dickinson University Press, 1983). Jay Monaghan's *Custer: The Life of General George Armstrong Custer* (Boston: Little, Brown, 1959), one of the better biographies, devotes more than half its pages to Custer's Civil War service in presenting a sympathetic interpretation.

George Crook

by Jerome A. Greene

Courtesy Fort Laramie National Historic Site, National Park Service

He stood as an anomaly among frontier military leaders. Relentless in pursuit of hostile Indians, he became their tireless defender in more tranquil times. An innovative warrior, he dealt imaginatively with tribesmen in peacetime, and he spent three-quarters of his career in positions related to the military administration of Indian affairs. Though foremost a soldier, George Crook held views on Indians that differed markedly from those of many of his army contemporaries. Militarily, he was a pragmatist whose methods were often criticized by traditionalists in warfare, despite his long field experience. His detractors included subordinates as well as superiors, but his defenders numbered worthy colleagues and men high in government. Lacking the flamboyance of some other military leaders, Crook pursued his goals with a quiet diligence that was widely misinterpreted. His aide once described him as being ''plain as an old stick.'' It is this accurate yet wholly deceptive characterization of the man that has endured to the present.

George Crook was born September 8, 1828, near Taylorsville in eastern Ohio, the ninth of the ten children of Thomas and Elizabeth Matthews Crook. George matured in this rural setting. His education was limited, and as a youth he showed little interest in books. He probably would have become a farmer had not fateful circumstances intervened. In 1848 he was interviewed by Congressman Robert P. Schenk, who was attempting to fill a vacancy at West Point. Upon Crook's assurance that he would try the military curriculum, Schenk nominated the nineteen-year-old to the Military Academy.[1]

Crook arrived at West Point in early June 1848. His career there was remarkably unremarkable. He excelled in no particular academic discipline; he consistently ranked low academically and graduated thirty-eighth in his class of forty-three in 1852. His personal conduct, however, was exceptional, with few demerits received in four years. His taciturn nature led to only minimal interaction with his fellow cadets, although he did make friends with several—Philip H. Sheridan, in particular—whose careers would one day make their impact on his own.[2]

After graduation, Brevet Second Lieutenant Crook joined the Fourth Infantry on the Pacific Coast, where he participated in numerous campaigns against warring native tribes only recently exposed to white civilization in the wake of the California gold rush. Promoted to second lieutenant in July 1853, he served principally in the rugged area of the California-Oregon boundary. His experiences there formed the rudiments of his knowledge of Indians.[3]

By the mid-1850s the land was being overrun by white settlers, and lawlessness was rampant. Crook learned of many instances where Indians were killed indiscriminately by whites who went unpunished. The result was war, and soldiers who sympathized with the Indians were sent to fight them.[4] Crook took part in several expeditions that went after the Rogue River and Pitt River tribes, and while scouting in June 1857 the young officer received a severe arrow wound in his right hip.

Nevertheless, the unjust treatment of the Northwest Indians during this period profoundly affected Crook and set the tone of his convictions on Indian-white relations. In 1858, on an expedition against the Rogue River tribes, he proved himself an able diplomat; rather than attack a village that harbored several Indian murderers, Crook tactfully negotiated with the camp leader to secure the culprits without bloodshed.[5]

After the outbreak of the Civil War in 1861, Crook returned to the East as a captain in the Fourteenth Infantry. In September he accepted the colonelcy of the Thirty-sixth Ohio Volunteer Infantry Regiment. During 1861–62 he served in the mountain country of West Virginia and distinguished himself at Lewisburg, where he defeated a Confederate force. Crook soon won several brevets as well as promotion to brigadier general of volunteers. As commander of a brigade in the Ninth Corps, he participated in the actions at South Mountain and Antietam. His work in West Virginia bore marked similarity to his earlier campaigns in the Northwest, for he was largely concerned with hunting down bushwhackers who had taken advantage of wartime conditions to kill and rob with impunity.

In 1863, Crook commanded a division at Carthage, Tennessee, before being appointed to the Second Cavalry Division, which he led at Chickamauga in September and later at McMinnville and Farmington, Tennessee. Ordered east in February 1864, Crook led forays against railroads operating between Lynchburg, Virginia, and eastern Tennessee. Appointed commander of the Department of West Virginia in August, Crook subsequently commanded the Army of West Virginia during Major General Philip H. Sheridan's Shenandoah campaign. He took part in engagements at Berryville, Opequan, Winchester, Fisher's Hill, and Cedar Creek; in October 1864 he was promoted to major general of volunteers. On February 21, 1865, Crook and another general officer were captured by Confederates and sent to Libby Prison. Exchanged scarcely a month later, Crook assumed command of the cavalry of the Army of the Potomac, leading it at Dinwiddie Court House and in nearly all the final actions leading to Appomattox. He finished the war a major general of volunteers with regular army brevets up to and including that of major general.[6]

Despite his laurels, Crook had mixed feelings about his Civil War service. Particularly irritating to him were the rampant cronyism and political favoritism whereby inexperienced and inept civilians were placed in high military grades because of their personal contacts. "It was galling to serve under such people," wrote Crook. Distressing, too, was the revelation of what the war did to people he admired. On at least one occasion, Sheridan—his West Point friend—lied to him and denied him credit while at the same time promoting himself. Crook never forgot the slight, and relations between the two men were strained ever after.[7] A positive feature of Crook's tenure in the East was his introduction to Mary T. Dailey, apparently in Maryland in 1865; they were married on August 22 of that year. No children were born of the union, and Mary Crook played only a peripheral role in her husband's career. Except for occasional visits to his western garrisons, she remained at a family estate near Oakland, Maryland.[8]

In January 1866, Crook, like hundreds of other officers, was mustered out of the volunteer service and reverted to his regular army grade of captain. Whereas the Civil War proved to be the capstone of many army careers, for Crook it was but a hiatus from frontier duty. In July 1866 he became lieutenant colonel of the newly formed Twenty-third Infantry, intended for duty in the Northwest.[9] He arrived to command the District of Boise, Idaho Territory, in December 1866, during a time of scattered Indian disturbances throughout the region of northern California and Nevada, eastern Oregon, and southern Idaho. Within a week he was in the field, leading a company of cavalry in pursuit of Indians.

Over the next 20 months Crook conducted intense operations against the Paiutes, Klamaths, and related tribes. Refining his earlier west coast techniques, Crook employed Wasco, Warm Springs, and Shoshone scouts against the Paiutes. He began an extensive use of pack mules, which permitted him to move freely far beyond his supply base. And he campaigned in the dead of winter, striking at tribes in heretofore sacrosanct cold-weather encampments, killing men, capturing women and children, and destroying provisions.[10]

Crook's command of 200 soldiers and Indian scouts engaged the Paiutes and their allies frequently during the course of the campaign. On six occasions Crook personally led his men into combat, impressing them with his purpose and zeal. A final winter offensive began from Camp Warner, Oregon, in March 1868, when Crook's troops—their faces smeared with burnt cork to retard snowblindness—again took the trail. On March 17 the command struck the Paiutes a decisive blow, and within three months the tribesmen sought peace. Meeting with them at Camp Harney, Oregon, in July, Crook exhibited the hard-line diplomacy that became his hallmark in Indian negotiations: he brusquely informed them that he was sorry they wanted peace because once they were all dead, the government's problem would be solved. After several hours the Indians managed to "convince" Crook to end the war, and he was able to solicit scouts from among the Paiutes for an expedition against a neighboring tribe before settling the rest of them on reservations. For this performance, Lieutenant Colonel Crook was made temporary commander of the Department of the Columbia, a signal recognition not lost on the officers who were bypassed for this honor. He remained in Portland two years, during which time he quelled disturbances among the Umatilla and Nez Perce Indians.[11]

In appearance at this time Crook, standing a bit over six feet tall, was broad shouldered and sinewy. His features were pronounced—large aquiline nose, piercing blue-gray eyes, and firm mouth. His blond whiskers were several inches long and parted at the chin; in the field he often wore them braided and tied at either side of his face. On campaign Crook never dressed in full uniform, favoring a flannel shirt, brown canvas overalls, a slouch hat, and moccasins.[12]

Like his clothes, Crook's manner reflected his aversion to authority. He disliked ceremony and preferred to command by example rather than by order. His manner was quiet and deliberate, and he seldom advanced his opinions. Yet though he was innovative in developing campaign procedures, Crook ultimately became inflexible in their use. His stubbornness sometimes tested the limits of official military tolerance, but such tenacity may account for the success of his methods.[13]

Crook's achievements in the Northwest ensured a demand for his services in other quarters. By the early 1870s the Territory of Arizona was experiencing difficulties with several hundred Coyotero Apache and Yavapai tribesmen who persisted in killing settlers, stealing livestock, and otherwise harassing citizens. On two occasions Crook, fatigued from his recent campaigns and unfavorably disposed toward the climate of the Southwest, turned down command of the Department of Arizona, but in 1871, President Ulysses S. Grant ordered him to take charge of the department by virtue of his brevet rank of major general.[14]

Reaching his new post in September 1871, Crook had barely begun planning a campaign against the Apaches when Vincent Colyer, prominent humanitarian and secretary of the Board of Indian Commissioners, arrived in Arizona. Colyer was the embodiment of the administration's so-called peace policy, under which warring tribes were to be corralled on reservations administered by religious groups. Clothed with presidential authority, Colyer had been sent to persuade the Indians to surrender themselves at reserves established in the territory. Fearing a setup by peace policy advocates, Crook politely gave Colyer every assistance but made clear his disagreement with the federal emissary's methods. The peace policy, he believed, was too idealistic to be applied, much less understood, in Arizona. Unswayed, Colyer eventually met with some of the Indians, who promised to remain peaceful. Colyer's mission was followed by that of another humanitarian, Brigadier General Oliver O. Howard, who came to Arizona with even more authority than his predecessor. Crook, again concerned that any movement by his soldiers would be construed as purposeful disruption of President Grant's conciliation program, patiently awaited Howard's departure. Like most humanitarians, Howard was convinced that the Indians could be dealt with from the start by using trust and peaceful means instead of force—a concept Crook thought naive and dangerous. Justice and humanity, he believed, would come to warring tribes only after they had experienced military defeat.[15]

In November 1872, immediately following the peace missions, Crook launched his campaign against the hostile Apaches. Initially a winter operation designed to seek out the tribesmen wherever they went, the Tonto Basin expedition lasted almost 18 months. During this time, units of the First and Fifth Cavalry, accompanied by Indian guides, tracked isolated groups of Apaches through the Mogollon country of south central Arizona. Crook prosecuted the campaign with the same vigor he had shown in the Northwest. He employed pack mules to sustain his operations, and he directed his men to advance on hostile rancherias at night and burn them. As victories multiplied, Crook began adding surrendered Apaches to his commands, thereby intensifying the demoralization of the hostiles. Finally, in April 1873, the Apaches and Yavapais sued for peace. Crook met with many of the Indians at Camp Verde, promised to protect them if they stopped their violence, and sent selected emissaries to confer with those who had not come in. He vowed to destroy all Indians who refused to surrender. The campaign ended Apache resistance in western Apacheria and brought relatively uninterrupted peace to Arizona for several years. In recognition of his success, Crook was promoted past colonel to brigadier general on October 29, 1873.[16]

The Tonto Basin campaign represented the highest development of Indian warfare methodology as it existed in the 1870s. It bore Crook's stamp of ingenuity and witnessed the refinement of techniques he had previously adopted in

Idaho and Oregon. The acquisition of breechloading firearms and fixed ammunition to replace bows and arrows had made the hostile warriors formidable adversaries, and their ability to traverse the most difficult terrain increased their advantage significantly. Crook's response was unrelenting pursuit: "In fighting them we must of necessity be the pursuers," he observed of the Apaches, "and unless we can surprise them by sudden and unexpected attack, the advantage is all in their favor."[17]

Crook's expeditions exhibited several unusual features. He made drastic cuts in the gear carried by his officers and men, permitting only minimal clothing and bedding. Always advancing, he kept his troops at the ready and "strong enough to receive a shock and move on." He preferred campaigning when winter gripped the tribesmen and hindered their movements. To ensure the success of his various columns, Crook selected trusted officers of mature judgment who displayed interest in the Indians. He issued few orders and preferred to conduct his operations independently, away from all supervision and possible interference by superiors.[18]

All of these procedures complemented Crook's two major innovations, the extensive use of pack animals and the regular employment of Indian scouts. Under his close direction, the organization, equipment, and utilization of pack mules became an art; it was, said his aide, John Bourke, "the great study of his life." While mules had always been used to some extent by the army, Crook became interested in the potential of a highly developed system for use in Indian campaigning. He had organized three government-owned pack trains in 1867 under civilian Thomas Moore, who continued as Crook's chief packer over the next two decades. Crook regarded the trains as "an important adjunct" in Indian warfare and believed "that a pack-train can only be efficient when composed of mules expressly selected and used solely for that purpose."[19]

On the trail, the superiority of pack trains over more conventional supply wagons was readily apparent. The surefooted mules were not restricted to flat valley floors but could traverse the most rugged mountainous terrain. They carried loads averaging 250 pounds apiece and were capable of taking on 100 pounds more if necessary. Hardy beasts, they required only native grasses as fodder and easily kept pace with the cavalry horses. Their mobility permitted Crook wide freedom of movement and enabled him to pursue his campaigns for extended periods with persistent dispatch. Whenever troops came under attack, it became Crook's policy to herd the mules to the rear where they—and the supplies—would be safe. Through his efforts the pack train service was refined into a productive component of the Indian-fighting army and one that was increasingly emulated by other military leaders.[20]

Crook's employment of Indian scouts was equally important to his success. This practice, too, dated from his years in the Northwest, where he had used warriors from friendly tribes to run down the Paiutes and their allies. The concept was not an original one; Indian scouts had assisted army units throughout American history, but Crook's use of them was predicated on his belief that it could contribute to the psychological disintegration of hostile tribes. Preferably, scouts were enlisted from among elements of the tribe being pursued, for their presence promoted internal dissension among the hunted. The recruitment of scouts from the enemy tribe also effectively reduced the number of warriors the troops must fight. Crook's first unit of Apache scouts, conpensated with regular soldiers' pay, so benefited his campaign that further companies were recruited from among the Coyotero and White Mountain tribes. The Apache scouts, backed by ever-present supplies and ammunition, were relied upon to use their individuality, intuitive prowess, and qualities of endurance to seek out their kinsmen.[21] Crook employed Indian scouts less successfully in his campaigns on the northern plains—particularly against Utes, Shoshones, Sioux, and Northern Cheyennes—but his achievements in Arizona in the 1870s and 1880s prompted calls for a formal Indian auxiliary force and led in the 1890s to efforts to organize companies of Indian soldiers within established army units. These attempts waned, however, as large-scale Indian campaigning became a thing of the past.[22]

Few senior army officers subscribed to Crook's enthusiasm for employing Indian scouts, and Crook spent much time defending his policy to his superiors. His success in the Southwest notwithstanding, he won few converts. The Apache scouts were presumed to be unreliable, a condemnation Crook was quick to discount, but there appears to have been some basis for this opinion: on expeditions into Mexico they occasionally stole livestock and murdered citizens without punishment. While Crook stubbornly defended them, he failed to convince those whose decisions most mattered, and the disagreement that later evolved was the most tragic personal rebuff in Crook's career.[23]

In addition to its military value, the use of the scouts supported Crook's philosophy that the demise of traditional Indian lifeways must precede successful acculturation. Exposed to the rudiments of white civilization and accountable for their actions as individuals, Indian scouts became equal to white men—a notion Crook cultivated among them, for he believed it made them see beyond tribal superstition and think for themselves. His views coincided with the government's aim to force tribes upon reservations and to assimilate them through programs of land severalty and self-government. Crook remained convinced that only the army, secure from the vagaries of domestic politics, could provide the absolute honesty and firm control necessary to solve all Indian troubles— on and off the reservations—and thereby effect the final change.[24]

Final change meant forced acculturation of the Indians into the dominant culture. Throughout his life Crook evinced deep respect for the Indian lifeways with which he associated, and he was regarded by many as the country's foremost authority on Indians. In an era rife with Darwinian influences, however,

Crook believed in the superiority of the Caucasian race, perceiving the Native Americans to be at a lower evolutionary stage, advancement from which depended upon native ambition. Nor did Crook share the scientific curiosity in Indians shown by some of his subordinates.[25]

Feeling that the tribes could be considered "children in ignorance," Crook advocated patience in their acculturation, believing that tendencies toward regression were ever present. He tried to make them see that without acculturation their demise was certain and to convince them that their self-interest lay in education in the white man's ways. They must channel their energies into such productive agrarian vocations as raising stock. The effect would be a further breakdown of tribalism. Crook held the view that the Indians were latent capitalists and that the existence of a cash market for their goods would encourage their cultural and economic transformation. As they became acculturated, they would seek the legal protection afforded by enfranchisement. Citizenship would bring the vote, and the Indians, at long last, would become bona fide "Americans."[26]

In Arizona, Crook got the opportunity to apply his principles. As department commander he led an all-out military campaign to forcibly subdue the Apaches and make them accept reservation status. Once they were in custody, he undertook a program designed to change their lifeways. To promote self-government and discipline among the tribesmen, Crook selected groups of his Apache scouts to serve at the agencies as salaried police. True to his own cultural prejudices, though ostensibly to protect the Indians from themselves, Crook outlawed such tribal customs as a man's cutting off the nose of an unfaithful wife. He advanced the rights of the women to equal protection and decreed that they be humanely treated. Crook also introduced a system of jury trial among the Indians, letting them decide cases of petty offenses. He imposed strict methods of physical accountability, inaugurating a tag system for the different bands so that unauthorized absences by individuals might quickly be detected.[27]

Central to all this, however, was Crook's plan to introduce the Apaches to capitalism by the fruits of their labor. On the reservation he urged them to take up farming and stock-raising. He introduced ideas of husbandry among them, furnished them the requisite livestock and implements with which to practice it, and—hoping to make the Indians see that the advantages of peace outweighed those of war—promised them a market for all their produce. Through Crook's policy of firmness and fairness, and with his personal monitoring, the Apache program worked.[28]

In March 1875, Crook was reassigned and left Arizona to command the Department of the Platte, headquartered in Omaha. The Lakotas, or Teton Sioux, of the northern plains were threatening trouble over the Black Hills, part of western Dakota Territory but assigned to Crook's new administrative domain. In 1868 the government had established a reservation for these people that embraced this tract, but the discovery of gold in the area produced a full-scale invasion by whites. Before long, serious complaints were registered against the free-roaming Sioux by the white trespassers as well as by peaceful tribes along the upper Missouri River. The Indian Bureau demanded the return of the Sioux to the agencies in Dakota Territory and Nebraska. Their noncompliance early in 1876 led the War Department to initiate operations against the hostile, or nonreservation, Sioux.[29]

Several army columns made preparations to go after the Indians, and first into the field was Crook's 900-man contingent, which struck north from Fort Fetterman, Wyoming Territory, on March 1, 1876. Crook hoped to find the Sioux still in winter quarters and deliver a demoralizing blow. On March 17 a force of six cavalry companies from his command under Colonel Joseph J. Reynolds fell upon a snowy encampment along Little Powder River in southeastern Montana Territory—but the village contained mostly Northern Cheyennes rather than Sioux. At first Reynolds's soldiers routed the Indians and drove them from the village. But while the troops burned the camp, the warriors counterattacked and recaptured most of their ponies. Few casualties occurred on either side. Learning of the encounter, the loss of the enemy horses, and the burning of the camp and its supplies, Crook was furious. He later brought charges that forced Reynolds to resign from the army. Probably because of freezing weather rather than Reynolds's defeat, however, Crook abandoned the campaign and led his troops back to Fort Fetterman. News of the battle emboldened tribesmen at the Red Cloud and Spotted Tail agencies in Nebraska who subsequently joined the hostiles. If nothing else, the Crook-Reynolds campaign helped bring the Northern Cheyennes into the Great Sioux War.[30]

Crook reopened his offensive in late May, again driving north toward the Bighorn–Yellowstone region of Montana to cooperate with columns under Brigadier General Alfred H. Terry and Colonel John Gibbon. Unable to enlist either Sioux or Cheyenne scouts, he took with him a large group of Crows and Shoshones. The hostiles under the Oglala Crazy Horse and other leaders met his advance on June 17 along Rosebud Creek and, in a spirited contest of several hours duration, forced Crook into a stalemate.

Rosebud proved to be an unusual encounter and one with repercussions for Crook's career. For one thing, the hostiles initiated the combat, meeting over 1,000 soldiers on a field of their choosing. First into the fray were Crook's Crow and Shoshone scouts, who relished the chance to confront their old enemies. For the soldiers, the engagement consisted of a number of well-directed cavalry charges to clear warriors from the high ground surrounding the troops. Fighting ranged over a broad area of rugged terrain that favored the large number of well-armed and unusually unified Indians. But in his direction of affairs Crook allegedly sent out conflicting orders, then sent part of his command into

retreat. He was later accused of failing to support his Indian auxiliaries. Ultimately, the hostiles withdrew, leaving the army in possession of the field. Instead of heading north again, however, Crook—fearing an ambush by the
Sioux—turned his men about and marched with his wounded back to his base
camp along Goose Creek in Wyoming to replenish rations and await
reinforcements.[31]

The Rosebud encounter tarnished Crook's reputation. It was the only major
battle with the Indians in 1876 in which he personally commanded, and though
he may have won a tactical victory in holding his ground, strategically he was
defeated. Crook's failure on the Rosebud had a critical impact, for a week later
Custer fell at the Little Bighorn. Almost immediately there were questions regarding Crook's actions. His behavior in the Rosebud fight drew "unmeasured
condemnation" from officers stationed at Fort Fetterman.[32] Some cited his failure to move on immediately afterward to join Terry and Gibbon as a cause for
the Custer catastrophe: by advancing, he might have so occupied the Indians as
to diminish their strength at the Little Bighorn on June 25. In later years, Crook
tended to blame certain subordinates for the reversal and revealed a petty side to
his character in responding to criticism of his performance. The controversy
haunted him for the rest of his life.[33]

With his second offensive stymied and with the reluctant concurrence of
Lieutenant General Sheridan, commander of the Division of the Missouri,
Crook passed several weeks at his base camp anxiously awaiting fresh cavalry
and infantry troops. It was a bad decision, for it allowed the hostiles unre-
stricted movement. Finally, in early August, supported by the newly arrived
Fifth Cavalry, Crook left Goose Creek and moved north with 2,000 men of the
Bighorn and Yellowstone Expedition to find the Sioux and Cheyennes. Besides
the Fifth Cavalry, the command consisted of various companies of the Second
and Third Cavalry and the Fourth, Ninth, and Fourteenth Infantry. Crook was
accompanied by a contingent of Ute and Shoshone scouts as well as by his pack
train. Employing past procedures, he ordered the command stripped of all but
the essentials in food, clothing, and supplies.[34]

Crook joined General Terry, his senior in rank, in the parched terrain south
of the Yellowstone River. The two commanders conferred, then moved their
columns east to Powder River before turning to the Yellowstone. There
Crook's Indian scouts abandoned the campaign. Operating in the Department
of Dakota under Terry clearly bothered Crook, who yearned to renew his independence. After refitting his command, he left Terry behind and headed east.
Soon the weather turned bad, and over the next three weeks Crook's soldiers
endured the "Mud March" as they trailed the Indians into Dakota Territory.
When rations ran out, Crook directed his troops to eat meat from the exhausted
mounts that had to be shot along the way. Eventually the growing plight of his
soldiers made Crook dispatch a unit under Captain Anson Mills to collect provi-

sions in the Black Hills mining settlements. En route, on September 9, Mills discovered and attacked a sizable Indian village, scattering its occupants. Crook's expedition reached the site in time to repel a counterattack by warriors from nearby camps. The Battle of Slim Buttes yielded few casualties on either side and involved only an extended skirmish, but it proved to be the army's first significant victory in a project heretofore plagued with disaster and bad luck. Following Slim Buttes, Crook's army pressed on to the Black Hills and Camp Robinson, Nebraska.

Crook later presided over a winter expedition into Wyoming's Bighorn country, during which Colonel Ranald S. Mackenzie attacked a large camp of Northern Cheyennes on the Red Fork of Powder River. The fight against Chief Dull Knife effectively ended Cheyenne participation in the war; in its aftermath most of the surviving tribesmen either surrendered or froze to death. Troubled once more by freezing temperatures and discouraged by mounting logistical expenses, Crook led his command home to Fort Fetterman in December.[35]

With the exception of Mackenzie's victory, Crook's performance in 1876 drew mixed reviews. Many officers and men who accompanied him on the starvation march condemned his management of the expedition and pronounced harsh judgment on his leadership ability. In his persistence to strike the hostiles a fatal blow, Crook somehow lost the combination of methodology and common sense that had prevailed in Arizona. The Sioux and Cheyennes moved and fought differently from the Apaches and, when challenged, were more given to direct confrontation with the troops. Crook's Indian scout policy faltered with his enlistment of Shoshones rather than Sioux, and it failed altogether when they left him at the Yellowstone. As a consequence, so badly did Crook miscalculate his enemy that at least one senior officer on the expedition reportedly considered bringing charges against him for incompetence in command.[36]

In 1877, Colonel Nelson A. Miles headed the closing operations of the Great Sioux War while Crook dealt with the disaffected Sioux at the Red Cloud and Spotted Tail agencies. With control of the tribesmen vested in the army, he urged the government to recognize as their spokesman the more "progressive" Brulé leader, Spotted Tail, rather than the Oglala traditionalist chief, Red Cloud. Yet it was Red Cloud who succeeded in convincing Crazy Horse and his followers to surrender in May 1877. Then when Crook did succeed in enlisting Sioux scouts, Crazy Horse became indignant and precipitated a crisis at the agencies. Hoping to stem the turbulence, Crook directed Crazy Horse's arrest; on September 5, 1877, the chief was stabbed while being disarmed. He died that night.[37] Ironically enough, his death was partly caused by Crook's attempts to effect his scout policy among the Sioux.

Crook returned to Omaha and assumed the administrative duties of department commander. It was during this period that his views of Indian affairs crystallized and he became more outspoken. When troubles with the Bannocks and Northern Cheyennes surfaced in 1878 and 1879, Crook sided with the Indians in his official reports. His clearest statement in regard to Indian policy, however, involved members of the small Ponca tribe. The Poncas had been removed to the Indian Territory in 1877, forcibly driven from their reservation on the Nebraska–Dakota line to make way for the Sioux. After two difficult years in which many Poncas died, a group of about 30 Indians led by Chief Standing Bear headed back to Nebraska, where, by order of the War Department, they were arrested by troops of Crook's command.

While he dutifully followed orders, Crook in fact sympathized with the Poncas, for their situation pointed up the lack of the legal protection that Indians needed, in his view, if acculturation were to succeed. Seizing the moment, Crook managed a delay in returning the Ponca tribesmen to the Indian Territory and sought legal assistance on their behalf. He enlisted the help of Omaha newsman Thomas Henry Tibbles, who, aided by concerned lawyers, obtained a writ of habeas corpus from U.S. District Court Judge Elmer Dundy. Tibbles also generated national publicity.

At issue in the two-day trial that opened on April 30, 1879, was the government's contention that the Indians, being neither persons nor citizens under the law, had no right to file suit against the government. Standing Bear's attorneys argued that the tribe could not be removed against their will in peacetime: the Indian was shown to be a person within the definition of the habeas corpus act; enforced removal therefore constituted deprivation of personal liberty and made his suit legitimate. Judge Dundy found in Standing Bear's favor, a landmark ruling that affected the government's role in Indian matters thereafter. In December, Crook was appointed to a commission which recommended that the tribesmen be allowed to remain in Nebraska, that they be indemnified monetarily for their losses, and that schooling and farming supplies be arranged for them.[38]

Crook was recalled to Arizona as department commander in 1882 when discontentment among the reservation Apaches and raiding by Chiricahuas between Arizona and Mexico threatened to undo the peace imposed during his previous tour. When Crook undertook an inspection of the agencies and military posts preparatory to outlining a course of action, his mere presence at the agencies allayed much of the unrest, and he had little difficulty reinstituting his earlier programs. The main problem, however, lay with the Chiricahua Apaches, who had to be stopped from raiding, robbing, and killing in the United States and then withdrawing into the wild sanctuary of Mexico's Sierra Madre. After one especially bloody foray by Apaches under Chato in the spring of 1883, Crook planned a retaliatory campaign designed to seek out the Indians in their refuge. Existing conventions between the United States and Mexico specified that troops from either country might pursue hostile Indians into the other.[39]

After outfitting an expedition of nearly 200 Warm Springs Apache scouts, one troop of cavalry, and 350 pack mules, Crook crossed into Mexico on May 1, 1883. His campaign proved quick and conclusive. On May 15 the scouts surprised a rancheria high in the mountains, killing nine warriors and capturing supplies and equipment. Crook's force moved steadily forward, hoping to follow up with similar assaults. The Apaches sent women to tell Crook they wanted to surrender; he demanded to speak to the leaders. When they finally appeared, Crook told them, with his customary frankness, that he preferred to fight it out. The Chiricahuas begged for peace, however, and after securing a promise that the remaining tribesmen would bring themselves in to the San Carlos Agency, Crook reentered the United States with 52 men and 273 women and children.[40]

Crook now moved to solidify the military presence at the agencies. In July 1883 he persuaded authorities in Washington to let him reimpose his acculturation procedures on the Apaches without interference from civilian agents. To encourage the Indians' familiarity with self-government, he permitted them to select community sites where they might settle on the reserve, making their leaders responsible for their behavior. He reintroduced the police system, using Apache scouts to oversee events in the scattered enclaves. In time, Crook believed, all this would lead to enfranchisement, the Indians' ultimate salvation.[41]

Unfortunately, while Crook's program introduced the Indians to another mode of living, it also helped rupture relations between his officers and the civilian agents. The attitude in Washington toward his Apache policies grew unsympathetic under Sheridan (who had become commanding general), who had always opposed the use of Indian auxiliaries. Before resolution could be attained, a band of Chiricahuas led by Geronimo fled the reservation, and President Grover Cleveland ordered full control of the agencies placed in the hands of the military authorities.[42]

Geronimo's outbreak from the San Carlos Agency occurred May 17, 1885. With him went a number of malcontent leaders plus assorted women and children. For the next 11 months Crook pursued these renegades, who took refuge again in the Sierra Madre and crossed into the United States at will to conduct raids. Columns of Apache scouts were sent into Mexico; in January 1886, one headed by Captain Emmett Crawford was erroneously attacked by Mexican irregular troops, and Crawford was killed. Finally, in March, Geronimo faced Crook below the border to negotiate his future. The government wanted all the Chiricahuas removed to the East, said Crook. He demanded Geronimo's unconditional surrender but got only his agreement to spend two years in confinement before returning to the reservation. Crook opposed the removal plan, since it also entailed sending his own Chiricahua scouts to prison. Not only did it fail to discriminate between renegades and nonrenegades, but it subtly cast discredit on Crook's program. When Crook telegraphed Sheridan the news of

Geronimo's capitulation, Sheridan rejected the terms, specifying nothing less than the Apaches' unconditional surrender or their destruction. Crook was now expected to disavow the established agreement, something he refused to do.[43]

Meanwhile, to Crook's dismay, Geronimo and some of his men staged a drunken revel and fled. He wired the news to Sheridan, who shot back an angry message that read in part: "It seems strange that Geronimo and party could have escaped without the knowledge of the scouts," a remark that seriously challenged Crook's procedures by questioning the loyalty of his scouts. Further, Sheridan reminded Crook that he had many regular troops at his disposal "and ought to be able to do a great deal with such a force." Affronted by the implicit censure, Crook wired back on April 1: "I believe the plan upon which I have conducted operations is the one most likely to be successful in the end. It may be, however, that I am too much wedded to my own views in this matter, and as I have spent nearly eight years of the hardest work of my life in this department, I respectfully request that I may now be relieved of its command."[44] The next day, Sheridan ordered Brigadier General Nelson A. Miles to complete the operation against Geronimo, and Crook was reassigned to the Department of the Platte, his relationship with Sheridan forever breached. Miles, with larger conventional forces and fewer scouts but otherwise using methods not radically different from those of Crook, succeeded in compelling the remaining hostiles to surrender in September 1886.[45]

The end of the Geronimo campaign and the removal of the Chiricahuas to Florida signaled the start of a feud between Crook and Miles that lasted until Crook's death. Crook could not accept the fate of these Indians; he saw their removal as unwarranted and a reflection on his own credibility with them. Miles obviously relished his new-found fame as Geronimo's conqueror, a designation Crook rejected. Gradually, the rift widened into a quarrel over who should receive the most credit for effecting the surrender, Crook for initiating the campaign that resulted in the submission of the largest number of the hostiles, or Miles for prosecuting it to its conclusion.[46]

Crook returned to Omaha under a cloud. He could not contain his sense of frustration over Sheridan's refusal to sustain his work with the Apaches. Within a few months of his transfer he wrote two significant dissertations explaining his Apache policy and what it had accomplished in Arizona. "The Apache Problem", his apologia, appeared in the *Journal of the Military Service Institution of the United States* in October 1886. It was followed by his *Resumé of Operations against Apache Indians, 1882–1886,* first published in Omaha in 1886 and then, over Sheridan's objection, by the Government Printing Office the next year.[47] Primarily, the *Resumé* was Crook's means of conveying his conviction that he was right and venting his indignation at Sheridan. Crook defended the trustworthiness of the scouts and argued that the success of the army against the Apaches rested with their employment. He concluded by asserting that Miles's success in obtaining Geronimo's surrender was due to his reversion to Crook's methods.[48] Far from suppressing the controversy surrounding Crook's departure from Arizona, publication of the *Resumé* only fueled the breach between Miles and Crook on the one hand, and between Crook and Sheridan on the other.

Partly because of his concern over the Apache prisoners, Crook became more deeply involved in the Indian rights movement and entered into lengthy correspondence with its leaders. In their eyes Crook stood out as a soldier enunciating compassion and intelligence in matters of Indian administration. His role in the Standing Bear case had influenced organization of the Indian Rights Association, a group with which he became philosophically allied; if he differed materially, it was only in his belief that military force was necessary to bring the Indians to the point where their acculturation might be attempted. By the late 1880s, however, the western tribes were mostly subdued, so that this difference of opinion mattered little.[49]

In April 1888, President Cleveland promoted Crook to major general and appointed him commander of the Division of the Missouri. While Crook was the senior brigadier in the service, his advancement over the heavily favored Miles represented partial atonement for his treatment in Arizona. He and his wife moved to Chicago and took up residence in the Grand Pacific Hotel. His health had begun to fail, and a physical examination disclosed lung and heart irregularities. Yet Crook remained active in conducting the affairs of his division, and his headquarters soon acquired his stamp of informality: everyone wore civilian clothes.[50]

In 1889, Crook served on a commission to the Sioux to obtain their consent to a congressional bill under which they would relinquish 11,000,000 acres of the Great Sioux Reservation and which provided for allotment in severalty. From June until August he labored to convince the tribesmen at the six Dakota agencies to ratify the measure. He argued forcibly that the Indians would get no better deal and should sign the agreement before the government simply took their land. He repeatedly told the Indians that their acceptance of the act would in no way alter their rations. But once the required signatures were obtained and the bill became law, Congress cut appropriations for the agencies, an act that reduced beef rations. "It will be impossible to convince them," mourned Crook, "that it is not one result of their signing."[51] Efforts were made to relieve the ensuing economic and spiritual crisis among the Sioux — but not soon enough to head off the confrontation at Wounded Knee in 1890.

During this period Crook also gave increased attention to the imprisoned Chiricahua Apaches. In 1886 both the renegades and the reservation Indians, as well as many of Crook's former scouts, had been confined in Florida. Provisions of the surrender specifying that Geronimo and his followers were to be reunited with their families were violated. A number of warriors were incarcerated at Fort Pickens, while the majority of adults languished in Fort Marion—both coastal locations where moist malarial breezes debilitated tribesmen accustomed to an arid mountain environment. Many died. Still irked by Miles's treatment of some of his trusted scouts, as well as by violations of the surrender accord, Crook enlisted the help of Herbert Welsh and the Indian Rights Association in getting the government first to reunite the families and later to remove the Apaches to the supposedly more salubrious climate of Mount Vernon Barracks, near Mobile, Alabama.

Their condition did not improve, however, and late in 1889 Crook obtained permission to seek out a more suitable home for the Apaches. When he visited his old friends and former adversaries at Mount Vernon Barracks, Chato, Chihuahua, and other leaders greeted him in a gesture of affection and respect. Crook's report of the meeting was instrumental in getting presidential support for a measure to remove the Apaches to Fort Sill, Indian Territory. Since passage of such legislation would, in a sense, vindicate Crook over Miles, while repudiating the policies of the now deceased Sheridan and former President Cleveland, the proposal generated much opposition among Democrats and supporters of Miles. In reopening the debate over Geronimo's surrender, Miles, with backing from the western press, attempted to point up the disloyalty of the Apache scouts, a contention Crook termed false. The controversy intensified with the Senate's introduction of a resolution for the removal west of the Indians. Among friends, Crook missed few opportunities to criticize Miles's deceit and Sheridan's thanklessness on the Apache issue.[52]

Early in 1890, Crook's heart condition worsened; it was compounded by influenza contracted during a trip to Fort Sill in conjunction with the proposed transfer of the Apaches. The long years of exposure in the West were catching up, and Crook began to tire easily. He grew anxious over the Apache situation, his conflict with Miles, and the antagonism that had greeted his Apache proposals in the West. Crook suffered a heart attack and died in his Chicago hotel suite on March 21, 1890. Funeral services were held at the hotel; the honorary pallbearers included an assemblage of old military friends and supporters, among them former president Hayes. Three days after his death, Crook was buried at Oakland, Maryland, in a low-key ceremony attended by civil and military luminaries from Washington. In November his remains were transferred to Arlington National Cemetery.[53]

Crook's death postponed action on the Senate resolution for the removal west of the Apaches. With his voice silenced, the legislation fell idle, not to be revived and passed until four years later. In 1894 the Apaches were transferred to Fort Sill, where they remained prisoners of war for the next two decades. Had he lived, Crook would likely have continued his quest to improve their condition, rectify past wrongs, and seek justice in their treatment. For nearly 30 years he had immersed himself in matters pertaining to the control and cultural transition of American Indians, gaining broad experience with the tribesmen in peace and war. Although stoic on the surface and seemingly impervious to criticism, he was in fact deeply affected by it. Possibly, in agonizing over the repudiation of his methods in 1886, Crook viewed any success in the Apache prisoner controversy as vindication not only of his policies but of his career.

As wartime adversary and peacetime friend of the Indians, Crook remained committed to the welfare of the people he came to understand perhaps better than any other white man of his day. His stubbornly held convictions encouraged development of a unique methodology which, however successful, proved too much for an army entrenched in procedural conservatism. Nonetheless, no army officer of the late nineteenth century ever matched Crook's record in Indian affairs, either in his extensive campaigns and negotiations or in his efforts to promote acculturation on the reservation. As a contemporary observer concluded: "Crook, in his quiet, steady way, did more to settle the Indian difficulty than Custer and all the other dashing cavaliers of the American army put together."[54]

Notes

1. These facts of Crook's early life are drawn from his own *General George Crook: His Autobiography,* ed. Martin F. Schmitt (Norman: University of Oklahoma Press, 1960), xvi–xviii; and Gustave J. Fiebeger, "George Crook," in Allen Johnson and Dumas Malone, eds., *Dictionary of American Biography,* 11 vols. (New York: Scribner, 1933–58), 2:563.

2. Crook, *Autobiography,* xix–xx; John F. Finerty, *War-Path and Bivouac; or, The Conquest of the Sioux* (Norman: University of Oklahoma Press, 1961), 318; *Army and Navy Journal,* March 22, 1890; George W. Cullum, *Biographical Register of the Officers and Graduates of the U.S. Military Academy, at West Point, N.Y., from Its Establishment, March 16, 1802, to the Army Re-Organization of 1866–67,* 2 vols. (New York: Van Nostrand, 1868), 2:329.

3. Crook, *Autobiography,* 10; John G. Bourke, *On the Border with Crook* (New York: Scribner, 1891), 110; James T. King, "George Crook, Indian Fighter and Humanitarian," *Arizona and the West* 9 (Winter 1967): 336.

4. Crook, *Autobiography,* 11, 15–16; Thomas W. Dunlay, "General Crook and the White Man Problem," *Journal of the West* 18 (April 1979): 4.

5. Crook, *Autobiography,* 61–62.

6. This brief account of Crook's Civil War career is drawn from Fiebeger, "George Crook," 563; Finerty, *War-Path and Bivouac,* 318–19; and Mark M. Boatner III, *The Civil War Dictionary* (New York: David McKay, 1959), 209.

7. Crook, *Autobiography,* 98, 127, 134n, 141.

8. Ibid., 306.

9. Charles King, "George Crook," *War Papers Read before the Commandery of the*

State of Wisconsin, Military Order of the Loyal Legion of the United States (Milwaukee, Wis.: Burdic, Armitage, & Allen, 1891), 257–58; Fiebeger, "George Crook," 563; *Records of Living Officers of the United States Army* (Philadelphia: L. R. Hamersley, 1884), 9.

10. William R. Parnell, "Operations against Hostile Indians with General George Crook, 1867–68," *United Service* 1 (May–June 1889): 482–83, 491; John G. Bourke, "General Crook in the Indian Country," *Century Magazine* 41 (March 1891): 644; C. King, "George Crook," 258; Oliver Knight, *Following the Indian Wars: The Story of the Newspaper Correspondents among the Indian Campaigners* (Norman: University of Oklahoma Press, 1960), 33, 39.

11. Parnell, "Operations against Hostile Indians," 628, 634; Robert M. Utley, *Frontier Regulars: The United States Army and the Indian, 1866–1890* (New York: Macmillan, 1973), 180–81; Bourke, "General Crook in the Indian Country," 649–50; Knight, *Following the Indian Wars*, 39; Crook, *Autobiography*, 159; Finerty, *War-Path and Bivouac*, 320; C. King, "George Crook," 258–59.

12. Bourke, "General Crook in the Indian Country," 652–54; Bourke, *On the Border with Crook*, 110, 268; Oliver O. Howard, "Major-General George Crook, U.S.A.," *Chatauquan* 11 (June 1890): 327; Finerty, *War-Path and Bivouac*, 6; Crook, *Autobiography*, 193n; Azor H. Nickerson, "Major General George Crook and the Indians," typescript, Crook-Kennon Papers, U.S. Army Military History Institute, Carlisle, Pennsylvania; J. W. Vaughn, *With Crook at the Rosebud* (Harrisburg, Pa.: Stackpole, 1956), 23.

13. C. King, "George Crook," 267; Utley, *Frontier Regulars*, 179; J. King, "Indian Fighter and Humanitarian," 335.

14. C. King, "George Crook," 259–60; Utley, *Frontier Regulars*, 193; Henry P. Walker, "George Crook: 'The Gray Fox.' Prudent, Compassionate Indian Fighter," *Montana, the Magazine of Western History* 17 (April 1967): 3; John Morgan Gates, "General George Crook's First Apache Campaign (The Use of Mobile, Self-Contained Units against the Apache in the Military Department of Arizona, 1871–1873)," *Journal of the West* 6 (April 1967): 310.

15. J. King, "Indian Fighter and Humanitarian," 340–41; Utley, *Frontier Regulars*, 194, 196; Henry E. Fritz, *The Movement for Indian Assimilation, 1860–1890* (Philadelphia: University of Pennsylvania Press, 1963), 117; Ralph H. Ogle, *Federal Control of the Western Apaches, 1848–1886* (Albuquerque: University of New Mexico Press, 1970), 113.

16. Crook, *Autobiography*, 176, 177, 179, 182, 183n; Bourke, "General Crook in the Indian Country," 656, 660; C. King, "George Crook," 261; Gustave J. Fiebeger, "General Crook's Campaign in Old Mexico in 1883. Events Leading Up to It and Personal Experiences in the Campaign," in John M. Carroll, ed., *The Papers of the Order of Indian Wars* (Fort Collins, Colo.: Old Army Press, 1975), 194–95; Fritz, *Movement for Indian Assimilation*, 130–31; Gates, "Crook's First Apache Campaign," 314, 316–17, 318; Walker, "The Gray Fox," 7; Utley, *Frontier Regulars*, 194–98; Ogle, *Federal Control of the Western Apaches*, 113, 116–17; George Crook Appointment, Commission, and Personal File, Records of the Office of the Adjutant General, Record Group 94, National Archives (hereafter cited as Crook ACP File); Fiebeger, "George Crook," 56.

17. George Crook, "The Apache Problem," *Journal of the Military Service Institu-*

tion of the United States 7 (October 1886): 260–62; Crook, *Autobiography,* 54. See also, "Report of General George Crook," in *Report of the Secretary of War, 1880* (Washington: Government Printing Office, 1880), 80.

18. C. King, "George Crook," 260–61; Bourke, "General Crook in the Indian Country," 645, 647, 656; William H. Bisbee, "Lieutenant Fountain's Fight with Apache Indians at Lillie's Ranch, Mogollan Mountains, December 9, 1885, and at Dry Creek, N.M., December 19, 1885," in Carroll, *Papers of the Order of Indian Wars,* 89; Bourke, *On the Border with Crook,* 109, 112, 234, 250–51; J. King, "Indian Fighter and Humanitarian," 337–38; Dan L. Thrapp, *General Crook and the Sierra Madre Adventure* (Norman: University of Oklahoma Press, 1972), 106; Gates, "Crook's First Apache Campaign," 313, 318.

19. Bourke, *On the Border with Crook,* 138–39, 150; Crook, "Apache Problem," 264; Henry W. Daly, *Manual of Pack Transportation* (Washington, D.C.: Government Printing Office, 1910), 17; J. A. Breckons, "The Army Pack Train Service," *Recreation* 6 (June 1897): 428.

20. Bourke, *On the Border with Crook,* 151, 166, 353; Daly, *Pack Transportation,* 18; Breckons, "Army Pack Train Service," 428; Gates, "Crook's First Apache Campaign," 312, 313, 318; Walker, "The Gray Fox," 6, 7; Utley, *Frontier Regulars,* 48–49.

21. Bourke, *On the Border with Crook,* 202–3; Crook, *Autobiography,* 163, 166; Crook, "Apache Problem," 260, 263, 264; John Bigelow, *On the Bloody Trail of Geronimo* (Los Angeles: Westernlore Press, 1968), 44, 46, 51; Ogle, *Federal Control of the Western Apaches,* 223; Gates, "Crook's First Apache Campaign," 311, 312, 318; J. King, "Indian Fighter and Humanitarian," 338, 339; Dan L. Thrapp, *The Conquest of Apacheria* (Norman: University of Oklahoma Press, 1967), 97, 100.

22. John S. Gray, *Centennial Campaign: The Sioux War of 1876* (Fort Collins, Colo.: Old Army Press, 1976), 112, 116–17, 227; William H. Powell, "The Indian as a Soldier," *United Service* 3 (March 1890): 229–38. A detailed examination of the recruitment and use of Indian scouts (first authorized by the army in 1866), along with their military role and contributions and the attitudes exhibited toward them by the officer corps, appears in Thomas W. Dunlay, *Wolves for the Blue Soldiers: Indian Scouts and Auxiliaries with the United States Army, 1860–90* (Lincoln: University of Nebraska Press, 1982).

23. Nelson A. Miles, *Personal Recollections of General Nelson A. Miles* (Chicago: Werner, 1896), 452; Utley, *Frontier Regulars,* 55.

24. Crook, *Autobiography,* 214, 229; Bourke, *On the Border with Crook,* 225; Lummis, *Dateline Fort Bowie: Charles Fletcher Lummis Reports on an Apache War,* ed. Dan L. Thrapp (Norman: University of Oklahoma Press, 1979), 120; Robert M. Utley, "The Celebrated Peace Policy of General Grant," in Roger L. Nichols and George R. Adams, eds., *The American Indian: Past and Present* (Waltham, Mass.: Xerox College Publishing, 1971), 187, 188, 190; Dunlay, "Crook and the White Man Problem," 7.

25. Fiebeger, "General Crook's Campaign in Old Mexico," 194; Dunlay, "Crook and the White Man Problem," 9; Bourke, "General Crook in the Indian Country," 653; Bourke, *On the Border with Crook,* 225; Thomas C. Leonard, "Red, White and the Army Blue: Empathy and Anger in the American West," *American Quarterly* 26 (May 1974): 181.

26. Bourke, *On the Border with Crook,* 112, 142–44, 215–16, 218, 226; J. King,

"Indian Fighter and Humanitarian," 344–45, 346; Fiebeger, "George Crook," 564; Dunlay, "Crook and the White Man Problem," 5, 6; Fritz, *Movement for Indian Assimilation*, 203.

27. Bourke, *On the Border with Crook*, 17, 213, 219; Ogle, *Federal Control of the Western Apaches*, 118–19.

28. Bourke, *On the Border with Crook*, 112, 131, 213–14, 221; Bourke, "General Crook in the Indian Country," 660; Crook, "The Apache Problem," 267; Howard, "Major-General George Crook," 328; J. King, "Indian Fighter and Humanitarian," 342; Dunlay, "Crook and the White Man Problem," 6.

29. "Report of General Crook," in *Report of the Secretary of War, 1876* (Washington: Government Printing Office, 1876), 500–501. An extremely critical view of Crook's involvement in this episode and throughout the ensuing Sioux War is in Gray, *Centennial Campaign*, esp. 19–20.

30. J. W. Vaughn, *The Reynolds Campaign on Powder River* (Norman: University of Oklahoma Press, 1961), 61, 159–60; James C. Olson, *Red Cloud and the Sioux Problem* (Lincoln: University of Nebraska Press, 1965), 217–18, 221; Gray, *Centennial Campaign*, 45, 47.

31. Bourke, *On the Border with Crook*, 316; "Report of General Crook," in *Report of the Secretary of War, 1876*, 500; Crook, *Autobiography*, 196; Gray, *Centennial Campaign*, 123, 124; James T. King, "General Crook at Camp Cloud Peak: 'I Am at a Loss What to Do,'" *Journal of the West* 11 (January 1972): 116, 117, 122, 127. The most complete account of the Rosebud Battle is in Vaughn, *With Crook at the Rosebud*, 47–147.

32. Helena, Montana, *Daily Independent*, June 30, 1876, quoted in Vaughn, *With Crook at the Rosebud*, 160.

33. Crook, *Autobiography*, 196; Vaughn, *With Crook at the Rosebud*, 165–66; J. W. Vaughn, *Indian Fights: New Facts on Seven Encounters* (Norman: University of Oklahoma Press, 1966), 144.

34. Crook, *Autobiography*, 200; Charles King, *Campaigning with Crook and Stories of Army Life* (New York: Harper, 1890), 158; Utley, *Frontier Regulars*, 268; J. King, "General Crook at Camp Cloud Peak," 124, 126; Jerome A. Greene, *Slim Buttes, 1876: An Episode of the Great Sioux War* (Norman: University of Oklahoma Press, 1982), 12.

35. Gray, *Centennial Campaign*, 212–13, 218, 225–26, 227, 233, 345; Greene, *Slim Buttes*, 29, 30, 33–116.

36. Finerty, *War-Path and Bivouac*, 204; Greene, *Slim Buttes*, 37, 68, 112, 113.

37. Utley, *Frontier Regulars*, 282; Olson, *Red Cloud and the Sioux Problem*, 233, 234, 238.

38. James T. King, "'A Better Way': General George Crook and the Ponca Indians," in Richard N. Ellis, ed., *The Western American Indian: Case Studies in Tribal History* (Lincoln: University of Nebraska Press, 1972), 76–87; Crook, *Autobiography*, 234; Fritz, *Movement for Indian Assimilation*, 190. See also Thomas Henry Tibbles, *The Ponca Chiefs: An Account of the Trial of Standing Bear*, ed. Kay Graber (Lincoln: University of Nebraska Press, 1972).

39. Crook, *Autobiography*, 243; Fiebeger, "Crook's Campaign in Old Mexico," 196–97; James E. Serven, "An End to the Apache Warpath," *Smoke Signal* 22 (Fall

1970): 26, 27; Odie B. Faulk, *The Geronimo Campaign* (New York: Oxford University Press, 1969), 35, 36; Ogle, *Federal Control of the Western Apaches,* 219.

40. Fiebeger, "Crook's Campaign in Old Mexico," 197–200; Crook, *Autobiography,* 249; Lummis, *Dateline Fort Bowie,* 104–6; Serven, "An End to the Apache Warpath," 12, 27, 28. The most complete contemporary account of the expedition is in John G. Bourke, *An Apache Campaign in the Sierra Madre: An Account of the Expedition in Pursuit of the Hostile Chiricahua Apaches in the Spring of 1883* (New York: Scribner, 1886). A modern and thorough treatment is in Thrapp, *Sierra Madre Adventure.*

41. Fiebeger, "Crook's Campaign in Old Mexico," 201; Crook, *Autobiography,* 249; Lummis, *Dateline Fort Bowie,* 100–101, 110; Serven, "An End to the Apache Warpath," 26; Faulk, *Geronimo Campaign,* 35–36; Thrapp, *Sierra Madre Adventure,* 177, 178; J. King, "Indian Fighter and Humanitarian," 345–46; Ogle, *Federal Control of the Western Apaches,* 216, 217, 222–23.

42. Fiebeger, "Crook's Campaign in Old Mexico," 201; Ogle, *Federal Control of the Western Apaches,* 229–30, 231; Utley, *Frontier Regulars,* 377–78, 382.

43. A number of the Indians under Chihuahua, Nana, and lesser chiefs who subsequently surrendered on the terms originally granted by Crook were sent to Florida, where they were permanently incarcerated: Lummis, *Dateline Fort Bowie,* 53. Crook ever after felt that he had lied to these people.

44. Crook, *Autobiography,* 264–65.

45. This synopsis of Crook's role in the Geronimo campaign is drawn essentially from "Report of Brigadier-General Crook," in *Report of the Secretary of War, 1886* (Washington: Government Printing Office, 1886), 154–55; Lummis, *Dateline Fort Bowie,* 28–29; Thrapp, *Conquest of Apacheria,* 348–49, 350; Serven, "An End to the Apache Warpath," 28–29, 34; Utley, *Frontier Regulars,* pp. 383–86, 392; Leonard Wood, *Chasing Geronimo: The Journal of Leonard Wood, May–September, 1886,* ed. Jack C. Lane (Albuquerque: University of New Mexico Press, 1970), 9–10.

46. Washington *Evening Star,* March 21, 1890; Dan L. Thrapp, *Al Sieber, Chief of Scouts* (Norman: University of Oklahoma Press, 1964), 357n, 358n; J. King, "Indian Fighter and Humanitarian," 347; John A. Carroll, "Commentary on the Crook–Miles Controversy," *Smoke Signal* 15 (Spring 1967): 114, 115.

47. See George Crook, *Crook's "Resumé of Operations against Apache Indians, 1882 to 1886"* (London: Johnson–Taunton Military Press, 1970), 2, 5; Crook, *Autobiography,* 267; Faulk, *Geronimo Campaign,* 184. The controversy sparked numerous pro-Crook and pro-Miles accounts over the next several decades: see e.g., Bourke, *On the Border with Crook;* Miles, *Personal Recollections;* and Britton Davis, *The Truth about Geronimo* (New Haven, Conn.: Yale University Press, 1929).

48. Crook's *"Resumé of Operations",* 23, 24–25.

49. Crook, *Autobiography,* 270, 271; Dunlay, "Crook and the White Man Problem," 4; J. King, "A Better Way," 87; J. King, "Indian Fighter and Humanitarian," 347.

50. Bourke, *On the Border with Crook,* 486; C. King, "George Crook," 265; Crook, *Autobiography,* 281; Faulk, *Geronimo Campaign,* 185.

51. Bourke, *On the Border with Crook,* 486; Jerome A. Greene, "The Sioux Land Commission of 1889: Prelude to Wounded Knee," *South Dakota History* 1 (Winter 1970): 48, 51, 55–57, 65; Olson, *Red Cloud and the Sioux Problem,* 313, 317. The

transcript of the proceedings is in U.S. Senate, *Reports Relative to the Proposed Division of the Great Sioux Reservation, and Recommending Certain Legislation,* 50th Cong., 1st sess., no. 51.

52. Crook, *Autobiography,* 291, 292, 300; Bourke, *On the Border with Crook,* 485; Howard, "Major-General George Crook," 329; Washington *Evening Star,* March 21, 1890; C. King, "George Crook," 264–65; Faulk, *Geronimo Campaign,* 186, 187; Dunlay, "Crook and the White Man Problem," 8, 9; Richard N. Ellis, "The Humanitarian Generals," *Western Historical Quarterly* 3 (April 1972): 172.

53. Howard, "Major-General George Crook," 326; *Washington Evening Star,* March 21, 1890; *Army and Navy Journal,* March 29, 1890; Crook, *Autobiography,* 300; Bourke, *On the Border with Crook,* 487, 489–91; Crook ACP File; *Army and Navy Journal,* November 15, 1890.

54. Finerty, *War-Path and Bivouac,* 317.

John G. Bourke

by Joseph C. Porter

Historians remember Captain John Gregory Bourke for his service on the staff of General George Crook and as the author of three books that became classics in the literature of the Indian Wars.[1] In his own lifetime Bourke was best known as an ethnologist and folklorist who enjoyed an international reputation, yet he spent his adult years in the army; indeed, his accomplishments as a scholar were a direct result of his military career. Bourke is an example of a facet of military history in the nineteenth century when the army was a primary tool of the expansion of Anglo-Americans into the western frontiers. Since army officers were often among the first with technical or scientific training to encounter little-known areas, they frequently functioned as scientists or explorers, gathering information, specimens, and artifacts. The army savants were a response to the need for information; as the frontier areas were settled, their importance declined. Bourke's career also illustrates the military, scientific, and humanitarian problems arising from American movement into Indian lands after the Civil War.

Bourke was born in Philadelphia on June 23, 1846. His parents were upper-middle-class Irish immigrants with aspirations for their children. Devoutly Roman Catholic and dedicated to learning, they hired a Jesuit to instruct the eight-

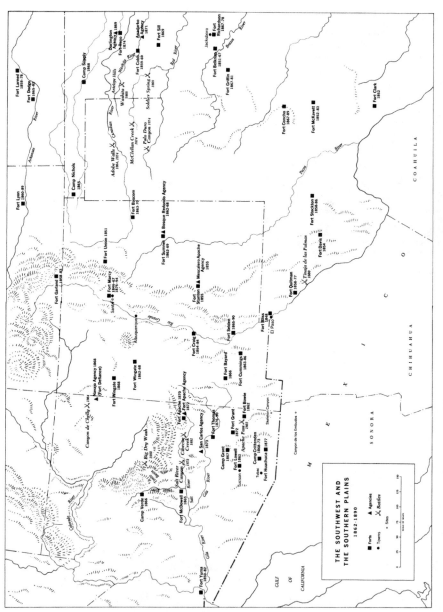

The Southwest and Southern Plains, 1862–90. *From Robert M. Utley, The Indian Frontier of the American West, 1846–1890 (Albuquerque: University of New Mexico Press, 1984). Reprinted by permission of the University of New Mexico Press.*

year-old John in Greek, Latin, and Gaelic. In 1855 he began studies at Saint Joseph's College in Philadelphia. Another year of study would have earned him the Bachelor of Arts degree, but he left Saint Joseph's abruptly in the autumn of 1859 after quarreling with a teacher.[2]

He planned to re-enter school, but as he later recalled, "the outbreak of the Rebellion made all the boys in the city crazy."[3] At 16, he lied about his age and enlisted in the Fifteenth Pennsylvania Volunteer Cavalry. Private Bourke first saw action at the Battle of Stones River, Tennessee, from December 29, 1862, to January 2, 1863, where he earned the Medal of Honor; the citation reads simply, "Gallantry in Action."[4] During the Battle of Chickamauga, Georgia, his unit was at the point where a strong Confederate attack forced the Union armies to retreat on September 29, 1863; he recalled the Union soldiers "reeling back like a demoralized mob to Chattanooga."[5] Bourke endured the Confederate siege of Chattanooga and later arrived in Atlanta with General William T. Sherman's forces.[6]

Two weeks after his nineteenth birthday, Private Bourke was mustered out of the volunteer service. That autumn he entered the United States Military Academy at West Point, and he graduated eleventh in a class of 39 in June 1869.[7]

Bourke was 23 years old when he received his commission as a second lieutenant in the Third Cavalry. His personality and character had been shaped by his upbringing, his Civil War experience, and his West Point education. He was dedicated to what he believed was the northern way of life, centered on the solid middle-class virtues of yeoman farmers, small businessmen and middling professional people. These values—inspired by his parents, emphasized at Saint Joseph's College, and reinforced at West Point—defined Bourke's outlook. As a private soldier he fought for these ideals against the "slavocracy," and as an army officer he wished to implant his vision of civilization in the West. Perhaps this idealized middle-class society never really existed except in Bourke's mind, but it served as the basic motivation in his military career.

A fascination with the land, history, and peoples of the American West, a habitual tendency to observe his surroundings closely, and the boredom of garrison life on the frontier prompted Bourke to keep extensive diaries. He began to take descriptive notes as soon as he arrived in New Mexico in 1869, and by 1872 his journals had settled into a pattern of detailed observation and personal opinion. Because of his skill as a chronicler, they became more than an account of an army officer's life on the frontier. The portrait of Bourke that emerges from the diaries is that not of a solitary officer in a remote region but of a highly literate man living in an area that the army was attempting to incorporate into national life. He was committed to shaping the western frontier to his notions of Anglo-American civilization. He believed that he was both a participant in and a student of the settlement of the last continental frontier, and he initially hoped that his diaries would record the development of civilization in the West. When his early vision was not realized, the diaries reflected his disillusionment as he observed the American West that actually came to be.

Bourke reported to Fort Craig, New Mexico, in the autumn of 1869. From 1870 until 1873 he fought fierce Apache warriors who were defending their lands against Hispanic and Anglo intruders.[8] By autumn of 1870 he was an experienced Indian fighter, his troop commander calling him an "excellent officer."[9]

Despite the fighting, little was accomplished, and in 1871 the army made a decision that had direct ramifications for Bourke's future military and scientific career: it sent the unorthodox George Crook to try to duplicate against the Apaches his previous successes over Indians in Oregon, Idaho, and California.[10] The army ordered Crook, then only a lieutenant colonel, to assume command of the Department of Arizona, normally a position for a brigadier general.

Crook required officers of experience to serve as his aides, and Bourke joined his staff in September 1871.[11] From then on, the career of Bourke became inexorably linked to the fortunes of Crook. For the next 15 years Bourke served Crook as advisor, confidant, amanuensis, and henchman, and his expertise in the nineteenth-century science of ethnology formed the intellectual rationale of Crook's Indian policies.

After assessing the situation in Apacheria, Crook saw that soldiers alone could not defeat tough warriors who could cover 75 to 100 miles a day across terrain and in a climate where the American soldier, as Bourke put it, "droops and dies." Crook believed that only Apaches themselves were capable of subduing their hostile brethren. Since their diffuse social organization made it possible to persuade the warriors of one Apache band or group to fight against other bands and groups, he decided to enlist Apaches as scouts or auxiliaries, and then send mixed units of soldiers and warriors after the hostiles.

Serving with these commands, Bourke found himself not only fighting against Apaches but also living with and fighting alongside other Apaches. He spent the winter of 1872–73 in the field; on December 28, 1872, he was at the bloody battle in Salt River Canyon which demonstrated that Crook's plan worked. Led by the Apache scouts, the soldiers could and would reach anywhere within Apacheria. Crook combined the threat of annihilation with the offer of a just peace for any hostiles who surrendered.

By early April 1873 the major military offensive was over, and Bourke noted that they had "terminated the first and only successful campaign against the Apaches since the acquisition of the Gadsden Purchase."[12] His ebullience was well founded. His conduct during the winter of 1872–73 had earned him four commendations for "bravery and gallantry," with Crook lauding his "conspicuous zeal in carrying out field duties."[13] The ambitious Bourke was on the staff of an officer whose spectacular success against the Apaches gave both men much visibility. In recognition for his work in Arizona, Crook was promoted from lieutenant colonel to brigadier general in October 1873.[14]

In 1875, Bourke moved to the Great Plains when Crook assumed command of the military Department of the Platte, with headquarters in Omaha, Nebraska. In 1876, Bourke participated in four of the major battles of the Great Sioux War. He was with the Bighorn Expedition commanded by Colonel Joseph J. Reynolds, which—after 17 days of driving snowstorms and subzero temperatures—attacked a Cheyenne village on the Powder River on March 17, 1876; the fight was a disaster for the soldiers. On June 17, Bourke fought at the Battle of the Rosebud in Montana, and during that fight he led an attack of Crow and Shoshone auxiliaries against the Cheyennes.

Bourke was in the field for five months that summer. He endured Crook's "Horse Meat March" in late August and early September 1876, during which, units from Crook's command attacked a Sioux village at Slim Buttes, South Dakota, on September 9. He was with the Powder River Expedition when Colonel Ranald Mackenzie ordered the attack on the Cheyenne village of Chief Dull Knife at dawn on November 25, 1876.[15]

The defeat of Dull Knife marked the end of one stage of Bourke's military career. He would be involved as an observer, not a combatant, with the Northern Cheyenne flight from the Indian Territory in 1878, the Ute War in Colorado in 1879, and the Apache campaigns of the 1880s; his last fight against Indians was in the Cheyenne village on November 25, 1876. Already his interest in ethnology was beginning to compete with his soldierly aspirations. He never questioned the sacrifices made by the army during the Great Sioux War, but he began to look behind the battles and to question the reasons for the bloody impasses that cost both Indians and soldiers so dearly. He had been fighting Indians since 1869, and the end of the Great Sioux War signaled a change in his relationship with the Native Americans. After 1876 he went to them as a student of their cultures, not as an enemy soldier.

Bourke's transformation from cavalry officer to ethnologist was not sudden; rather, it was a gradual process that began in Apacheria in 1872 and was completed at Camp Robinson, Nebraska, in the spring of 1877. His inclination toward observation and study predisposed him to intellectual pursuits, but it was his battlefield experiences that made him an ethnologist. In 1869, Bourke believed that "the only good Indian was a dead Indian and that the only use to make of him was that of a fertilizer."[16] He was caught up in the prevailing white attitude toward the Apaches and the violence of Indian fighting. When his cavalry troop killed a warrior in 1870 and an Apache scout with the unit presented him the scalp and ears, Bourke (doing himself no credit, as he later admitted) accepted them. He mounted the ears in a frame and used the scalp as a lamp pad. When an acquaintance who spotted those "ghastly trophies" nearly fainted, Bourke "saw at once how brutal and inhuman I had been and ordered them buried."[17]

Crook's use of Apache auxiliaries sparked Bourke's scientific curiosity about the Indians. Ironically, his gradually changing view came from serving with the Apache scouts while the army was tracking down and killing hostile Apaches. Suddenly Bourke found himself living and working side by side with dozens of Apaches "of whom many had never been thrown into contact with a white man."[18] The warriors might be helping the army, but they diligently followed their own customs. Daily contact with the Indians did little to alter previous misconceptions and stereotypes among some soldiers, but Bourke noticeably began to change his opinion of the Apaches and eventually of all Indians.

His initial interest was due not to any abiding desire to study Apaches systematically, but to a personal curiosity about the habits of his new comrades in arms, who just happened to be Indians. Within two weeks of joining a column of soldiers and warriors in 1872, Bourke had begun to compile his first vocabulary of the Apache language. The warriors perceived and appreciated his interest, and during the winter of 1872–73 they dubbed him "Nantan Hosh Dijoolé" or Captain Cactus.[19] His attention spread to other tribes, and in 1874, during a visit to the Hopis, Bourke made his first detailed ethnographic notes on a people other than the Apaches.[20]

Bourke had a similar experience with each plains tribe he met. The battlefield forged his initial unflattering opinions into respect for the warriors. Personal companionship with auxiliaries and reservation Indians modified his notions, leading him to appreciate the Indian cultures. His transformation from a brash young officer who believed that the "only good Indian was a dead Indian" to a serious scholar of Native American cultures and an advocate of Indian rights was at first tentative, but after spending the winter of 1876–77 with the Lakotas and the Northern Cheyennes at Camp Robinson, his conversion was complete.

Bourke's first efforts in ethnology began with the Apaches. His fluent command of Spanish enabled him to talk with Mexican captives raised among the Apaches and to begin his first fieldwork among them in the early 1870s. He also did research among the Papagos, Hualpais, Navajos, and Hopis during his first tour of duty in the Southwest. After moving to Nebraska he worked among the Crow, Shoshone, Arapaho, Lakota, Northern Cheyenne, Ponca, and Omaha tribes.

Bourke's personal characteristics and values governed his contact with Native Americans. As he lived with the Apache scouts or sat in a Cheyenne or Arapaho tepee and dined on deer brains, buffalo intestines, or stewed pup, his direct personal experiences coalesced with the intellectual tradition that dominated nineteenth-century ethnology.

Bourke and his contemporary ethnologists did not regard themselves as mere dabblers or amateurs. They believed that they were establishing a science of man. If ethnology was new, they fused it with an old but still vital research strategy that dated back to the Enlightenment of the eighteenth century. It was the advocates of this intellectual approach — Bourke prominent among them — who defined the standards of research, determined the questions to be asked, and published the monographs — in short, dominated American anthropology for a generation after the Civil War. The ethnologists — military or civilian — were a crucial part of the nation's response to the Indians.[21]

The ethnological methodology derived from the eighteenth-century Enlightenment included a "philosophical outlook which placed heavy emphasis on description and classification."[22] This created a "kind of naive rationalistic empiricism — belief that the method of pure empiricism consistently pursued would lead to a rational understanding of the Universe."[23] This empirical bent exercised an influence on ethnology until the early twentieth century.

The ethnologists also had a model into which they strove to fit their data, a theory of man and society that had originated in Scotland in the eighteenth century, where a group of Scottish thinkers had developed a research strategy based on the assumption that the fundamental unit of study must be groups of people, or "society."[24] They also argued that all people, in all places, at all times were basically similar, and that racial differences did not affect that basic unity of human nature.

Their belief in the unity of mankind compelled the Scottish thinkers and their intellectual descendants to confront the variety of cultural differences that existed around the world and throughout history: how, for example, were the differences between Aztecs, ancient Hebrews, Apaches, and nineteenth-century Europeans to be explained? In response, the Scots and their nineteenth-century followers argued that all human society represented "progress" from "rudeness" or "savagery" to "civilization." Because humanity was universally the same, the path of all groups to civilization would be similar; therefore, a variety of cultures existed not because people were unalike but because their societies were at different stages of social development. The ethnologists of Bourke's generation saw in nonindustrial cultures the living history of their own civilization. When he was talking to a Crow or a Lakota warrior, Bourke was conversing not only with a friend and a fellow fighting man but also, in his opinion, with a living historical specimen.

Two contradictory tendencies existed within this ethnological outlook: ethnocentrism and cultural relativity. The ethnologists believed that Euro-American culture represented the highest level of social evolution and provided the standard against which to measure the "rudeness" or "civilization" of other societies; nevertheless, because humanity at each stage of social development fashioned institutions and mores consistent with its level of social advancement, the habits and practices of one society should not be judged by those of another. The Scottish tradition that influenced Bourke and his fellow ethnologists predated and weathered the impact of Romanticism and Darwinism on other fields of scholarship. The Victorians who accepted the Scots' ideas rejected the racist theories of humankind that were becoming current among their contemporaries: apparent differences between peoples were due to varying degrees of social evolution, not to innate racial characteristics. Bourke, even during his most strained relations with Indians, never resorted to racial explanations.

Since society was the Scots' focus of study, they theorized that "modes of existence" or styles of subsistence were the bedrock of any culture. Consequently, Bourke and his contemporaries diligently studied hunting and gathering, herding, agriculture, and commerce. Bourke was sickened at the sight of warriors mutilating their fallen enemies, but he did not ascribe this practice to any inherent racial or cultural defect. Instead, he argued that the warriors of the plains were at the hunting stage of human progress, and that their behavior was consistent with the economic demands of hunting, "for the law of Nature has made all hunters Ishmaelites and they must for self-preservation exterminate all interlopers into their hunting grounds."[25] Bourke doubted that "civilized" society could claim moral superiority: "We enlightened people who prate so much about our goodness and elevation would do just the same thing, under the same circumstances," he wrote. "We have but little more morality than the savage mean as he is; but we have a great deal more bread and butter."[26]

The ethnologists became embroiled in the same problems of the red-white conflict that touched Bourke's life as an army officer. The centuries of struggle between the Indians and the intruders had entered its last military phase. The 1870s demonstrated that white expansion into Indian lands could not be stopped. Having seen the Indian country change radically even within a decade, Bourke realized that continuing white settlement had ended hopes for an Indian "preserve" in the West. The wars of the 1870s vividly underscored the need for a change in government policy toward the Indians. To well-meaning humanitarians and reformers it seemed that the only alternative to the physical extermination of the Indians was to "civilize" them; the Indians could be saved only if they abandoned their tribal cultures and became red white men. Given this view, the ethnologists' schema of social evolution became more than an intriguing scientific theory; as one historian has written, when "a comprehensive Indian policy was drawn up in the 1880s, [this] hierarchy of progress was adopted."[27] Concern with "civilizing" the Indians signaled the end of the military offensive and the mounting of a different kind of assault, based on white expectations that red cultures should vanish. Ironically, then, while some demanded the extermination of the Indians, self-proclaimed humanitarians called for an acculturation that would end their traditional way of life.

Bourke and his fellow ethnologists believed themselves charged with two related missions. They hoped first that their studies could serve an immediate utilitarian purpose: they would use their ethnological knowledge to determine proper Indian policy scientifically. It was Bourke's expertise in anthropology that provided the intellectual framework for Crook's Apache policies. The primary concern of Bourke and others who regarded themselves as friends of the Indians was not the continued integrity of tribal cultures. Rather they wanted to assure the circumstances and to protect the rights that would encourage the Indians to follow the theoretical path from "savagery" to "civilization."

The ethnologists' second interest in the Indians transcended the practical problems of policy. Since they assumed that white expansion would inevitably destroy tribal ways of life, the Gilded Age anthropologists felt compelled to analyze aboriginal cultures before they disappeared. The devastating impact of white settlement on the tribes of the trans-Mississippi West after the Civil War added greatly to their sense of urgency. Bourke and his contemporaries believed that it was imperative to study these "vanishing" cultures—the living prehistory of Victorian civilization and the *raison d' être* of their ethnological theory—before it was too late.

In late 1880 and early 1881, Bourke's scientific efforts came to the attention of Major John Wesley Powell, director of the Bureau of Ethnology at the Smithsonian Institution, who invited Bourke to join him in an ethnological expedition to the Southwest in the summer of 1881.[28] Reluctant to place himself under the aegis of the Bureau of Ethnology, Bourke suggested to Lieutenant General Philip H. Sheridan, commander of the military Division of the Missouri, that the army itself detail him to duty as an ethnologist.[29]

The "Memoranda for Use in Obtaining Information concerning the Indian Tribes" that Bourke showed to Sheridan was the result of his practical fieldwork experience and his reading of ethnological literature. The first of its 18 sections dealt with "tribes" and the "limit of present and former ranges and . . . affiliations and relations with other tribes." Other areas of investigation included "Toys, Games, Musical Instruments, and Modes of Recreation," "Courtship, Marriage, and Divorce," "Implements and Utensils of War and Peace," "Food," "Kinship," "Tribal Government," "Therapeutics," and "Religion, Superstitions, Myths."[30] Each section included detailed questions that Bourke had devised.

The completeness of the "Memoranda" and the fact that a scientist of Powell's stature was seeking Bourke's services prompted Sheridan to grant Bourke duty as an ethnologist. Crook had also supported Bourke's request. Sheridan allowed him flexibility, limiting him only to the tribes south of the Union Pacific Railroad; the general ordered another officer, Captain William P. Clark, to study the tribes north of the railroad.[31] He and Bourke had served together in the Sioux War when Clark had commanded the Indian scouts. In

1881, while Bourke was in Chicago to visit Sheridan, Clark was working on his book about the sign language of the plains Indians.[32]

Sheridan ordered post commanders to give Bourke all of the assistance necessary for his work. Rations, the use of army ambulances, mules, drivers and orderlies, weapons, ammunition, and railroad transportation were arranged for Bourke and his cargo of artifacts. Sheridan also gave him adequate time to conduct research, and control over his own notes and the publication of his findings — matters crucial to any scholar. "Take your time," Sheridan told Bourke. "I want you to make a success of this and I'll back you up in every possible way."[33]

Bourke wasted no time. He had reported to Sheridan on March 25, 1881, and within six days he set out on a tour that ranged from Idaho to El Paso, Texas. Because of his familiarity with Shoshone scouts during the Great Sioux War, Bourke started with the Bannocks and Shoshones at the Fort Hall Reservation in Idaho.

In June 1881 he conducted his most significant fieldwork among the Sioux when he observed the Oglala Sun Dance near Camp Robinson, Nebraska. This ceremony had intrigued Bourke since his first contact with the plains Indians. It was fortunate that he made systematic notes of it when he did, for after 1883 the government forbade the Sun Dance. It was of such great importance to the Sioux, however, that they surreptitiously continued to hold the ceremony away from prying white eyes.

The central ritual of the Sun Dance was performed on the third day of Bourke's visit, June 22, 1881. The prospective dancers, 26 warriors, were gathered in the dance arena. Bourke learned that the dancers had vowed to undergo the ordeal "to propitiate the powers above for dangers feared or to thank them for favors already received"; they had fasted for three days in preparation, being allowed very little food, water, or sleep. The Oglalas promised Bourke "every facility in acquiring a knowledge of this great dance." His position on Crook's staff prompted their willingness to cooperate; they wished Bourke to "tell Wi-chakpa-yammi [General Crook] that we know he is our friend and we know you are his Mini-ho-a man [ink man: that is, secretary or aide-de-camp] and as you have come from him we want you to see all."[34]

Bourke watched as attendants laid each dancer supine on a bed of sage and the medicine men sharpened their knives. Murmuring a prayer, a medicine man bent over the dancer "taking up as much of the skin of the breast under the nipple of each dancer as could be held between his thumb and forefinger of [his left hand] while with the right he boldly and coolly but leisurely cut the quivering form, making an incision under his thumb not less than an inch and a quarter to an inch and a half long."[35] The medicine man plunged wooden skewers horizontally through the bleeding cuts, and the skewers were attached to leather or woven horsehair thongs that dangled from the top of the dance pole or Sacred Tree. Holding a flute made from the wing bone of an eagle between their teeth and a cottonwood sapling in their hands for balance, the dancers assumed a stance that Bourke compared to the military position of attention. Playing the flute and dancing a jerky, stiff-legged step, they leaned back against the pull of the thongs, trying to tear themselves free of the Sacred Tree.

The medicine men and managers of the ceremony gave Bourke free access to the arena so that he could follow every step of the rite, and various Oglala dignitaries and other informants explained difficult points and volunteered information about confusing aspects. Realizing that the Sun Dance was too elaborate for one person to see all, Bourke posted other observers in key positions, later incorporating their notes into his own. Six other army officers, his interpreter, and the Indian agent aided him. He also collected a number of artifacts relating to the ceremony.

His report of the Sun Dance revealed the full range of Bourke, the ethnologist: his skill at detached, systematic observation, his friendship for and personal interest in the Oglalas, and the influence of the current ethnological notions upon his work. No more than any other anthropologist of any generation could Bourke escape his own intellectual heritage, which shaped the questions he asked and therefore the answers he found. He viewed the event through the eyes of a Victorian-era anthropologist, grounded in the tenets of his science. Amid the pageantry, festivities, and serious ceremonial importance of the Sun Dance, Bourke, consistent with his notions of progressive social development, saw himself surrounded not merely by 8,000 Sioux Indians but by the living social roots of his own culture.

His use of the word ''savage'' to describe the rites must therefore be viewed in the context of anthropological theory: it was a scientific classification defining one of the stages through which societies progress. Bourke demonstrated this view in an exchange with an Oglala chief, Red Dog, who was worried that the ethnologist would not understand the Sun Dance.

''My friend,'' said Red Dog, ''this is the way we have been raised. Do not think us strange. All men are different.''

''You speak truly,'' Bourke responded as he watched a warrior succeed in tearing himself free from the Sacred Tree. ''All men are different. This is your religion, the religion of your grandfathers. Our grandfathers used to be like yours hundreds and thousands of years ago, hut now we are different. Your religion brought you the buffalo. Ours brought us the locomotives and the talking wires.''[36]

He believed that, given time, the Sioux would follow the prescribed route to ''civilization,'' but unlike some other ethnologists and reformers, Bourke doubted that the process could be hurried; he strongly disagreed with efforts to coerce changes in tribal cultures.

Example rather than force or decree, he argued, should be the method to convince the Indians to follow the road away from ''savagery.'' Bourke believed that the Oglala Sun Dance itself verified his cautiously optimistic predictions. Some of the aged medicine men had grumbled to him about the decline of the dance from older standards. It was now hard to get the pipestone for the sacred medicine pipes and difficult to procure enough buffalo heads for the ceremony—facts that pointedly demonstrated the changes overtaking the Sioux. The old men told Bourke that the ritual had become a shadow of its former self. He thought that the Sun Dance "is sad enough, horrible enough, but it is slipping away so rapidly that another lustrum will witness its extirpation."[37]

In addition to his work among the Bannocks, Shoshones, and Oglalas, between April and November of 1881 Bourke visited the Navajos, and 22 pueblos in Central Arizona, western New Mexico, and along the Rio Grande. The physical and mental demands of fieldwork were nearly as arduous as those of a military campaign, involving little sleep, frequent lack of food, and the emotional strain of living with peoples different from himself. He drove himself so hard that nervous and physical exhaustion became his constant companions.

Fieldwork among the Pueblo Indians brought special problems: the plains Indians, the Navajos, and the Apaches had openly cooperated with his research, but the Pueblos skillfully guarded their culture. What Bourke regarded as the zealous pursuit of scientific data was pure and simple insult to them.

Nevertheless, he achieved valuable results, particularly in recording the details of Pueblo material culture. In his two visits to the Hopis this anthropological pioneer demonstrated that Hopi culture deserved serious study: his hundreds of pages of notes and sketches became the draft of his first book, *The Snake Dance of the Moquis of Arizona*. Published in the United States and Great Britain in 1884, *The Snake Dance* established his international reputation as an anthropologist.[38]

Three visits to the Zunis opened a new line of inquiry for Bourke: the ritual use of human excrement and urine in cultures around the world. A brief essay, "The Urine Dance of the Zuni Indians of New Mexico," won him election to membership in the American Association for the Advancement of Science.[39] After further research, Bourke wrote *Scatalogic Rites of All Nations*, a massive study that was translated into a German edition with a preface by Sigmund Freud.[40]

The situation in Apacheria, meanwhile, had so deteriorated that Crook was ordered back to Arizona; Bourke returned with him to Whipple Barracks near Prescott, Arizona, on September 4, 1882.[41] He was back at the scenes of his first action as an army officer and with the Indians who had first interested him in ethnology. Although still an officer on Crook's staff, ethnology remained his primary concern, even during the war against the Chiricahua Apaches led by Geronimo. Between 1882 and 1886, Bourke's research among the Western Apaches and the Chiricahua Apaches strengthened his reputation; books and articles from his pen during these years convinced important people to support his scientific efforts.

Bourke's second tour of duty in Arizona revealed that he had matured as a fieldworker since leaving the Southwest in 1875. During the early 1870s he had displayed a genuine but undisciplined curiosity about the Western Apaches; when he returned to them in 1882, he was a veteran scientist. Between 1882 and 1886 his military duties were almost subordinate to his investigations of Apache culture and history. He never doubted the superiority of his own civilization, but the Western Apaches and the Chiricahua Apaches forced him into his closest empathy with any Indian people. Bourke became such a familiar sight as he took notes among the Indian rancherias that the Apaches called him *naltsus bichidin,* the paper ghost or paper medicine man.[42]

An interest in all facets of Native American life and his zeal to collect facts led Bourke to attempt to survey entire Indian cultures; however, two projects dominated his efforts among the Apaches, compiling an Apache dictionary and grammar, and studying the significance of their medicine men.

Major Powell of the Bureau of Ethnology initially encouraged Bourke to study the Apache language, and by the spring of 1886 he had compiled a list of approximately 2,500 Apache words. Evidence indicates that the Bureau of Ethnology planned to publish Bourke's Apache grammar and vocabulary.[43] His finished manuscript was sent to the Bureau, but unaccountably, it has never been found. Bourke studied the Apaches' language at a critical time in their history, and he rendered the words and thoughts of the last generation of preservation Western and Chiricahua Apaches. Fortunately, a 49-page fragment of a draft of the vocabulary was found in the Bourke collection at the Nebraska State Historical Society,[44] but these pages and the rough notes scattered through his diaries and notebooks are all that remain of the years of effort that Bourke devoted to the Apache language.

Bourke could not ignore the importance of medicine men. The Apaches regarded the universe as essentially hostile, and "life is conceived as a path along which individuals must be constantly helped by ritual devices," anthropologist Morris E. Opler writes of the Chiricahuas. "This trail must be followed exactly as the heroes of mythical times are said to have journeyed along it."[45] Ritual strictures, prescribed by the medicine men, reached into the most routine aspects of daily life, and Bourke watched as warriors greeted the morning sun with a pinch of *hoddentin* (a sacrificial meal or powder) and a prayer. Medicine men governed the proper behavior of war parties, and Bourke learned the significance of dances, "seeing" the enemy, sweat lodges (in which Bourke participated with the Apaches), amulets, and war shirts. Ritual warpath language was spoken once a war or raiding party crossed south of the Gila River.[46]

Several Western Apache and Chiricahua Apache medicine men and two medicine women were Bourke's informants. He asked questions and then listened, making little effort to guide the discussions. He assured accuracy by having different medicine men provide information on the same points.[47] No individual could discuss completely the role of medicine men within Apache culture, however, for each was intensely specialized—in control of one "power'' or gift—and not prepared to talk knowledgeably about the skills of another. Some cured specific ailments or diseases. Others, like Geronimo, were shamans of war. Frequently, the medicine men performed rituals on Bourke before imparting information. They believed that talking about ''power'' was fraught with grave danger, and they wanted to protect themselves and the ethnologist.

Given the precepts of his science, Bourke's genuine fondness for the Western and Chiricahua Apaches as individuals and admiration for their cultures placed him in a contradictory position. The Apaches enjoyed a special place in his esteem that they never relinquished to any other group of Indians; he was not indulging in hyperbole when he talked about his friends among them. After he left the Southwest in 1886, he maintained contact with these friends through white frontiersmen, and years later individual Apaches were still sending their photographs to Bourke. When he believed that the Chiricahua Apaches were victims of injustice, he spent years in a futile effort to help them.

Ironically, however, as the conservative Bourke studied the Apaches, their culture seemed to coincide more closely with his personal middle-class values than did the white society of the burgeoning southwestern frontier. Fieldwork had revealed some common ground between him and the Indians: he and the Apaches loathed liars. The Apaches placed as high a value on chastity and strict sexual practices as did the straitlaced Bourke. Even if they were at the theoretical level of ''savagery,'' Bourke found them honorable, truthful, industrious, intelligent, valorous, chaste, and patriotic—qualities that he cherished but found lacking in the frontier population of the 1880s.

Yet his acceptance of the Apaches remained on a personal level: he did not modify his definition of their culture as a rung on the ladder to civilization, or openly admit that a dilemma existed. In the 1880s he predicted that within five more years ''the savage, as a savage, will have disappeared from within our boundaries.''[48] It was the medicine men, often his friends, who blocked the path to civilization. ''The 'Medicine Men' are as a rule the most intelligent and most astute men of the tribe; no wonder then that they have gained so much power; a power which must be shattered before the Indian can be fairly placed on the road to civilization,'' Bourke wrote in 1885. ''So long as the 'medicine men' exist, the Indians can never follow the white man's road.''[49] His monograph ''The Medicine Men of the Apache'' detailed his argument.

For Bourke the tragedy was that the Indians, whom he had come to know so well, were never treated with the honesty and justice that he believed should be the basis of civilization. He eventually became a militant defender of Indian rights not because he had changed his ideas of cultural evolution but because he maintained them. When Bourke became convinced that narrow-minded greed, blatant opportunism, and self-serving politics—rather than a desire to ''civilize'' the Indians—dominated government Indian policy, he became an outspoken critic of that policy. When he began to battle for Indian rights in the 1880s, he was fighting against the sabotage of his own values.

Since ethnology had its utilitarian emphasis, Bourke hoped to provide solutions to the problems of setting Indian policy. General Crook had developed his own unique ideas of Indian management, which he sought to implement among the Western Apaches, but it was Bourke who articulated the theoretical basis of the Crook plan for "civilizing" the Apaches. Bourke and Crook advocated a laissez-faire approach, letting the Apaches govern themselves as much as possible. They wanted the army to provide a cash market for Western Apache crops and livestock. Since the army required grain, forage, and beef, Crook thought that these products could be purchased from the Indians. Bourke believed that agriculture and stock-raising could replace raiding as the economic staff of Apache life. The pecuniary astuteness of the Western Apaches impressed many observers, and their agricultural efforts in 1875 convinced Bourke that with a little encouragement and agricultural training, they could soon completely support themselves. Otherwise, he argued, the Western Apaches should be left alone; they had no need for an Indian Bureau to feed or clothe them.

Bourke encouraged Crook's use of enlisted Apache scouts in the army. Like agriculture, he insisted, such employment would help the Apaches advance along the path of social development. The scouts were ruthlessly effective in tracking down and killing Indian offenders, and their salaries introduced working capital among the Apache tribes. "By the Crook method of dealing with the Savage, he was, at the outset, de-tribalized without knowing it; he was individualized and made the better able to enter the civilization of the Caucasian, which is an individual civilization," Bourke described the idea behind the policy. "As a scout, the Apache was enlisted as an individual: he was made responsible individually for all that he did or did not."[50]

Actually, however, it can be argued that the recruitment of Indian scouts reinforced traditional Apache culture. Becoming a scout provided an exhilarating break from the routine of reservation life for an Apache warrior, and despite Bourke's notions about "de-tribalization," the Apache complex of war strictly governed the scouts. White officers and Apache first and second sergeants commanded the scout companies. The sergeants were experienced warriors who normally would have led raiding or war parties. The Western Apache clan system dictated enlistments in much the same way that it had the formation of war or raiding parties. Clan "brothers" enlisted as a group, and Bourke learned that the scouts camped by clan and advanced into battle by clan, led by their own sergeants. What Bourke hoped would undermine tribal values, therefore, may in fact have enhanced them. He saw the use of scouts as a lever to ease the warriors toward civilization; the Apaches saw an opportunity that they pragmatically adopted to their own customs.[51]

By 1886, Bourke's reputation as a scholar was such that Francis Parkman had become his patron. Parkman asked his friend William Endicott, then secretary of war, to allow Bourke to continue his studies in Washington, D.C., with the support of the War Department.[52] During and after his five-year sabbatical in the capital, Bourke was active in scientific and intellectual circles. In 1891 he published *On the Border with Crook,* which quickly became a classic on the history of the Indian wars. He did extensive research about the history of Spain in North America. Folklore had interested him for years, and in 1891— when he was reassigned to Fort Ringgold, Texas—he began extensive investigations into the folklore of the lower Rio Grande Valley. In 1893 the Department of State appointed him curator of its exhibit at the Columbian Exposition in Chicago: La Rabida, a facsimile of the monastery in Spain that had sheltered Christopher Columbus during his darkest hours. In 1895, Bourke was elected secretary of the Anthropological Section of the American Association for the Advancement of Science. That same year he became president of the American Folk-Lore Society.

But while Bourke's intellectual pursuits flourished, his military career did not. For the last decade of his life he was a strident critic of the imprisonment of the Chiricahua Apache tribe in Florida and Alabama, and his efforts on behalf of the Indian prisoners made him unpopular with several influential people— including his former patron General Sheridan and President Grover Cleveland. With the death of George Crook in 1890, Bourke lost a powerful advocate within the military establishment. Despite 34 years of service and his excellent record, he never rose above the rank of captain.

Not until the last year of his life, when he became bitter about his lack of promotion, did Bourke seriously consider pursuing ethnology outside the army. For most of his career he had felt no conflict between his military duties, his scholarship, and his endeavors to reform Indian policy. In 1896, however, he planned to retire from the army and devote his time to writing. Rigorous campaigns and fieldwork had severely taxed him, and for 15 years he had suffered poor health. He died before he could leave the service—on June 8, 1896, 15 days short of his fiftieth birthday.

Bourke's death and the closing years of the nineteenth century coincided with the end of the era of the soldier-scientist who had explored the wilderness, mapped the terrain, and studied the Native Americans during a century of continental expansion.

Notes

1. John G. Bourke, *An Apache Campaign in the Sierra Madre: An Account of the*

Expedition in Pursuit of the Hostile Chiricahua Apaches in the Spring of 1883 (New York: Scribner, 1886); John G. Bourke, *Mackenzie's Last Fight with the Cheyennes: A Winter Campaign in Wyoming and Montana* (Governor's Island, N.Y.: Military Service Institution, 1890; rpt., Bellevue, Neb.: Old Army Press, 1970); John G. Bourke, *On the Border with Crook* (New York: Scribner, 1891; rpt., Lincoln: University of Nebraska Press, 1971).

2. Diary 88 (October–November 1888), 45–49. Bourke faithfully kept his diary from his arrival in the Southwest in 1869 until his death in 1896. The volumes encompassing the years 1869–72, probably lost or stolen during his life, have vanished. With the exception of the entries for December 1–16, 1888, all the surviving volumes are in the library of the United States Military Academy, West Point, New York. This research is based on the Bell & Howell microfilm edition of the West Point volumes. Citations here follow the USMA classification by volume number (with the inclusive dates for each one) and page.

3. Diary 88, 52.

4. Letter to author from Brigadier General William E. Carraway, April 9, 1976 (the late General Carraway was a student of the history of the Fifteenth Pennsylvania Volunteer Cavalry); Diary 90 (February–March 1889), 13–14.

5. Diary 31 (August 19–October 11, 1879), 234.

6. Ibid.

7. Colonel Edwin V. Sutherland, "The Diaries of John Gregory Bourke: Their Anthropological and Folklore Content" (Ph.D. diss., University of Pennsylvania, 1965), 7.

8. The Southern Athapascans included the Navajos and six distinct Apache tribes. Bourke was most involved with the Western Apaches (further divided into the White Mountain, the Cibecue, the San Carlo, the Southern Tonto, and the Northern Tonto groups) and the Chiricahua Apaches (a name applied to four related groups: the Bedenkohes, the Chokonens, the Chihennes, and the Nednais). For a good introduction to the history and culture of these two Apache tribes and their conflict with outsiders, consult Grenville Goodwin, *The Social Organization of the Western Apache* (Chicago: University of Chicago Press, 1942); Morris E. Opler, *An Apache Life Way: The Economic, Social, and Religious Institutions of the Chiricahua Indians* (Chicago: University of Chicago Press, 1941); and Dan L. Thrapp, *The Conquest of Apacheria* (Norman: University of Oklahoma Press, 1967).

9. First endorsement by Howard Cushing on Bourke letter to Adjutant General, September 9, 1870, personal file, John Gregory Bourke, Box 863, Record Group (RG) 94, National Archives (NA).

10. The best sources on Crook are Bourke, *On the Border with Crook;* and Martin F. Schmitt, ed., *General George Crook: His Autobiography* (Norman: University of Oklahoma Press, 1960, 1986).

11. General Orders No. 18, September 1, 1872, Headquarters, Department of Arizona, Drum Barracks, California; a copy is pasted in Diary 1 (November 20, 1872–April 6, 1873).

12. Diary 1, 175.

13. General Orders No. 14, April 9, 1873, Department of Arizona, Prescott, Bourke personal file, Box 863, RG 94, NA.

14. *Crook, Autobiography,* 183n.

15. Bourke, *Mackenzie's Last Fight,* 23.

16. Bourke, *On the Border with Crook,* 115.

17. Diary 92 (May 12–June 23, 1889), 65.

18. Diary 46 (August 28–September 2, 1881), 2125.

19. The name was given him by his Western Apache friends and later picked up by the Chiricahua Apaches as well. *Nantan* means chief or captain; Bourke translated *hosh dijoolé* (in his rendering, ''hüzdichúli'' or ''justa-chuli'') as Turk's head cactus. The Turk's head, or bisnaga—also known as the eagle claw cactus—is a bluish, sparsely spined barrel cactus with wide, curved spines that resemble an eagle's claws. The Apaches must have had Bourke's huge waxed cavalry mustache in mind when they nicknamed him. (For the information on the Turk's head cactus, I thank ethnobotanist Karl Scherwin, Department of Anthropology, University of New Mexico.) *The Western Apache Dictionary* (Fort Apache: White Mountain Apache Culture Center, 1972) defines *hosh dijoolé* as the strawberry or porcupine hedgehog cactus.

20. Diary 2 (September 22–October 20, 1874), 101–25.

21. These assumptions about the intellectual behavior of the ethnologists were shaped by Thomas S. Kuhn, *The Structure of Scientific Revolution* (Chicago: University of Chicago Press, 1970).

22. Brook Hindle, *The Pursuit of Science in Revolutionary America* (Chapel Hill: University of North Carolina Press, 1956), 12.

23. George H. Daniels, *American Science in the Age of Jackson* (New York: Columbia University Press, 1968), 66.

24. This brief summary of the Scottish contribution to social science theory is based on Gladys Bryson, *Man and Society: The Scottish Inquiry of the Eighteenth Century* (Princeton, N.J.: Princeton University Press, 1945); David Kettler, *The Social and Political Thought of Adam Ferguson* (Columbus: Ohio State University, 1965); Louis Schneider, ed., *The Scottish Moralists: On Human Nature and Society* (Chicago: University of Chicago Press, 1967); Douglas Sloan, *The Scottish Enlightenment and the American College Ideal* (New York: Teacher's College Press, Columbia University, 1971); John B. Stewart, *The Moral and Political Philosophy of David Hume* (New York: Columbia University Press, 1963); Alan Swingewood, ''Origin of Sociology: The Case of the Scottish Enlightenment,'' *British Journal of Sociology* 21 (1970): 164–80.

25. Diary 15 (December 4–December 28, 1876), 1492–93.

26. Ibid.

27. Brian W. Dippie, ''The Vanishing American: Popular Attitudes and American Indian Policy in the Nineteenth Century,'' (Ph.D. Diss., University of Texas, 1970), 133.

28. Powell to Bourke, March 3, 1881, Bureau of American Ethnology (BAE) Correspondence, Letters Sent, Box 3, National Anthropological Archives (NAA), Smithsonian Institution. Major John Wesley Powell (1834–1902) was a well-known western explorer, geologist, and ethnologist. In 1869, Powell and nine other men spent three months on a voyage of exploration down the Green River and the Colorado River. Powell was a politically astute bureaucrat who played an important role in the creation of the United States Geological Survey and the Bureau of Ethnology in 1879; he served as director of the bureau from 1879 until his death, and as director of the geological survey from 1881 to 1894. See William Culp Darrah, *Powell of the Colorado* (Princeton, N.J.:

Princeton University Press, 1951); and Wallace Stegner, *Beyond The Hundredth Meridian: John Wesley Powell and the Second Opening of the West* (Boston: Houghton Mifflin, 1953).

29. Diary 38 (January 6–March 8, 1881), 1118–19. For Sheridan, consult Paul Andrew Hutton, *Phil Sheridan and His Army* (Lincoln: University of Nebraska Press, 1985).

30. Diary 38, 1118–19, and Diary 39 (March 15–May 18, 1881).

31. Special Orders No. 33, March 26, 1881, Headquarters Military Division of the Missouri, Chicago (pasted in Diary 39); Philip H. Sheridan to Bourke, March 19, 1881, J. M. Christlieb Collection, Center for Great Plains Studies, University of Nebraska, Lincoln.

32. William P. Clark, *The Indian Sign Language with Brief Explanatory Notes of the Gestures Taught Deaf-Mutes in Our Institutions for Their Instruction, and a Description of Some of the Peculiar Laws, Customs, Myths, Superstitions, Ways of Living, Code of Peace and War Signals of Our Aborigines* (Philadelphia: L. R. Hamersley, 1885). Clark's study was reprinted by the University of Nebraska Press in 1982.

33. Special Orders No. 33, March 26, 1881, Headquarters Military Division of the Missouri, Chicago; Diary 39, 1138.

34. Diary 40 (May 18–June 21, 1881), 1459; Diary 41 (June 21–July 20, 1881), 1520.

35. Diary 41, 1515–16.

36. Diary 41, 1523–24. Clark, in *The Indian Sign Language*, 21, notes that Red Dog was a Hunkpapa who lived with and became a leader among the Oglalas.

37. Diary 41, 1530.

38. John G. Bourke, *The Snake Dance of the Moquis of Arizona* (New York: Scribner, 1884).

39. Diary 74 (June 22–October 11, 1884), 56.

40. John G. Bourke, *Scatalogic Rites Of All Nations: A Dissertation upon the Employment of Excrementitious Remedial Agents in Religion, Therapeutics, Divination, Witchcraft, Love Philters, etc., in All Parts of the Globe* (Washington, D.C.: W. H. Loudermilk, 1891); the German edition is John G. Bourke, *Der Unrat in Sitte, Brauch Glauben und Gewohnheitrecht der Volker* (Leipzig: Ethnologischer Verlag, 1913).

41. Diary 58 (August 22–September 5, 1882), 49.

42. Diary 59 (September 8–October 15, 1882), 96.

43. Bureau of Ethnology to Bourke, f. 4, MS 28, John G. Bourke Collection, Nebraska State Historical Society.

44. Carol J. Condie, ed., *Vocabulary of the Apache of 'Indé Language of Arizona & New Mexico Collected by John Gregory Bourke*, with biographical notes by Joseph C. Porter (Greeley: University of Northern Colorado, Museum of Anthropology, 1980).

45. Opler, *Apache Life Way*, 15.

46. *Hoddentin*, the sacrificial powder of the Apaches, was said to have been strewn by Assanut-li-je over the surface of the sky to make the Milky Way: John G. Bourke, "The Medicine Men of the Apache," in *Ninth Annual Report of The Bureau of Ethnology, 1887–1888* (Washington, D.C.: Government Printing Office, 1892), 507. Also see Keith H. Basso, ed., *Western Apache Raiding and Warfare: From the Notes of Grenville Goodwin* (Tucson: University of Arizona Press, 1971), 265.

47. Bourke, "Medicine Men of the Apache," 500.

48. Diary 78 (October 26–November 18, 1885), 96.

49. Diary 78, 75.

50. Bourke, *On the Border with Crook*, 225.

51. For more detail on the Apache scouts, see Thomas W. Dunlay, *Wolves for the Blue Soldiers: Indian Scouts and Auxiliaries with the United States Army, 1860–90* (Lincoln: University of Nebraska Press, 1982), 165–86.

52. Joseph C. Porter, ''John Gregory Bourke, Victorian Soldier Scientist: The Western Apprenticeship, 1869–1886'' (Ph.D. diss., University of Texas, Austin, 1980), 558–79.

Benjamin H. Grierson

by Bruce J. Dinges

Courtesy Fort Davis National Historic Site,
National Park Service

Benjamin H. Grierson was an unusual soldier on the post–Civil War frontier. A music teacher and unsuccessful merchant before the war, he became a Northern hero as the result of a spectacular raid through Mississippi in the spring of 1863. At the close of the sectional conflict he turned in the stars of a major general of volunteers for the silver eagles of a colonel in the regular army. During almost a quarter-century as commander of the legendary "buffalo soldiers" of the Tenth Cavalry—one of the army's two black mounted regiments—he experienced frustration, fatigue, criticism, boredom, prejudice, and tragedy at remote outposts. While promotion and public acclaim rewarded the exploits of a handful of flamboyant Indian fighters—the likes of Custer, Mackenzie, and Miles— Grierson marched with those officers who followed just a step behind the cutting edge of the Indian frontier. It was his unglamorous task to maintain peace, map and explore new territory, cut roads, string telegraph lines, and enforce government policy toward the Indians. An intelligent, complex individual, he embodied a peculiar blend of single-minded self-interest, obligation to family, fierce political partisanship, commitment to liberal ideals, and devotion to duty. Neither by temperament nor training a model soldier, Grierson nonetheless made significant contributions to the settlement of the trans-Mississippi West.

Nothing in Grierson's background suggested future prominence as a military figure. The youngest of five surviving children of Scots-Irish immigrants, Robert and Mary (Sheppard) Grierson, he was born in Pittsburgh, Pennsylvania, on July 8, 1826, and three years later moved with the family to Youngstown, Ohio. At the age of eight he survived a near-fatal kick from a horse. Although he acquired only a common school education, Grierson possessed a quick mind and a facile intellect. He composed music at an early age and mastered a wide variety of musical instruments.

About 1850 the Grierson family migrated to Jacksonville in west central Illinois, where Ben quickly established a reputation as an accomplished music teacher and bandleader. On September 24, 1854, he married his childhood sweetheart, Alice Kirk, and shortly thereafter entered into partnership in a mercantile business at Meredosia on the Illinois River. The firm of Grierson & Walihan foundered in the Panic of 1857, and on the eve of the Civil War the partners declared bankruptcy. In the meantime, Grierson had become passionately involved in Republican politics. As a party workhorse, he made important contacts with the likes of senatorial candidate Abraham Lincoln and future Illinois governor Richard Yates.

At the outbreak of the Civil War, Grierson owed his military rank to these political connections. Summoned to Springfield by Governor Yates, he joined the staff of Brigadier General Benjamin M. Prentiss at Cairo as a volunteer aide in May 1861. Later, as major and then colonel of the Sixth Illinois Cavalry, he demonstrated surprising aptitude. Major General William T. Sherman described him as "the best cavalry commander I have yet had," and appointed him Chief of Cavalry for the Fifth Division, Army of the Tennessee.[1]

Grierson catapulted into national prominence as the result of his sweep from La Grange, Tennessee, to Baton Rouge, Louisiana, in late April 1863. In 16 days, his small brigade sliced through the heart of Mississippi, tearing up railroad tracks and telegraph lines, confiscating horses and mules, and destroying arms and supplies. With a dazzling combination of speed and deception, Grierson diverted Confederate attention from the Union movement across the Mississippi below Vicksburg. Ulysses S. Grant characterized the raid as "one of the most brilliant cavalry exploits of the war"; as the first example of "what might be done in the interior of the enemy's country without a base from which to draw supplies," it had a crucial impact on Grant's strategic thinking. Grierson was rewarded with a commission as brigadier general of volunteers.

Grierson gained a reputation as a somewhat eccentric cavalryman, who carried a jew's harp in his pocket and occasionally stopped at plantation houses to relax and to entertain the inhabitants on the piano. In campaigns against Nathan Bedford Forrest in northern Mississippi, he also demonstrated reliability, even when his immediate superiors failed—often spectacularly—to corner the elusive Confederate cavalry. After Grierson conducted a second devastating raid through Mississippi in the winter of 1864–65, Grant assigned him, as brevet major general of volunteers, to organize the cavalry for Major General E.R.S. Canby's movement on Mobile, Alabama. Grierson had scarcely taken to the field when the Confederate armies capitulated. At his own request, he remained on duty to organize cavalry at New Orleans for the invasion of Texas. Relieved by Major General Philip Sheridan, he commanded the district of Northern Alabama at Huntsville until January 15, 1866. Subsequently, he was promoted to the full rank of major general of volunteers (retroactive to May 27, 1865) and released from volunteer service on April 30, 1866.

With recommendations from Grant and Sherman, Grierson was commissioned colonel of the Tenth Cavalry on July 28, 1866, and ordered to Fort Leavenworth, Kansas, to supervise recruitment and organize his regiment. In a letter to Major General Winfield Scott Hancock, commanding the Department of the Missouri, Sherman succinctly summarized Grierson's attributes as a soldier: "You have only to tell him what to do," he advised Hancock, "and he will do it with a will." Command of the Tenth Cavalry—one of two new mounted units composed of black enlisted men and white officers—was not considered a plum assignment; a number of officers had accepted lesser rank with white regiments rather than serve with blacks. Grierson, however, embraced the challenge enthusiastically and took immediate steps to ensure that blacks would enter the service on an equal footing with their white counterparts. In a stern letter he reminded Lieutenant Nicholas D. Badger, the recruiting officer at Louisville, Kentucky, that "the word 'Colored' is not to be borne upon any paper relating to or connected with the regiment, —its only official designation being the Tenth Regiment of Cavalry U.S. Army." When the post commander, Colonel William Hoffman, refused to allow Negro troopers to appear alongside white soldiers on the Fort Leavenworth parade ground, Grierson defied the order and protested to department headquarters the application of "invidious distinctions" between white and black troops. Grierson barely evaded court-martial, but by his early and forceful stand he upheld the dignity of the regiment and served warning that the Tenth would not be pushed around.[2]

Grierson's arrival on the frontier coincided with a critical period in Indian-white relations. Hancock's ill-advised and poorly executed campaign during the spring of 1867 sparked a full-scale war on the central and southern plains. To the north, Cheyenne and Arapaho warriors threatened Kansas communities and harassed detachments of the buffalo soldiers guarding the Kansas Pacific Railroad. To the south, companies of the Tenth took station in the Indian Territory, where the Kiowas and Comanches freely raided the exposed settlements in Texas. In late October, in the treaties of Medicine Lodge Creek, the hostile tribes agreed to settle on two large reservations in the Indian Territory, away from major roads and the line of the railroad; not until the summer of 1868, however, did Congress appropriate money to implement the Medicine Lodge treaties, by which time the Indians had grown restless and apprehensive. General Sheridan, Hancock's successor in command of the Department of the Missouri, then prepared to drive the Indians onto their reservations. In May 1868, as Sheridan concentrated troops for a winter campaign, he ordered Grierson to move his headquarters from Fort Riley, Kansas, south to Fort Gibson on the Arkansas River.

Grierson's assignments and accomplishments in the Indian Territory established the pattern of his military career over the subsequent two decades on the southern plains and in the Southwest. While Sheridan assembled troops to take the field, Grierson scouted south and west from Fort Gibson in search of a site for a new military post in the heart of the Kiowa-Comanche reservation. After a month of exploration, he compiled a detailed report outlining new roads, describing the condition of existing forts, and commenting on Indian affairs. For the new army garrison, he recommended a site proposed by General Randolph Marcy 16 years earlier, near the junction of Medicine Bluff and Cache creeks and north of the point where the Comanches crossed the Red River on their raids into Texas.[3]

Sheridan placed Grierson in charge of construction of the post. First designated Camp Witchita, it was soon renamed Fort Sill to honor Brigadier General Joshua W. Sill, a West Point classmate of Sheridan's who was killed at Stones River, Tennessee, in 1862. Grierson relished the assignment and routinely worked late into the night going over blueprints and assigning work details. By the summer of 1871, the fort boasted stone stables and storerooms, comfortable officers' quarters, and barracks housing ten companies of the Tenth Cavalry, comprising 27 officers and 695 enlisted men. Sherman described Fort Sill as "one of the best if not the very best [post] on the frontier," and congratulated Grierson on a job well done.[4]

Meanwhile, however, as military commander at Fort Sill, Grierson was wedged between the proverbial rock and a hard place, and his predicament illustrated the problems involved in implementing federal policy toward the southern plains tribes. At the outset, personality conflicts and loosely defined limits of authority created confusion. As commander of the District of the Indian Territory, Grierson shared with Colonel William B. Hazen, Indian superintendent of the Southern Military District, the responsibility for distributing rations and keeping the peace among the Cheyennes, Arapahos, Kiowas, Comanches, and Kiowa-Apaches who were being driven onto the reservations set aside by the Medicine Lodge treaties. Hazen possessed an uncanny ability to generate controversy, and relations between the two officers soon soured. Although Hazen initially expressed satisfaction that "Grierson takes hold with a right good will," before long he complained of the colonel's seeming reluctance to chastise marauding Indians. Grierson echoed Hazen's pleas for more and improved rations for the tribes but protested that Hazen repeatedly over-stepped his authority in attempting to deal with Indians who were off the res-ervation and therefore under military jurisdiction.[5]

In July 1869, Lawrie Tatum, a hard-nosed Iowa Quaker, replaced Hazen as agent for the Kiowas and Comanches. The change heralded the inauguration of the Grant (or Quaker) peace policy, under which the supervision of Indian affairs was entrusted to a Board of Indian Commissioners composed of repre-sentatives of the various religious denominations. To implement the new policy in the Indian Territory, the adjutant general issued orders that Indians on their reservations would not be interfered with by the military, except at the specific request of the agent or the Bureau of Indian Affairs. In effect, the order made the Fort Sill reservation a staging area for Kiowa and Comanche raids into Texas and a haven for returning marauders.

Because of his Republican principles and his unbounded admiration for Grant, Grierson embraced the peace policy with an enthusiasm unusual in an army officer. The cooperation between Grierson and Tatum was productive; as the two men consulted on matters of mutual concern and agreed on short-range measures and long-term policy. Realistically, however, the warrior tradition of the Kiowas and Comanches, the proximity of their reservation to the Texas frontier, and the limitations of the peace policy itself afforded little chance for success. Grierson and Tatum pleaded for an adequate ration for the Indians as a means of curbing depredations, and when rations were not immediately forth-coming, Grierson requested that the government abide by the terms of the Medicine Lodge Treaty and allow the Kiowas and Comanches to hunt buffalo as far north as the Canadian River. "It is true the Indians have not strictly ful-filled their part of the treaty," he admitted, "yet the Government have [sic] failed to comply, in full, with a single provision of the same." Two companies of the Tenth Cavalry patrolled the Red River, but so long as the soldiers were occupied in building Fort Sill, Grierson was powerless to prevent Indians from crossing over into Texas.[6]

Grierson's efforts to abide by the spirit as well as the letter of the peace poli-cy placed him in a awkward position with some of his military superiors. When, in the summer of 1869, Fort Sill became part of Hazen's District of the Lower Arkansas, Grierson interpreted the reorganization as a step toward re-moving him from command and wrote in calculated anger to Tatum: "It seems . . . that I too must be considered *too much* of a *Quaker* myself or *peace man* to be left here in charge of military affairs on this Reservation. If I had launched out and killed a few Indians—on the principal [sic] of the Irishman at the *Fair*—which was, 'wherever he saw a head to hit it'—I would no doubt be considered *successful,* and it would have then been unnecessary to place another officer over me as an intermediate commander between me and Dept. Hd. Qrs.'' He assured Tatum that so long as he retained command, he would ''pursue such a course as to control the Indians & prevent depredations, without losing sight of the object contemplated by the phylanthropic [*sic*] and good people of the land, —*without bringing on a war for the purpose of gaining an opportunity of killing off Indians*.'' Tatum wrote a strong endorsement of the efficient management of military affairs at Fort Sill. Grierson breathed easier when, on December 9, 1869, the District of the Lower Arkansas was discontinued.[7]

Grierson likewise curried favor with the Board of Indian Commissioners. In correspondence with Felix Brunot, the board's secretary, he painted an optimistic picture of affairs on the reservation and predicted ultimate success if the measures that the commissioners had recommended for increasing rations and for appropriations for agency farmers and agricultural implements were approved. Brunot personally interceded on Grierson's behalf with Commissioner of Indian Affairs Ely Parker and with President Grant and General Sherman.[8]

But events on the Kiowa-Comanche reservation belied Grierson's assurances that the peace policy was succeeding. The Kiowas in particular continued their raids into Texas, and a correspondent of the *Army and Navy Journal* reported Grierson's disapproval ''of the Indian troubles here being made public.'' To curtail depredations, Grierson and Tatum adopted a hard line with marauding Indians, insisting that captives and stolen stock be surrendered without compensation, withholding rations and annuities from Indians off the reservation, and demanding the breakup of rings of traders who exchanged guns and ammunition for stolen mules. These stern measures, however, produced few results.[9]

Blood flowed on the Texas frontier during the summer of 1870, and the press and citizens directed a steady stream of abuse at Grierson. Terrorized settlers in northern Texas accused the Fort Sill commander of supplying the Indians with arms and ammunition, and the Texas legislature threatened to investigate his management of Indian affairs. Major General John Pope, then commanding the Department of the Missouri, defended his subordinate and expressed dismay that army officers had joined in the chorus of criticism. He reminded the critics that neither he nor Grierson had ''the least authority over the Indians on the reservations . . . not even the power to prevent hostile parties of Indians from organizing and setting out on a raid into the settlements, until such Indians have passed beyond the limits of the reservations.'' By that time, Pope lamented, it was frequently no longer a question of control or prevention ''but of pursuit in general fruitlessness.''[10]

Affairs on the Fort Sill reservation climaxed in May 1871, when Grierson assisted Sherman in arresting Satanta, Satank, and Big Tree for leading the Warren Wagon Train Raid in north Texas. In a dramatic confrontation on the porch of the commanding officer's quarters, Grierson seized the barrel of a carbine that the Kiowa chief Lone Wolf had leveled at Sherman and wrestled it out of the Indian's hands. The arrest of the Kiowa chiefs, and the subsequent killing of Satank when he attempted to escape, had far-reaching consequences. Although the peace policy remained in effect, the Department of the Interior reluctantly admitted that "lenient measures and forbearance" had failed among the Kiowas and Comanches on the reservation and acknowledged that "severe treatment would seem to be the only wise and proper course to pursue to compel right conduct on their part." Therefore, Secretary of the Interior Columbus Delano instructed the Commissioner of Indian Affairs to allow the military to enter the Indian Territory "at all times in the pursuit and arrest of predatory and criminal Indians and for the purpose of recovering property and captives held by such Indians."[11]

Meanwhile, Sherman ordered Fort Sill reinforced. In the summer of 1871, Grierson and Colonel Ranald Mackenzie of the Fourth Cavalry launched a joint expedition from Fort Sill and Fort Richardson, Texas, against Kicking Bird and the Kiowas, who had bolted from the reservation with a herd of stolen mules. As he approached the Kiowa camp, Grierson received word from Tatum that the Indians had agreed to return the animals. Immediately, he alerted Kicking Bird to move his people onto the reservation and out of the way of Mackenzie. Mackenzie was furious at missing the opportunity to chastize the Kiowas and never forgave Grierson for sending the warning.[12]

Given the restrictions on the military under the peace policy, Grierson's actions were prudent and as effective as his limited resources allowed. The Commissioner of Indian Affairs concluded in 1871 that although the year had been marked with "gross outrages" on the Texas frontier, still "there would doubtless have been a serious war inaugurated . . . but for the watchfulness of the military and the agent in charge of their [the Kiowa-Comanche] agency." General Pope similarly commended Grierson for exercising good judgment in "his delicate and critical relations with the Kiowas and Comanches."[13]

Mistrust of Grierson's management of affairs at Fort Sill, however, may have influenced Brigadier General Christopher C. Augur, in March 1872, to assign him the task of removing unauthorized settlers from along the Missouri, Kansas & Texas Railroad, which was then building through the eastern section of the Indian Territory. Augur's instructions removed Grierson from Fort Sill at a time when Tatum was reporting the Indians beyond his control and when a military showdown appeared imminent. Sheridan approved the transfer of regimental headquarters and four troops of the Tenth Cavalry from Fort Sill to Fort Gibson and the resurrection of the District of the Indian Territory under Grierson's command. But he also cautioned Augur "not to let Grierson make too much out of Gibson. He is fond of the place & will get his whole regiment there if half a chance is given to him." Grierson's connection with Fort Sill ended, as the post was excluded from the District of the Indian Territory. To his subordinates, it appeared that Grierson had been "shelved." If so, he made no complaint; he promptly removed the settlers, and in early September 1872 he arranged a truce that averted bloodshed between rival factions of the Creek Nation.[14]

After six years of hard, frustrating, and virtually uninterrupted service in the Indian Territory, Grierson accepted General Sherman's offer of assignment as superintendent of the General Mounted Recruiting Service at St. Louis in December 1872. Sherman proposed the change as a well-deserved rest "after the confusion of an Indian life." And, apart from a minor furor when Grierson refused to accept a writ of habeas corpus to turn over a deserter to civil authorities, the St. Louis assignment was indeed a pleasant interlude that placed him close to his family and the comforts of civilization.[15]

Tension had long been smoldering among junior officers of the Tenth Cavalry, however, and scandal surfaced at Fort Sill in the colonel's absence. Although an excellent organizer, Grierson was a notoriously lax disciplinarian, and during most of his long tenure as commander of the Tenth, the regiment was openly divided between pro- and anti-Grierson factions. At Fort Gibson in the summer of 1872, he had alerted Augur to "a very decided spirit of insubordination made manifest at Fort Sill by Officers of my regiment . . . whose only aim seems to be a mad desire to push themselves forward by endeavoring to pull me down." Discipline and morale deteriorated further under Grierson's temporary successor, Lieutenant Colonel John W. "Black Jack" Davidson. When a series of embarrassing social improprieties among officers and ladies came to light during the summer of 1874, Sheridan moved swiftly to break up "the nest at Fort Sill." In November he ordered the regimental headquarters to Fort Concho, Texas, and scattered all but two companies of the Tenth Cavalry among the posts in West Texas.[16]

Grierson, whose tour of duty at St. Louis expired at the close of 1874, took the transfer of the regiment personally and complained to Sherman that Sheridan failed to appreciate him and that he was being "shoved aside by Mackenzie," the new commander at Fort Sill. More galling, he arrived at Fort Concho in April 1875 as companies of the Tenth Cavalry prepared for an extended scout of the Staked Plains under the command of the coarse and corpulent Colonel William R. Shafter of the Twenty-fourth Infantry. Grierson was near apoplectic over the assignment of an infantry officer to command the cavalry and privately protested the action as "an outrageous injustice to all the Field Officers of the Regt." He viewed the order as the latest in a long string of abuse heaped upon him by "*Sherry-dan,*" dating back to the close of the Civil War and designed to force him out of the army. "Thank God," he informed his wife, "my back is not broken, and mark what I tell you, sooner or later, I will get even with this man."[17]

For Grierson—exiled to the barren reaches of West Texas, separated from his wife and children, and feeling persecuted—the early days at Fort Concho were the nadir of his military career. "There is not an officer here," he told Alice, "who is not disgusted with the Country, the Dept., & the Army, and the half of them would resign . . . if they were not so infernally poor." Grierson requested a transfer to the Fifth Cavalry upon the retirement of Colonel William H. Emory in July 1876 (the command went to Sheridan's protégé Wesley Merritt) and seriously pondered resigning, but with no assurance of an income awaiting him in civilian life, he concluded to remain in the service. And yet, he confessed, "I do not feel myself to be such an enthusiastic soldier as heretofore." Still determined to do his duty, he nonetheless admitted that in the future he might be less inclined "to volunteer extra work, [or] to suggest or recommend anything beyond what I know & feel I am in duty bound."[18]

To boost his flagging morale, and to keep his troopers occupied and out of the saloons and brothels in the adjacent community of San Angela (present-day San Angelo), Grierson turned his attention to rebuilding and refurbishing the dilapidated military post. The activity proved beneficial, and Alice expressed pleasure at hearing that her husband was back in his "element," supervising workmen. Under Grierson's command, Fort Concho became the focal point of the army's presence in West Texas.[19]

Grierson's great contribution to the settlement of West Texas commenced on January 22, 1878, when Brigadier General E. O. C. Ord issued orders establishing the District of the Pecos. Although Ord distrusted black soldiers, the demands of settlers, railroad construction crews, and mail contractors for protection from Indian incursions compelled him to devise a plan for defense for the trans-Pecos region. To Grierson he entrusted the sparsely settled area extending from Fort Concho west nearly to El Paso and from the Texas–New Mexico border south to the Rio Grande. Ord's strategy was to deny Indians access to the handful of waterholes that dotted the arid plains. From forts and subposts, patrols were to fan out over the country scouting for Indian signs, exploring and mapping the unknown reaches of West Texas, opening wagon roads, escorting the mails, and stringing telegraph lines.

Grierson vigorously tackled the new assignment. Company commanders took to the field with rigid instructions to compile accurate journals of their marches — recording mileage, describing topography and natural resources — and to prepare detailed maps. Grierson himself made frequent explorations and tours of inspection throughout the district, and submitted a lengthy report on its geology, geography, flora, and fauna. Ord was pleased at the "earnest and successful efforts to develop the resources of the country" and congratulated Grierson on his "arduous and energetic services" — a compliment that Grierson accepted with skepticism. Despite assurances that the Tenth Cavalry had accomplished more than any other regiment in the department, he suspected that Ord "would sooner have White troops in Texas" and predicted that "he will trade us off for the 4th Cavalry if he can."[20]

Yet Indian depredations continued in southern New Mexico and West Texas, and in April 1880, Grierson marched with 280 troopers of the Tenth Cavalry to the Mescalero Agency near Fort Stanton, New Mexico. Victorio and his band of Mimbres Apaches had been using the agency as a refuge, and Grierson assisted Colonel Edward Hatch (who had served under him on the great raid in Mississippi) and the black troopers of the Ninth Cavalry in disarming and dismounting the Indians on the reservation. Hatch bungled the operation, and a number of Indians fled into the mountains. Grierson, however, reserved his criticism for the Department of the Interior, which had allowed the Mescalero Agency to become "virtually a supply camp for Victorio's Band" while their families were being fed and "kindly cared for" at the San Carlos Agency in Arizona. Privately, he characterized the department as a "Hydra Headed Monster," and like most army officers he viewed the division of Indian affairs between civilians and the military as cruel and inefficient. "The Indian Bureau hold the Indians up," he observed, "& the War Dept. knock down & drag out." It would be more humane, Grierson concluded, "to turn everything relating to Indian affairs" over to the War Department, where the Indians would be more honestly and fairly treated and "would have much less cause for complaint."[21]

To capture Victorio and the renegades from the Mescalero Reservation, Sheridan ordered the Tenth Cavalry back into New Mexico in late May. Grierson objected that the movement would expose the entire Rio Grande frontier to Indian incursions, and prevailed upon Ord to have the order rescinded. The wisdom of his advice was demonstrated in late July, when Victorio emerged from Mexico and entered West Texas. In a brief but adroitly managed campaign—the only campaign he would ever conduct against hostile Indians—Grierson outmanuevered, outmarched, and twice ambushed the Apaches. At Tenaja de las Palmas on July 30, he displayed considerable personal bravery in holding a hastily fortified position with only nine men (including his 19-year-old son Robert) until reinforcements arrived. Several days later, he marched 65 miles in 21 hours and surprised the Indians in Rattlesnake Canyon, northwest of Van Horn. Denied access to waterholes, and facing soldiers and a commander who were thoroughly familiar with the environment and terrain of the trans-Pecos, Victorio fled to his death at the hands of Mexican troops south of the border.[22]

Grierson felt that he never received the credit due him for ending the Indian threat in West Texas and opening the region to settlement. In an odd compliment, Ord congratulated him on "a short, sharp, and successful campaign" but recommended that the Tenth Cavalry be transferred out of the Department of Texas. General Augur, Ord's successor, acknowledged Grierson's success when, on February 1, 1881, he abolished the District of the Pecos. In relinquishing district command, Grierson assessed the achievements of the previous three years. In addition to constructing barracks and quarters at various posts and guarding the mails, the troops had explored and mapped thousands of square miles of West Texas. The resources of the trans-Pecos had been made known, and with the end of the Indian menace, settlers were migrating to the region in growing numbers. "A settled feeling of security, heretofore unknown," Grierson noted, prevailed throughout West Texas, and he predicted "a rapid and permanent increase of the population and wealth of the state." Within a year two transcontinental rail lines traversed the trans-Pecos, linking Texas to the Pacific Coast and further stimulating settlement.[23]

Although calm returned to West Texas, life was seldom peaceful at Fort Concho, where Grierson was still stationed. San Angela, across the river from the fort, was a rough frontier town where saloons, gambling halls, and brothels provided ample opportunity for violence between soldiers, gamblers, and cowboys. Grierson contributed to strained relations between civilians and the military by meddling in politics in the southern and pro-Democratic community. During the 1876 presidential contest (one of the few in which he was unable to obtain a leave to return to Jacksonville and cast his ballot), he campaigned locally for Rutherford B. Hayes and announced the Republican victory with a cannon salute. He further irritated local residents when, in 1880, he opposed the removal of the post office from Fort Concho to San Angela. Grierson's enemies retaliated in letters to the San Antonio *Express* criticizing his conduct of the Victorio campaign.[24]

Long-standing antagonism between soldiers and civilians at Fort Concho and San Angela erupted during the first week of February 1881 in the so-called "San Angelo Riot." In retaliation for the gunning down of a private of the Sixteenth Infantry and a trooper of the Tenth Cavalry in San Angela saloons, white and black troops crossed the North Concho River on the evening of February 1 and seized the sheriff. Three nights later, troopers of the Tenth Cavalry, demanding "justice or death," riddled the Nimitz Hotel with bullets. Alarmed residents telegraphed for assistance to Governor O. M. Roberts, who dispatched a company of Texas Rangers to help restore order.

Perhaps fearful that calling attention to the troubles would fan the flames of prejudice against black troops, Grierson violated military protocol by failing to report the February 4 incident to department headquarters. General Augur first learned of the assault on the hotel on February 8, when Governor Roberts demanded an explanation. Grierson—who blamed the white troops for inciting the riot—responded with a long list of grievances and suggested that the Texas authorities take steps to prevent citizens from murdering soldiers. Augur absolved Grierson of blame but warned that any recurrence would result in the breakup of his command. He instructed Grierson to exchange the companies involved in the fracas with troops stationed at the outposts.[25]

As the Indian frontier dissolved in West Texas, the government decided in the summer of 1882 to abandon Forts McKavett and Stockton and to concentrate companies of the Tenth Cavalry and the Sixteenth Infantry at Forts Concho and Davis. Given his choice of headquarters, Grierson selected Fort Davis, 250 miles southwest of Concho. Since his first visit to the post in 1878, he had admired its commodious commanding officer's quarters and the scenic location in the majestic ranch country of the Davis Mountains. Always the builder, he envisioned the construction of a large permanent military installation and cherished hopes of establishing a ranching empire for himself and his four sons. During his tenure as post commander, a telegraph line was completed from the fort to Marfa on the Southern Pacific Railroad; a new water system was installed; and new barracks, officers' quarters, and warehouses were erected. As acting department commander during Augur's absence on leave in September and October 1883, Grierson pushed (unsuccessfully) for government purchase of land adjacent to the post and routinely approved requests for building materials. In February 1884, Fort Davis housed the largest garrison in its history — eight troops of the Tenth Cavalry and two companies of the Sixteenth Infantry, consisting of 39 officers and 643 enlisted men.

Grierson saw opportunity in the availability of thousands of acres of inexpensive state and railroad land. He also realized that a permanent military installation at Fort Davis would provide a lucrative market and enhance property values. Eventually, he acquired title to more than 45,000 acres in West Texas (fortunately for him, nineteenth-century Americans maintained rather relaxed standards of conflict of interest). He organized a railroad promotion company, and worked unsuccessfully to link Fort Davis with the railroad at Marfa. Invariably, his actions as a military commander complemented his interests as a rancher.[26]

Grierson was a devoted husband and father whose involvement in land speculation grew out of personal tragedy. Two of his children had died in infancy; the only daughter, 13-year-old Edith, succumbed to typhoid fever at Fort Concho in 1878. Charlie, the eldest Grierson son, was stricken with a serious mental disorder (probably manic-depressive psychosis) while a cadet at West Point the previous year; he later returned to complete his studies and upon graduation was assigned as a second lieutenant to his father's regiment. In 1882 the second son, Robert, was similarly afflicted while enrolled as a first-year medical student at the University of Michigan. Fearing that the episodes had been brought on by stress and overwork, Grierson hoped that ranching would prove therapeutic for the older boys and prevent similar attacks in his two younger sons, Benjamin Henry, Jr. (Harry), and Theodore McGregor (George). Grierson never realized his dream of wealth, however, for in April 1885 the Tenth Cavalry was ordered to Arizona, and without his personal supervision the ranch business declined. When the army abandoned Fort Davis in 1891, any lingering visions he still entertained of building a personal fortune in West Texas were dispelled.[27]

Grierson's lax and familiar method of command had contributed to the transfer of the Tenth. Comfortably ensconced at Fort Davis and absorbed in his ranching interests, he turned much of the day-to-day administration of the regiment and post over to a small group of favorites. Lieutenant John Bigelow, Jr., recorded during the winter of 1884–85 that matters in the "Friendless Tenth" had degenerated into "a contest for supremacy, if not for existence in the regiment, between the good element and the bad and that the two elements are pretty evenly matched." Prompted in large measure by Major Anson Mills, Grierson's temperamental and headstrong second-in-command, a flurry of charges and countercharges involving officers at Fort Davis landed on the desk of the department commander, Brigadier General David S. Stanley. In recommending a change of station for the Tenth Cavalry, Stanley explained that the command had become " 'localized' to an extent such as to have an effect prejudicial to the public interest on several of its officers," and expressed regret at the demoralization of "a regiment which had rendered much valuable and severe service."[28]

Grierson was disappointed with his new assignment. He had hoped to establish regimental headquarters at either Fort Grant or Fort Huachuca; instead, the department commander, Brigadier General George Crook, scattered the troops of the Tenth among the posts in southern Arizona and ordered the colonel— with the regimental staff, band, and one troop—to Whipple Barracks, headquarters of the Department of Arizona near Prescott. Within weeks the buffalo soldiers took to the field after Geronimo and a small band of Chiricahuas who had bolted from the San Carlos Reservation. Far removed from the scene of hostilities and with little to occupy his time, Grierson watched in thorough boredom as the Apache leader eluded his pursuers. "I am very well satisfied," he lamely consoled himself, "that I am in no way connected with this Indian Mess . . . as no glory or credit has as I can see been gained by any one except the Indians."[29]

Grierson was again involved with the Indian question after April 1886, when Brigadier General Nelson A. Miles replaced Crook in Arizona. In June the new department commander dispatched Grierson to investigate troubles between white settlers and the Hualapai Indians along the Colorado River. Grierson's calm and evenhanded settlement of the difficulty impressed Miles and led him to rely upon the colonel's diplomatic talents. In July, Miles transferred the headquarters of the Tenth Cavalry to Fort Grant, and the following November he assigned Grierson to command the District of New Mexico at Santa Fe.

Immediately, Grierson confronted a complicated fight to resolve the grievances of the Jicarilla Apaches. In 1880, President Rutherford B. Hayes had set aside a reservation for the Jicarillas in northern New Mexico; however, stockmen and settlers—with the support of Secretary of the Interior Henry M. Teller—had succeeded in having the tribe relocated on the Mescalero Reservation in southern New Mexico. During the fall and winter of 1886 dissatisfied Jicarillas left the reservation and appealed to Governor Edmund G. Ross and General Miles to be allowed to move elsewhere and take up lands in severalty.

Grierson became an articulate champion of the Jicarillas, recommending that land immediately be set aside on their old reservation, where they might enjoy "the quiet homes to which they are, — as wards of the nation, — so justly entitled." On February 11, 1887, President Grover Cleveland responded to the Jicarillas' petition and established another reservation for them in the vicinity of Amargo, New Mexico. Subsequently, however, New Mexico delegate Anthony Joseph, acting on behalf of stock raisers and settlers in northern New Mexico, succeeded in having the $1,500 that Congress had earmarked for removal of the tribe stricken from the Indian appropriation bill.

Undaunted, Grierson in April 1887 assisted Special Indian Agent H. S. Welton in moving 500 Jicarillas with their possessions and livestock to the new reservation. Pending congressional appropriation, Grierson accepted personal responsibility for the pay and expenses of a surveyor to fix the boundaries; he then supervised the removal of fraudulent settlers. The Commissioner of Indian Affairs credited the military with much of the success of the settlement of problems in New Mexico. Nonetheless, Grierson expressed concern that the Jicarillas had been attached to the Southern Ute Agency. He pointed an accusing finger at Ute Agent C. B. Stollsteimer and the powerful mercantile and cattle-raising Archueleta family, whom he correctly identified as conniving to steal the Jicarillas' land.

Grierson devoted similar careful attention to problems on the Navajo reservation in northeastern Arizona and northwestern New Mexico. A particularly volatile situation existed along the San Juan River in the northeast corner of the reservation, where settlers blocked Navajo access to water. In August 1887, Grierson restored the strip to the Indians. The same year, he investigated four violent confrontations between tribesmen and whites on the reservation. "In such incidents," he reported, "the Indians, usually the greatest sufferers, have seldom been the aggressors"; in fact, he praised the Navajos for unusual patience under trying circumstances. To alleviate problems, he urged appropriations for the construction of tanks and reservoirs, and an enlargement of the boundaries of the Navajo reserve.[30]

On November 24, 1888, Grierson succeeded Miles as commander of the Department of Arizona. His 18-month tenure as department commander was unremarkable. Between February and November of that year, he and Miles — now commanding the Division of the Pacific — had been working to secure their mutual promotions; their foremost priorities were to "make no mistakes, and maintain peace in the Departments." An escape from Fort Grant in December 1888, the robbery of Paymaster Joseph Wham in southern Arizona the following May, and the rampage of the Apache Kid during the spring of 1890 were minor annoyances that were routinely handled by commanders in the field.

Grierson conducted several inspections of posts and reservations in Arizona, but the bulk of his days were filled with the tedium of administrative routine. Beyond supervising quartermaster, commissary, paymaster, and ordnance offices, he plotted elaborate field maneuvers, assigned officers to organize and test a heliograph system, and promoted cooperation between the regular army and the California National Guard.[31]

Grierson also devoted considerable attention to the welfare of the Indians within his department. Above all, he pleaded for fairness and justice in dealing with the tribes. The government, in his estimation, had a solemn duty "to properly care for and protect them and leave nothing undone for their advancement, in order that at least the remnant of a people, who, long neglected and much abused, may in time be raised to the honorable and enviable position of citizens of one great Republic." He therefore endorsed the policy of converting nonessential military posts into industrial schools, where Indians could learn the trades supposedly necessary to transform them into civilized members of society. Likewise, he recommended that the Indians be encouraged in agricultural pursuits and their lands protected from avaricious whites by the issuance of titles to individual tribesmen. "With such recognized claims and needful assistance rendered to them under the supervision of honest, capable agents and practical farmers; with liberal appropriations for schools . . . at suitable points throughout their reservations, and more attention given the important matter of education," Grierson predicted that "they would very soon become self-sustaining, and within a reasonable time be prepared to embrace the rights and advantages of citizenship."[32]

While Grierson shared the humanitarian outlook of the Indian reformers of the late nineteenth century, he embraced as well many of the racial stereotypes of his generation. In 1890 the War Department requested the opinions of the nine division and department commanders on an experiment to enlist tribesmen in all-Indian units of the regular army. Grierson was among six ranking officers who opposed the plan. Principally, he objected that the Indian soldiers would be recruited from among the most restless and unruly members of the various tribes; in effect, the proposal offered a reward for bad behavior. But he also argued that certain "well known traits of character" unsuited Indians for military duty; these included "sullenness, indifference, inordinate superstition," and other "savage propensities." Blacks, by contrast, he characterized as cheerful, kind, generous, and obedient; for these reasons, they were peculiarly fitted for the role of common soldier, "they being superior in some respects to the white men now enlisted." Despite these obvious prejudices, Grierson could not pass up an opportunity to call again upon the government to redress wrongs being perpetrated upon Indians and blacks alike. The unsatisfactory condition of Indian affairs, he charged, was due mainly to government mismanagement and the unjust actions of rapacious frontiersmen. Blacks had proved their worth as soldiers, yet "they are still by local restrictions denied many of the privileges afforded to white men notwithstanding the Government has the inherent right and power to fully protect the humblest citizen throughout its entire domain."[33]

Grierson's plea for justice came near the close of a military career spanning three decades and after a quarter-century of intimate association with blacks and Indians on the frontier. Since 1873, he had also waged a dogged campaign for what he saw as justice on his own behalf. Like most officers, he watched with a keen eye the infirmities and advancing ages of those above him on the ladder of rank. When a vacancy seemed imminent, he deluged congressional delegations with letters and copies of his military record. He also sought the endorsements of prominent senior army officers and politicians. General Sherman repeatedly assured Grierson of his high professional and personal regard but would not take sides in recommending officers for promotion. It was with considerable frustration and finally outright anger that Grierson suffered the advancement over his head of Ranald Mackenzie in 1882 and Wesley Merritt in 1887. Fearful of perhaps never achieving brigadier rank through regular channels, he lobbied for passage in Congress of proposals to loosen the protocol of promotion. Even with the support of Miles, Grierson approached retirement as the only colonel commanding a department.[34]

Not until April 5, 1890, did Grierson receive the coveted star of a brigadier general—a rank he scarcely had time to exercise, as he was retired on July 8 at the mandatory age of 64. For a number of years thereafter he divided his residence between his sons' ranch at Fort Davis, Texas, and his home in Jacksonville, Illinois. Alice had died in 1888, and in 1897 Grierson married Lillian Atwood King, a widow. He offered his services during the Spanish-American War, and in 1900 applied for the Medal of Honor for "distinguished and conspicuous gallantry" during his 1863 raid through Mississippi; neither request was approved. By 1908, Grierson exhibited symptoms of senile debility, and his business affairs were placed in the hands of a trustee. He died on August 31, 1911, at his summer home at Omena, Michigan, and the body was returned to Jacksonville for burial. At the age of 85, he had been one of only six surviving major generals of the Civil War.[35]

Grierson retired from the army in the same year that the Census Bureau announced the close of the frontier. His military career had encompassed the entire quarter-century of post–Civil War expansion. A jocular, amiable man when he entered the regular army, he left it saddened and disappointed. Grierson created a number of his own problems; others were symptomatic of difficulties affecting the army and the conduct of Indian affairs. As a non–West Pointer, he was an outsider who had few intimate contacts within the military establishment or in Washington, D.C. As the commander of black troops, he struggled against prejudice and endured isolation at remote frontier posts. Concerned over injustices perpetrated against black and red men, he was a perceptive critic but seldom in a position to influence policy.

Although little appreciated, Grierson's accomplishments were nonetheless significant. Under his command, the Tenth Cavalry carved a proud record and proved the worth of blacks as soldiers. Today, the active military installation at Fort Sill, Oklahoma, and the reconstructed buildings at Forts Concho and Davis in Texas stand as monuments to his skill as a builder. As commander of the District of the Pecos, he ended the Indian threat in West Texas and opened a vast region to settlement. In Arizona and New Mexico he was an effective defender of the rights of Indians against efforts to deprive them of their lands. An unorthodox soldier, Grierson was a competent and reliable subordinate, whose personal misfortune it was to excel at the least glamorous tasks that the army undertook in the country's effort to advance settlement on the frontier.

Notes

1. Grierson's early life and his Civil War service (summarized here) are in Benjamin H. Grierson, "The Lights and Shadows of Life: Including Experiences and Remembrances of the War of the Rebellion," typescript, Benjamin H. Grierson Papers, Illinois State Historical Library, Springfield (a microfilm copy of this collection is in the Southwest Collection, Texas Tech University, Lubbock); and Bruce J. Dinges, "The Making of a Cavalryman: Benjamin H. Grierson and the Civil War along the Mississippi, 1861–1865" (Ph.D. diss., Rice University, 1978). Also see D. Alexander Brown, *Grierson's Raid: A Cavalry Adventure of the Civil War* (Urbana: University of Illinois Press, 1954). For a fictional account of the raid, see Harold Sinclair, *The Horse Soldiers* (New York: Harper, 1956); the novel was made into a 1959 film starring John Wayne. Grierson's domestic life is described in William H. Leckie and Shirley A. Leckie, *Unlikely Warriors: General Benjamin H. Grierson and His Family* (Norman: University of Oklahoma Press, 1984). There is no evidence to support the often repeated story that Grierson was afraid of horses.

2. William T. Sherman to Winfield S. Hancock, January 25, 1867, Benjamin H. Grierson Papers, Newberry Library, Chicago. Correspondence relating to recruitment and organization of the Tenth Cavalry is in Letters Sent, Tenth U.S. Cavalry, Record Group (RG) 98, National Archives (NA). For literature and sources on black soldiers in the West, see William H. Leckie, *The Buffalo Soldiers: A Narrative of the Negro Cavalry in the West* (Norman: University of Oklahoma Press, 1967); Arlen L. Fowler, *The Black Infantry in the West, 1869–1891* (Westport, Conn.: Greenwood Publishing, 1971); and John M. Carroll, ed., *The Black Military Experience in the American West* (New York: Liveright, 1971).

3. Grierson to Chauncey McKeever, July 4, 1868, Letters Received, Department of the Missouri, RG 393, NA.

4. Sherman to Grierson, June 23, 1871, Grierson Papers, Newberry Library. See also W. S. Nye, *Carbine & Lance: The Story of Old Fort Sill,* centennial ed. (Norman: University of Oklahoma Press, 1969), 100–106, 120–22.

5. William B. Hazen to Philip H. Sheridan, March 18, 1869, Box 6, Philip H. Sher-

idan Papers, Library of Congress. In 1867, Grierson had served on the court-martial board that tried Lieutenant Colonel George A. Custer, whom he grew to detest. In 1879 he performed a similar duty in the case of Hazen and Colonel David S. Stanley.

6. Grierson to W. G. Mitchell, February 22, 1870, Letters Received, Department of the Missouri, RG 393, NA. Lee Cutler, "Lawrie Tatum and the Kiowa Agency, 1869–1873," *Arizona and the West* 13 (Autumn 1971): 228–33. Tatum's own account is in Lawrie Tatum, *Our Red Brothers and the Peace Policy of President Ulysses S. Grant* (Philadelphia: John C. Winston, 1899; rpt., Lincoln: University of Nebraska Press, 1970).

7. Grierson to Lawrie Tatum, September 30, 1869, Grierson Papers, Newberry Library; Tatum to Enoch Hoag, October 16, 1869, enclosed in Hoag to Ely Parker, October 18, 1869, Letters Received, Office of Indian Affairs, RG 75, NA (microfilm 234, roll 376).

8. The Brunot-Grierson correspondence is in Grierson Papers, Newberry Library.

9. *Army and Navy Journal,* September 17, 1870.

10. "Indian Depredations in Texas," *House Misc. Docs.,* 41st Cong., 2d sess., no. 142; newspaper clipping enclosed in J. J. Reynolds to E. D. Townsend, May 23, 1870, Letters Received, Department of Texas ("Indian File"), RG 393, NA; John Pope to Townsend, June 17, 1870, ibid. Grierson pointed out that frequently the marauders were whites disguised as Indians: Grierson to Townsend, July 18, 1870, ibid.

11. *Report of the Secretary of Interior, 1871* (Washington, D.C.: Government Printing Office, 1872), 419. Nye, *Carbine & Lance,* 123–47.

12. Grierson to Assistant Adjutant General, Department of the Missouri, September 21, 1871, Letters Received, Department of the Missouri, RG 393, NA; R. G. Carter, *On the Border with Mackenzie* (1935; rpt., New York: Antiquarian Press, 1961), 123–24; Ernest Wallace, *Ranald S. Mackenzie on the Texas Frontier* (Lubbock: West Texas Museum Association, 1964), 41–43.

13. *Report of the Secretary of Interior, 1871,* 419; Pope to J. B. Fry, October 2, 1871, Letters Sent, Department of the Missouri, RG 393, NA.

14. Sheridan to C. C. Augur, May 28, 1872, Box 7, Sheridan Papers; J. Will Myers to [John D.] Myrick, September 26, 1872, Letterpress Book, J. Will Myers Papers, Panhandle-Plains Historical Museum, Canyon, Texas; *Annual Report of the Commissioner of Indian Affairs, 1872* (Washington, D.C.: Government Printing Office, 1872), 41–42, 136–37. In November 1871 the Indian Territory had been transferred from the Department of the Missouri to the Department of Texas.

15. Telegram, Sherman to Grierson, December 30, 1872, Grierson Papers, Illinois State Historical Library; Sherman to Grierson, February 20, 1873, Grierson Papers, Newberry Library; St. Louis *Missouri Republican,* January 30, 31, February 2, 5, 1873.

16. Grierson to Augur, July 11, 1872, Press Copies of Letters Sent, District of the Indian Territory, RG 393, NA; Sheridan to William W. Belknap, November 8, 1874, Box 11, Sheridan Papers. Discipline problems are discussed in Bruce J. Dinges, "Scandal in the Tenth Cavalry: A Fort Sill Case History, 1874," *Arizona and the West* 28 (Summer 1986): 125–40.

17. Grierson is quoted in Augur to Sherman, February 1, 1875, Letters Sent, Department of Texas, RG 393, NA; Grierson to Alice Grierson, June 21, 1875, Fort Davis National Historic Site Papers, Southwest Collection, Texas Tech University, Lubbock.

18. Grierson to Alice Grierson, June 8, 17, 25, 1875, Grierson Papers, Illinois State Historical Library. Telegrams, Grierson to Ulysses S. Grant, April 15, 1875, and Grierson to Belknap, April 15, 1875, Benjamin H. Grierson Appointment, Commission, and Promotion File, G 553 CB 1865, Folder 4, Box 60, RG 94, NA (hereafter Grierson ACP File).

19. Alice Grierson to Grierson, May 27, 1875, Fort Davis National Historic Site Papers. A study of Grierson's military contribution in West Texas is Frank M. Temple, "Colonel Grierson's Texas Command" (master's thesis, Texas Tech University, 1959).

20. Thomas Vincent to Commanding Officer, District of the Pecos, February 11, 1880, Letters Sent, Department of Texas, RG 393, NA; Grierson to Alice Grierson, August 4, 1879, Grierson Papers, Illinois State Historical Library. A copy of Grierson's report on the natural resources of West Texas is in Grierson Papers, Newberry Library. See also Frank M. Temple, "Colonel B. H. Grierson's Administration of the District of the Pecos," West Texas Historical Association Year Book 38 (October 1962): 85–94.

21. Grierson to Assistant Adjutant General, Department of Texas, May 21, 1880, Letters Sent, District of the Pecos, RG 393, NA; Grierson to Alice Grierson, April 17, 1880, Grierson Papers, Newberry Library.

22. Grierson to Assistant Adjutant General, Department of Texas, September 20, 1880, Letters Sent, District of the Pecos, RG 393, NA; Douglas C. McChristian, "Grierson's Fight at Tenaja de las Palmas: An Episode in the Victoria [sic] Campaign," Red River Valley Historical Review 7 (Winter 1982): 45–63; Frank M. Temple, "Colonel B. H. Grierson's Victorio Campaign," West Texas Historical Association Year Book 35 (October 1959): 99–111.

23. Ord to Adjutant General, Military Division of the Missouri, October 1, 1880, in Annual Report of the Secretary of War, 1880, 4 vols. (Washington, D.C.: Government Printing Office, 1880), 1:110–11; General Orders 1, District of the Pecos, February 7, 1881, copy in Grierson Papers, Illinois State Historical Library.

24. Correspondence on the post office fight is in Papers Relative to Removal of Post Office from Fort Concho, RG 393, NA.

25. "Memoirs of William George Wedemeyer . . . 1836–1902," 2 vols., typescript, 2:102–7, California State Historical Society, San Francisco; Susan Miles, "The Soldiers' Riot," Fort Concho Report 13 (Spring 1981): 1–20.

26. Post Returns, Fort Davis, Texas, February 1884, RG 393, NA (microfilm 617, roll 298); Mary L. Williams, "Empire Building at Fort Davis," manuscript, Fort Davis National Historic Site, Texas. Bruce J. Dinges, "Colonel Grierson Invests on the West Texas Frontier," Fort Concho Report 16 (Fall 1984): 1–14.

27. Leckie and Leckie, Unlikely Warriors. Both Charlie and Robert died in mental institutions. Harry and George, considered eccentric by their neighbors, remained on the remnants of the Grierson property in Fort Davis until their deaths in 1934 and 1950, respectively.

28. Douglas C. McChristian, ed., Garrison Tangles in the Friendless Tenth: The Journal of First Lieutenant John Bigelow, Jr., Fort Davis, Texas, (Mattituck, New York: J. M. Carroll, 1985), 27. David S. Stanley to Adjutant General, Division of the Missouri, December 19, 1884, Letters Sent, Department of Texas, RG 393, NA.

29. Grierson to Charlie Grierson, February 21, June 15, 1885, Fort Davis National Historic Site Papers, Southwest Collection, Texas Tech University.

30. Copies of Grierson's annual reports for 1887 and 1888, and "Special Report" regarding removal of intruders from the Jicarilla Reservation, October 1887, are in Grierson Papers, Illinois State Historical Library. See also Veronica E. Velarde Tiller, *The Jicarilla Apache Tribe: A History, 1846–1970* (Lincoln: University of Nebraska Press, 1983), 83–106.

31. Nelson Miles to Grierson, March 14, 1889, Grierson Papers, Newberry Library; Donald Chaput, "Los Angeles and the Department of Arizona," *Southern California Quarterly* 57 (Spring 1975): 19–21.

32. *Annual Report of Colonel B. H. Grierson . . . Commanding Department of Arizona, 1889* (n.p., n.d.), passim. Copy in Grierson Papers, Illinois State Historical Library.

33. Grierson to Adjutant General, March 8, 1890, Letters Sent, Department of Arizona, RG 393, NA.

34. Correspondence relating to Grierson's long struggle for promotion is in Grierson ACP File.

35. Telegram, Grierson to War Department, April 5, 1898; Grierson to Adjutant General, February 23, 1900; Charles Grierson to Adjutant General, November 1, 1911 (all in Box 62, RG 94, NA); Jacksonville, Illinois, *Daily Journal*, September 11, 1911.

Ranald S. Mackenzie

by J'Nell L. Pate

Quiet, reticent men quite frequently exhibit greater abilities of organization, accomplishment, and leadership than do their more flamboyant contemporaries who use every opportunity to call attention to themselves by their outgoing personalities. The successes of the former sometimes reach greater heights, yet often they remain less known and less acclaimed by history. Such was the fate of Ranald Slidell Mackenzie, brevet major general of volunteers during the Civil War, colonel of the Fourth United States Cavalry, 1870–82, and brigadier general in the United States Army at the time of his retirement in 1884.

Mackenzie performed his duties consistently and competently, although he revealed himself to be irascible, irritable, and a high-strung worrier at the same time. A harsh disciplinarian, he tirelessly and unmercifully pushed his men on field campaigns. While Mackenzie's career is not well known in the twentieth century, during his own lifetime he was highly recognized, particularly by citizens on the Texas frontier.[1]

Mackenzie graduated first in his West Point class and was commissioned a second lieutenant June 17, 1862, entering the Corps of Engineers. His record reads like a chronicle of famous Civil War battles: Kelly's Ford, Second Bull Run, Fredericksburg, Chancellorsville, Gettysburg, Wilderness campaign,

Spotsylvania, Todd's Tavern, Petersburg, Opequan, Winchester, Fisher's Hill, Cedar Creek, Five Forks, and the surrender at Appomattox Court House. During these not quite three years of service Mackenzie suffered six wounds—including the loss of two fingers on his right hand that caused the Indians in the West to call him "Bad Hand"—and earned rapid promotions, ending the war as a brevet major general of volunteers and a brevet brigadier general in the regular army. He commanded a cavalry division in the Army of the James attached to General Philip H. Sheridan's army.

Following the war, Mackenzie served in the engineer corps in Portsmouth, New Hampshire, for 14 months as a captain before being promoted to colonel of the newly formed Forty-first Infantry, a black regiment whose command others had refused. When he assumed command of the Fourth United States Cavalry on December 15, 1870, he was the second youngest colonel in the service. Over the next 12 years he distinguished himself and his regiment in Indian campaigning, participating in five successful Indian battles: McClellan's Creek in the Indian Territory, September 29, 1872; Remolina, Mexico, May 18, 1873; Tule Canyon in the Texas Panhandle, September 26, 1874; Palo Duro Canyon, Texas Panhandle, September 28, 1874; and the Dull Knife fight at Willow Creek, Wyoming, November 25, 1876.

Quite possibly of more significance than Mackenzie's successful Indian fights was the peace he maintained without resorting to force, often where others before him had failed. Upon arriving with his 577 black troopers of the Forty-first Infantry on June 27, 1867, at Fort Brown, Texas, Mackenzie faced resentment from unreconstructed Confederates in the nearby community of Brownsville. Despite continuing harassment from the editor of the local paper, the Brownsville *Daily Ranchero,* and "varying degrees of prejudice and hostility [against the black troops] at every post that adjoined a settlement" during the regiment's service on the Texas border, "there is not a single substantiated record of any act of violent reprisal on their part."[2] Mackenzie improved the quality of men joining the Forty-first by having its recruitment station transferred to the North. His troopers performed varied duties, including guarding property after a hurricane, guarding river crossings, maintaining pickets to stop border violations, escorting wagon trains, building roads, guarding lonely stage stations, and such other monotonous jobs as post construction and repair.[3] His Forty-first has been called "one of the crack regiments of the Army" during the years it served on the Texas frontier.[4]

In the fall of 1869 the Forty-first and Thirty-eighth were consolidated to form the Twenty-fourth Infantry under Mackenzie. While he commanded Fort McKavett, Texas, with his infantry, local citizens looked beyond their prejudice to realize that their settlement remained well protected in Mackenzie's hands and began to admit it.[5]

Then, on December 15, 1870, Mackenzie accepted the colonelcy of the Fourth Cavalry, which became the command that brought him lasting fame as an Indian-fighting cavalry officer. He and his men spent most of the next two years at Fort Richardson in northern Texas, 60 miles south of the Indian Territory, engaging in two long and frustrating field expeditions in 1871 and 1872. The latter expedition failed to find the Comanches but did shatter the myth that the Staked Plains were uninhabitable. People had argued for a number of years that the area could not sustain a large body of Indians for any length of time. Mackenzie found the headwaters of the Brazos, the Pease, and the Wichita rivers; his discovery of ample water and game proved that Indians could live there.[6]

Mackenzie fought the first of his major Indian battles on September 29, 1872, at McClellan's Creek in the Indian Territory. He had been ordered to find the nonreservation Kwahadi Comanches. At about four o'clock in the afternoon of September 29, Colonel Mackenzie and his command reached the crest of a wooded hill above McClellan's Creek, some seven miles from its juncture with the north fork of the Red River. Below, Mackenzie saw an Indian village of 262 lodges. His 284 men would face approximately 500 Comanches.

Mackenzie ordered three companies to charge straight toward the camp while a fourth company went after the horse herd. In the 30-minute battle Mackenzie's men completely devastated the village, burning about 100 lodges, killing 24 Comanches, and capturing 124 women and children. Mackenzie lost two troopers, and two others sustained wounds. The soldiers captured nearly 3,000 horses, but on the night after the battle, Indians stampeded the herd and recovered them. Mackenzie sent his prisoners to Fort Concho, Texas, with two companies of the Fourth Cavalry.[7]

Commissioner of Indian Affairs Francis Walker wrote in his annual report that year that the "chastisement" inflicted on the Kwahadi Comanches at McClellan's Creek by Colonel Mackenzie surely must have convinced the tribes that the government meant business. Walker called it the "most successful" expedition yet conducted on the northern and western borders of Texas, around Fort Sill, and in the Indian Territory.[8]

Indian agents and Interior Department officials had persuaded a delegation of prominent Indian chiefs from Fort Sill to travel to Washington, D.C. during the fall of 1872, and they were there when the McClellan's Creek fight occurred. When Commissioner Walker received word by telegraph of the capture of the 124 women and children, he informed the chiefs in the delegation that all who remained outside the reservation would be treated similarly.[9] The particular band that Mackenzie had attacked had never surrendered to reservation life but did so in the fall of 1872 because they lacked supplies and wished to obtain the release of the women and children;[10] in addition, they surrendered several white captives in exchange.[11] Mackenzie had given the army and the Indian Bureau a bargaining tool. As a result, Indian depredations in northern Texas practically ceased during that fall and winter.

Hostile conditions still existed on the southern Texas border along the Rio

Grande River, so in 1873 the army sent Mackenzie and the Fourth Cavalry there to restore order. As General William T. Sherman explained: "In naming the 4th for the Rio Grande the President is doubtless influenced by the fact that Col. MacKenzie [sic] is young and enterprising, and that he will impart to his Regiment his own active character."[12] Mescalero Apaches, Kickapoos, and Lipan Apaches who resided in northern Mexico were crossing the river to raid Texas settlements, then hastening back to their own side of the river, avoiding patrols from Forts Brown, Duncan, Clark, and other scattered posts. In 1872 an average of 5,000 Texas cattle had been stolen monthly.[13]

Mackenzie was stationed at Fort Clark in Kinney County, 125 miles west of San Antonio and only 18 miles north of the Rio Grande. Lieutenant General Philip Sheridan and Secretary of War William W. Belknap traveled to Fort Clark and conferred personally with Mackenzie about the situation, telling him to do whatever was necessary to halt the depredations. [14]

Soon afterward, upon hearing of a raid by a party of Lipans, Mackenzie assembled six companies—approximately 360 men, including 17 officers, 24 Seminole scouts, and 14 civilians. They crossed the Rio Grande near the town of Quemado, Texas, and headed south. The night remained warm, the moon partially hidden in light haze. The column rode rapidly, and Mackenzie soon ordered the men to drop their packs of food because the heavily laden mules could not keep up the pace. To succeed in his plan for a surprise attack, Mackenzie knew he must reach the Indian villages by daybreak.[15]

The column reached Remolina, 40 miles south of the border, about seven o'clock on May 18, 1873, and found Lipan and Kickapoo bands camped in three villages of coarse grass huts about a mile apart. Mackenzie organized the command into platoons. The first platoon delivered its fire, wheeled to the right, and then turned and ran the length of the first village. Each platoon did the same. Some of the guides tried to persuade Mackenzie to send part of his troops around behind the encampment to cut off any Indian escape to the mountains, but he refused to divide his command while on foreign soil so far away from his supply base. He also believed the Kickapoos to be more numerous than they were, even though he apparently knew that he was striking the villages while most of the fighting force remained away on a raid. Mackenzie thus exhibited a bit of his cautious nature that stood him and his men in good stead. Quite likely he would have preferred to attack the Lipans and Mescaleros, but the Kickapoos received the brunt of the attack because their village lay first in the long string of huts.[16]

The sudden charge on the village resulted in a complete victory. After the initial attack, much of the fighting continued on foot. Mackenzie ordered his men to search the three villages thoroughly and then burn them. The men found contracts for cattle at specific prices, proving that the Indians were selling stolen Texas cattle to the Mexicans, who provided a willing market. The colonel and his men took 40 captives, mostly women and old men, and found 19 Indians dead after the battle. One soldier died and two suffered wounds.[17] Mackenzie sent the prisoners, all Kickapoos, to their reservation in the Indian Territory, from which they had been absent for several years.

The successful Remolina raid created an even greater stir than had McClellan's Creek. Early reactions were unfavorable. Two of Mackenzie's officers protested bitterly that he had risked their lives by crossing the border without specific orders to do so—which technically was true, but he had verbal assurance from General Sheridan and the secretary of war that he would be supported in whatever he did to clean up the situation. Angry Mexican officials protested to the United States government that the raid was a violation of the rights of a neutral neighbor. Citizens throughout Texas feared an attack from Mexico in retaliation, and newspapers predicted a conflict.[18] One critic even theorized that President Grant had urged Mackenzie to instigate war with Mexico to draw attention away from the Credit Mobilier scandal and to assure his continuance in power.[19]

Before Mackenzie's raid into Mexico, Commissioners Henry M. Atkinson and Thomas G. Williams had been negotiating return of the Kickapoos to their reservation in the Indian Territory, and the Indians were angered that at the very time they were dealing with U.S. commissioners, officers of the same government attacked them. The commissioners at first requested that the Indian captives be turned over to Mexican authorities as an inducement to the Kickapoos to return to the United States, but the army would not release them, and the commissioners later admitted that Mackenzie's raid helped rather than hurt the removal.[20]

Most army personnel applauded Mackenzie's raid, too, and when favorable results rather than retaliation followed, praise poured in from all sides. On June 2, 1873, the Texas Legislature passed a resolution extending the "grateful thanks of the people of the State" to Mackenzie and his men.[21] The frontier citizens who feared that Mackenzie's action would precipitate war remained in the minority; most south Texans rejoiced that the colonel had dealt the outlaw Indians well-deserved punishment, and one contemporary newswriter recorded that more newspapers praised his action than condemned it.[22]

A full year later officials still commended Mackenzie's raid because they saw the positive results: "Affairs of the Rio Grande line, especially on the Upper Rio Grande, have become almost entirely settled since the handsome chastisement given to the Indians near Santa Rosa, in Mexico by Colonel Mackenzie, Fourth Cavalry."[23] The secretary of war's report mentioned that the Kickapoos had returned to their reservation on December 20, 1873, and that Mexican authorities were cooperating to prevent future Indian raids.

Mackenzie remained in southern Texas during the year following the raid, except for a four-month leave from September to January 1874 because of severe rheumatism problems. His army superiors, however, soon needed him to deal with troubles in the Indian Territory and the Texas Panhandle. Large numbers of Kiowas, Comanches, and Cheyennes began leaving the Fort Sill Reservation in the summer of 1874 for several reasons. Buffalo hunters had invaded their hunting ground, precipitating a fight in June at Adobe Walls in the Texas Panhandle. The Quaker peace policy of the Grant administration had proved unworkable, because the well-intentioned agents frequently could not handle their charges. A lack of sufficient supplies for Indian allotments bred discontent, and railroad construction crews had crossed land in the Indian Territory that had been promised to the tribes by the Medicine Lodge Treaty of 1867.

A large military campaign to round up the truant Indians commenced late in the summer of 1874, involving some 2,000 soldiers under the overall command of General Sheridan. From Fort Leavenworth, Kansas, General John Pope directed troops from the Department of the Missouri and commanded Colonel Nelson A. Miles, Lieutenant Colonel Thomas H. Neill, and Major William R. Price. General Christopher C. Augur commanded the Department of Texas from San Antonio, with direct control over Colonel Mackenzie, Lieutenant Colonel John W. Davidson, and Lieutenant Colonel George T. Buell.[24] The military strategy was to keep the Indians in the south so that they could not join the northern plains tribes.[25] One of the six commands remained near Fort Sill; the other five converged from as many directions to surround the Indians in the Texas Panhandle. Mackenzie's unit was the largest body of troops and engaged the hostiles in the only major military action.

Commanding 13 companies of cavalry and infantry plus 31 Tonkawa scouts, Mackenzie searched the headwaters of the Red River for the runaway Indians. From the time he joined his men in their field camp on September 19, 1874, until he returned to his post in late December, he relentlessly pursued the fugitives.

On September 26, Indians attacked Mackenzie's scouts and later that night engaged his entire command, which was camped near Tule Canyon, without inflicting much damage. They withdrew after a three-hour battle lasting well past midnight. Mackenzie then ordered Sergeant John B. Charlton and two Tonkawa scouts to follow the Indians who had attacked in order to locate their camp. Charlton and the scouts returned late on the evening of September 27. At dusk Mackenzie ordered his command to saddle up; leaving a troop each of cavalry and infantry to guard supply wagons at Tule Canyon, he led 400 troopers due north at a rapid pace. After riding all night, they reached a point overlooking Palo Duro Canyon at daybreak. Stretching three miles down the canyon were the five villages of Kiowas, Cheyennes, Arapahos, and Comanches that his scouts had located the previous day.

The scouts discovered that the only way to descend to the floor of the canyon was by single file on a rocky buffalo trail, so Mackenzie ordered the Tonkawas down to open the fight. They got about two-thirds of the way down the trail before an Indian sentinel spotted them and shouted the alarm; that sentinel became the first to die. An Indian later reported that those first shots failed to arouse most of the Indians because they thought it was only someone out hunting deer.[26] The last of the soldiers reached the bottom of the canyon an hour after the first ones and immediately formed columns and charged. Dim sunlight and rifle smoke in the air made vision difficult. Mackenzie yelled orders from the middle of the fighting, often personally looking out for his men and moving them out of danger.[27]

The Indians held their ground for a time and fought desperately to allow their women, children, and pack animals to escape by hidden retreats known only to them. Soon, however, they fell back to the head of the canyon in the face of steady fire from the soldiers. They retreated in the open along the banks of the Prairie Dog Fork of the Red River. Mackenzie and his men pursued the Indians until sunset, following them through the pass and keeping on their trail a short distance. They turned back because the men had not eaten in 25 hours and the casualties needed attention. Only one soldier died in the fight, but several had sustained severe wounds.

Mackenzie ordered the men to burn everything of value in the five camps before assembling back on the plains above the canyon. There he formed the troops into a large parallelogram around 1,400 captured Indian ponies, and this "living corral" marched over 20 miles to Tule Canyon with the ponies inside.[28] Learning from the experience of having the Indians recapture their horses after the McClellan's Creek fight, Mackenzie ordered the bulk of the Indian ponies shot after letting his scouts select about 350 of the best to keep.

News of Mackenzie's successful battle spread rapidly. Even the *New York Times* picked it up from a Texas paper and carried the story on page one two weeks later.[29] The Indians never recovered from the blow Mackenzie struck on September 28, and began turning themselves in to their reservations a few families at a time. Mackenzie and his men kept after them, harrassing them for 61 days on the trail. In all, the soldiers marched more than 900 miles, fought five engagements, killed nine Indians, took hostiles prisoner, and captured some 1,600 horses—all in the face of the "most adverse weather conditions imaginable," for they sloshed through mud, snow, and sleet much of the time.[30]

Of the entire 1874 Red River War, 25 engagements occurred between Indians and U.S. troops, 20 of these on Texas soil, but Mackenzie had discovered the main camp in the Panhandle and thus precipitated the largest engagement. General Sheridan called the Red River War the "most successful of any Indian campaign in this country since its settlement by the whites" and gave "much credit to the officers and men engaged in it."[31] Following the conclusion of the fall campaign, Sheridan sent Mackenzie back to the Indian Territory in 1875 to guard the Indians on the reservation. The colonel probably rejoiced to be able to remain in one spot for a while, for of 45 months between March 1871 and December 1874, he had spent 18 of them in the field.[32]

From his headquarters at Fort Sill, Mackenzie sent scouts out to persuade stragglers to report to the reservation;[33] the last band, that of Mow-way, finally surrendered in June 1875. The line of settlement on the Texas frontier had not moved any farther west than Fort Griffin and the area around it, but after Mackenzie and the army drove the Indians back to the Indian Territory — and Mackenzie kept them there — the Texas Panhandle was quickly opened to settlement. Many ranches made their appearance; that of Charles Goodnight in Palo Duro Canyon was the first.

In order to keep the Indians on the reservations in the Indian Territory, Mackenzie knew that they needed to be well fed and taught an occupation. With money he received from selling confiscated Indian ponies, Mackenzie purchased 3,500 sheep and 600 head of cattle in New Mexico for the Indians to raise (unfortunately, they did not like mutton and would not adapt to being sheep herders). He also assisted the Indian agent at Fort Sill in procuring needed supplies. The colonel successfully kept 8,500 Indians quiet with only 400 troops for an entire year — a feat never before accomplished at Fort Sill.[34]

Texans wanted Mackenzie back within their borders, particularly on the Rio Grande frontier, and the adjutant general of Texas, William Steele, wrote army headquarters on May 30, 1876, asking for Mackenzie's reassignment. Governor Richard Coke endorsed the letter. General S. B. Maxey in Washington seemed willing, for he wrote: "The troubled condition of the Rio Grande border demands an officer of great prudence and discretion coupled with unflinching courage and firmness. Such we have found in McKenzie[sic]."[35]

The army did not send Mackenzie back to the Rio Grande at that time, however, for he was needed in the Great Sioux War to the north. After the Cheyennes and Sioux destroyed George Armstrong Custer's Seventh Cavalry at the Little Bighorn River on June 25, 1876, Lieutenant General Philip H. Sheridan ordered Mackenzie to Camp Robinson, Nebraska. He arrived in mid-August with six companies of the Fourth Cavalry to form part of Brigadier General George Crook's Powder River expedition. Mackenzie assumed command of 18 companies of the Third, Fourth, and Fifth Cavalry, the Fourth Artillery, and the Ninth and Fourteenth Infantry.[36]

The hostiles had scattered into several different camps. Troops captured the village of Sioux chief American Horse at Slim Buttes, South Dakota, in September. Two Moon of the Cheyennes camped near the Tongue and the Rosebud Rivers. A large village belonging to Dull Knife's Cheyennes moved from the Powder River, and the army had no idea where he had gone. Dull Knife and his Northern Cheyennes had left the Red Cloud Agency in June 1876 when the government attempted to remove them to the Indian Territory.[37]

When Red Cloud, who had taken his camp 23 miles east of the Red Cloud Agency, refused to return, Crook sent Mackenzie after him with six companies of the Fourth Cavalry and two of the Fifth. Mackenzie surrounded the camp on October 23, 1876, and—without firing a shot—forced Red Cloud to return to Camp Robinson. Mackenzie did have to set fire to some of the lodges, however, before the women would pack their belongings and move.[38]

Mackenzie's cavalry formed the advance column of General Crook's winter campaign, commencing November 14, 1876, to round up the remaining hostiles. Crook specifically instructed Mackenzie to locate Dull Knife. The colonel moved his expedition to the Crazy Woman Fork of the Powder River on November 22 and established a camp, where he left his wagons under a strong guard. Then he set out early on November 24, marching 12 miles up the Crazy Woman Fork. His Pawnee scouts under Captain Luther North and Major Frank North discovered an Indian village, presumed to be Dull Knife's. It was almost nightfall when Mackenzie learned of their discovery, and his men were tired from their march. He halted his command to wait for darkness and for the moon to rise. Then he ordered the men out at full moonlight and reached Dull Knife's camp just at daybreak on November 25. At sunrise his men charged into a wide valley where the Indians had been dancing and playing drums all night; they had just retired when the troops attacked. The charge lacked the advantage of complete surprise, for Mackenzie's scouts got mired in the mud and called attention to their presence. The Cheyennes had little time to salvage their property, however, as they hurried to the safety of bluffs and rocks behind the village.

Mackenzie's men destroyed 173 lodges, captured 700 Indian ponies, and killed and wounded about 40 Cheyennes. His losses totaled one officer and six men killed, plus 26 wounded—more casualties than in all his other Indian engagements combined.[39]

When the troopers piled all the Indian belongings in the center of the camp preparatory to burning the village, they discovered many articles that had belonged to Custer's Seventh Cavalry. Some of his men later expressed concern that Mackenzie did not press an advantage with the Cheyennes and follow them farther, but he "lived up to his reputation as a conservor [sic] of manpower."[40] He knew that his exhausted men needed rest. Mackenzie's battle with Dull Knife's band constituted the only real engagement of Crook's Powder River expedition, although the troops remained in the field through most of December.

After the Montana and Wyoming campaigns, Mackenzie returned to Fort Sill in the late spring of 1877, where he again assisted the agent in procuring enough supplies to keep the Indians satisfied and thus prevent them from having an excuse to flee the reservation.

Because the army had left only a skeleton force on the Rio Grande, raiders again became bold. Thus in December 1877—to the great relief of the settlers in southern Texas—Mackenzie was transferred back to the Rio Grande. Close to five years after his Remolino raid, in the late spring of 1878, Mackenzie crossed the Rio Grande again with 11 companies of cavalry. He was compelled to abandon his chase of Kickapoo Indians and Mexican cattle thieves and return to the Rio Grande when his guide became ill and his water supply dwindled. At the river on his return, Mackenzie exchanged verbal challenges with a Mexican force that did not want him to pass. Mackenzie prepared for battle and gave every indication that he would order his men to fire before the Mexican officer gave in and let the Americans cross the river. Mackenzie's presence on the border helped decrease Indian raiding across the river. He was always quick to back his words with action if necessary and actively sought opportunities to encounter Mexican and Indian bandits.

In September 1879 a Ute outbreak at the White River Agency in Colorado resulted in the death of 12 whites and the wounding of 43 others. Mackenzie was transferred to Fort Garland, Colorado, to help counter the rebellious Utes. Texas Congressman C. Upson wrote the secretary of war on October 4, 1879, protesting Mackenzie's removal from the Rio Grande. Upson wanted him back as soon as the Colorado crisis ended, claiming that the peace on the Rio Grande had been assisted "in no little degree, by the presence of that daring officer and his brave troops."[41] General Sherman replied that "Mackenzie can't be everywhere."[42] In fact, Mackenzie had made such an impression in Texas that when the 1877 army appropriation bill failed in Congress, the Texas delegation had agreed to support it provided the colonel and his regiment were ordered back to Fort Clark, Texas.[43]

This time, however, Mackenzie had to deal with the Utes before returning to Texas. In May 1880 he moved 200 miles to the Los Pinos Agency on the Ute reservation near present Ouray, Colorado. His task in September 1881 was to remove 1,458 Utes from their homeland in the more fertile area of southwestern Colorado to a new reservation in Utah. Quite understandably, they did not want to go.

Mackenzie placed his troops on a mesa overlooking the Uncompahgre River, spreading them out so the Utes could witness his strength. He threatened to seize their guns and livestock if they refused to move. His nine companies of cavalry and nine of infantry made an impressive show. Meanwhile, he rushed construction of a telegraph line 80 miles long so he could be in contact with the War Department in Washington. The Utes remained under the Department of the Interior, and a commission composed of prominent citizens had been unsuccessfully attempting to move them to their new reservation. The military possessed no authority until a hostile act occurred, but Mackenzie saw no reason to wait for hostilities to commence if he could prevent them. With the new telegraph, he was able to find out instantly when the Secretary of the Interior relinquished control over the matter to the War Department. Once this occurred, Mackenzie called in 20 of the Ute chiefs and firmly told them that he would see them moved to their new reservation. The only question they had to decide was whether they would go peaceably or be forced. His firmness paid off. He later commented that the Ute removal was his greatest accomplishment, for he had quite possibly averted an Indian war by his decisiveness.[44]

Following Mackenzie's successful conclusion of the Ute question, he was assigned to command the District of New Mexico, headquartered at Santa Fe. His long-anticipated promotion to brigadier general came through on October 26, 1882. Hoping for more leisure time free from campaigning, he brought his mother and spinster sister Harriet out to Santa Fe to live with him. But his health began to trouble him more than usual (he had suffered bouts of rheumatism for years), and when his mother died, he remained depressed for months. He also began to complain to his superiors of apparent slights and seemed to show hints of a persecution complex.[45]

In November 1883, Mackenzie was appointed commander of the Department of Texas with headquarters at San Antonio, and there he met a woman whom he had known before her marriage 14 years earlier. The 32-year-old Mrs. Florida Tunstall Sharpe was a widow with a 12-year-old son. The general and Mrs. Sharpe soon became engaged, and Mackenzie bought a ranch near the town of Boerne for their future home. The wedding never took place, however, for Mackenzie began to exhibit symptoms of deteriorating mental health and suffered a complete collapse in December. Military doctors and his sister Harriet arranged for him to be sent by train to an asylum in New York, his home state. A military commission examined Mackenzie in the spring of 1884 and on March 24 officially retired him at age 43, after 22 years of service.[46] Eventually, he was able to leave the asylum; he lived with his sister and a cousin until his death on January 19, 1889, at age 48. A full military burial followed at West Point.

Quite clearly, this was a sad and untimely end to a brilliant military career. Had Mackenzie remained healthy, he would have been only 58 at the time of the Spanish-American War and no doubt would have played a prominent role, as did William R. Shafter, who had been lieutenant colonel in the Fourth Cavalry under Mackenzie during the Texas campaigns.

Unfortunately, however, his nervous, irritable temperament had marred much of Mackenzie's life. He rarely seemed happy. A wife and family might have put the pressures of a busy career into a different perspective, but as Mackenzie told the commission that ended his military career, the army was his life. The pressures of command placed a severe strain on Mackenzie's nervous system, while others seemed to enjoy and even glory in their position and accomplishments. For example, George Custer and Nelson Miles both welcomed journalists on their campaigns; Mackenzie refused to allow any with him.

Enlisted men serving under Mackenzie did not always like him. While they respected his authority and bragged of being a part of the Fourth Cavalry, they complained of his harsh discipline. Sergeant John B. Charlton, who became quite close to Mackenzie, labeled him "an unappreciative, hard man."[47] What precipitated this remark in Charlton's memoirs was his recalling the incident when the colonel placed him under arrest for failing to come back when Mackenzie called him in the heat of battle during the Palo Duro Canyon fight. Charlton's immediate superior, Lieutenant William Thompson, released him within two hours after the arrest.

On the other hand, officers who served under Mackenzie and later wrote reminiscences had nothing but praise for their former commander. Thompson, who later became a major, wrote that Mackenzie had the ability to impart a high sense of duty to all who served under him, mainly by his own example of discipline and efficiency. "He was a man of very deep and intense feeling, of a high-strung and nervous temperament, and those who did not understand him fully, gave him the credit of bordering upon the martinet; but all who did understand his character, knew him to be a man of such a noble heart and of such courage that it was impossible for him to possess a particle of such a spirit."[48]

Robert G. Carter, whose *On the Border with Mackenzie* remains the most detailed memoir by one of Mackenzie's junior officers, was frank about his irritability but still lavishly praised the man. Most of Mackenzie's superiors— Ulysses S. Grant during the Civil War, William T. Sherman and Philip H. Sheridan during the Civil War and Indian campaigns—knew him by his accomplishments, and all praised him. Sheridan considered Mackenzie his favorite field commander and knew he was "the very man" to deal with Red Cloud and his Sioux in 1876.[49] Grant called him "the most promising young officer in the Army."[50]

One superior officer was an exception, however: Colonel Joseph J. Reynolds, commander of the Department of Texas in 1871. When Mackenzie bypassed regulations in obtaining forage for his animals for a field expedition, because he rightly suspected Reynolds of taking kickbacks from contractors, Reynolds—probably to protect himself against complaints to higher authorities—preferred charges against Mackenzie for a violation of regulations, but the charges were later dropped.[51] The Belknap scandal in 1876 brought Reynolds's activities to light and left Mackenzie's reputation unblemished. The incident revealed his own sensitive pride and devotion to the army, however, as well as furnishing "a glimpse at the vein of self-pity in Mackenzie's personality" that grew more pronounced from that time forward.[52] Newspaper attacks against the army in 1876 upset him, particularly charges against the character of the soldiers at Fort Sill while he commanded the post.

From the distance of nearly a century, historians can reach a better perspective of Mackenzie's place in history. He was one of the first officers to "advocate an offensive war" against the Indian encampments along the edge of the Staked Plains rather than defensive measures to protect the frontier settlements.[53] Add to that the fact that he "whipped the Fourth into the best cavalry regiment in the army'' and one can begin to grasp his value to the Indian-fighting troops.[54]

Some of his contemporary officers gained fame for a single major campaign or notoriety for a huge debacle, yet when one summarizes Mackenzie's entire career—Civil War service, five successful Indian battles, innumerable encounters, and peacekeeping activities—the image of a constant, efficient soldier emerges. Mackenzie was the troubleshooter upon whom the army could depend when hostilities erupted anywhere in the West. They trusted him to handle the situation, whether it involved thieves on the Texas border, renegades from the Indian Territory, northern Sioux and Cheyennes, rebellious Utes, or raiding Apaches. His superiors, and citizens in the areas involved, were always satisfied with his actions. Mackenzie could be counted on to take the offensive and fight. During his relatively short 22-year military career, Mackenzie forged a record that his contemporaries who served twice as long might envy.

Notes

1. Ernest Wallace, ed., *Ranald S. Mackenzie's Official Correspondence Relating to Texas, 1871–1873* (Lubbock: West Texas Museum Association, 1967), vii.

2. Wayne R. Austerman, "Ranald S. Mackenzie and the Early Years on the Border," *Red River Valley Historical Review* 5 (Fall 1980): 79.

3. Ibid., 76, 78, 79. See also Paul W. Carlson, "William R. Shafter: Military Commander in the American West" (Ph.D. diss., Texas Tech University, 1973), 77–78.

4. Arlen L. Fowler, *The Black Infantry in the West, 1869–1891* (Westport, Conn.: Greenwood Publishing, 1971), 18.

5. San Antonio *Daily Herald,* November 26, 1869.

6. Lessing H. Nohl, Jr., "Bad Hand: The Military Career of Ranald Slidell Mackenzie, 1871–1889" (Ph.D. diss., University of New Mexico, 1962), 66.

7. Wallace, *Mackenzie's Official Correspondence, 1871–1873,* 141–45. See also "Record of Engagements with Hostile Indians in Texas, 1868–*1882,*" *West Texas Historical Association Yearbook* 4 (October 1933): 104. Nohl, "Bad Hand," calls this Mackenzie's most significant battle because of its impact on deliberations with the chiefs in Washington.

8. *Annual Report of the Secretary of the Interior for 1872* (Washington, D.C.: Government Printing Office, 1872–73), 396, 481–82.

9. Galveston *Daily News,* October 27, 1872.

10. Lawrie Tatum, *Our Red Brothers and the Peace Policy of President Ulysses S. Grant* (Philadelphia: John C. Winston, 1899), 135.

11. Thomas C. Battey, *The Life and Adventures of a Quaker among the Indians* (Boston: Lee & Shepard, 1891), 83–89, 99.

12. Wallace, *Mackenzie's Official Correspondence, 1871–1873,* 162.

13. Galveston *Daily News,* March 30, 1872.

14. Robert G. Carter, *On the Border with Mackenzie* (Washington, D.C.: Eynon, 1935), 422–23. As General Philip Sheridan forwarded Mackenzie's report of April 22, 1873, he wrote on it: "There is in my opinion only one way left to settle the Mexican frontier difficulty, that is, to cross the Rio Grande and recover our property, and punish the thieves": Wallace, *Mackenzie's Official Correspondence, 1871–1873,* 163.

15. Carter, *On the Border with Mackenzie,* 434–36.

16. Ibid., 447–48. See also Nohl, "Bad Hand," 97; and Arrell Gibson, *The Kickapoos, Lords of the Middle Border* (Norman: University of Oklahoma Press, 1963), 238.

17. Wallace, *Mackenzie's Official Correspondence, 1871–1873,* 170. Also "Department of Texas," *Army and Navy Journal,* June 28, 1873, p. 728.

18. Dallas *Herald,* May 31, 1873; Fort Worth *Democrat,* May 31, 1873; Galveston *Tri-Weekly News,* May 30, 1873.

19. Dallas *Herald,* July 26, 1873.

20. *Annual Report of the Secretary of the Interior for 1873* (Washington, D.C.: Government Printing Office, 1874–75), 539.

21. Wallace, *Mackenzie's Official Correspondence, 1871–1873,* 171–72; Carter, *On the Border With Mackenzie,* 463.

22. San Antonio *Daily Express,* June 3, 1873.

23. *Annual Report of the Secretary of War for 1874* (Washington, D.C.: Government Printing Office, 1874), 58.

24. William H. Leckie, *The Military Conquest of the Southern Plains* (Norman: University of Oklahoma Press, 1963), 83–84.

25. Joe F. Taylor, ed., "The Indian Campaign on the Staked Plains, 1874–75, Military Correspondence from War Department Adjutant General's Office, File 2815–1874," *Panhandle Plains Historical Review* 34 (1960): 40.

26. Wilbur Nye, *Carbine & Lance* (Norman: University Oklahoma Press, 1943), 222. Mumsukawa, a Comanche, furnished a detailed account.

27. Sergeant John B. Charlton, "Battle of Palo Duro Canyon," *Frontier Times* 24 (April 1947): 370. See also Waco *Daily Examiner,* October 16, 1874; and Galveston *Daily News,* October 22, 1874.

28. Carter, *On the Border with Mackenzie,* 493.

29. *New York Times,* October 12, 1874.

30. Adrian Norris Anderson, "Colonel Ranald S. Mackenzie on the Texas Frontier, 1873–1874," (Master's thesis, Texas Technological College, 1963), 111. See also Nohl, "Bad Hand," 140. Nohl called Mackenzie "unimaginative" for not using hardy Indian ponies that could subsist on grass and bark, as Colonel Nelson A. Miles did. Instead, Mackenzie had to rely on the forage of Lieutenant Henry W. Lawton's wagon train, and the army was always short of supplies, although Lawton did a masterful job. Mackenzie's weakened horses remained a problem in the fall of 1874.

31. *Annual Report of the Secretary of War for 1875* (Washington, D.C.: Government Printing Office, 1875), 58.

32. Anderson, "Mackenzie on the Texas Frontier," 120.

33. Fort Sill, I.T. 1874–1877, vol. I, April 23, 27, 1875, pp. 177–80, Fort Sill, Oklahoma.

34. *Annual Report of the Secretary of the Interior for 1875* (Washington, D.C.: Gov-

ernment Printing Office, 1875), 775, 777. See also *Letter on Affairs at Fort Sill, House Exec. Docs.*, 44th Cong., 1st sess., no. 175, p. 4.

35. Ernest Wallace, ed., *Ranald S. Mackenzie's Official Correspondence Relating to Texas, 1873–1879* (Lubbock: West Texas Museum Association, 1968), 199–200.

36. *Annual Report of the Secretary of the Interior for 1876* (Washington, D.C.: Government Printing Offices, 1876–77), 457.

37. George E. Hyde, *Red Cloud's Folk* (Norman: University of Oklahoma Press, 1937), 287.

38. George Bird Grinnell, *Two Great Scouts and Their Pawnee Battalion* (Cleveland, Ohio: Arthur H. Clark, 1928), 253–55.

39. Captain Joseph H. Dorst, "Ranald Slidell Mackenzie," *Journal of the United States Cavalry Association* 10 (December 1897): 377. See also Robert M. Utley, *Frontier Regulars: The United States Army and the Indian, 1866–1890* (New York: Macmillan, 1973), 283–84.

40. Nohl, "Bad Hand," 214. See also Oliver Knight, *Following the Indian Wars* (Norman: University of Oklahoma Press, 1960), 290; and Grinnell, *Two Great Scouts*, 269–73.

41. Wallace, *Mackenzie's Official Correspondence, 1873–1879*, 224.

42. Sherman's comment on letter, October 17, 1879, ibid., 226.

43. Carter, *On the Border with Mackenzie*, 210.

44. Dorst, "Ranald Slidell Mackenzie," 379.

45. Mackenzie to Pope, July 7, 1882, Adjutant General's Office, Letters Received, cited in Nohl, "Bad Hand," 309.

46. Dorst believed that strenuous field service, inflammatory rheumatism, the results of his seven wounds that made field service painful, and the mental strain of command combined with Mackenzie's conscientious and nervous nature to take its toll over the many years: "In seeking the source of the disease that caused his retirement and resulted in his death, the physicians attached much weight to this accident [a head injury received in a fall from a wagon in 1875 that left him incoherent for days] and to the sunstroke received in his childhood" ("Ranald Slidell Mackenzie," 381). Nohl, after examining the actual medical report, said the doctors diagnosed a disease usually called "general paresis" or "general paralysis of the insane"; 30 years later the medical world would know that in a high percentage of cases general paresis originates in syphilitic infections: "As unlikely as it may seem that the straight-laced general contracted syphilis, the evidence strongly suggests that such was the case." At one time or another, Mackenzie exhibited almost all the classic symptoms of general paresis: irritability, restlessness, poor emotional control, dipsomania, delusions of grandeur and persecution, slurred speech. His writing grew more disorganized and practically illegible; later in life he could barely walk ("Bad Hand," 329).

47. John B. Charlton, *Old Sergeant's Story*, ed. Robert G. Carter (New York: Frederick H. Hitchcock, 1926), 110.

48. Major W. A. Thompson, "Scouting with Mackenzie," *Journal of the U.S. Cavalry Association* 10 (December 1897): 433.

49. Paul Andrew Hutton, *Phil Sheridan and His Army* (Lincoln: University of Nebraska Press, 1985), 322, 354.

50. U.S. Grant, *Personal Memoirs*, 2 vols. (New York: Charles L. Webster, 1886),

2:541. Even the Indians apparently became impressed by Mackenzie, for James Mooney in *Seventeenth Annual Report of the Bureau of American Ethnology*, 414, said that for years any Mexican captive with fingers missing was called "Kinzi" (cited in Nohl, "Bad Hand," 121).

51. "Charges and Specifications preferred against Col. Ranald S. Mackenzie," Adjutant General's Office, Letters Received, cited in Nohl, "Bad Hand," 55.

52. Ibid., 158.

53. Anderson, "Mackenzie on the Texas Frontier," 119.

54. Utley, *Frontier Regulars*, 216.

William B. Hazen

by Marvin E. Kroeker

The history of the American frontier is so replete with colorful figures that many of them have been all but forgotten, among them even those who were once widely known. William B. Hazen, Indian fighter, Indian superintendent, post commander, chief signal officer, and controversialist, is one of these.

Hazen's was a complex character. Some contemporaries considered him a courageous crusader; others saw him as a chronic troublemaker. He constantly battled the establishment and was the central personality in several courts-martial and congressional inquiries. Ambrose Bierce, who probably knew him as well as anyone, described him as "aggressive, arrogant, tyrannical, honorable, truthful, courageous—a skillful soldier, a faithful friend and . . . the best hated man I ever knew."[1] These qualities made for a stormy but productive career.

Born on September 27, 1830, in Hartford, Vermont, Hazen was a descendant of Edward Hazen, who settled at Roly, Massachusetts, in 1649. In 1834 his parents, Stillman and Ferona Hazen, moved their family to a farm between Garrettsville and Hiram, Ohio. Here, in a rural religious environment, Hazen grew to manhood. Here also he formed a mutually beneficial friendship with a young man destined to become Hiram's most famous son, James A. Garfield.

Like a number of his eighteenth-century Hazen forebears, young Bill chose a military career. His efforts to enter West Point were unsuccessful at first; however, a few months before his twenty-first birthday he was named to replace a nominee who had failed the entrance examination. Although his academic record was not outstanding, he left West Point a totally committed militarist.[2]

Second Lieutenant Hazen's first assignment after graduation in 1855 was to a Fourth Infantry unit garrisoned at Fort Lane, Oregon. This southern Oregon post was situated in a region seething with Indian-white unrest and violence. The heart of the problem was that too many whites were harassing Indians who were unwilling to forsake their ancestral lands for the convenience of foreign intruders. And, too often, greed prevailed over ethics. The result was a protracted period of conflict called the Rogue River Wars, lasting from 1850 to 1856.

The army's role was to protect the whites—although, officially, friendly Indians were also to be protected. Indeed, peaceful Indians were often in more danger than peaceful whites. Hazen would find that same situation elsewhere in subsequent years, and it always bothered him. The editor of the *Oregonian* apparently reflected the views of the general populace when he declared that there was not one friendly Indian in the country. "These inhuman butchers and bloody fiends must be met and conquered, vanquished—yes, EXTERMINATED."[3]

As the general warfare intensified, Joel Palmer, superintendent of Indian affairs, decided to adopt measures that would prevent Indian extermination. He arranged to relocate Indians on the newly created Grand Ronde Reservation on the Oregon coast. Lieutenant Hazen helped implement this early experiment with the closed reservation system in the West. He headed the military escort that accompanied the first contingent of Indians to Grand Ronde and then for 13 months commanded the troops posted there to police the reservation. He laid out a site for a post, later called Fort Yamhill, and built a blockhouse. Here also he first witnessed the incompetence and frustrations of Indian Bureau officials and the demoralizing impact of reservation life on Indians.[4]

Participation in the Rogue River Indian Wars, even in a minor role, and the more important assignment at Grand Ronde (which won the young lieutenant a commendation from General John E. Wool, Commander of the Department of the Pacific) proved valuable experience and good preparation for similar service later.[5]

In the spring of 1857, Hazen was transferred to the Eighth Infantry, then actively engaged in the military effort to subjugate the Indians on the Texas frontier. The southern plains tribes were challenging the advance of the whites with unprecedented intensity as they saw their hunting lands appropriated, their game growing scarce, and a steady stream of settlers and soldiers threatening to oust them from the country. Surely in such a vast expanse there should have been space for both Indians and whites, but neither one would make room for the other.

When Hazen arrived at Fort Davis, Texas, in February 1858, Indian raiding activity was reaching a peak. General David E. Twiggs, Commander of the military Department of Texas, decided on a more aggressive policy. Beginning in the spring of 1858, he ordered the troops at the frontier posts to engage in active campaigns of pursuit and punishment until all the Indians were thrashed into submission. "As long as there are wild Indians on the prairie," he stated, "Texas can not be free from depredations." This military strategy was followed until November 1859, at which time the frustrated general declared it to be a failure and ordered the troops to go back to a "defensive system."[6]

During the time of the chase-and-destroy policy, Hazen personally commanded four separate expeditions against Indian raiding parties. The first was an arduous 450-mile march along the edge of the arid Pecos Plains in pursuit of a party of Mescalero Apaches who had attacked a mail train near Fort Davis. On June 10, 1858, Hazen's detachment located their sizable encampment in the Guadalupe Mountains and in a surprise attack destroyed their lodges, camp equipment, and a large supply of food. The Indians fled without inflicting any casualties, but while the troops were returning to Fort Davis, two soldiers were shot dead in the darkness of night by nervous recruits who mistook them for Apaches. In his official report, Hazen grumbled, "I never saw so worthless a set of men thrown together in my life." Fighting Indians, he decided, was safer than traveling with green soldiers. (His report also contained some pertinent observations about the discouraging agricultural potential of the western plains—a subject he would continue to study and write about extensively in later years.) For his successful expedition against the Apaches, Hazen was cited in General Orders.[7]

In May 1859, a detachment from Fort Inge under the command of Hazen defeated a small Kickapoo raiding party on the West Fork of the Nueces. Four Indians were killed in a brief fight, and none escaped without serious injury. For this "highly creditable" performance Hazen was again cited in General Orders, and "for gallant conduct in two engagements with Indians in Texas" he was breveted a first lieutenant.[8] This was the first brevet awarded an officer since the Second Seminole War for service against Indians.

In the fall of 1859, Hazen had two encounters with Comanches who were harassing settlers in the Uvalde area. On the first occasion he recovered a large herd of stolen horses but was unable to administer any significant physical damage on the fleet raiders. The second clash, occurring on the headwaters of the Llano, was in retaliation for the killing of two settlers near Fort Inge. Commanding a force of 39 volunteers and regulars, Hazen engaged a well-armed and disciplined party of eight warriors, killing all but one; however, he and three volunteers were wounded in the fierce close-range combat. With bullet wounds in his hand and side, 85 miles from the nearest fort, Hazen's life was in peril. After some confusion and delay in the rescue operation, the stricken officer was finally transported to San Antonio for extended hospitalization.[9]

Hazen's scouting skill and dashing courage against the redoubtable Comanches caught the attention of his superiors. Colonel Robert E. Lee, department commander, Lieutenant Colonel Joseph E. Johnston, department inspector, and the army headquarters all accorded him official recognition. In a unique gesture, the citizens of San Antonio presented him a sword and a resolution expressing their "high esteem and admiration" for protecting "our Western frontier from the ravages of hostile Indians."[10]

The near-fatal wound terminated Lieutenant Hazen's brief but action-packed career in Texas. On January 28, 1860, he began a year's leave of absence to recuperate. The lingering effects of his wounds were to cause him frequent misery, and the Comanche bullet that he carried in his body ultimately contributed to his death.

When the Civil War broke out, First Lieutenant Hazen (promoted April 1861) was an instructor of infantry tactics at West Point; five months later, however, he was appointed colonel in command of the Forty-First Ohio Volunteer Regiment. He first saw action at Shiloh, where his performance (typically) evoked considerable controversy and acrimonious debate, particularly after the war. He then fought at Stones River, where he gained national acclaim for his valiant stand at Round Forest and where the oldest Civil War monument is dedicated to "Hazen's Brigade." He also led troops at Chickamauga, Missionary Ridge, Pickett's Mill, and Fort McAllister.[11]

At Missionary Ridge, Hazen's men suffered heavy losses as they swarmed up the hill to seize a Confederate artillery battery. Afterward, Hazen and General Philip H. Sheridan clashed head on over the question of who got to the crest of the ridge first, and the animosity continued throughout their careers.[12]

The official record of Hazen's Civil War career abundantly reveals intelligence, initiative, and courage. He rose from the position of brigade commander to divisional commander in the Army of the Tennessee, and at war's end was commander of the Fifteenth Corps. A spit-and-polish disciplinarian, he rigorously enforced military rules and regulations. According to Colonel G. C. Kniffen, he was a cold, capable leader whom his men hated but admired. An aide to General William T. Sherman described him as a resolute, self-assured, and brave commander.[13] As he advanced in rank from lieutenant to major general of volunteers, Hazen developed a tendency to find fault even with superiors; an egotistical and outspoken perfectionist, he became greatly irritated if military matters—however minor—were not carried out efficiently and "by the book." When he saw—or presumed to see—such faults, he unhesitatingly pointed the finger. This trait, combined with a stubborn adherence to personal convictions, held significant implications for his postwar career in the West.

In 1866, Hazen, then a colonel in the reorganized regular army, returned to the West as acting assistant inspector general of the Department of the Platte. An initial assignment was to assess the growing restiveness of the Indians residing in the Powder River region of the northern plains, and coincidentally to evaluate the capabilities of the troops posted in the area. His inspection took him from Fort Laramie up the Bozeman Trail to Forts Reno, Phil Kearny, and C. F. Smith. He then treked 185 tortuous miles northwestward to Camp Cooke on the upper Missouri River before proceeding down through the gold regions of Virginia City, Montana, and into Utah to Salt Lake City.

The October 16, 1866, report of his expedition, along with the maps drawn by his companion and former Civil War aide Ambrose Bierce, not only provided valuable details on the military situation but also assessed the economic potential of this vast plains region. Hazen's report strongly urged the government—then evaluating its Indian policy—to adopt a reservation system for the plains tribes. Ever since his grim encounters with the Red Raiders in Texas, Hazen had believed the plains Indians to be irredeemably savage; what he saw and heard from soldiers and travelers along the Bozeman Trail seemed only to reinforce this stereotyped image. He denounced the Indian of the plains as "a dirty beggar and thief, who murders the weak and unprotected . . . keeps no promises, and makes them only the more easy to carry on his murder and pillage." Allot each tribe its reservation, he advised; give them food and clothing; and then make "vigorous, unceasing war on all that do not obey and remain upon their grounds." The troops, he cautioned, should be commanded by officers who knew how to fight Indians. Civil War experience alone would be of little use in combatting fleet, mounted bands of guerrilla warriors. If adopted, Hazen believed, the reservation system would in a few years solve the Indian problem. "When once thoroughly whipped there will afterwards be no trouble . . . we would only have him on our hands as a peaceable pauper, in place of a thieving, murdering one, and at half the cost."[14]

His attitude toward the lands occupied by the Indians was also negative. He characterized the region west of the hundredth meridian as almost totally devoid of agricultural potential. "Of this entire country one-half may be considered of no value," while the other half was grazing land that could support only "a scanty pastoral population." These barren lands would never be of much use, Hazen declared, and "no amount of railroads, schemes of colonization or government encouragement can ever make more of it." He deplored misleading information being published about the high plains, stating that "every one interested in this country systematically deceives everybody else with regard to it."[15] His outspokenness on this subject became his hallmark.

Hazen's inspection report of 1866 became a part of the official record studied by government officials responsible for the formulation of Indian policy. Military men and humanitarians alike seemed agreed that the Indians' nomadic way of life should end and that they be required to conform to the "superior culture'' of the white majority. Confining Indians to restricted reserves would not only bring peace to the West, many believed, but also foster Christian civilization among the ''red heathen.'' These views became the basis for developing a reservation policy for the plains Indians.

In October 1867 and April 1868, a peace commission negotiated with western tribal leaders at both Medicine Lodge, Kansas, and Fort Laramie for the assignment of fixed, limited reservations. By the terms of the resulting Medicine Lodge Treaties, the Kiowas, Comanches, Kiowa-Apaches, Cheyennes, and Arapahos agreed to accept reservations in western Indian Territory. The Indians pledged peace with the United States, and the government promised to provide the means necessary to acculturate the natives.[16]

Implementation of the treaty terms became the joint effort of the Bureau of Indian Affairs and the army. Lieutenant General William Sherman, commander of the Division of the Missouri, was authorized to appoint a special military commander to administer affairs within the Indian Territory. Sherman selected Hazen, whose views on Indians coincided with his own, to head this command, designated as the Southern Indian Military District.[17] At the time of his appointment Hazen was colonel of the Thirty-Eighth Infantry, a black regiment that he had commanded since March 1867.

By September 1868, when Hazen assumed his new duties, Sherman and Major General Philip H. Sheridan had decided on a punitive winter campaign to drive the recalcitrant Cheyenne and Arapaho bands to their reservation. Indian Bureau officials demanded assurances that the Kiowas and Comanches, who had been peaceful since Medicine Lodge, would be protected. Sherman agreed that the friendly tribes should be spared from the war.

Hazen's first assignment was to segregate the peaceful tribes from those declared hostile. Fort Cobb, near the confluence of Cobb Creek and the Washita River, was chosen as the site for Hazen's headquarters and the rendezvous for the peaceful Indians. The task of contacting the many scattered Kiowa and Comanche bands in Kansas and the Indian Territory and persuading them to make camp near Fort Cobb was extremely difficult, but by November 20, 1868, many of the principal chiefs had brought in their bands.[18]

Hazen's task at Fort Cobb was formidable. The thousands of Indians surrounding the fort looked to him for subsistence and direction. No Indian Bureau agents were present to carry out the treaty provisions; Agent Edward Wynkoop resigned because he feared he was being used by the military as ''a decoy to lure Indians into a trap.'' In addition to Kiowas and Comanches as his charges, Hazen had bands of many other local tribes on his hands. Some Indians, not surprisingly, did not trust him because he was an arm of the hated military establishment. Only by a skillful balancing of tactful diplomacy and forceful threats was he able to prevent serious trouble from erupting.[19]

A serious dilemma confronted Hazen when Black Kettle and Big Mouth, representing Cheyenne and Arapaho bands, arrived at his headquarters on November 20, 1868, seeking protection from Sheridan's army. Black Kettle, a survivor of the 1864 Sand Creek Massacre, was a peace chief committed to settling on the reservation as agreed to at Medicine Lodge. He stated that he wanted peace but that he was speaking only for his band, not for the people north of the Arkansas who were at war. The problem was that the Cheyenne and Arapaho tribes were beyond Hazen's authority, since the army had declared war on them. He advised Black Kettle to return to his camps on the upper Washita, contact Sheridan in that area, and surrender to him. If peace were made from that quarter, then Hazen said he would provide for them at Fort Cobb. Disappointed, the old chief headed back for his encampment in western Indian Territory.

Hazen had "followed the book," but he seemed uneasy about it. In his lengthy report of November 22 he informed Sherman of Black Kettle's offer to surrender his band at Fort Cobb and suggested that Sheridan should make peace with the "distinct bands" of Black Kettle and Big Mouth because they seemed sincerely serious of peacefully settling down. Although he believed he had dealt with the chiefs according to military policy, he asked Sherman to give him "definite instructions in this and like cases."[20]

One day after he got back to his camp, Black Kettle and many of his band were slaughtered by Lieutenant Colonel George A. Custer's troops on the Washita River. The chief's death led to a new wave of criticism against the military handling of the Indians. Indian Bureau officials, former agent Wynkoop, and others decried a policy that led to the killing of a prominent chief who, they claimed, had been earnestly striving for peace. Sheridan retorted that Black Kettle was nothing but "a worn out and worthless old cipher." Sherman sought to defend the army's role by asserting that Black Kettle's camp was not friendly and that Custer was not like John Chivington, the perpetrator of the Sand Creek Massacre.[21]

Hazen also jumped to the defense of the army. In a letter to Sherman dated December 31, 1868, he stated that he wished to refute the reports "that Black Kettle's camp, destroyed by Custer, were peaceable Indians on their way to their reservation. In his talk with me . . . Black Kettle stated . . . that their people did not want peace with the people above the Arkansas." This was not only a distortion of Black Kettle's speech but a direct contradiction of Hazen's official report of November 22. Since Hazen had a reputation for preparing official reports with meticulous care, it would appear that the purpose of this letter was to close ranks behind General Sherman, whom he admired. And in defense of his own actions, he insisted to James Garfield, chairman of the House Military Affairs Committee, that he had not misled the chief into a false sense of security but had specifically told him that troops were approaching the Washita and that "they were liable to attack him at any time."[22]

On December 16, when Hazen learned that Sheridan and Custer were moving troops down the Washita, he was immediately concerned for the safety of the Kiowa and Comanche camps situated along the river valley. Fearing that Sheridan might attack the Indians resting under his promise of security, Hazen dispatched runners with a letter to the general stating that "all camps this side of the point reported to have been reached are friendly, and have not been on the warpath this season."[23] Sheridan and Custer were obviously incensed by the message. An all-out attack on a Kiowa village was to have commenced that day. Custer claimed that Kiowas had been engaged in the Battle of the Washita and therefore did not deserve protection. In his reports and later accounts he bluntly charged that Hazen had been "completely deceived" and "misled" by the Indians and had seriously erred in preventing the planned attack. Sheridan regretted losing an opportunity to fight Indians but did not feel he could ignore a letter from Sherman's special agent. Nevertheless, he believed that labeling the Kiowas "friendly" was ridiculous and subsequently charged that if Hazen had not interfered, "the Indian problem on the Texas frontier" would have been solved at that time.[24]

The fact is that Hazen's decisive action averted an uncalled-for confrontation that would have resulted in the slaughter of innocent Indians who had put their trust in officials assigned to "lead them on the road to civilization." If Sheridan had carried out his planned attack, he would have been vulnerable to many of the charges leveled against Chivington at Sand Creek. The reputation of the army, already tarnished, would have suffered even more. Hazen later defended his actions in a thoroughly documented response to Custer's memoirs. His pamphlet, *Some Corrections of "My Life on the Plains"* (1875), showed that, contrary to Custer's assertions, the Kiowas as a tribe had lived up to their agreements of 1867 and had not participated in the Washita battle. On the night of November 26, the chiefs Custer assumed had joined in that clash were sleeping at Fort Cobb; they did not leave for their camps on the Washita until midmorning of the following day, several hours after the battle. Any failure to protect these Indians would clearly have violated the agreement made with them by the military and the directives given Hazen by General Sherman. Hazen declared that the official records revealed the false imputations and "mischievous errors" propagated by Custer and Sheridan.[25]

By the spring of 1869 most of the southern plains tribes were located on their reservations. When Fort Sill was established as a permanent military post, Hazen moved his agency headquarters to the same site. In administering reservation affairs, Hazen tried to deal firmly but justly with his wards. He even invited the United States Indian Commission, a private organization of humanitarians, to investigate reservation conditions; when Vincent Colyer arrived to do so, Hazen conveyed his frustrations over the Indian Bureau's inability to properly manage the new system.

Hazen's services as commander of the Southern Military District were concluded on June 30, 1869. By that time Quaker agents were on hand to expand the work he had begun. His judicious administration at Fort Cobb and Fort Sill, his courage and firmness in the face of danger, and his farsighted plans for the bands under his jurisdiction won him the praise of military superiors and Indian Bureau officials, and even some words of approbation from Indians. Although he would have preferred to see the army take over Indian affairs, he was confident that the appointment of Quakers would be a definite improvement over the previous system, which he called a "burlesque upon the government and a swindle upon the Indian." Conquered, demoralized, and destitute, these tribesmen could use a "wholesome example of Christian morality" to set them on the white man's road.[26]

In 1869, Hazen was appointed colonel of the Sixth Infantry and commanded this regiment for the rest of his western career, serving at Fort Gibson, Indian Territory; Fort Hays, Kansas; Fort Buford, Dakota; and Fort White River, Colorado. While at Fort Gibson he served in a dual capacity as commander of the post and as Indian superintendent for the Southern Superintendency (an agency formed to implement treaty obligations). As a member of the Hazen-Field Commission he tried to get a substantial monetary settlement of $1.8 million for the loyal Creeks based on a provision in their 1866 Reconstruction Treaty. Thanks to a loophole in the treaty, the government determined that it needed to pay only $100,000. Hazen agreed with the Creeks that they deserved the full amount, but there was nothing he could do about it.[27] He was more successful in getting lands set aside for the Wichitas, who had been lost in the bureaucratic shuffle when reservation boundaries were drawn in the Indian Territory. He also tried to persuade the Interior Department not to award land grants to railroads building through eastern Indian Territory that would lead to the disintegration of the land base of the Five Civilized Tribes. According to Ely S. Parker, the Seneca commissioner of Indian affairs, Hazen's insightful views "materially guided" the bureau's policy toward Indians in the Southwest.[28]

In the latter months of 1870, Colonel Hazen served as an observer of the Franco-Prussian War. He visited battle fronts and interviewed Count Otto von Bismarck and Field Marshal Helmuth von Moltke. Two years later he published *The School and the Army in Germany and France,* in which he made a number of comparisons between the German and American armies that provoked the wrath of his colleagues. He criticized the American staff departments, condemned political favoritism, and damned the "indolence, ignorance, and shiftlessness" of American officers.[29] Yet the *Army and Navy Journal* carried extensive excerpts from the work and praised the author for "the moral courage to speak his whole mind without regard to personal consequences."[30]

Meanwhile, in 1871, Hazen married Mildred McLean, the 21-year-old daughter of Washington McLean, owner of the Cincinnati *Enquirer*. Not only did the prominent McLean family have considerable influence in the Democratic Party; Mildred's brother John married the daughter of Edward Fitzgerald Beale and became the owner of the Washington *Post*. "Millie" accompanied her 41-year-old husband to Fort Gibson, where accommodations for even a society girl were quite comfortable. When the Sixth Infantry moved to Fort Hays in late 1871, she found conditions more primitive but still bearable.

Early in 1872, Hazen once again became involved in a controversy that had far-reaching consequences. While posted at Fort Sill in 1869, he had begun to sniff out irregularities in the post tradership operations and, to his dismay, discovered evidence of kickbacks paid by traders to get post monopolies. Even more shocking, the evidence pointed directly at Secretary of War William W. Belknap. He knew that to get involved would jeopardize his career, but his strong convictions would not permit him to remain silent.

In February 1872, therefore, he mailed his friend Garfield the damaging evidence, including an excerpt from a contract between John S. Evans, the Fort Sill trader, and C. P. Marsh, a close friend of Belknap, which required Evans to pay $12,000 annually for the exclusive privilege of trading on the military post. It further stated that Evans was to pay Marsh "so long as William W. Belknap is Secretary of War."[31] Outraged, Garfield conferred with John Coburn, then chairman of the House Military Affairs Committee, and informed Hazen: "Coburn and I have today agreed that we will double teams, on the subject; and if we can get solid ground to stand on, will drive a six horse team through the whole establishment."[32]

In March 1872, Hazen testified publicly before Coburn's committee on army-staff matters, with the understanding that the post trader abuses would be raised "incidentally" during his testimony. He was led to believe that this procedure would make it a committee matter and protect him from charges that "he was out to get the Secretary of War." During the hearing, Hazen presented sufficient evidence to indicate that the system administered by the secretary offered abundant opportunity for graft, but strangely, Coburn raised no questions that sought to establish Belknap's involvement in the contractual arrangement at Fort Sill. Apparently something had occurred to cause Coburn and Garfield to rein in their "six horse team."[33]

Immediately after Hazen's appearance before the committee, Belknap drafted a departmental order that he hoped would mollify and disarm his critics. The directive prohibited licensed traders from "farming out" (leasing) their operations to a second party. The wording of the order showed Belknap to be both devious and shrewd, as it in no way affected Marsh's lucrative arrangement or—as was later revealed—his own substantial share of the kickbacks. The Fort Sill tradership was not being "farmed out"; Evans held the license but was being forced to pay bribes to Marsh to keep it from being awarded to someone else, and Marsh was sharing the bribe money with Belknap. Yet Garfield and Coburn declared the departmental order "a complete remedy of the evils complained of." Thus the heat was temporarily off the corrupt official.[34]

Hazen, however, soon felt the wrath of the secretary of war: learning who was responsible for stirring up the commotion, Belknap reportedly vowed to "send him to Hell." Instead, he was sent to Fort Buford—a remote "Siberia" in Dakota Territory—apparently as revenge for his criticism, though Belknap denied that he had anything to do with Hazen's transfer.[35]

It is not clear why Garfield and Coburn did not investigate the tradership corruption more thoroughly and pursue their obvious suspicions of Belknap's involvement. In 1876, when the House of Representatives finally presented impeachment charges against Belknap, there were accusations by the press that both men had contributed to a cover-up of the secretary's wrongdoing. In letters issued simultaneously to selected newspapers, clearly indicating collaboration on their part, Coburn and Garfield categorically denied the charges. Coburn stated, "I never heard of or saw any accusation against the Secretary of War. . . . General Hazen never intimated in the remotest degree that Belknap was guilty of a corrupt disposition." Garfield admitted that Hazen had disclosed to him the terms of a contract between Marsh and Evans and that he was "willing to testify on the subject," but he said that nothing "in the testimony" of Hazen "indicated or suggested any corruption on the part of the Secretary of War"; the "attempt to make it appear that I did not do my whole duty is absurd."[36]

Both letters are marked by falsehood and dissimulation. Garfield's version must have particularly hurt Hazen, but recognizing the political implications for his friend, he apparently decided not to press the issue. Besides, it became clear during the impeachment trial that Belknap, who had resigned his position, held Hazen primarily responsible for his downfall, thereby highlighting the colonel's courageous stand in behalf of honesty in the conduct of military affairs. Unfortunately for the cause of justice, however, the Grant administration refused to file criminal charges against Belknap.[37]

When Hazen learned in May 1872 that the Sixth Infantry would be transferred to Fort Buford, he was extremely distraught. He considered it a "banishment" and realized that the isolation would be particularly hard on his young wife. He complained to Garfield that they would be "six months without mails" and "generally out of the world." Moreover, he was experiencing pain and partial paralysis from the wounds he had received in Texas and feared that the extreme cold of the north would further aggravate the problem.[38]

The grim hardships of frontier army life struck Mildred and William Hazen with full force: shortly after their arrival at Fort Buford, their infant child died. In addition, Hazen's own physical condition worsened, yet despite the recommendations of four medical doctors, his application for leave was stymied by his superior, General Sheridan. The division commander finally relented but noted for the record: ''The disability which Colonel Hazen now has seems to have come on him about the time his regiment was ordered to . . . Dakota . . . and I find it impossible to remove from my mind the impression that this . . . is the foundation of his present disability.''[39] The implication was doubly rankling to Hazen because he believed that Sheridan had collaborated with Belknap in sending him to Dakota in the first place. It strengthened his opinion that Sheridan was ''a selfish, weak unscrupulous man . . . without a particle of administrative capacity.''[40]

While detachments of the Sixth Infantry engaged in escort duty for railroad surveying parties, chased Indians, and policed reservations, Hazen got involved in another fight, this time in the newspapers and magazines. The controversy was over whether the high plains could support any agriculture except grazing. Hazen contended that accounts of the fertility and abundance of the region were deceptively designed to help the railroads sell land, fleece immigrants, and bilk bond buyers. Financier Jay Cooke, in an effort to promote settlement of the Northern Pacific Railroad lands, advertised the northern plains as a ''Fruitful Garden'' and maintained that thanks to an ''aerial Gulf Stream'' the winters were generally mild. Hazen, in a long letter to the New York *Tribune* in February 1874, refuted these claims; he declared that most of the land was arid ''and will not, in our day and generation, sell for one penny an acre, except through fraud and ignorance.'' His pessimistic evaluation stirred up a literary war as western editors, railroad owners, land agents, and other interests sought to counter the charge.[41]

George A. Custer joined in the rebuttal with a lengthy article in the Minneapolis *Tribune,* criticizing his fellow officer's ''misrepresentations,'' ''distortions,'' and ''ignorance'' of the facts. Custer's impressions of the country stemmed from his experience as a member of the Northern Pacific's surveying party in 1873 and of the Black Hills expedition in 1874. His observations were clearly intended to reinforce the representations made by the railroad promoters.[42]

In the early 1870s there was still surprisingly little accurate information on the potential of the Great Plains. Since Hazen's service had taken him into every plains state or territory between the Rio Grande and Canada, he had the credentials to speak with some authority on western lands. Indeed, he developed a keen scholarly interest in the subject. In January 1875, his article ''The Great Middle Region of the United States, and Its Limited Space of Arable Land,'' published in the *North American Review,* provided a scientific description of the region, including extensive meteorological data that formed the basis for his belief that the lands beyond the hundredth meridian were generally incapable of agricultural production. After this article appeared, and when provoked by critics who questioned his motives and veracity, Hazen published *Our Barren Lands,* a strident rebuttal in defense of his views and reputation.[43]

Some historians have suggested that Hazen's writings were motivated by vindictiveness due to his "exile" rather than by a spirit of public concern. The evidence does not sustain that interpretation. His views had evolved over a long period of time, study, and personal experience. Although overly pessimistic about the future of the high plains—he did not foresee dry-farming techniques and extensive irrigation projects—his works provided an informed and comprehensive treatise on the western lands that was more widely read at the time than the reports by John Wesley Powell and other government surveyors and explorers. His words of warning in part prevented blind emigration to the inhospitable limits of the arid lands, at the same time directing attention to the more valuable portions of the West.

In 1877, Colonel Hazen got a welcome reprieve from Fort Buford when he was named attaché to the American legation in Vienna, Austria. The primary purpose of the assignment was to secure a military observer of the Russo-Turkish War. The only person happier about the nomination than Hazen was his wife, who had found the social life at Fort Buford too limited for her tastes. She and their new young son accompanied him to Europe. The fact that the minister to Austria-Hungary was Edward F. Beale, father-in-law of John McLean, probably helped Hazen get the appointment. Mildred Hazen enjoyed the pleasures of the rich, and in Europe the Hazens mingled freely with the social elite. She became a convert to Catholicism while in Vienna—at least partly to be able to attend church with the Austrian upper classes.[44]

Five months after his return from Austria, Hazen became entangled in a bizarre, irregular court-martial instigated by Colonel David S. Stanley. A pawn of the vindictive Belknap, Stanley accused Hazen of cowardice during the Civil War at Shiloh, imposture at Stones River, falsifying reports on Missionary Ridge, and committing perjury in the Belknap trial. Hazen retaliated by accusing Stanley of libel, and a double court-martial was ordered by General Sherman, beginning in April 1879. Stanley was found guilty of unbecoming conduct and reprimanded. A mass of testimony offered by Hazen's counsel was arbitrarily ruled out during the Stanley trial, the court stating that such testimony might properly be introduced during Hazen's trial. But the court then ruled that he could not be tried, since the statute of limitations was already exceeded. Only partially vindicated, Hazen was furious at Sherman because he had deliberately ignored the statute of limitations in ordering him to be arraigned in the first place.[45] Convinced that he had been unable to defend his record effectively in court, Hazen wrote *A Narrative of Military Service* (1885), a lengthy documented book detailing his Civil War career.

Although he decried political favoritism, when James Garfield was elected president in 1880, Hazen requested an appointment as brigadier general and chief signal officer. Respecting his fellow Ohioan's abilities, the President-elect informed President Rutherford Hayes that he wanted Hazen promoted and nominated to fill the vacant position. Hayes complied, although, according to his diary, it was against the "wish" of General Sherman.[46] Thus, in December 1880, after two decades of service on the frontier, Hazen left the Great Plains for his new post in Washington, D.C.

Hazen's tenure in the Signal Service was turbulent from beginning to end. Highly placed enemies in military and political circles, stunned by his promotion, seemed intent on totally destroying his reputation and effectiveness. President Garfield's assassination in 1881 left him even more vulnerable to open criticism. The result was that he was forced to spend much of his time defending the office before congressional committees.

When he assumed his duties, Hazen found the Signal Corps in a state of disarray, with a lack of organization, discipline, and harmony that fostered cliques and inefficiency. A hard-nosed administrator, he moved with dispatch to rectify these problems, in the process discharging 30 men from the service.

The most important activities of the Signal Corps related to its function as the national weather service. Congress had established the Weather Bureau as part of the Signal Service in 1870, but not much was accomplished until Hazen took charge. He was determined to improve the scientific character of the weather service and to enhance its practical usefulness. Two major advances were the recruitment of qualified personnel for the corps and the promotion of scientific experimentation, research, and publication. Indicating his continuing interest in the West, Hazen designated western military posts to monitor and report official rainfall records.

Other accomplishments during Hazen's administration included the adoption of International Bureau of Weights and Measures standards, the formation of state weather services, and research cooperation with the National Academy of Sciences and the Smithsonian Institution. The corps also assisted in devising and securing the adoption of the standard meridian time zones.[47]

The most publicized project during Hazen's tenure was the Signal Service expedition to the Arctic during the International Polar Year. In the summer of 1881, Lieutenant Adolphus W. Greely and a 25-man team proceeded to Lady Franklin Bay, Grinnell Land, to establish an observation station. In 1882 a relief ship sent to deliver supplies failed to reach the party. It was crucial for the team members' survival that they receive supplies the following year. Hazen entrusted this assignment to an experienced corpsman, Lieutenant Earnest Garlington. When Garlington unexpectedly ran into summer ice and storms, his judgment failed him: unable to reach Greely, he returned home without leaving a cache of supplies at a predetermined location, as instructed.[48]

As soon as the shocking news of the failure reached him in September 1883, Hazen urged Secretary of War Robert Lincoln to dispatch another rescue mission immediately. Several men with Arctic experience volunteered their services, but Lincoln, who had never been in favor of "this costly . . . wild goose chase into nowhere," seemed in no hurry to act; finally, he decided that a second attempt would not be feasible that year. It was not until June 22, 1884, that Greely and his party were located, and by then there were only seven survivors. Before long, accusations began to circulate that members of the party had engaged in cannibalism.[49]

In his annual report of 1884, Hazen defended himself against blame for the problems of the Arctic expedition. He claimed that if the War Department had followed his advice in September 1883, the Greely party would have been rescued intact: a good sealing ship departing from Saint John's, Newfoundland, could have safely reached the men; there had been four such vessels available, and veteran sealing masters were convinced that the attempt would have succeeded. He concluded with the hope that "this whole matter" would be thoroughly investigated by Congress.[50]

Lincoln's annual report of 1884 called Hazen's comments "extraordinary" and "hardly excusable." He defended his decision and implied that the tragedy was due in large part to Hazen's own bungling.[51] Since the Greely rescue, the *New York Times* had repeatedly called for Hazen's ouster, blaming the debacle on "the carelessness and stupidity . . . the miserable blunders" of the Chief Signal Officer.[52] Now, it appeared to Hazen, even the secretary of war was trying to make him the scapegoat, although Greely himself, who had worked closely with him in formulating the details of the expedition, never once laid any blame at the feet of Hazen.

When Hazen's call for an investigation went unheeded, the distraught officer unburdened himself "in an unguarded moment" to a reporter of the Washington *Evening Star*. He recited his frustrations with Lincoln's apathy toward the Arctic venture and the fate of its members; Lincoln had wrongfully permitted the "odium of neglect" to rest upon him, Hazen said, whereas the blame for the loss of lives rested with the lethargic secretary of war. The *Evening Star* published the story on March 2, 1885, only a few days before Lincoln was due to be replaced by the incoming Grover Cleveland administration. Acting quickly, the incensed secretary ordered court-martial proceedings against Hazen, charging him with insubordination, and then left office.[53]

Although Hazen probably did not deliberately seek a court-martial, as some speculated, it appears that once the order was issued, he saw the proceedings as the only way he had to vindicate himself and his office; when rumors circulated that the Cleveland administration might dissolve the court-martial, Hazen personally asked the new secretary of war, William Endicott, to let his case go to trial.[54]

Hazen was, as expected, found guilty and reprimanded. According to Frederick Logan Paxton, however, "the feeling was general among experts, including Greely, that Hazen was clearly in the right."[55] And scientist Cleveland Abbe wrote that in defending himself, Hazen was able to expose publicly "the true reasons of the failure of the War Department to properly support and succor the Signal Service Expedition."[56] Having suffered only a verbal spanking while gaining widespread public support, Hazen felt that he had obtained a "real vindication."[57]

General Hazen's career ended on January 16, 1887, when he died unexpectedly as a result of complications from his old bullet wound and a diabetic condition. He was survived by his wife Mildred and son John, who were wintering in Europe at the time of his death. John McLean Hazen died in 1898—the only direct descendant of William B. Hazen. A year later Mildred Hazen married Admiral George Dewey, the hero of Manila Bay.

William B. Hazen's career in many respects was not unlike that of his contemporaries in the frontier military. His ability, writings, travels, influential marriage and friends, however, clearly set him apart from the average officer of his day—as did his notorious penchant for controversy. Squabbles among army men were not uncommon in that period, but no other officer so persistently took on the establishment, and so consistently emerged so totally undaunted, his integrity unscathed. Sherman, Sheridan, Custer, and—as noted by Ambrose Bierce—"a countless multitude of the less luckless had the misfortune, at one time and another, to incur his disfavor, and he tried to punish them all." As a result, "he was accused of everything, from stealing to cowardice, was banished to obscure posts, 'jumped on' by the press, traduced in public and in private, and always emerged triumphant. . . . Duty was his religion, and like the Moslem he proselyted with a sword."[58]

Imbued with the principles of honesty and accountability, Hazen served as the army's conscience at a time when mediocrity was the hallmark of the military. His very memory was a "terror to every unworthy soul in the service."[59] When he saw graft and deceit, waste and inefficiency, negligence and shoddy performance of duty, his principles would not permit him to look the other way.

Hazen's initially severe attitude toward Indians moderated with experience (as was true of several army officers). He originally supported the reservation system because he saw it as the way to end the Indian military menace, not as a way to acculturate the natives. Later he came to believe that with proper management, many tribesmen might actually become self-sufficient—but not if they were expected to become farmers on the dry plains, where the reservations were established and where even experienced white farmers could barely, if at all, eke out a living. He saw this as a critical policy flaw that government officials and humanitarians failed to recognize.

In the 1880s, while the western frontier was rapidly shrinking, Hazen pioneered new frontiers for the military and the nation. The Signal Service Expedition explored land farther north than anyone else had reached and, despite the problems encountered, gathered information that prepared the way for later explorations. A lake near the top of the earth bearing Hazen's name serves as a frigid monument to his contribution in expanding human knowledge of this far northern frontier.[60]

Hazen's personal and professional qualities gained him both friends and enemies. He was often opinionated and unyielding when discretion might have been the better part of valor; even his best friends found him one of the most exasperating of men. Yet he was right more often than he was wrong, and his integrity is difficult to question. General Sherman, despite occasional differences with his volatile subordinate, said of Hazen: His military record from the day of his first commission is perfect, and is such as any man may be proud of. He is an officer of the highest professional attainments and of the best possible habits."[61] These words, written less than two years before Hazen's death, would have served as a fitting epitaph for the veteran frontier soldier.

Notes

1. Ambrose Bierce, *Collected Works,* 12 vols. (New York: Gordian Press, 1966), 1:283–84.

2. W. H. Tucker, *History of Hartford, Vermont* (Burlington, Vt.: Free Press Association, 1889), 360–62.

3. *Oregonian,* October 20, 1855, cited in Robert C. Clark, "Military History of Oregon, 1849–1859," *Oregon Historical Quarterly* 36 (March 1935): 30.

4. Joel Palmer to Brevet Major General John E. Wool, December 1, 1855, *House Exec. Docs.,* 34th Cong., 3rd sess., no. 93, pp. 24–25. See also Stephen Beckham, *Requiem for a People: The Rogue Indians and the Frontiersmen* (Norman: University of Oklahoma Press, 1971).

5. Headquarters, Department of the Pacific, to Captain A. J. Smith, December 3, 1856, Letter Book, Department of the Pacific, 1856, Adjutant General's Office (hereafter AG), Record Group (hereafter RG) 98, National Archives (hereafter NA).

6. Brevet General D. E. Twiggs to Hardin R. Runnels, September 9, 1858, cited in Walter Prescott Webb, *The Texas Rangers* (Boston: Houghton Mifflin, 1935), 160; Twiggs to Colonel L. Cooper, Headquarters of the Army, November 9, 1859, in an endorsement on Major William French to Lieutenant J. A. Washington, Headquarters, Department of Texas, November 5, 1859, Letters Received, Department of Texas, November 5, 1859, Letters Received, Department of Texas, AG, RG 94, NA.

7. W. B. Hazen to Lieutenant and Adjutant William E. Dye, June 22, 1858, Letters Received, Department of Texas, AG, RG 94, NA; General Order no. 5, Headquarters of the Army, New York, November 10, 1859, AG, RG 94, NA.

8. Hazen to Captain R. P. Maclay, May 23, 1859, Letters Received, Department of Texas, AG, RG 94, NA; General Order no. 5, Headquarters of the Army, New York, November 10, 1859, AG, RG 94, NA.

9. Hazen to R. P. Maclay, October 7, 1859, in W. B. Hazen, *A Narrative of Military Service* (Boston: Ticknor, 1885), 431; Hazen, Report of the Operations of a Scout, October and November, 1859, to Captain J. Withers, Assistant Adjutant General, Headquarters, Department of Texas, December 20, 1859, Letters Received, Department of Texas, AG, RG 94, NA.

10. Lieutenant Colonel J. E. Johnston to the Assistant Adjutant General, Headquar-

ters of the Army, November 14, 1859, Letters Received, AG, RG 94, NA; General Order no. 16, Headquarters, Department of Texas, October 30, 1860, cited in M. L. Crimmins, "Colonel Robert E. Lee's Report on Indian Combats in Texas," *Southwestern Historical Quarterly* 39 (July 1935): 23–24; General Order no. 11, Headquarters of the Army, November 23, 1860, AG, RG 94, NA; Hazen, *A Narrative of Military Service*, 436.

11. Hazen, *A Narrative of Military Service*, 26–28, 34–35, 72–73; Benson J. Lossing, *The Pictorial Field Book of the Civil War*, 3 vols. (Hartford: T. Belknap, 1874), 2:546–47.

12. Hazen, *A Narrative of Military Service*, 176, 178–79; Philip H. Sheridan, *Personal Memoirs of P. H. Sheridan, General, United States Army*, 2 vols. (New York: C. L. Webster, 1888), 1:320.

13. William M. Lamars, *The Edge of Glory: A Biography of General William S. Rosecrans, U.S.A.* (New York: Harcourt, Brace, 1961), 229; George Ward Nichols, *The Story of the Great March from the Diary of a Staff Officer* (New York: Harper, 1865), 92.

14. Hazen to Brevet Major H. G. Litchfield, Acting Assistant Adjutant General, Department of the Platte, October 16, 1866, *House Exec. Docs.*, 39th Cong., 2 sess., no. 45, pp. 5–6.

15. Ibid., 2–3.

16. Charles J. Kappler, *Indian Affairs, Laws and Treaties*, 5 vols. (Washington, D.C.: Government Printing Office, 1903–41), 2:977–78, 983–89.

17. General Order no. 4, August 10, 1868, Headquarters, Division of the Missouri, in *Annual Report of the Commissioner of Indian Affairs to the Secretary of the Interior for the Year 1868* (Washington, D.C.: Government Printing Office, 1868), 85.

18. Thomas Murphy to Charles E. Mix, September 19, 1868, in ibid., 75; Sherman to J. M. Schofield, September 17, 1868, ibid., 77; *Annual Report of the Secretary of War for the Year 1868* (Washington, D.C.: Government Printing Office, 1868), 4; Hazen, *Some Corrections of "My Life on the Plains"* (1875), reprinted in *Chronicles of Oklahoma* 3 (December 1925): 300–301; Hazen to Sherman, November 10, 22, 1868, typescript, Sherman-Sheridan Papers, University of Oklahoma.

19. Edward W. Wynkoop to Peter Cooper and others, December 23, 1868, Philip H. Sheridan Papers, Library of Congress; Hazen to Sherman, November 7, 1868, Sherman-Sheridan Papers.

20. Hazen to Sherman, November 22, 1868, Sherman-Sheridan Papers.

21. Sheridan to Sherman, November 1, 1869, *Annual Report of the Secretary of War, 1869–70* (Washington, D.C.: Government Printing Office, 1870), 47.

22. Hazen to Sherman, December 31, 1868, Sheridan Papers; Hazen to James A. Garfield, January 17, 1869, James A. Garfield Papers, Library of Congress.

23. Hazen to the officer commanding troops in the field, December 16, 1868, Sheridan Papers.

24. Report of Operations of the Command of Brevet Major General George A. Custer, from December 7 to December 22, 1868, Sheridan Papers; George A. Custer, *My Life on the Plains; or, Personal Experiences with Indians* (New York: Sheldon, 1874; rpt., Norman: University of Oklahoma Press, 1962), 291; Sheridan, *Personal Memoirs*, 2:334.

25. Hazen, *Some Corrections of "My Life on the Plains,"* 384, 393–94.

26. Hazen to Sherman, June 30, 1869, in *Annual Report of the Commissioner of Indian Affairs for the Year 1869* (Washington, D.C.: Government Printing Office, 1869), 393–96.

27. Hazen to E. S. Parker, February 14, April 30, 1870, Office of Indian Affairs, 1824–81, MSS Creek Agency, Letters Received, RG 75, NA (microcopy 234, roll 232); J. D. Cox to the Commissioner of Indian Affairs, September 5, 1870, ibid.

28. Enoch Hoag and Hazen to Parker, June 13, 1870, Southern Superintendency, Letters Received, RG 75, NA (microcopy 234, roll 839); Parker to Hazen, January 10, 1870, Finance and Miscellaneous, Letters Sent, RG 75, NA (microcopy 21, roll 93).

29. William B. Hazen, *The School and the Army in Germany and France* (New York: Harper, 1872), 222–46.

30. *Army and Navy Journal,* July 20, 1872.

31. Hazen to Garfield, February 4, 1872; copy of letter of R. H. Pratt to Hazen, November 25, 1871, enclosure, Garfield Papers.

32. Garfield to Hazen, February 13, 16, 1872, Garfield Papers.

33. *House Report,* 42nd Cong., 3rd sess., no. 74, pp. 170–80.

34. Copy of circular issued by Department of War, March 25, 1872; Garfield to John Coburn, April 8, 1876, Garfield Papers.

35. Regular Army Organization Returns, Sixth Infantry, April 1872, AG, RG 94, NA; *New York Times,* March 4, 1876.

36. Coburn to editor, Cincinnati *Commercial,* March 30, 1876, reprinted in *New York Times,* April 5, 1876; Garfield to Coburn, April 8, 1876, Garfield Papers.

37. The official record of the Belknap trial is found in *Congressional Record: Proceedings of the Senate, Trial of William W. Belknap,* 44th Cong., 1st sess., 1876.

38. Hazen to Garfield, May 5, 1872, Garfield Papers; copy of a certificate on health of William B. Hazen, May 8, 1872, AG, RG 94, NA.

39. Hazen to the Assistant Adjutant General, Department of Dakota, July 5, 1872, Letters Received, AG, RG 94, NA; endorsement of Lieutenant General Sheridan, July 26, 1872, ibid.

40. Hazen to Garfield, July 23, 1871, Garfield Papers.

41. Jay Cooke and Company, *The Northern Pacific Railroad: Its Route, Resources, Progress and Business* (Philadelphia: n.p., 1871), 48; "Poetry and Philosophy of Indian Summer," *Harper's New Monthly Magazine* 43 (December 1873); New York *Tribune,* February 7, 1874.

42. Minneapolis *Tribune,* April 17, 1874.

43. W. B. Hazen, "The Great Middle Region of the United States, and Its Limited Space of Arable Land," *North American Review* 120 (January 1875): 1–34; W. B. Hazen, *Our Barren Lands: The Interior of the United States West of the 100th Meridian, and East of the Sierra Nevadas* (Cincinnati: Robert Clarke, 1875).

44. Ronald Spector, *Admiral of the New Empire: The Life and Career of George Dewey* (Baton Rouge: Louisiana State University Press, 1974), 107–8.

45. Transcript of the Stanley-Hazen Trial, Records of the War Department, Office of the Judge Advocate General (Army), General Courts-Martial, 1812–1938, RG 153, NA; General Court-Martial, Order No. 35, Headquarters of the Army, June 18, 1879, AG, RG 94, NA.

46. Hazen to Garfield, November 3, 5, 1880, Garfield Papers; T. Harry Williams, ed., *Hayes: The Diary of a President* (New York: McKay, 1964), 307.

47. General Hazen's Testimony, Disbursements of Public Moneys of the Chief Signal Officer, United States Army, April 3, 1886, *House Misc. Docs.,* 49th Cong., 1st sess., no. 255, p. 145; Cleveland Abbe, "William Babcock Hazen," *Popular Science Monthly* 21 (May 1887): 113–17.

48. A. L. Todd, *Abandoned: The Story of the Greely Arctic Expedition, 1881–1884* (New York: McGraw-Hill, 1961), 16–23, 47–49, 66; Annual Report of the Chief Signal Officer, 1882, in *Annual Report of the Secretary of War, 1882* (Washington, D.C.: Government Printing Office, 1882), 67; ibid., *1883,* 8; ibid., *1884,* 14–21; John Caswell, *Arctic Frontiers: United States Explorations in the Far North* (Norman: University of Oklahoma Press, 1956), 96–108.

49. Todd, *Abandoned,* 67; Caswell, *Arctic Frontiers,* 109; John S. Goff, *Robert Todd Lincoln* (Norman: University of Oklahoma Press, 1969), 135–37; Winfield S. Schley, *Report of Winfield S. Schley, Commander, U.S. Navy, Commanding Greely Relief Expedition of 1884* (Washington, D.C.: Government Printing Office, 1887), 44.

50. Annual Report of the Chief Signal Officer, 1884, in *Annual Report of the Secretary of War, 1884* (Washington, D.C.: Government Printing Office, 1884), 14–21; General Hazen's Testimony, Disbursements of Public Moneys, 144–45.

51. *Annual Report of the Secretary of War, 1884,* 25.

52. Todd, *Abandoned,* 288.

53. General Hazen's Testimony, Disbursements of Public Moneys, 144; Todd, *Abandoned,* 306–8.

54. General Hazen's Testimony, Disbursements of Public Moneys, 144.

55. In Allen Johnson and Dumas Malone, eds., *Dictionary of American Biography,* 11 vols. (New York: Scribner, 1958), 4:479.

56. Abbe, "William Babcock Hazen," 114.

57. An account of the trial is found in T. J. Mackey, *The Hazen Court-Martial* (New York: Van Nostrand, 1885); General Hazen's Testimony, Disbursements of Public Moneys, 144.

58. Bierce, *Collected Works,* 1:283–84.

59. Ibid., 283.

60. Todd, *Abandoned,* 46; General Hazen's Testimony, Disbursements of Public Moneys, 145. For an evaluation of the scientific knowledge gained from the expedition, see Caswell, *Arctic Frontiers,* 111–13.

61. Washington *Post,* March 16, 1885.

Nelson A. Miles

by Robert M. Utley

The Indian stood impassively facing the white general. For a moment each stared into the eyes of the other. Then the Indian laid his rifle at the feet of the soldier chief. The surrender of Kicking Bear to Major General Nelson A. Miles on January 15, 1891, marked the collapse of the Sioux Ghost Dance troubles. All morning Indians had been streaming into the Pine Ridge Agency, the climax of a movement of several days' duration that brought some 4,000 people back to their homes. "It was a grand sight to see them slowly marching along for three hours up and down the hills," wrote a newspaper correspondent, "and as General Miles said, a sight never again to be witnessed in Indian warfare on this continent."[1]

The general was right. The surrender of Kicking Bear, chief apostle of the Ghost Dance religion among the Sioux, signified the end of major Indian warfare in the United States. Of all the military leaders who had labored to this end, none boasted a brighter record than Nelson A. Miles. By 1891 the ceremony enacted with Kicking Bear had become a familiar experience to Miles; indeed, Kicking Bear himself had surrendered to him once before, on the Yellowstone in 1877, together with other Sioux and Cheyennes who had helped to crush Custer a year earlier. So in 1877 had Chief Joseph of the Nez Perces, with a

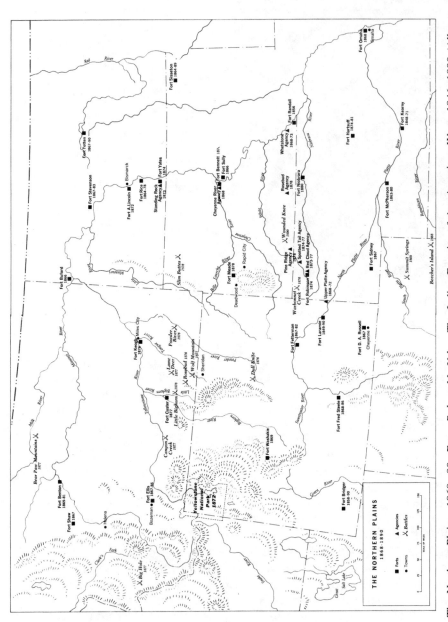

The Northern Plains, 1868–90. *From Robert M. Utley,* The Indian Frontier of the American West, 1846–1890 *(Albuquerque: University of New Mexico Press, 1984). Reprinted by permission of the University of New Mexico Press.*

moving speech ending with the memorable words, "From where the sun now stands I will fight no more forever." So in 1886 had Geronimo: "This is the fourth time I have surrendered," the Apache observed. "And I think it is the last time," the general replied, correctly.[2]

Although the Indian wars were over, Miles would rise still higher, to the top command of the United States Army. It was an impressive ascent from youthful beginnings as a clerk in a Boston crockery store, but still not as high as his ambition dictated. His future career, like his past, would be marred by controversy and endless discord with associates. For in Nelson A. Miles vanity and ambition powered a fierce competitiveness that drove him to revel tastelessly in his own genuine abilities and successes while minimizing or denying those of others. "Brave Peacock," Theodore Roosevelt would call him, not inaccurately.[3] Unfortunately for his place in history, the image obscures a record of notable achievement.

Miles came to the frontier army in 1866 without West Point credentials but with an extraordinary Civil War record. Self-education had prepared him for the war. While clerking in Boston, he had attended night school, read deeply in military history, mastered military principles and techniques, and even paid an old French veteran to teach him drill and discipline. He marched off in 1861 as a lieutenant of Massachusetts volunteers. Courage, leadership, professional knowledge, hard work, and ambition brought the young officer to the notice of superiors, and he rose swiftly. By Appomattox he had made himself a popular hero—four times wounded; veteran of every major battle of the Army of the Potomac except Gettysburg; successful regimental, brigade, division, and (briefly) corps commander. Promotion to major general of volunteers came in October 1865, and three brevet commissions covered him with further honors.

Not only was the general an authentic hero; he looked like one. Tall, muscular, broad-shouldered, well-proportioned, with intense blue eyes and jaunty mustache, he made a dashing figure in his blue and gold uniform with starred shoulder straps and chest full of brass buttons. He was 26 years old.

Miles had found his calling. He wanted to be a career soldier, and his record in the volunteers assured him a commission in the postwar regulars. He sought a brigadier's star—a presumptuous goal in the shrunken peacetime army even for one of his conspicuous attainments. The colonel's eagles that he accepted with bad grace represented a higher rank than others with greater seniority and superior records could win.

Even this distinction came not solely in recognition of wartime services. Miles had learned one of the immutable truths of his times: ability helped, but high-level influence was essential. He enlisted the support of an imposing roster of military and political luminaries in behalf of his candidacy, and his colonel's commission owed as much to this as to his war record. Miles would become one of the army's most ardent practitioners of influence peddling.

Marriage appeared to enhance the possibilities, although it is unlikely that cynicism formed part of the motivation. On June 30, 1868, he wedded Mary Hoyt Sherman, whose uncles were Ohio Senator John Sherman and Lieutenant General William Tecumseh Sherman. Less than a year later, with the inauguration of Ulysses S. Grant to the presidency, "Cump" Sherman became general-in-chief of the army. At once Miles began to importune his wife's uncle for official favors. Until 1883, when he stepped down as head of the army, Sherman stubbornly fended off these advances. Indeed, such was Sherman's distaste for favoritism that the family connection often proved as much liability as asset.

Assigned to command the Fifth Infantry at Fort Hays, Kansas, Miles fretted in idleness and boredom while others gained public notice—George Crook against Apaches in Arizona, Ranald S. Mackenzie against Comanches in Texas, Eugene A. Carr against Cheyennes in Colorado, George A. Custer against Cheyennes in the Indian Territory. Of all his rivals for fame and preferment, Miles held Crook in lowest esteem. When Grant and Sherman discovered that Crook knew how to fight Indians, they promoted him from lieutenant colonel to brigadier general over the heads of Miles and every other full colonel in the army, an act that Miles bitterly protested to Sherman as proof of West Point bias. Custer, on the other hand, had won Miles's sincere respect and affection. Slightly younger even than Miles, he also had been a major general and war hero, and now served as lieutenant colonel of the Seventh Cavalry. The two became fast friends during the summer of 1869, when the Seventh camped near Fort Hays.

Finally, in the Red River War of 1874–75, Miles got his first opportunity for distinction. Like most Indian outbreaks of the period, the Red River War sprang from the mounting pressures and restraints of life on the reservation. Cheyennes, Arapahos, Kiowas, and Comanches bolted from their reservations in the Indian Territory and fled westward to the vast table of the Staked Plains, in the Texas Panhandle. Lieutenant General Philip H. Sheridan, commanding all the territory east of the Rocky Mountains, worked out a plan of operations with his principal subordinates. From Texas and the Indian Territory, Brigadier General Christopher C. Augur would launch three columns toward the Staked Plains; from New Mexico and Kansas, Brigadier General John Pope would dispatch two. Converging on the Indians, the five columns would harass and, if possible, battle them into submission. Command of Pope's Kansas column, more than 700 men of the Sixth Cavalry and Fifth Infantry, went to Miles.

South from the Arkansas River, Miles's men tramped through day after blistering day of August 1874. Streams and water holes dried in the merciless drouth, and great clouds of locusts stripped the prairies to dust. Men opened the veins of their arms to moisten swollen lips and tongues. Finally, on August 30, they flushed the enemy, some 200 Cheyennes posted on a line of hills along the eastern base of the Staked Plains caprock. Deploying the infantry in the center and a cavalry squadron on each flank, Miles bombarded the Indians with howitzer and Gatling-gun fire, then charged. The Cheyennes fell back to another line of hills. Miles repeated the movement. Kiowas and Comanches joined the fight, augmenting the warrior force to 600. For five hours the troops drove the Indians from one position to another. Then, their families safely out of danger, the warriors scaled the caprock and scattered over the Staked Plains. The soldiers destroyed the villages and other property abandoned by the Indians in their flight.

With contact made, Miles now found himself halted. Having exhausted his supplies and outrun his supply line, he could not press his advantage. He had to turn back to his supply base on the Canadian River. Moreover, the drouth suddenly broke. Cold rain drenched the troops, sent the streams over their banks, and turned the virtually grassless plains to mud. Warriors swarmed on his supply line. Finally he reached his base, where he went into camp and fumed over the continuing shortages that immobilized him while the other columns searched out the Indians.

As usual, Miles looked for, and found, scapegoats for his misfortune. The supply problem was real and a disgrace, the result mainly of a system that placed chief reliance on civilian transportation contractors independent of military control. But Miles saw his affliction in more personal terms as "gross mismanagement somewhere in our rear" — probably, he thought, on the part of Pope's quartermaster, Colonel Stewart Van Vliet. For that matter, Pope himself — an even more temperamental officer — incurred Miles's scorn: instead of looking to his columns, he was off touring the East. "It required a peculiar kind of genius," Miles wrote Mary, "to conduct an Indian campaign from West Point or Boston." He made the same complaint to Sherman and suggested that "this whole Indian region" be organized as a separate department, with himself in command.[4] To aggravate still further Miles's ill humor, Colonel Ranald S. Mackenzie and the Fourth Cavalry surprised an Indian camp in Palo Duro Canyon on September 28; they routed the inhabitants and destroyed all their provisions and possessions, including a herd of 1,400 ponies. Like Crook, Mackenzie was an officer against whom Miles felt especially competitive.

Yet in the end Miles made the largest contribution, not by a flashy stroke like Mackenzie's but by stubborn perseverance in the face of adversities of distance and weather that drove the other columns back to their forts. A few bands of fugitives had begun to drift into the agencies as early as October, following the battles with Miles and Mackenzie and, especially, the autumn storms. But other bands remained out through the winter, and Miles, his supply problems eased, went after them. Through driving blizzards and bitter cold, the expedition kept to the field in December and January. "But the troops did not seem to suffer or complain," Miles wrote Mary, "and it was quite amusing to hear them singing 'Marching Through Georgia' way out on these plains."[5] Cold, hunger, and above all the constant fear of a surprise attack by bluecoats who refused to call off the chase finally drained the Indians of the will to resist. During February and March 1875 they surrendered by the hundreds at Fort Sill and the Darlington Agency. By June the last had given up, ending warfare on the southern plains.[6]

Despite his successes in the Red River War, Miles could not break free of the obscurity that so oppressed him. While Mackenzie won acclaim for Palo Duro Canyon, Miles got very little for the fight of August 30 (which did not even have a name) or for the punishing winter operations that wore down the last holdouts. Pope seemed intent on denying Miles his rightful credit. On top of this indignity, Crook's Arizona triumphs earned him command of the Department of the Platte—Sioux country—a post Miles very much coveted. He failed even to get his regiment assigned to one of the three big expeditions Sheridan assembled in 1876 to war on the Sioux and Northern Cheyennes of Montana—until after he opened a newspaper one July day to read news that shocked the nation. Sheridan's Sioux operations had met disaster. The golden-haired Custer—popular idol, protégé of Sheridan, intimate of Miles—had fallen with a good portion of his regiment at the Little Bighorn.

With half his regiment (the rest was to follow), Miles ascended the Missouri and Yellowstone by steamboat as part of the reinforcements for Brigadier General Alfred H. Terry, whose campaign had also come to grief on the Little Bighorn. Anxious to be after the Indians who had slain his friend Custer, Miles found a singular lack of urgency. "I never saw a command so completely stampeded as this," he wrote Mary.[7] When Terry joined with General Crook on August 10, Miles's disgust deepened. Caution afflicted Crook, too, the result of a mauling the Sioux had dealt him on the Rosebud a week before the Custer disaster. Together, Crook and Terry counted almost 4,000 men. Miles judged their column too unwieldy and too hesitantly led ever to catch the swift-moving Indians. Seeking a way out, he persuaded Terry to send him back to the Yellowstone to prevent the Indians from fleeing north toward the British possessions.

True to Miles's predictions, Crook and Terry bogged down in mud, disputation, and dejection, and by the middle of September they had abandoned the field altogether. Not Miles. On Sheridan's orders, he was to hold the Yellowstone Valley through the winter. Thus freed from the interference of demoralized superiors, he intended to make the most of the opportunity.

Throwing up a rude cantonment on the Yellowstone at the mouth of the Tongue River, Miles kept resolutely after the Indians. "They expected us to hive up," he wrote Mary, "but we are not the hiving kind."[8] In October his detachments skirmished with Sitting Bull's Sioux north of the Yellowstone, and twice the colonel parleyed inconclusively with this mightiest of all Sioux chiefs. Later in October some 2,000 Sioux surrendered to Miles and promised to return to their agencies, but few did. Through the fall months and into the winter his hardy foot soldiers, never more than 500 strong, remained in the field. Enveloped in huge coats of buffalo fur, they faced the stinging blizzards and numbing temperatures of a Montana winter.

To the south, Crook also took the field, with Mackenzie as his striking arm. On November 25, 1876, Mackenzie surprised Dull Knife's Cheyenne village on the Red Fork of Powder River. In desperate fighting his cavalrymen drove the Indians from their tepees into the frozen wilderness without food or shelter. By late December, however, Crook had retired from the field.

The operations of Miles and Crook, combined with the rigors of winter, kindled peace sentiment among the hostiles. On December 16 a delegation of Sioux chiefs approached the Tongue River cantonment to have a talk with the soldier chief, but when Crow Indian scouts fired on them, they hastily withdrew. Angrily, Miles dismounted the Crows and sent their ponies to the Sioux in apology—to no avail.

Once again, as the new year opened, Miles ventured from his base, marching up the Tongue in search of Crazy Horse's village, which now sheltered the Cheyennes impoverished by Mackenzie's blow. On January 8 he encountered Crazy Horse and some 500 Sioux and Cheyenne warriors in the Battle of Wolf Mountain, which ended in a violent snowstorm as bursting artillery rounds and charging infantry drove the Indians from the field. Back at his headquarters, Miles wrote exultantly to Mary that he "had taught the destroyers of Custer that there was one small command that could whip them as long as they dared face it."[9]

Jubilantly, Miles boasted of his successes in long letters to General Sherman. He coveted either of two positions, he had written back in November— secretary of war or command of a department; he hoped Sherman might help him obtain one. Now, in the aftermath of Wolf Mountain, he answered Sherman's frosty response by declaring that he had "fought and defeated larger and better armed bodies of hostile Indians than any other officer since the history of Indian warfare commenced," and also that he had "gained a more extended knowledge of our frontier country than any living man." He supposed secretary of war was out of the question, but surely his record entitled him to departmental command. His own department commander, General Terry, had not properly supported him; indeed, there was "criminal neglect of duty" at the St. Paul headquarters of the Department of Dakota, "or there is a determination that I shall not accomplish anything." Crook, commander of the Department of the Platte, had turned in an even sorrier performance than Terry. "A man who was a failure during the war and has been ever since," Crook in his recent campaign had "accomplished nothing but give the Indians renewed confidence." The only solution was for Sherman to place Miles in charge. This could be done by what Sherman must have judged a breathtaking rearrangement of the army's command structure: pack Pope off to New York, give Pope's departmental command at Fort Leavenworth to Terry, and transfer elsewhere the two colonels in the Department of Dakota who ranked Miles, thus leaving him the senior officer. "If you will give me this command *and one-half the troops now in it, I will end this Sioux war once and forever in four months.*"[10]

Actually, Sherman and Sheridan were already discussing a more modest plan to enlarge Miles's responsibilities and resources, but events overtook its execution. Disheartened by the winter's setbacks, the Indians once again debated peace or war. Sitting Bull, hounded by Miles's detachments, called off the war altogether and went north to live in the land of the "Great Mother," Queen Victoria. In the village of Crazy Horse, once more on the Little Bighorn, the peace faction gained strength. At this juncture Miles himself put out a peace feeler, sending his interpreter to escort some Cheyenne women captured at Wolf Mountain back to their people and sound out the possibilities of negotiation. In response, some chiefs came over to talk with Miles. He bluntly informed them, as he wrote Mary, "that there could be but one big chief in this part of the country, and that I proposed to occupy that position."[11] They disliked his demand for unconditional surrender, but they kept on talking. In fact, chiefs came and went through February and March and into April, conferring with Miles and gaining more and more confidence in him. "Bear's Coat," they called him, in recognition of the huge fur overcoat that protected him from the Montana winter.

The chiefs procrastinated because of other peace feelers coming from the south, from Crook. In the middle of February a delegation of agency Sioux headed by Spotted Tail, Crazy Horse's uncle, set forth to coax the hostiles in. Spotted Tail carried word that Crook would do everything he could to prevent them from being moved to the Missouri River, where many officials wanted them settled. Miles, still insisting on unconditional surrender, viewed with distress Crook's attempt to steal "his" hostiles. If it succeeded, he told Mary, "Crook will go out to meet them and claim the credit of bagging them. Yet he has had no more to do with it than if he had been in Egypt."[12]

Miles's fears were justified. Throughout April, in large bodies and small, 3,000 Sioux straggled into their agencies in Nebraska and Dakota and gave up. On May 6, at the Red Cloud Agency, Crazy Horse threw three rifles at the feet of General Crook, a bitter blow for the hard campaigner up on the Yellowstone. Even so, some 300 Cheyennes and a handful of Sioux, drawn by the magnetism of their winter adversary, surrendered to Bear's Coat rather than Crook.

Bear's Coat had one final chance. Lame Deer's Sioux band had refused to give up. On May 7, his infantry now backed by cavalry, Miles found and attacked Lame Deer's village on Muddy Creek, a tributary of the Rosebud River. Cut off and surrounded, Lame Deer and his head warrior laid their rifles on the ground in front of Miles's horse. At this moment a scout rode up and covered the two Indians with his rifle. Fearing they were to be killed, they swiftly retrieved their weapons, and Lame Deer fired point-blank at Miles. He dodged, and the bullet struck and killed a cavalryman behind him. Both Indians were riddled with bullets.

The Battle of Muddy Creek was the last engagement of the Sioux War. Yet the war could not be regarded as truly over so long as Sitting Bull remained in Canada, for at any time he might return to his homeland. Miles, from his Yellowstone base—soon named Fort Keogh—would have Sitting Bull as his special charge. But not before fate again awarded him opportunity.

In far-off Oregon and Idaho that summer of 1877, war broke out with the Nez Perces. Under Chief Joseph and other able leaders, some 800 people fought off army pursuers and made a desperate leap across the Rocky Mountains and Yellowstone National Park to the Montana plains. In close pursuit but never quite able to catch up struggled a force commanded by Brigadier General Oliver O. Howard, the one-armed "praying general" of Civil War note, whom Miles had once served as aide-de-camp. Colonel John Gibbon fell upon the Nez Perces at Big Hole but got badly bloodied. They slipped around another blocking force, then beat it off at Canyon Creek. On September 17 a courier rode into Miles's post with a dispatch from Howard. Describing the latest developments, it stated that the Indians were now fleeing toward the Canadian border and asked if Miles could try to head them off.

Miles needed no coaxing. Before the next dawn he had ferried five companies of infantry and two troops of cavalry across the Yellowstone. Picking up more cavalry along the way, he hastened northwest, crossed the Missouri River, and on September 30 caught the quarry in camp at the northern base of the Bear Paw Mountains. He struck at once but found the Nez Perces a skilled and tenacious foe. Their deadly defensive fire cut down 60 attackers, of whom six were officers and 12 noncommissioned officers. Finding assault too costly, Miles had to settle for a siege. Maddeningly, it dragged on day after day as Howard's column drew closer. But upon arrival, the generous Howard kept in the background. When at last, on October 5, Chief Joseph came forward to utter his eloquent words of surrender, it was to the victor of Bear Paw rather than the tired general who had toiled in his wake across 1,700 miles of wilderness.

Characteristically, Miles marred his triumph by boasts that excluded Howard and his troops from any share of the credit. Stung by the ingratitude (especially since he had just endorsed Miles for promotion), the general and his friends struck back. The controversy grew so public and so unseemly that finally Sherman himself had to order it ended. [13]

For the next three years, 1877–80, Miles aggressively patrolled the international frontier. He ached to dart across the boundary and smash Sitting Bull's Sioux as Mackenzie had once done to the Kickapoos on the Mexican border, but Sherman made it clear that any violation of British territory would land him in serious trouble. When, however, the hungry Sioux came south in the spring of 1879 to hunt buffalo, they found Bear's Coat waiting. Expertly, he drove them back to their sanctuary.

Meantime, emboldened by his continuing success, Miles stepped up his campaign for promotion. Admiring Montanans joined in the agitation, and many of the army's generals as well as such political figures as the governor of Massachusetts penned endorsements. "I have told him plainly," an exasperated Sherman fumed to Sheridan, "that I know of no way to satisfy his ambitions but to surrender to him absolute power over the whole Army with President and Congress thrown in."[14] Miles's persistence also aroused resentment among other aspiring colonels. A story making the rounds had the equally ambitious Mackenzie nervously pacing in front of his tent one night; an officer asked what he was doing. "Nothing much," replied the colonel. "I was only looking for that star; I don't see it tonight." "You can't see that star now," quipped the officer, "there's Miles between you and the star."[15] Indeed he was. Moved by the appeals of Miles and his supporters, President Rutherford B. Hayes forcibly retired Brigadier General Edward O. C. Ord, an old friend and classmate of Sherman's, and gave Miles the star for which he had so strenuously labored.

Posted to command the Department of the Columbia, the new brigadier was thus not on hand a few months later, in July 1881, when Sitting Bull led the remnant of his people across the boundary to surrender. He should have been, for more than any other officer Miles had brought about the successful conclusion of the Sioux hostilities. His operations against the Sioux and Nez Perces in 1876–79 certified him to top rank among the army's Indian fighters. In them he displayed the traits that had earned him distinction in the Civil War and that had been apparent, at least to him, on the southern plains—energy, aggressiveness, perseverance, boldness, imagination, and innovation. In particular, he had belied the conventional wisdom that only cavalry could prevail over Indians; afoot or mounted on captured Indian ponies, his infantry recorded one success after another. Exasperating as Miles could be, both Sherman and Sheridan had to concede that he got results.

For the next five years Miles served as a department commander, first in the Pacific Northwest and then at Fort Leavenworth, Kansas, stirring from office routine only when vacancies opened in the grade of major general. Although "Cump" Sherman had retired, John Sherman remained a leader in the Senate. Miles could also draw on another family connection, for in 1878 Mary's sister became the wife of Pennsylvania's powerful Senator Don Cameron, son of old Simon Cameron and briefly Grant's secretary of war. To Miles's disgust, however, the promotions went to Terry and Howard.

In 1886, Sheridan—now general-in-chief—ordered Miles to head the Department of Arizona. It was a large irony, for he replaced George Crook under circumstances bound to intensify their longtime enmity. In 1882, Crook had returned to Arizona to war on the Apaches, who under Geronimo and other chieftains were terrorizing settlements from privileged refuges in Mexico. In four years, relying heavily on pack trains for mobility and Apache scouts rather than regular soldiers, he had earned much favorable notice. Twice, with the approval of the Mexican government, he had dug Geronimo and his followers out of lairs high in the formidable Sierra Madre and persuaded them to surrender, but each time they had bolted back to their mountain hideaways. Sheridan distrusted the Indian scouts, and when Geronimo slipped from Crook's grasp a second time, he issued orders that led Crook, tired and disconsolate, to ask for a transfer.

Sensitive to Sheridan's views, Miles turned the spotlight from scouts to regulars. Forming a tightly knit strike force under Captain Henry W. Lawton, he sent it into Mexico. Through the brutally hot summer of 1886, Lawton combed the Sierra Madre in an ordeal as exhausting as it was seemingly futile. Regulars, Miles discovered, could keep the fugitives on the move but could not close with them in a fight. In the end, taking care not to let the shift be too visible, he began to make greater use of Apache scouts. He also summoned Lieutenant Charles B. Gatewood, a Crook protégé experienced in dealing with Apaches, to try to seek out Geronimo for peace talks.

Gatewood found Geronimo deep in the wilds of Mexico, but it was a Miles innovation that enabled him to succeed in his mission. This was nothing less than the deportation to Florida of all the Chiricahua and Warm Springs Apaches—Geronimo's people—on the San Carlos Reservation. When Gatewood informed Geronimo that the reservation no longer contained any of his division of the Apache tribe, he agreed to meet with Miles and discuss giving up the warpath. The surrender took place at Skeleton Canyon, Arizona, on September 4, 1886. Miles ensured lasting peace by packing Geronimo and his companions off to Florida to live with their kinsmen.[16]

So once again Miles had won, a victory celebrated by grateful Arizona citizens and made doubly sweet by the contrast with Crook's apparent failure. Again there was controversy—over division of honors between Crook and Miles and their disciples, and over the exile of the Apaches to Florida. Even Crook's faithful Indian scouts had been sent east, a matter of special resentment to him. It only aggravated the quarrel that when Terry retired, Crook rather than Miles advanced to major general.

In the spring of 1890, however, a sudden heart attack struck Crook dead. Miles was the senior brigadier in the army. In a final irony of the Crook-Miles rivalry, the second star for which seniority qualified him grew dim as, despite the energetic support of Senators Sherman and Cameron and influential Californians like Leland Stanford and George Hearst, President Benjamin Harrison looked elsewhere. The President, Sherman confided, thought Miles "if not disobedient, at least a troublesome man to get along with.''[17] Alarmed, Miles hastened to Washington to counter this impression, which he attributed to Howard and the friends of Crook. Presenting himself at the White House, he talked his way into the good graces of the President and emerged, after all, with the prized promotion.

Major General Miles had scarcely sewn on his new shoulder straps and moved into Crook's old Chicago office to head the Division of the Missouri when troubling reports came from the Sioux reservations in Dakota. A new religion had taken hold. As taught by its originator, a Nevada Paiute, the Ghost Dance religion sought the return of the old free life by nonviolent means. But among the Sioux it combined with hunger, disease, despair, and a host of festering grievances to produce a volatile mixture. By November 1890 the dance faction had so undermined the authority of some of the agents and so alarmed neighboring settlers that the President ordered troops to the reservations.

Miles hastened to Dakota to take personal command. The appearance of soldiers had stampeded the dancers, who had withdrawn to a remote corner of the Pine Ridge Reservation. Moreover, on December 16, on the Standing Rock Reservation, Indian police attempting to arrest Sitting Bull had shot and killed the old chief, who since his surrender had never wavered in his resistance to white authority. Seeking a peaceful resolution of the crisis, Miles concentrated on diplomacy. The policy seemed about to succeed, with the Sioux making their way slowly and apprehensively toward the Pine Ridge Agency, when disaster struck. On December 29, Colonel James W. Forsyth and the Seventh Cavalry clashed with Big Foot's Sioux band at Wounded Knee. Some 200 people, including many women and children, fell under a murderous barrage from cavalry carbines and rapid-fire cannon.

Wounded Knee shattered Miles's peace offensive as angry Indians once more stampeded. Furious, he brought formal charges against Forsyth but failed to make them stick. Meanwhile, in the early days of 1891, he revived his peace program. Gathered in a huge village north of the Pine Ridge Agency, the Sioux quarreled among themselves. Expertly, Miles exploited the divisions; he sent in conciliatory messages urging surrender and promising kind treatment. At the same time he drew a circle of 3,500 soldiers even more tightly around the village. Slowly the Indians moved toward the agency as the chiefs debated and disputed. Thus combining force and diplomacy in just the right proportion, Miles turned the deadly incident at Wounded Knee into a complete surrender at Pine Ridge.[18]

The surrender marked the end of major Indian hostilities in the United States, and the grand review that Miles staged on January 21 captured something of this significance while also saluting his own contribution to it. With Sioux stolidly watching from the hills and a winter gale whipping the brightly colored capes of the soldiers, regiment after regiment paraded before their commanding general. Sabers flashed, rifles were presented, guidons whipped in the fierce wind. A band played Custer's old battle air, "Garryowen," as the Seventh Cavalry trooped by and the deadly cannon—their carriages riddled by Sioux bullets—brought up the rear. Miles, his hat hung on his saddle pommel and his gray hair tossing in the wind, could scarcely contain his excitement over the spectacle. "It was the grandest demonstration by the army ever seen in the West," wrote a correspondent, and it was, as the general sensed at the time, the last of the frontier era.[19]

This was Miles's grandest moment, the culmination of a distinguished career as a field commander through four years of the Civil War and 25 years of Indian wars. What followed was bitter anticlimax, especially for a man of his soaring ambition.

As early as 1888, California interests had advanced Miles's name for the presidency, and throughout the 1890s he doubtless had no more difficulty visualizing himself as President than he had had in 1876, a frontier infantry colonel, as secretary of war. However, as an ascerbic old campaigner who knew Miles well observed, "The Cameron & Sherman influence isn't to be sneezed at, and he's got it. But he will never warm the presiding seat in the cabinet of these United States."[20] In truth, neither major party ever seriously considered him as a nominee.

In 1895, Miles did attain the top command of the army—successor to Washington, Scott, Grant, Sherman, and Sheridan—but his term was an unrelieved frustration. In the Spanish-American War, President William McKinley's administration denied him any real authority and relegated him to the command of an almost unnoticed expedition against Puerto Rico. Instead of glory, he gained uncomplimentary notice from a bitter public quarrel with the secretary of war and a ruthless, unjust attack on the commissary general in the scandal over "embalmed beef."

Even his elevation in 1901 to the newly restored grade of lieutenant general brought small satisfaction. Almost at once he earned the displeasure of President Theodore Roosevelt by taking sides in a feud between admirals and by criticizing U.S. policy in the Philippines. He also opposed the long-overdue reform of the War Department, which called for converting the commanding general into a chief of staff. And finally, when he reached the mandatory retirement age of 64 in 1903 and stepped down as the last commanding general in the army's history, the President declined to send the customary congratulatory message, and the secretary of war absented himself from the retirement ceremony.

Miles lived out his remaining years quietly in Washington, D.C. World War I brought persistent applications for active duty from the old general, but they were politely turned aside. No longer a center of controversy, he became a venerable figure out of the past, a reminder of the war to save the Union, of the Old Army, and of the frontier West that he had played so conspicuous a part in opening to settlement.

The end, at the age of 85, could not have been more fitting. In the spring of 1925 he took his grandchildren to the circus. The band played the national anthem. Standing erectly at attention, rendering the military salute to the flag, he collapsed with a heart attack. The burial at Arlington National Cemetery featured the impressive ceremonial homage he would have considered his due. He might also have felt a small sense of vindication in the graveside attendance of President Calvin Coolidge.

Notes

1. Charles G. Seymour, "The Sioux Rebellion: The Final Review," *Harper's Weekly* 35 (February 7, 1891): 106.

2. *Personal Recollections and Observations of General Nelson A. Miles* (Chicago: Werner, 1896), 527; this was reprinted with an introduction by Robert M. Utley by Da Capo Press in 1969. Also see Nelson A. Miles, *Serving the Republic: Memoirs of the Civil and Military Life of Nelson A. Miles* (New York: Harper, 1911).

3. Quoted in Virginia Johnson, *The Unregimented General: A Biography of Nelson A. Miles* (Boston: Houghton Mifflin, 1962), 353. Though uncritical, this book is invaluable for extensive quotations from Miles's colorful letters to his wife, Mary. Also see Peter R. DeMontravel, "The Career of Lieutenant General Nelson A. Miles from the Civil War through the Indian Wars" (Ph.D. diss., St. John's University, 1983); and Newton F. Tolman, *The Search for General Miles* (New York: Putnams, 1968). The Miles Papers have recently been presented to the Library of Congress.

4. Johnson, *Unregimented General*, 59; Nelson A. Miles to William T. Sherman, September 27, 1874, vol. 37, William T. Sherman Papers, Library of Congress.

5. Johnson, *Unregimented General*, 69.

6. Details of the Red River War can be found in James L. Haley, *The Buffalo War: The History of the Red River Indian Uprising of 1874* (Garden City, N.Y.: Doubleday, 1976); William H. Leckie, *The Military Conquest of the Southern Plains* (Norman: University of Oklahoma Press, 1963); W. S. Nye, *Carbine & Lance: The Story of Old Fort Sill* (Norman: University of Oklahoma Press, 1969); and Robert C. Carriker, *Fort Supply, Indian Territory: Frontier Outpost on the Plains* (Norman: University of Oklahoma Press, 1970).

7. Johnson, *Unregimented General*, 93–94.

8. Ibid., 110.

9. Ibid., 152.

10. Miles to Sherman, November 18, 1876, vol. 45; Miles to Sherman, January 20, February 1, 2, March 14, 29, April 8, 30, 1877, vol. 46, Sherman Papers.

11. Johnson, *Unregimented General*, 158.

12. Ibid., 161.

13. A good biography of Oliver O. Howard is John A. Carpenter, *Sword and Olive Branch: Oliver Otis Howard* (Pittsburgh, Pa.: University of Pittsburgh Press, 1964). The literature on the Nez Perce War is voluminous. Three monographs deserve special attention: Alvin M. Josephy, Jr., *The Nez Perce Indians and the Opening of the Northwest* (New Haven, Conn.: Yale University Press, 1965); Merrill D. Beal, *"I Will Fight No More Forever": Chief Joseph and the Nez Perce War* (Seattle: University of Washington Press, 1963); and Mark H. Brown, *The Flight of the Nez Perce* (New York: Putnam, 1967).

14. Sherman to Philip H. Sheridan, March 9, 1879, Box 39, Philip H. Sheridan Papers, Library of Congress.

15. Charles J. Crane, *Experiences of a Colonel of Infantry* (New York: Knickerbocker Press, 1922), 113.

16. Details of the final Geronimo campaign can be found in Britton Davis, *The Truth about Geronimo,* ed. M. M. Quaife (Lincoln: University of Nebraska Press, 1976); Angie Debo, *Geronimo: The Man, His Time, His Place* (Norman: University of Oklahoma Press, 1976); Dan L. Thrapp, *The Conquest of Apacheria* (Norman: University of Oklahoma Press, 1967).

17. Quoted in Johnson, *Unregimented General,* 262.

18. For the Ghost Dance troubles, see Robert M. Utley, *The Last Days of the Sioux Nation* (New Haven, Conn.: Yale University Press, 1963).

19. Seymour, "Sioux Rebellion," 106.

20. Quoted in John M. Carroll, ed., *The Benteen-Goldin Letters on Custer and His Last Battle* (New York: Liveright, 1974), 233.

Frank D. Baldwin

by Robert C. Carriker

Frank Dwight Baldwin was one of the best-known military figures in the trans-Mississippi West during the post–Civil War era. To the enlisted men and officers of the Fifth Infantry he was an outstanding leader who commanded detachments in the Indian Territory expedition of 1874 and the Sioux campaigns against Sitting Bull. To the ordinary western homesteader of the 1870s and 1880s, Baldwin was a hero. News of his exploits against hostile Indians were widely repeated on both sides of the hundredth meridian. Frank Baldwin was a respected and revered frontier figure in his time.

Baldwin's major distinction to military historians today is barely more than the fact that he was one of only two regular army officers who twice received the Medal of Honor.[1] Yet an examination of his full service record reveals not only a brave soldier but a capable officer as well, in one of the most diverse careers in the frontier army. When it was required, Baldwin campaigned against the Indians with a vengeance. He could also be sympathetic to the Indian's situation, however, as when he arranged treaty revisions for the mid-Columbia tribes of the Pacific Northwest, or safely resettled the Nez Perce in their homeland. For four years in the 1890s, Baldwin served as agent for the Kiowa-Comanche reservation, protecting those tribes from traders, cattlemen, "sooners," and timber thieves. Beyond this, Baldwin's career is worthy of a review in that he was typical of many other junior officers in the post–Civil War army whose rise through the ranks was tied to the coattails of a major figure. Like his mentor, Nelson A. Miles, Baldwin's army career fluctuated with the political tenor of the times.

Frank Baldwin was born June 26, 1842, at Manchester, Michigan, in a family whose heritage in America was traceable to colonial Connecticut. He was educated in Constantine, Michigan, and attended college briefly. Still, he seemed destined to be a farmer.[2]

Events at Fort Sumter, South Carolina, changed Baldwin's career plans forever. Like thousands of others, Baldwin answered Abraham Lincoln's call for volunteers in April 1861, enlisting in the Second Michigan Infantry. Michigan units, however, were not well organized, and the Second Infantry first merged with the Chandler Horse Guards and then disbanded. It was not until August 5, 1862, that the determined youth finally attached himself to a permanent regiment, enrolling as a second lieutenant with the Nineteenth Michigan Infantry.[3]

The Army of the Ohio, to which the inexperienced Nineteenth was attached, hurriedly trained in Kentucky and then went on active duty in Tennessee. In 20 months Baldwin saw action only twice, and both times he was taken prisoner. The first time he spent two months at Libby Prison in Richmond before he was freed in a prisoner exchange. He was captured again while defending a railroad bridge across Stones River near Murfreesboro. This time, the Confederates deemed Baldwin and the other prisoners unworthy of further effort and released them all at sundown, minus their personal and military effects.[4]

In time the Nineteenth moved to Chattanooga, where it joined General William T. Sherman's army in its sweep across Georgia. As the number of battles increased and their intensity grew, Baldwin found his stride as a soldier. From May 1864 until April 1865, Baldwin participated in 15 engagements against the Confederates. He distinguished himself in several battles, most especially at Peachtree Creek, near Atlanta, where he led his company in a countercharge and, in spite of a withering fire, broke through the enemy lines to singlehandedly capture two officers from a Georgia regiment.[5] Before Sherman's march to the sea was completed, Baldwin was promoted to captain; by the time the war was over he was a lieutenant colonel of volunteers.

Discharge from the army did not sit well with Baldwin. For many youths the cruel combat of the Civil War was enough to stifle any future desire for uniformed adventure. But for Baldwin it was the reverse. A brief fling at farming, even a return to college, could not measure up to the enterprising life he had known in the military. When the opportunity to enter the regular army as a second lieutenant in the Nineteenth Infantry offered itself in February 1866, Baldwin did not hesitate to accept. It was a fateful decision. Though many times he would risk his life during several decades of Indian fighting, and though he often felt slighted when lesser men were promoted ahead of him, Baldwin never regretted his long association with the United States Army. He would retire after 40 years, in 1906, as a brigadier general.

During Baldwin's initial assignment in Arkansas the bloated post–Civil War army reorganized itself several times. The result was that the 24-year-old second lieutenant became a first lieutenant in the Thirty-seventh Infantry and was ordered to Kansas for immediate duty protecting stagecoaches traveling through Indian country.

Fort Ellsworth was not only deep in Cheyenne and Arapaho country; it was also perched on the edge of what was considered to be the Great American Desert. It was a dangerous and desolate spot. Yet escort duty was seldom boring, thanks to the Indians and the wolves.[6] Still, Baldwin was lonely. Following his parole from Libby Prison in 1863, he had met Alice Blackwood, a schoolmate of his sister. In the months between the end of the Civil War and his appointment to the regular army, he had courted the young lady, and the misery of his Kansas experience now caused him to propose marriage. On January 10, 1867, Frank and Alice were wed in Northfield, Michigan. Alice, a spunky young lady who had already been to California, insisted on joining her husband in Kansas.[7]

In the spring following the couple's arrival in Kansas, Baldwin's unit was transferred to New Mexico Territory. While en route to Fort Wingate, on October 12, 1867, Alice delivered the Baldwin's only child, Juanita Mary, in Trinidad, Colorado Territory. Growing family responsibilities, plus an unstable situation in the constantly reorganizing army, caused Alice to urge Frank to rethink his commitment to a military career.[8] Frank remained firm, however. He liked his life of independent action, and he was sure his administrative and leadership talents would shortly bring him advancement. Besides, he believed opportunities for promotion would soon be enhanced by his transfer to the Fifth Infantry in yet another reshuffling of regiments. But Baldwin was too optimistic; he remained mired in the ranks of junior officers.

In June 1874, Baldwin received special orders from Colonel Nelson A. Miles to report for duty at Fort Dodge, Kansas. A general outbreak of Indians across the southern plains had forced Lieutenant General Philip H. Sheridan to send a massive military force into the field. Brigadier General John Pope, of the Department of the Missouri, and Brigadier General C. C. Augur, of the Department of Texas, were ordered to coordinate the attack in the Red River War. Each commander would employ three columns, one of which, the Indian Territory expedition under Pope, was to be led by Colonel Miles.[9] Miles and Baldwin had served together in Kansas in 1869, and the colonel could see in his subordinate outstanding leadership ability. Baldwin was slight in appearance, being just over five feet eight inches in height, but his steely gray eyes intimated a determination of purpose that even the rawest recruit instantly recognized and respected. Miles asked Baldwin to serve as his chief of scouts. Thus began a partnership that would last until both men retired from the army.

As a concession to his wife, Baldwin embarked upon his new assignment carrying pen, ink, and paper in addition to his military equipment. Alice disapproved of Frank's stagnant military career but felt that something might be gained from it if he could record his experiences for future publication. Frank promised to describe all of his activities in a pocket diary like the one he had meticulously kept during the Civil War. Later, it was agreed, Alice, an aspiring writer, would "enlarge and embellish" her husband's diary for publication.[10] Presumably, Frank would distinguish himself in Miles's campaign and gain promotion in the army, while Alice would be launched on a literary career.

The objective of the Indian Territory expedition was to move south of Fort Dodge, toward the Red River, sweeping the Texas Panhandle clean of hostiles. The scouts comprised 20 Delaware Indians whom Baldwin recruited from near Coffeeville, Kansas, 15 white trailers enlisted at Dodge City, and two dozen or so specially selected army volunteers. For the seven months of the Indian Territory expedition, the scouts normally operated outside the full command, seeking the best trails, locating water holes and camping spots, and reporting Indian movements. Their advanced position often put them in direct conflict with hostile warriors.

On August 30, for example, they were three miles in front of Miles's main command, exploring a range of low hills bordering the Red River, when they exchanged gunfire with the rear guard of a Cheyenne band. Within moments several hundred Indians had reversed direction and charged the small band of scouts, "swooping over the hill like a Kansas cyclone," Baldwin recorded. The scouts managed to hold their position until Miles came forward with 400 cavalrymen and three howitzers; then they moved out once more in the advance, chasing the Cheyennes from ridge to ridge until night began to fall. Dark smoke on the sunset horizon told Miles that the Indians were burning their lodges and whatever else might impede their flight away from the relentless pursuit.[11]

Similarly, on November 8, Baldwin and his scouts stumbled upon Grey Beard's camp on McClellan's Creek, Texas. There was no time to wait for the main command, so Baldwin launched an attack using nine wagons and his entire command of scouts, plus a company of infantry at his disposal, about 125 men in all. The Indians, several hundred strong, were stunned by this impulsive action but fought bitterly to keep Baldwin away from the camp. The initial penetration made by the surprise charge, however, plus well-directed howitzer fire, enabled Baldwin to enter the village, where he discovered two white captives, Julia and Adelaide German, ages five and seven. Twice the Indians attempted to retake their camp, but they were forced into retreat and followed so closely by Baldwin's command that the scouts were able to use revolvers.[12]

The scouts also carried messages between the commands. For these assignments, Baldwin did not permit volunteering; each man took his turn for dangerous missions, no excuses permitted. Not the least of the many individual demonstrations of resourcefulness exhibited by the scouts came from Baldwin himself. In company with three others, Baldwin left Miles's command in the Texas Panhandle at dusk on September 6 and rode nearly nonstop to Camp Supply, 180 miles distant, in three and a half days. The first morning out the scouts were discovered by Indians, and from then on they were almost continually pursued. Rains swelled the streams, forcing numerous fords; worse, it caused the scouts to stumble blindly into an Indian camp from which they escaped only by bravado and the fact that most of the Indians were in their lodges, taking refuge from the downpour.[13]

In spite of his exemplary performance in the field, the chief of scouts remained unrewarded by departmental headquarters. Miles was certainly appreciative of Baldwin's efforts and did what he could to advance him, but the post–Civil War army was highly political. Miles could recommend a promotion, but he could not approve one. He could, however, let Lieutenant Baldwin have all the responsibility he could handle. Prior to his rescue of the German sisters in the "Charge of the Wagon Train," as the incident became popularly known, Baldwin wrote to his wife: "The general certainly is doing everything for me in the way of giving me a chance. Just think of it. I am now to have a major's command and there is a major and a captain in camp."[14] Moreover, when the Red River War ended in February 1875, Miles recommended that Baldwin be awarded the brevet rank of captain for his services in carrying dispatches to Camp Supply, September 6–10, and the rank of major for the engagement at McClellan's Creek on November 8. Neither of these recommendations was acted upon at Department of the Missouri headquarters.

The bond between Miles and Baldwin was unaffected by this slight, and the two shared many hours together at Fort Leavenworth following the Indian Territory expedition. Soon, Miles was regarded as Baldwin's patron, so it came as no surprise that Baldwin was appointed Miles's battalion adjutant when the Fifth Infantry was ordered into the field against Sitting Bull following the Battle of the Little Bighorn.

The movement of troops to the northern plains in July 1876 was awkward and inefficient. Unusually hot temperatures and a lack of reliable information about the status of the Indians in the vicinity kept tempers short. Arrival at the Yellowstone expedition headquarters did nothing to relieve the tension. Baldwin was eager to get moving against the Indians and shared Miles's concern over the lack of initiative displayed by Brigadier General Alfred Terry.

The full command's first march down the Rosebud River set the tone for the rest of the campaign. Arrangements were inadequate for 1,700 troopers and 200 wagons, and the overly cautious Terry moved as though he "expected to be taken in by Indians every moment. I don't think there is any use in warning about our getting into a fight with the Indians for I don't believe we will see an Indian during the thirty-five days we are expected to be out,'' Baldwin decided. So it went for the entire summer.[15]

Baldwin's attitude improved in the fall, when orders arrived informing the Fifth Infantry that it would be one of three units to remain on the Yellowstone River for the winter. Baldwin anticipated that without the interference of others, Miles and the experienced Fifth Infantry would soon locate and defeat the Indians in their winter camps.

One such foray began on November 6. The difficulty of moving 440 men and 38 wagons between the breaks of the upper Missouri River combined with capricious, inclement weather to make the Fort Peck expedition a miserable experience. But it was not a failure. At one point, in an effort to clarify conflicting reports on the location of Sitting Bull's village, Miles split his command, allowing Baldwin to take 109 men with him to the Milk River. Temperatures below zero put a crust on the two feet of snow, cutting the men's legs, but that was overlooked when Sitting Bull's camp was sighted early on the morning of December 7. The Sioux were provoked, ''brisk fire'' was exchanged, and things went well for the Fifth. But this was, after all, Sitting Bull; rather than risk being sucked into a trap, Baldwin broke off the engagement. Later that night the temperature dropped to 40 degrees below zero, and Baldwin prudently ordered his force back to Fort Peck.

After resupplying and resting his men, Baldwin pushed on yet another 100 miles in pursuit of Sitting Bull. On December 18 his scouts located a camp of 122 lodges near the head of Redwater Creek. This time the Indians chose not to fight and gathered up their families and ponies for flight. Baldwin's men destroyed all of the lodges, robes, food, and horses that remained. Once again Baldwin had proved himself to be Miles's most effective subordinate in the field. His small command had traveled more than 325 miles in severe winter weather, kept the Indians moving, twice met them in battle, and captured large quantities of supplies. Miles personally ordered a relief expedition into the field to escort the heroes back to their cantonment on the Tongue River.[16]

Baldwin's introductory months on the northern plains were instructive to an already accomplished Indian fighter. Another area in which he was also growing in wisdom was in dealing with the press. Crook, Custer, Terry, Pope, and others frequently used the newspapers to publicize their activities; why should not Baldwin do the same? The Omaha *Herald* received a copy of Baldwin's official report to Miles on the Fort Peck expedition and was quick to editorialize on the effectiveness of Baldwin's small command. The Battle at the Redwater was labeled a ''signal victory'' that was ''eliciting the admiration of the whole country.'' But Baldwin perhaps overdid it. The newspaper's editor commented that ''while the army officers here hold Lieutenant Baldwin in great respect and none of them willingly questions his veracity, the question is being discussed in a serio-comic manner of withdrawing all the troops from the frontier, excepting the redoubtable Lieutenant, and letting him finish this war in short order."[17]

In January 1877, Miles turned his attention from Sitting Bull to Crazy Horse, and Baldwin, as usual, commanded a key company. Before the month was out, he and his company of the Fifth Infantry logged 233 miles in the field and had one more encounter with the Sioux. At the two-day Battle of Wolf Mountain, the Sioux and Northern Cheyennes took the offensive and attacked Miles's camp, but to no advantage. Once again, Miles, in a critical moment of the battle, counted on Baldwin to lead the charge that dislodged the Indians from high ground above the camp.[18] In the following months, Miles used the carrot as well as the stick to bring several bands of Sioux and Cheyennes back to their reservations. Sitting Bull, however, chose to retreat to Canada. Temporarily, in the spring of 1877, the Great Sioux War tapered off.

For the next several years Baldwin remained at the cantonment on the Tongue River (Fort Keogh), training scouts, seeing to supplies for several new posts in the vicinity, and enjoying the company of his wife and daughter, who had been permitted to join him when the hostilities died down. Periodically, there were Indian alarms. One came in August 1877, when Chief Joseph and his band of Nez Perces retreated across Montana. There was another scare in 1878, when it was rumored that Sitting Bull was assembling a huge band of hostiles along the Canadian border to swoop into American territory. Baldwin took no important role in the Nez Perce affair except to escort the surrendered tribesmen to the Indian Territory, but he made up for that in the renewal of the Sitting Bull campaign.

Several times each year from 1877 to 1880, Baldwin accepted the responsibility of leading expeditions into the field either to attempt to locate Sitting Bull's camp or to arrest the illicit traders who were selling guns to the Sioux. Baldwin believed certain reservation Indians were trading their government-issued "civilian clothes" to Canadians for arms and ammunition, which were then bartered to the dissident Sioux. Department policy forbade patrols north of the Missouri River, but Baldwin was an impetuous officer and frequently advanced small patrols all the way to the forty-ninth parallel. Sometimes this disregard of department policy was so flagrant that Miles had to reprimand him.[19]

In the fall of 1878, Baldwin was transferred to Fort Marion, Florida. Miles's effort to restrain his favorite subordinate was not at issue; rather, doctors had diagnosed a tubercular condition in Baldwin's right lung, and emergency medical leave was required. For Miles, and even Terry, there was a moment of embarassment. Baldwin was the epitome of Old Army spirit. He was 36 years old and had spent nearly 14 consecutive years on the Indian frontier in all manner of field assignments, yet he was still a junior officer. The bureaucracy was stirred to action: by the time Baldwin returned to Fort Keogh in June 1879, in slightly better health, he was wearing captain's bars.

Miles had immediate use for his new captain. Each spring brought fresh rumors of Sitting Bull's imminent attack upon American territory south of the "Dominion Line," and Baldwin resumed his practice of taking one or more patrols into the field north of the Missouri. His soldiers found no hostile camps in 1879, but they did arrest 829 illegal traders and confiscate 656 carts filled with contraband.

In the spring of 1880, Baldwin took to the field again and this time discovered a large camp of Indians along Little Porcupine Creek. His troops routed them and burned the camp. Within a short time almost 1,000 homeless Sioux surrendered at Fort Keogh.[20] Later, even Sitting Bull turned himself in to reservation authorities. Baldwin did not know it at the time, but he had made his final military campaign against the Indians.

In the fall, Baldwin's tubercular condition worsened, necessitating a second medical leave. This time, however, Miles personally saw to Baldwin's assignment as the American representative to a European military conference, so that he could spend a good part of the winter in the south of France. Baldwin gratefully accepted the gesture, and he and Alice began a grand tour of the continent. Baldwin's assignment came just as Miles was being promoted to the rank of brigadier general.[21]

When he returned from Europe in 1881, Baldwin joined Miles in the Department of the Columbia. Officially, he was an acting judge advocate: in reality, he once again served as a trusted aide to Miles, who commanded the department. In one instance, Baldwin prepared the way for a peaceful renegotiation of a treaty with Chief Moses and the mid-Columbia tribes. Miles also asked Baldwin to personally provide for the safe return of the Chief Joseph band of Nez Perce Indians to the Pacific Northwest after their eight-year exile in the Indian Territory; ironically, it was Baldwin who had escorted them there in 1877. In 1885 he met the band in Pocatello and brought them back to their reservations. Baldwin believed there was a time to fight and a time to heal, and he would tolerate no renewal of old grudges by unforgiving whites. His strategic placement of military detachments in Walla Walla, Spokane, and Umatilla ensured the safe passage of the Nez Perces back to their homeland.[22]

In the fall of 1885, when Miles left the Department of the Columbia and returned to the Department of the Missouri, Baldwin went with him. The following year Miles was transferred to the Department of Arizona; this time Baldwin, reluctantly, remained behind. He was reassigned to the frontier and spent short periods at Fort Custer in Montana Territory, Fort Totten in Dakota Territory, and Fort Davis in Texas.

In 1890, Miles was promoted to major general and took command of the Division of the Missouri. By this time many of his most strident antagonists were either dead or retired, and among the active officers he was the preeminent expert on Indian matters. Ever the politician, Miles understood that he now had the opportunity to exercise his influence as well as his judgment; accordingly, loyal friends such as Baldwin were honored. On a single day in February 1890, Baldwin received the brevet ranks of captain and major: the first for gallant service in actions against the Indians during the Indian Territory expedition of 1874, the second for similarly heroic actions against the Sioux at the Redwater and Wolf Mountain. Additionally, within a year, Baldwin was appointed acting inspector and acting judge advocate of the Division of the Missouri.

Simultaneously with Baldwin's appointment as an inspector, in January 1891, Miles received the full report of the battle that took place on December 29, 1890, at Wounded Knee Creek on the Pine Ridge Reservation in South Dakota. Indian anxieties, nurtured by the Ghost Dance religion and aggravated by the recent murder of Sitting Bull, helped precipitate an armed conflict between the Miniconjou Sioux and Colonel James W. Forsyth's Seventh Cavalry in which 146 Indians and 25 soldiers died.[23] In an effort to defuse an already perilous situation, on January 4, 1891, Miles ordered his trusted subordinate, Captain Baldwin, to join Major J. Ford Kent in a court of inquiry.

Never before, even on the field of battle among hostile Indians, had Baldwin been thrust so deeply into the center of conflict. The appointment of this perennial Miles loyalist as one of two inspectors was not lost on the general's critics. Moreover, the fact that Baldwin had a distinguished war record against Indians was worrisome to humanitarian groups. Everywhere controversy swirled. President Benjamin Harrison disapproved of any formal court of inquiry, but Miles required one anyway. After several days of testimony, Baldwin and Kent, sympathetic to fellow officers, minimized the impact of the battle in their preliminary report. But Miles's intense dislike for Forsyth was not satisfied. He prompted the court to reconvene for more testimony, and on January 18, Baldwin and Kent returned a strongly worded decision holding Forsyth responsible for the deaths at Wounded Knee.[24] In the end, both Lieutenent General John M. Schofield and Secretary of War Redfield Proctor overruled the court of inquiry and dismissed the charges against Forsyth.

Following the Wounded Knee episode, Baldwin was relieved to take the low-profile position of inspector of small arms practice for the Division of the Missouri. His duties were not excessive, and he was able to conduct a great deal of personal business.

Even more to his liking was the presentation on December 3, 1891, of a Medal of Honor for his actions at Peachtree Creek, Georgia, during Sherman's march to the sea. Miles, of course, recommended him for the honor, the fact that it was brought to the attention of the secretary of war more than a quarter-century later notwithstanding. By no strange coincidence, another application had been denied a month earlier for a Medal of Honor citing Baldwin's gallant though futile defense of the Stones River stockade near Murfreesboro in 1863.

By this time it was clear to Baldwin that promotion depended not only upon patrons and publicity but also upon awards. He soon became as persistent in his quest for honors as he once had been in seeking out Indian camps. In 1894, when Miles was in an even stronger position in the War Department, Baldwin requested his support for yet another Medal of Honor application, this one acclaiming his rescue of the German girls from Grey Beard's camp. The medal was denied in July, but after Miles rephrased his appeal, the secretary of war reversed himself and approved the issue of Baldwin's second Medal of Honor before the year was out.[25]

From 1894 to 1898, Baldwin was the agent for the Kiowa and Comanche reservation at Anadarko, Oklahoma Territory. As usual, Miles influenced the move; believing that the Bureau of Indian Affairs was the true source of Indian discontent on the reservations, he urged the appointment of military officers as agents, considering them better qualified than civilians to monitor Indian activity. An 1892 law permitted the President to appoint army officers as agents, and Grover Cleveland chose to do so for the Kiowa-Comanche reservation. The Kiowas and Comanches reluctantly sold their lands to the United States in 1892, but the ink was barely dry on the document before pressure to open them for settlement began to build. Meanwhile, Congress held up ratification of the agreement for eight years, and in the interval the Indians were harassed by a variety of frontier characters. It was into this situation that Baldwin found himself thrust in November 1894.

During his tenure at Anadarko, Baldwin spent most of his time serving eviction notices on sooners to the Kiowa and Comanche lands, controlling timber theft by whites, overseeing the writing of grass contracts with reputable cattlemen and the licensing of honest traders to deal with the Indians. More troublesome than all of these, in Baldwin's opinion, were the white husbands of Indian women who demanded equal land holdings with the native tribesmen. Baldwin bristled at their demands and refused to be intimidated. A group of these men responded by bringing suit against the agent, challenging his authority before his superiors, and even threatening violence in order to get their way. More than ever, Baldwin, the old warrior, realized that future Indian fights would take place in the courts, not in the countryside. It was a new era and one that he, a man of direct and decisive action, chafed under. Though wholeheartedly supported by both Miles and the Indian Rights Association, Baldwin would have preferred to fight his battles in the manner he knew best: on the battlefield. When at last too many complaints against him piled up, he asked for and was granted release in May 1898.[26] As a reward for his efforts, he was promoted to major in the Fifth Infantry.

Baldwin very much wanted to lead a battalion in the Spanish-American War. In an effort to hasten his chances, he transferred to a volunteer unit with the rank of lieutenant colonel. But he chose unwisely, for this outfit never got close to the field of battle — while Miles, who remained with the Fifth Infantry, led his troops in the conquest of Puerto Rico. Bitter at missing his chance for combat,

Baldwin sulked as an inspector in the Department of the Colorado and the Department of the Missouri until an opportunity arose for him to join a unit assigned to the Philippine insurrection. It was the only war he could find.

As it had done following the Civil War, the army underwent drastic reorganization after the Spanish-American War, and the eager Baldwin ended up as a colonel in the Twenty-seventh Infantry. His regiment sailed from America in January 1902 and arrived at Manila Bay within a month. Apparently Baldwin's leadership ability had not been diminished by his administrative assignments: with a willing though inexperienced regiment behind him, he defeated the Moros twice and made the Twenty-seventh the first troops on the south shore of Lake Lanano, Island of Mindanao. President Theodore Roosevelt sent him a congratulatory telegram, and the War Department responded with a promotion to brigadier general.[27] It was thus with a sense of triumph that Baldwin departed the Philippines in February 1903, for he was coming home not only a hero but also a general. Moreover, he had a new assignment as commander of the Department of the Colorado.

Baldwin retired from the United States Army on June 26, 1906, after 40 years of distinguished service. He made his home in Denver, but the pleasant surroundings of the Rocky Mountains did not make his departure from the regular army any more agreeable to him than when he had been mustered out of the volunteer army in 1866. It was not until 1917 that he received a reprieve: the governor of Colorado requested his assistance in preparing the state's National Guard for World War I, appointing him state adjutant general. Baldwin responded by doing an outstanding job of training the citizen-soldiers of his adopted state. When he retired for the final time in 1919, this time as a major general, he tried to adjust to a life of leisure and again attempted to write an autobiography, but he lacked enthusiasm for the project. The manuscript was still unfinished at his death in 1923.

Frank D. Baldwin's life and career contained elements of both normal and extraordinary military conduct. Many young men sought careers in the post–Civil War army and served with distinction. In his dedication to the service and his gallantry in combat, Baldwin was not unlike other military men. But there was something individualistic as well in his career. His contemporaries sometimes used the word ''verve.''

Baldwin had a contagious vigor in pursuing his goals. His men — whether in the Nineteenth Michigan Infantry, the Indian Territory scouts, the Fifth or the Twenty-seventh Infantry — instinctively understood his action-oriented personality; if they did not, Baldwin soon demonstrated it for them under actual field conditions. Miles recognized Baldwin's aptitude and used it to his own advantage. Baldwin was just as good for Miles's career as Miles was necessary to Baldwin's success.

In his own time Baldwin received the recognition that was due him. His bravery in the Civil War, the Red River War, and the Great Sioux War eventually netted him two brevet promotions and two Medals of Honor. The shame is that it took political interference to achieve honor for what should have been acknowledged on its own merits. But such was the age in which Baldwin lived. The post–Civil War army was as repressive in the department offices as it was uninhibited at frontier posts. It was on the frontier, in front of an independent command, that Baldwin earned his reputation.

When he died, Frank D. Baldwin proudly wore campaign ribbons from the Civil War, the Indian Wars, the Spanish-American War, the Philippine insurrection, and World War I. Newspaper accounts lauded his administrative position in Colorado during World War I and recalled his participation in the Philippine insurrection, but few persons in the Roaring Twenties remembered that in the 1870s Frank D. Baldwin had been one of the nation's greatest Indian fighters and had helped open the American West to settlement. One man did remember, however, and on behalf of thousands less eloquent but nevertheless grateful pioneers, he made Frank Baldwin's frontier military exploits the central theme of his eulogy before the funeral train carrying Baldwin's body departed Denver for Arlington National Cemetary. At the conclusion of his remarks, retired General W. S. Brown justifiably proclaimed: "A generation ago his name was a household word all along the frontier between the 100th meridian and the Rocky Mountains. In the development of the Great West few names stand higher than that of Frank D. Baldwin."[28]

Notes

1. Five men have received two Medals of Honor, but only Frank D. Baldwin and Thomas W. Custer were officers in the regular army, and Custer's medals were awarded posthumously. An act of Congress, July 1, 1918, now limits individuals to a single Medal of Honor.

2. Joseph Baldwin came as a free planter to Connecticut Colony on November 20, 1639. In time, members of the family drifted west. Francis Leonard Baldwin, the father of Frank, was born March 14, 1814, in Hope, New York. He moved to Michigan with his father in 1835; in 1841 he married Betsy Ann Richards and began to farm about four miles west of Manchester, Michigan, on land adjoining his father's property. Francis Leonard died on February 28, 1842, and his son Frank Dwight was born (in the log cabin his father had built) on June 26, 1842. Betsy Ann remarried and had two daughters, Rowena and Gertrude. Frank attended Hillsdale College for a short period before 1861. See C. C. Baldwin, "Baldwin Geneology," in Frank D. Baldwin Papers, Henry H. Huntington Library, San Marino, California.

3. Frank D. Baldwin, Diary (1862), and Frank D. Baldwin, "Autobiography," Baldwin Papers; *Record of Service of Michigan Volunteers in the Civil War* (Kalamazoo, n.d.), 4. The Nineteenth Michigan Infantry of 995 officers and men was composed of recruits from the Second Michigan Congressional District.

4. In 1891, Baldwin applied for a Medal of Honor for his part in defending the Stones

River Bridge. Therefore an excellent source of information on that battle is the Appointments, Commissions and Promotion File for Frank Baldwin (hereafter Baldwin ACP File), Records of the Adjutant General's Office, 1780s–1917, Record Group (RG) 94, National Archives (NA), which contains a dozen letters written to the secretary of war by eyewitnesses testifying to Baldwin's courage. The application was denied.

5. In 1891, Baldwin received a Medal of Honor for his bravery at Peachtree Creek. See Baldwin ACP File for 18 eyewitness statements. A summary of Baldwin's field service during the Civil War is in Frank Baldwin to C. Morris, September 20, 1866, Baldwin Papers.

6. Baldwin's several encounters with Indians and a particularly frightening chase by a pack of wolves across a deserted, snowy prairie can be found in Baldwin, "Autobiography," and an unnamed newspaper clipping from 1900 entitled "Thrilling Encounter," both in Baldwin Papers. See also "Interview of Frank D. Baldwin," by Thomas Dawson, March 28, 1922, in the Library of the State Historical Society of Colorado; and Nelson A. Miles, *Personal Recollections and Observations of General Nelson A. Miles* (Chicago: Werner, 1896), 129–30.

7. Alice Blackwood was born in 1845 in Ann Arbor, Michigan. Her parents, emigrants from New England, moved to California the same year and settled in Sacramento, where her father, Dr. Thomas Blackwood, became the first physician of that community. Alice and her sister were later returned to the care of an aunt in Michigan for the completion of their schooling. A summary of the life of Alice Baldwin can be found in the introduction to Robert C. and Eleanor R. Carriker *An Army Wife on the Frontier: The Memoirs of Alice Blackwood Baldwin 1867–1877* (Salt Lake City: Tanner Trust Fund, University of Utah Library, 1975).

8. See letters from Alice Baldwin to Frank Baldwin, December 3, 1870, January 20, 1871, and January 24, 1873, in Baldwin Papers.

9. For the causes, campaigns, and accomplishments of the Red River War, see William H. Leckie, *The Military Conquest of the Southern Plains* (Norman: University of Oklahoma Press, 1963); and James L. Haley, *The Buffalo War* (New York: Doubleday, 1976).

10. Baldwin actually wrote down his experiences twice: in both the shirt-pocket diary and a larger book into which he transcribed the daily diary entries when a relaxation in tempo permitted. After agreeing to "do as you suggest," Baldwin cautioned his wife to "remember that glory in my profession is won only in battle, though men may and will add to it by the skillful use of words": Frank Baldwin to Alice Baldwin, September 12, 24, October 6, 1874, Baldwin Papers. Alice later did write several stories about her husband's exploits during the Indian wars, but they were never accepted for publication. After Frank's death in 1923, Alice renewed her interest in writing and privately published Alice Blackwood Baldwin, *The Memoirs of the Late Major General Frank D. Baldwin* (Los Angeles: Westzel, 1929).

11. This and other activities of the scouting detachment can best be observed in publications by and about the scouts, including J. T. Marshall, *The Miles Expedition of 1874–1875: An Eyewitness Account of the Red River War*, ed. Lonnie J. White (Austin, Tex.: Encino Press, 1971); and Robert C. Carriker, "Mercenary Heroes: The Scouting Detachment of the Indian Territory Expedition, 1874–1875," *Chronicles of Oklahoma* 51 (Fall 1973): 309–24. See also Frank D. Baldwin, "The Battle of Red River, Texas,

August 30, 1874, the Part Taken by the Scouts,'' and ''Baldwin Indian Territory Expedition,'' in the William Cary Brown Collection, University of Colorado, Boulder.

12. The German family had been en route from Georgia to Colorado via Smoky Hill when they were attacked by Cheyennes on September 11, 1874. Five members of the family were killed, and four girls were taken captive; the older two were returned on March 6, 1875, at the Cheyenne and Arapaho agency. See Donald J. Berthrong, *The Southern Cheyennes* (Norman: University of Oklahoma Press, 1963), 395, 400–401. Baldwin received his second Medal of Honor in 1894 for the rescue of the German sisters; once again, eyewitness testimony is included in his ACP File, National Archives. See also a series of letters and Miles's official report in Box 134, Department of the Missouri, Letters Received, Records of U.S. Continental Commands, 1821–1920, RG 393, NA; Thompson McFadden, ''Diary of an Indian Campaign, 1874,'' ed. Robert C. Carriker, *Southwestern Historical Quarterly* 75 (October 1971): 198–232; and Baldwin, ''Autobiography,'' 402.

13. See Frank Baldwin, ''Daring Deeds of Army Scouts in Early Days,'' and ''Official Report as Bearer of Dispatches from General Miles Command, Butler County, Texas to Fort Leavenworth, Kansas, September 6 to 14, 1874,'' in Baldwin Papers; and W. C. Brown, ''General Baldwin's Scout in Panhandle of Texas, September 6 to 9, 1874,'' Brown Collection.

14. Frank Baldwin to Alice Baldwin, November 4, 1874, Baldwin Papers.

15. Frank Baldwin to Alice Baldwin, August 7, 1876, Baldwin Papers. Baldwin also wrote to Alice on August 4: ''They don't move with that vigor and life that would foretell success and it is rather discouraging to us who have had Indian experience and service under an active commander.''

16. The most revealing accounts of the Fort Peck Expedition come from Baldwin, Diary (1876); and Baldwin, ''Winter Campaigning against Indians in Montana,'' read before the Loyal Legion Comandery, Denver, Colorado, December 5, 1911, in Brown Collection.

17. The article added that ''the first report of Lieutenant Baldwin's exploit, written by himself, was such as to assure the incredulous that this Indian business was about terminated, and Sitting Bull had met a Waterloo defeat at the hands of the Lieutenant and 100 men'': Omaha *Herald*, January 23, 1877.

18. Baldwin, Diary (1877); ''Statement of Captain Frank D. Baldwin, Fifth Infantry, Regarding the Battle of Wolf Mountain,'' Brown Collection; Miles, *Personal Recollections*, 237–38; Baldwin Correspondence in Major George W. Baird Papers, Kansas State Historical Society, Topeka, Kansas.

19. Miles knew full well that Baldwin, once in the field, would go where Indian signs led him, departmental regulations notwithstanding. The irony of the situation is that Miles was himself ''a master at deliberately misunderstanding instructions and at exceeding authority just enough to get his way without provoking more than a reprimand from his superiors'': Robert M. Utley, *The Last Days of the Sioux Nation* (New Haven, Conn.: Yale University Press, 1963), 278–79. According to Baldwin's diary entry for March 29, 1878, Miles gave him ''secret instructions'' and then sent him to the Milk River area to hasten and encourage the surrender of the Sioux in that vicinity; officially, he was leading a telegraph and heliograph survey party. See Baldwin, Diary (1878), March 27 to May 20, and Baldwin, ''Autobiography,'' 583.

20. *A Synopsis of Military Operations of Nelson A. Miles* (Tucson: Arizona Historical Foundation Library, n.d.); Returns of the Fifth United States Infantry, Records of Adjutant General's Office, 1780s–1917, RG 94, NA; Letter of S. M. Miller, January 16, 1904, in Miller Collection, U.S. Army Military History Research Collection, Carlisle Barracks, Pennsylvania; Joseph Zimmerman to Frank Baldwin, June 5, 1918, Baldwin Papers.

21. Baldwin and Miles had been friends since 1869, and at one point Baldwin wrote to his wife: "The General has been exceedingly kind to me in every way and I know him like a brother. And if he should get his promotion I believe he would take me with him."

22. Miles, *Personal Recollections,* 397–415; Department of the Columbia, Letters Received, no. 1756, Records of U.S. Continental Commands, 1821–1920, RG 393, NA.

23. For Wounded Knee, see Utley, *Last Days of the Sioux Nation.*

24. *Annual Report of the Secretary of War, 1891,* 2 vols. (Washington, D.C.: Government Printing Office, 1891), 1:132–55; Division of the Missouri, Letters Received, "Papers relating to the investigation conducted by Major J. Ford Kent and Capt. Frank D. Baldwin into the Battle at Wounded Knee Creek," pp. 1–125, Letters Received, Division of the Missouri, Records of U.S. Continental Commands, RG 393, NA.

25. Baldwin ACP File.

26. Forrest D. Monahan, Jr., "The Kiowa-Comanche Reservation in the 1890's" *Chronicles of Oklahoma* 45 (Winter 1967–68): 451–63; Martha Buntin, "Kiowa Indians," and Kiowa Letterbook No. 44, both in the Indian Archives of the Oklahoma State Historical Society, Oklahoma City, Oklahoma; William T. Hagan, *United States–Comanche Relations* (New Haven, Conn.: Yale University Press, 1976), 222–47. See also the correspondence in Records of the Bureau of Indian Affairs, Letters Received 1895–98, RG 75, NA.

27. Baldwin, "Autobiography"; Frank D. Baldwin Collection, State Historical Society of Colorado Library; "Memorandum of Military Services of Brigadier General Frank D. Baldwin," Baldwin ACP File; Alice Baldwin, *Memoirs,* 98–102.

28. William C. Brown, "Eulogy for Frank D. Baldwin," Brown Collection.

Charles King

Courtesy Paul L. Hedren Collection

by Paul L. Hedren

GENERAL CHARLES KING TO BE RETIRED!

"Preposterous," retorted Wisconsin National Guard officials in 1921 when they learned that the government planned to relieve certain retired regular army officers serving with the state guards. The Wisconsonites, of course, had in mind their own Charles King, a legendary figure who had been with the guard since its formation. Their outcry came to the attention of Eli A. Helmick, inspector general of the army, who took it up with Major General James G. Harbord, deputy chief of staff. Harbord, an enthusiastic admirer of King, interceded by issuing the following notice: "The Chief of Staff directs that no action looking to the relief of General Charles King from duty with the National Guard of Wisconsin ever be taken without the personal action of himself or the Deputy Chief of Staff." Harbord then explained his staunch support. "I read General King's books before I came into the service. My first commission was in the 5th Cavalry. General King's name was a household word in that regiment, and his influence was still potent to work up enthusiasm among the youngsters in the regiment. . . . General King has ceased to be an officer, he is an institution."[1]

An institution? Such an accolade from Washington, D.C., was mighty praise for a 77-year-old "Indian fighter," who by 1921 was an anachronism in the age of airplanes and world wars. But to study King's career and to read his voluminous works about the Old Army is to discover a quality and far-reaching value that is equal to the acclaim. It was King who, more than anyone else, fashioned America's vision of the late nineteenth-century regular army: portraits in words of a hearty band of soldiers who fought monotony at home and a treacherous yet admired foe in the field; visions, too, of army women, the unrecognized partners in the military system, who in King's world danced their way into the hearts of men. These tales, which so excited readers three generations ago, are with us even today. The medium has changed, we watch stories about the cavalry and Indians on televison now. But the gaily attired troopers, the Irish top sergeant, the sensitive junior officers under reproach from a calloused senior—these images popularized by John Ford and John Wayne in their famous cavalry trilogy and by countless budget westerns and television serials—are figures from stories that Charles King told first.

But Charles King was more than a writer. For 70 years he wore the uniform of a soldier—a length of service unmatched in the history of the nation. He was a West Pointer, an artilleryman and cavalryman, a tactician, a campaigner who suffered war wounds, regimental adjutant of the Fifth U.S. Cavalry, adjutant general of the state of Wisconsin, and brigadier general of volunteers. He wore army campaign ribbons from the Civil, Indian, and Spanish wars, and the Philippine insurrection; the Victory Medal from World War I; and a silver star for an Apache fight in 1874. Together, these awards and this length of service form a distinction without equal in the annals of American military history.

King has been largely ignored for the past 60 years. At the turn of the century he commanded an international audience, and at home he was one of the nation's best-selling authors. Today a modest rediscovery is underway. Military and western historians return to King's books for details of army life offered by one who knew it well and had the literary skill to report it. Our interpretations of this colorful and controversial era are tempered by the passage of time. Yet it is always worthwhile exploring origins, and the search for General Charles King invites study of an intriguing and wonderfully complex gentleman, a soldier, writer, and historian of the first order.

Born in Albany, New York, on October 12, 1844, to a family whose antecedents included a delegate to the Constitutional Convention, a president of New York City's Columbia College, and a graduate of the United States Military Academy, young Charles exhibited a penchant for the military very early in life. As a lad he drilled with his father's militia companies; he was often introduced to military notables; and at the outbreak of the Civil War when his father, the West Pointer, returned to uniform as the first commander of the soon famed Iron Brigade, Charles joined his command as a drummer and mounted orderly. He had been pressing hard for admission to West Point, and with some luck, he received an "at-large" appointment from President Abraham Lincoln to the entering class of 1862.

Although King had an aversion to mathematics, his scholarship was generally good and his record at West Point characterized by steady achievement and promotion. By 1863 he was a cadet corporal, and that summer he was on hand to defend the academy from Southern sympathizers who threatened to steam up the Hudson River from New York City and burn the school. The threat never materialized, but the sight of loaded artillery pieces and cadets armed with ball cartridges left a considerable impression on King and his peers. By 1865, Charles was cadet adjutant, the highest rank in the corps of cadets.[2]

Holding such a prestigious position proved both an honor and a nightmare for young King. Theft of money and valuables was an age-old affliction at West Point. Culprits were occasionally caught—sometimes trapped by taking marked loot—and swift punishments meted out. Although hardly consistent with the ethics of jurisprudence, the academy staff condoned these summary courts, indeed often encouraged them. A blowup came when an innocent cadet was wrongly served.[3]

The central figure was second classman Orsemus B. Boyd, who was accused of stealing money after marked bills were discovered in his room. An unpopular cadet, Boyd was brought before the assembled battalion at evening parade wearing a placard "THIEF" on his back and was drummed off the post. But Boyd chanced upon West Point Superintendent George W. Cullum and told his story. A subsequent court of inquiry completely cleared Boyd as the victim of planted, not stolen, money. The court further recommended that the cadet leaders involved be brought to trial before a general court-martial. King, as adjutant, accepted complete responsibility. He and three others were sentenced to dismissal from the academy. Each sentence was later suspended, but King was stripped of his cadet adjutancy.[4]

The Boyd scandal markedly affected the principal participants. Boyd, believed guilty by many of his classmates even though exonerated by the court of inquiry, finished his West Point education as an outcast. This baseless reputation followed him to the frontier, where his many years of faithful service were characterized by scrupulous honesty until the day he died in 1885. Curiously, Boyd learned that the real thief, a cadet named John J. Casey, had confessed to the stealing, but he chose to do nothing about it. As for King, he never forgot the humiliation. Throughout the remainder of his life he offered accounts of the story to set the record straight, and even in his novels repeatedly used a plot structure patterned after the Boyd incident.[5]

Reduced to the ranks, Cadet King graduated in 1866, twenty-second in a class of 41 members. Although he had hoped to be assigned to the mounted service, specifically the First Cavalry, his appointment was to Light Battery K, First Regiment U.S. Artillery. Rather than join his unit directly, King remained at West Point through the summer of 1866 as a tactics instructor.[6]

From the fall of 1866 through 1868, Second Lieutenant King served with his battery in Louisiana. Gatling guns formed the armament of certain artillery units, and King, the junior officer of Battery K, commanded those rapid-firing weapons. Although never unleashed, King's Gatling section played an important role in the 1868 New Orleans racial riots. In January 1869, King transferred to Battery C, First Artillery, stationed at Fort Hamilton, New York. That summer he was detailed for a second time to West Point, where for the next two years he taught artillery and cavalry tactics as well as horsemanship. He was promoted to first lieutenant in the First Artillery on May 15, 1870.[7]

In 1871, King "grabbed at a chance to transfer into the cavalry"—the Fifth Cavalry, a crack outfit with a splendid reputation. King could not know he would have only a decade of service with the Fifth before battle wounds cut short his regular army career, but what a decade it was, with enough civil and military action to provide the grist for two-thirds of his novels.

The Fifth Cavalry was stationed in Nebraska when Lieutenant King joined it in the fall of 1871, just in time to hunt on the plains with the regiment's chief scout, William F. "Buffalo Bill" Cody. But the regiment soon received orders to take station in Arizona Territory. At the same time the regiment's colonel, William H. Emory, was returned to his brevet rank of major general and assigned to command the Department of the Gulf, then headquartered in New Orleans, and Emory selected King as his personal aide-de-camp. This second tour in the South was most memorable for King because of his marriage to Adelaide Yorke, daughter of sea captain Louis S. Yorke of Carroll Parish, Louisiana.[8]

The Fifth Cavalry had a lively time in the Apache campaigns of 1872 and 1873, recording 56 combat engagements. In the spring of 1874, King, then 29 years old, rejoined his Company K at Camp Verde, Arizona, and participated in the Apache fights at Stauffer's Butte on May 25 and Black Mesa on June 3. In the Stauffer's Butte engagement, 18 Apaches were killed and two rancherias destroyed. General George Crook was sufficiently impressed to recommend that King be breveted a captain for gallant and distinguished service. Congress did not consider Indian fighting worthy of brevet recognition, however, and failed to act on this and other recommendations until the early 1890s. By then King had earned his captain's bars and was retired from the regular army. Fearing that the comptroller might issue a declaration barring one who accepted the lower grade from receiving the retired pay and allowances of the higher—circumstances apparently not uncommon in those days—he declined the award.[9]

A more memorable and costly Apache fight took place on November 1, 1874, when King, leading 40 cavalrymen and Indian scouts, engaged Apaches at Sunset Pass near the Little Colorado River. King and Sergeant Bernard Taylor were attacked while scouting in advance of the detail. In the ensuing fight King received an arrow wound across the forehead and a crippling bullet wound in the right arm. But for the heroics of Taylor, who rescued him and carried him down the mountain, and Lieutenant George O. Eaton, who raced up with the command to drive off the attackers, King would have been killed.

King's arm was in serious condition. The bullet shattered the bone just below the shoulder and left an open, suppurating wound that intermittently discharged bone fragments; it left the young officer unfit for duty. In early 1875 he was admitted to the Presidio Hospital near San Francisco for additional treatment. His attending surgeons there concluded that it would be at least a year before he would have the use of his arm, so on April 11, 1875, he went on extended sick leave. Throughout the remainder of the year his wound expelled bone fragments and related matter, but by late 1875 it had healed sufficiently to warrant his return to active duty.[10]

News from the northern plains during the winter of 1875–76 probably had as much to do with King's return to service as did the slow but seemingly steady healing of his arm. In 1875 the Fifth Cavalry was relieved of its Arizona duties and directed to posts in Kansas, Colorado, and the Indian Territory. The Fifth missed the opening actions of the Great Sioux War, but as more and more troops were called into the fray, its participation became inevitable. King had rejoined Company K in the late fall of 1875 at Fort Riley and marched with it to Fort Hays in May 1876 as the regiment was consolidated in anticipation of fighting the Sioux. Confirming orders on June 5 directed regimental headquarters and eight companies to move by rail to Cheyenne, Wyoming Territory, and then on to Fort Laramie. In Cheyenne, King met Buffalo Bill Cody at the Union Pacific Railway depot and escorted the Fifth's favorite scout to the cavalry camp. At Fort Laramie, Lieutenant Colonel Eugene A. Carr, the battalion commander, prepared for field service along the Powder River trail, a feeder between the Nebraska Sioux agencies and the hostile camps in northern Wyoming and Montana.[11]

Patrolling in Wyoming and Nebraska passed uneventfully. No major parties of hostiles were encountered, although there were some minor skirmishes. The promotion of Wesley Merritt as colonel of the regiment on July 1 caused some stir among the men, but the news received on July 6 of Custer's defeat at the Little Bighorn was a matter of far greater consequence. Orders came directing the Fifth to General Crook's command on Goose Creek, near present-day Sheridan, Wyoming, but before they could be followed, a dispatch arrived on July 13 announcing that 800 potentially hostile Cheyennes had left the Red Cloud Agency for the northern camps. Merritt wasted no time backtracking to intercept the departing Indians, and after a forced march of 85 miles in 31 hours, he threw seven companies of the Fifth Cavalry in front of the Cheyennes at Warbonnet Creek, Nebraska.[12]

The fight on the Warbonnet was no more than a dawn skirmish between advance warriors from the Cheyenne village and several Fifth Cavalry companies; however, it had all the elements of frontier adventure that King later celebrated in his novels. It was here that seven companies of the regiment hid behind the cutbanks of the creek to surprise the advancing Indians. King alone was in a spotting position, crouched behind a hill waiting to unleash the fury of the cavalrymen. When the brief fight began, Buffalo Bill killed and scalped Yellow Hair, a Cheyenne warrior, proclaiming it the "first scalp for Custer."

Later both Cody and King made much of this little fight on the Warbonnet—Cody in his dramatic reenactments of the "duel" with Yellow Hair performed on stage and in his Wild West shows; King in countless versions of the skirmish penned for newspapers, magazines, and books—and in reality it was an episode worthy of acclaim. A sizable body of Indians had been prevented, at least temporarily, from joining the hostile camps in the north. Furthermore, the fight provided a significant psychological boost to the army after half a year of public criticism for their inability to handle the Sioux and Cheyennes. In King's estimation, it was "probably the one brilliant episode of the campaign."[13]

After Warbonnet, Merritt's command refitted at Fort Laramie and marched north to find Crook. Following his fight at Rosebud Creek, Montana, Crook had retired into Wyoming and established a base called Camp Cloud Peak, where he waited until August 3 for the Fifth Cavalry to join him. Then, with a burgeoning command numbering nearly 2,000, he set out after the Sioux. The hostiles by this time had broken up the large village that had massed against Custer at the Little Bighorn and had scattered across the plains. Crook headed toward the Black Hills rather than march directly to resupply at Fort Abraham Lincoln, near Bismarck, and when rations ran out, the soldiers resorted to eating horseflesh. Although the scouts found abundant Indian signs, the debilitated condition of the men, made worse by daily rains that turned the prairie to a quagmire, transformed the Black Hills march into a struggle for survival. The anguish of hungry men toiling through mud came to an end on September 13, when a beef herd and supply wagons from Deadwood reached Crook's command. "Discipline for a moment was forgotten," King recorded. "Men fought like tigers for crackers and plugs of tobacco," until officers restored order. "I know that three gingersnaps I picked up from the mud under the horses feet and shared with Colonel Mason and Captain Woodson—the first bite of bread we had tasted in three days—were the sweetest morsels we had tasted in years."[14]

Although the Fifth Cavalry's participation in the Great Sioux War was not over, the regiment's arrival in the Black Hills was about the end of it for Charles King. One last assignment came from General Crook, who asked him to prepare a map showing each day's march, the location of each fight, and other important details from the campaign. Crook knew of King's habit of keeping a daily diary and rough topographical notes. The request was received on October 24; King labored through the night, finishing the map just in time for Crook's departure early on October 25.[15]

The headquarters and several companies of the Fifth, including Company K, took up new garrison duties at Fort D. A. Russell, near Cheyenne. On October 5, King was formally appointed adjutant of the Fifth Cavalry, an assignment he had performed in an acting capacity through much of the summer.[16] He reveled in the responsibilities of the position. He had charge of the regiment's books, and he was keenly suited to tackle the army's endless paperwork—much of which was in arrears, as the regiment had been in the field for nearly six months.

As adjutant, King was in the thick of regimental business, and the unit seemed always on the move throughout 1877 and 1878. In late spring of 1877, five companies were sent to northern Wyoming and Montana to perform a reconnaissance of the 1876 battlefields and to guide Lieutenant General Philip H. Sheridan to the scene of the Custer fight and the Yellowstone River. In midsummer, Merritt, Carr, and King as acting assistant adjutant general were dispatched with five other companies on the Union Pacific Railroad to Omaha and Chicago to suppress labor riots in those cities. When they returned in August, they were immediately ordered northward to Fort Washakie, Wyoming, to organize a campaign against the Nez Perces, then in the midst of the flight to Canada. The Wind River expedition, as it was called, materialized with an impressive force made up of headquarters and 11 companies of the Fifth and one company of the Third Cavalry. But by the time they reached northwestern Wyoming, the Nez Perces had slipped through Yellowstone National Park and were back in Montana. King described the Fifth's participation in the Nez Perce War as a joyous outing which, in contrast to the 1876 campaign, was marked by abundant supplies, gorgeous weather, and marches through picturesque and beautiful country. [17]

For King himself, however, the pleasures of the Nez Perce campaign were tarnished by the torment from his old Apache wound. He later recalled how he had gone through the campaigns of 1876 and 1877 with his arm open and suppurating, and at one point he was particularly annoyed by a scrap of bone that projected so far as to catch in the sleeve of his undershirt; he finally extracted it with his teeth. [18] Yet the wound grew progressively worse. Each attending surgeon recorded how the bullet had so badly fractured the arm that there was considerable loss of bone, spotted necrosis, and the open, infected wound. In a letter to the adjutant general, King summarized his plight: "Nearly four years have elapsed, the wound has never healed, twenty pieces of bone have been discharged . . . the pain is constant and sometimes extreme, and I am assured by the surgeon that it will probably never be better." [19]

On January 28, 1878, King was relieved of his duties as regimental adjutant, and in June he requested that he be ordered before a retiring board. Colonel Merritt endorsed the application with a postscript declaring King entirely unfit for active service and urging his retirement in justice to his family. That fall a retiring board convened at Fort Leavenworth, Kansas, with Brigadier General John Pope commanding; after a short deliberation, it recommended that King be placed on the list of retired officers for disability from wounds received in the line of duty. [20]

To be official, the findings and recommendations of the retiring board had to be approved by the President. King was granted extended sick leave while he waited. Not coincidentally, he also stood high on the promotion list and received his commission as captain on May 1, 1879, just weeks ahead of the official retirement order. Nevertheless, he was sore at heart over having to leave his regiment and the profession he loved. King moved his family back to Milwaukee. The future was clouded, although an opportunity to get into railway engineering had surfaced in Wisconsin.[21] Another prospect glimmered, too: a chance to write, which seemed to offer acclaim, respect, and the financial security he sought.

What sparked King's interest in the literary field is not altogether clear. He remarked candidly in an interview published in *McClure's Magazine* that it was "circumstances, chiefly. . . . I wasn't long in finding out that keeping a family on retired captain's pay is a beggar's business. I had to go to work, so I took to writing."[22] This is an oversimplification: his first recorded attempt at a story came in the early 1870s while he was on staff duty in Louisiana. There he had written a full-length novel with a Reconstruction background, but it was rejected by the publishing firm of Harper and Brothers in 1873. The real stimulus probably came in 1879 when King returned from the frontier and was struck by the fact that even old friends and schoolmates knew nothing whatever about life in the Indian-fighting army: " 'How on earth do you kill time out there?' was the question, coupled with unflattering suggestions as to whiskey and poker. One night I broke loose and told them, and was astonished when a journalist present urged me to put it in writing for his paper."[23]

King's story of the Great Sioux War of 1876 appeared in Sunday sections of the Milwaukee *Sentinel* beginning in late 1879. The *Sentinel* collected the segments in 1880 and republished them as a pamphlet entitled *Campaigning with Crook: The Fifth Cavalry in the Sioux War of 1876*. The book was favorably received, and the 500 copies printed by the newspaper quickly sold out.[24] At the same time King placed several short stories in *United Service*, a monthly magazine that reviewed American military and naval affairs. Pleased with King's contributions, the editors of *United Service* asked whether he could write a serial for them to be run concurrently with an admiral's man-o'-war tale then in preparation. King promptly penciled two installments of a new story, and these were accepted by the magazine with a call for more. For 16 months, "Winning His Spurs" ran serially in the monthly. As payment, the *United Service* agreed to republish the story in paper binding, with King to receive a percentage of the proceeds. But the story also attracted the attention of the J. B. Lippincott Company, which offered to publish it in hard covers and pay a 10 percent royalty. Retitled *The Colonel's Daughter* (1883), the story was an instant success. With some 16 reprintings, and a German two-volume translation in 1885, it was and remains one of King's most readable fictional efforts.[25]

Spurred on by the good fortunes of "The Daughter," as King called it, Lippincott published *Kitty's Conquest,* his old Reconstruction novel, in 1884. And they asked for more, as did other publishers who sought to capitalize on a new author with a fresh story to tell. Over the next 34 years King's literary outpourings were truly remarkable. For five major publishers, led by Lippincott and Harper, and another half-dozen lesser houses, he produced 66 volumes: 53 works of fiction, four major historical or biographical books, and nine collections of short stories that were either all or in part his own. Two additional novelettes were published serially in magazines and never bound.

King's contribution to periodical literature is harder to assess, since these works are only now being catalogued. By his own conservative estimate, he contributed 250 short stories to *Cosmopolitan, Lippincott's Monthly Magazine,* the *Saturday Evening Post,* the various *Harper's* magazines, many military publications, and dozens of other weeklies and monthlies. Numerous additional articles were published in newspapers, and the frequency of his appearance in such children's publications as the *Youth's Companion* and *Harper's Round Table for Young Folks* attests to a following among the nation's youth, along with a frank realization that writing for children could be lucrative.

Although Captain King was not bound to the medium of fiction, or to stories about the Indian wars, some of his most creditable work was of that genre. "The Daughter" and its sequel *Marion's Faith* (1886) were two delightful stories about the —th Regiment of Cavalry in Arizona and on the northern plains. The —th Cavalry, of course, was King's own Fifth Cavalry, and the settings and events were taken almost directly from the regimental history. Some of the Fifth's officers, thinly veiled, were central characters; King appeared, too, masked as Lieutenant Billings. Dozens of Indian war novels followed with such titles as *Laramie; or, The Queen of Bedlam* (1889), *Captain Blake* (1891), *Foes in Ambush* (1893), and *A Trooper Galahad* (1899). Most were reprinted many times.

King also wrote about West Point and Reconstruction days, as well as ten novels about the Civil War. *The Iron Brigade* (1902) told of the boys from the Old Northwest who earned lasting fame during the "Rebellion." *Between the Lines* (1889) was particularly noted for its description of the cavalry fight at Gettysburg, which was labeled by Lord Wolseley, commander-in-chief of the British Army, the best thing of that kind he had ever read.[26] Perhaps not surprisingly, King also penned seven novels that used the Philippine insurrection for their setting. He has the distinction of being one of the few writers to incorporate that conflict in fiction.

Of King's historical works, *Campaigning with Crook* is the best and is still in print. It is a brilliantly written story of King's regiment in the Great Sioux War of 1876; together with the books written by Lieutenant John G. Bourke, aide-de-camp to General Crook, and reporter John Finerty, it offers complete primary coverage of the campaign after the Custer fight. *Trials of a Staff Officer* (1891) is a nine-episode autobiographical collection spanning King's Sioux War days and his early service with the Wisconsin National Guard. Two entries in particular, "The Adjutant" and "The Ordnance Officer," present glimpses into the trials and tribulations of regular army staff duty that are virtually unique to the literature of the Indian wars. Two other lengthy nonfiction volumes, *Famous and Decisive Battles of the World* (1884) and *The True Ulysses S. Grant* (1914), the latter a biography that also happened to be King's last book, suggest a range of interests broader than the little American army of the late nineteenth century.

The sheer volume of the King periodical stories hints at a wide range of reporting. While his stock piece was army fiction, King penned many nonfiction articles that offered either historical interpretation (as did "Custer's Last Battle" and "In Vindication of General Rufus King") or more straightforward reports ("Summit Springs," "The Leavenworth School," "The Story of a March").[27] At the same time he popularized some of his favorite haunts. Stories about West Point and Milwaukee appeared in several magazines, for instance, as did reports on Chicago and the Twin Cities in Minnesota. King also regularly contributed book reviews and commentary to magazines.

Beyond his own books and articles, many friends and associates asked that he lend his name to their works. W. A. Graham's *Story of the Little Big Horn,* James H. Cook's *Fifty Years on the Old Frontier,* Grace Hebard and E. A. Brininstool's *The Bozeman Trail,* and *The 32nd Division in the World War* each carried an introduction by King. Other volumes—such as Francis T. Miller, *The Photographic History of the Civil War,* and Theophilus F. Rodenbough, *The Army of the United States*—included his essays. Even the popular nineteenth-century army ballad "Forty Miles a Day on Beans and Hay" is known and sung today with an additional verse written by Charles King about fighting the Sioux with General Crook.[28]

King's literary efforts were widely reviewed, and the comments that appeared in magazines and newspapers help explain his enormous popularity among contemporaries. A critic for *Athenaeum* in 1894 wrote: "Capt. King has the happy knack of inspiring confidence in his ability to extricate his heroes and heroines from the appalling network of treachery into which they are beguiled. The reader soon realizes that virtue, as represented by gallant troopers and fair damsels, bears a charmed life, and that villainy, in the persons of Mexicans, Apaches, and deserters, is doomed in the long run to defeat and extinction."[29] Another commentator, writing for *Current Literature,* noted that King "has perhaps done more than any other man in this country to acquaint the public with life in the army. . . .To be sure, the vivid descriptions of scenes connected with the daily experience of the soldier would not be enough to establish a writer's reputation as a novelist, but Gen. King is a gifted story teller, and his works charm the reader as much as the ingenuity of the plot and the thrilling quality of the situation depicted as through the faithful presentation of the detail of military life in which they abound."[30]

The military press frequently commented on King's books, lending yet another perspective. The *Cavalry Journal*, for instance, noted of *The General's Double* (1898) that "the book is not to be read for the plot, as this merely furnishes an excuse for beautiful descriptions of actual occurrences. The word pictures are fascinating, and in many instances exciting."[31] King's name was common in the pages of the *Army and Navy Journal*, a widely read military weekly. Once when an anonymous letter to the editor assailed King's book *Waring's Peril* (1894) as a misrepresentation of social and official army life, the newspaper offered an immediate rebuttal. It explained that dramatic effect is essential to a novel and that the book's principal character, Sam Waring, if not a thorough army gentleman, was a type capable of producing "effective incident." "Capt. King," the *Journal* concluded, "is a born raconteur, and his books always afford entertainment for the passing hour."[32] More typical was a review concluding that "there is a delightful charm in all of Capt. King's books. His pictures of the old army are true, his sketches of characters just . . . his atmosphere is so clear, fresh and wholesome, that we seek not to discover the psychological reasons for the actions of the puppets on the mimic stage. His good people are truly good, and his bad people thoroughly bad."[33]

Interest in King and his work, however, waned in the twentieth century; he was remembered, if at all, as an "old Indian fighter of the Custer era" and scarcely as an author. Critics often categorized his writing as lightweight romantic fluff, material so topical in nature that it could no longer interest a nation with matured literary tastes.[34] Often ignored were more basic values, as acceptable today as they were three generations ago. Fiction carefully utilized, for instance, is recognized as workable primary source material; in King's case, it can tell us much about the army in the 40-year span from the Civil War to the turn of the century.[35] His carefully constructed word pictures, drawn as so many of them were from his diaries and life experience, are true images of a subject he knew well. As Don Russell, King student and author, concluded, "his stories are an exact reproduction of life in frontier army posts and on Indian expeditions. They form a highly valuable contemporary view of an aspect of Western life in a historic period. His books are not art; they are photography."[36]

Charles King, thrust into the civilian world after his retirement from the Fifth Cavalry, could not divorce the military. Although his physical condition precluded a career with the regular establishment, he soon found not one but two full-time positions that provided the satisfaction he needed. This was in addition to the growing demands of his writing career, which saw at its peak three and sometimes four books published each year.

King's first opportunity surfaced in Madison, Wisconsin. The laws of the United States required land grant colleges and universities to provide regular instruction in military science and tactics; since his retirement from the regulars, King had received two requests from western schools to take control of their military science departments. A similar request from Wisconsin's adjutant general that he take over the department at Madison—where the military duties had fallen to an unwilling professor in the department of civil engineering—could not be refused, and in 1880 he again donned the blue uniform of a soldier.

King faced an uphill battle at the university. Students and faculty alike were indifferent to military training; the weapons, accouterments, and uniforms on hand were virtually antiques. The indefatigable captain pushed hard for reform, eventually winning the school over. In May 1881 the university corps was inspected by the governor, his adjutant general, and Colonel John Gibbon of the Seventh U.S. Infantry. Gibbon had replaced Charles's father as the commander of the famed Iron Brigade during the Civil War, and to everyone's pleasure he was greatly impressed with the performance and discipline shown by the students.[37]

In 1881, in addition to his university duties, King began drilling Milwaukee's Light Horse Squadron, and the following spring he left the school to be appointed colonel and aide-de-camp to Wisconsin's governor, Jeremiah M. Rusk, thus beginning a 50-year affiliation with the national guard of his home state. King, always the drillmaster, sought to instill regular army discipline and regulation in the state forces. He insisted too that only authorized regular army tactics be taught in the armories and on the parade fields of Wisconsin. In 1883, King was appointed assistant adjutant general of the guard, and each spring he traveled statewide to make the inspections required by law. During the long winter months he repeated those rounds, spending three or four days with each unit, coaching and drilling. The transformation of the Wisconsin National Guard into a competent military force was long and arduous, yet by the eve of World War I—thanks to King's persistence and the continued support of the adjutant general and others—the War Department announced "that the organized militia of the State of Wisconsin may be taken as a model in training, equipment and basic administration."[38]

In addition to his increasing national guard responsibilities, King was induced in 1884 to join the faculty of the newly established St. John's Military Academy at Delafield, Wisconsin, as superintendent of the military department. St. John's, an Episcopalian preparatory school located between Milwaukee and Madison, soon acquired King's spit-and-polish stamp and proudly maintained it.[39]

President Benjamin Harrison named Lew Wallace (the Civil War general better known as the author of *Ben Hur*), Charles King, and five others to West Point's Board of Visitors in 1889. These boards were convened at the academy each June to attend the annual examinations and investigate the discipline, courses of instruction, and general administration at the military school, and then to make detailed reports to the President and Congress.[40] Several of the students and faculty who were at West Point at the time of King's extended visit later played important roles in his career. First classmen such as Alvin H. Sydenham and Charles D. Rhodes were eventual contributors to a number of King's edited volumes. So too was First Lieutenant John P. Wisser, who was detailed in 1889 to the school's department of chemistry, mineralogy, and geology. First Lieutenant William C. Brown, then the West Point adjutant, in addition to being a faithful correspondent of King's for over 50 years, was active with him in the search for the Warbonnet battle site in the 1920s and on numerous other historical projects.

Back in Wisconsin in 1890, King transferred from staff duty in the guard to line service as colonel commanding the Fourth Infantry, a Milwaukee regiment. In 1892 he was employed as the Commandant of Cadets at the Michigan Military Academy, Orchard Lake, Michigan. In July 1893, in fulfillment of a family promise, he retired from the national guard to take his wife and children abroad.[41]

Again, King's absence from the military did not last long; in 1895, Governor William H. Upham, a West Point classmate, appointed him adjutant general of the Wisconsin National Guard. A new governor came to office two years later, however, and despite the admonishment of the *Army and Navy Journal,* which hoped that the governor-elect of Wisconsin would ''have the good sense to recognize the fact that in Charles King the State has the best Adjutant General known to its history,'' he was not reappointed and again retired on January 4, 1897.[42]

With the outbreak of the Spanish-American War, state troops were mobilized to augment the small standing army. The individual states commissioned the regimental and company officers of their volunteer forces, but President McKinley was to select certain general and staff officers for each of the new divisions. In all, the President and the War Department controlled about 1,000 regular and volunteer commissions, and for these more than 25,000 applications were received, many supported with endorsements from influential politicians and businessmen. King threaded this bureaucratic maze with little difficulty, and his commission came promptly.[43] In late May 1898, with King's appointment virtually assured, his old Indian wars commander, Major General Wesley Merritt, wired the War Department requesting that his former adjutant be assigned to him in San Francisco for service in the Philippine Islands. When asked if that would be agreeable, King telegraphed Washington, ''Glad to serve with General Merritt, Philippines or anywhere.''[44]

In San Francisco, King formally received his commission as a brigadier general of volunteers, and on June 18 he was directed to organize the motley

state regiments arriving on the coast into combat-ready brigades. Across the
Pacific a tenuous alliance existed in the Philippines between the United States
naval forces commanded by Admiral George Dewey and the Filipino insurgents led by General Emilio Aguinaldo. Although the Spanish garrison in Manila was surrounded, the trust between the Americans and the insurgents was fast
diminishing; by the time Merritt arrived with land forces, the enemy was as
much Aguinaldo as the Spanish. The Battle of Manila on August 13 ended
Spanish resistance on the islands while King was en route by steamship. But the
dual claims of the Americans and the Filipinos over control of that country were
not yet resolved.[45]

After a two-and-a-half-month stopover in Honolulu, where General King
temporarily commanded the District of Hawaii, he finally reached Manila in
mid-November. He was immediately assigned to command the First Brigade,
First Division of the Eighth Corps, which was distributed along the Pasig River
southeast of Manila. The tension between the Filipino and American camps
came to a head on the evening of February 4, 1899. Sporadic firing began that
night and soon progressed toward King's troops. His orders were simply to
hold his position, but ascertaining particularly strong opposition on his left
flank near the river, he requested of Major General E. S. Otis—who by this
time had replaced Merritt in the islands—that he be allowed to advance and
make a broad sweeping movement in that direction. Otis approved the action,
and at dawn King's brigade of California, Idaho, and Washington volunteers
executed a perfect left-wheel maneuver that inflicted heavy casualties and
drove the Filipinos across the Pasig.[46]

King's action on February 5 was a glowing success. His troops killed 160
and wounded another 70 of the insurgents while suffering casualties of 17 killed
and 79 wounded. More important, his command took prisoners and captured
valuable arms and ammunition, as well as 2,000 bolos, the dreaded Filipino
long knives. King's immediate superior, Major General Thomas M. Anderson,
recommended that he be promoted to the full rank of major general in recognition for the battle, but this endorsement took much the same course as his Indian
wars brevet and was never acted upon.[47]

Sporadic fighting continued for several months, and King's command engaged in frequent skirmishes with the insurgents, but the incessant exposure
and rigors of the field had a telling effect on the 54-year-old officer. A serious
skin infection compounded by an alarmingly debilitated frame convinced army
doctors to urge him to return to the States. Eventually ordered home, King recovered quickly and once more faced the prospect of returning to civilian life.
He did explore, if briefly, the chance of obtaining an appointment to the regular
army, but that failed to materialize. Brigadier General King was honorably discharged from the volunteer forces effective August 2, 1899.[48]

Back in Wisconsin, King again threw himself into literary and local military affairs. His books were fresh with the flavor of the Philippine Islands, and he signed off as "General Charles King" rather than the "Captain" of previous decades. In 1901 he returned to St. John's Military Academy as a professor of military science, and in 1904 he was ordered to active duty with the Wisconsin National Guard in the inspector and instructor roles he knew so well. King's affiliation with historical and military organizations were of growing importance, too. He had long been active in the Military Order of the Loyal Legion, a society of Civil War officers, and he was an Original Companion in the Order of Indian Wars of the United States, a fraternity of frontier army officers. There were other groups as well, but he seemed particularly fond of these two: he was a contributor to the Loyal Legion's publications; in the Order of Indian Wars he was the group's historian in 1908–9 and senior vice-commander in 1921.

In 1913, King traveled to the Pine Ridge Reservation in southwestern South Dakota to meet an assembly of veteran Indian wars campaigners, including Nelson A. Miles, Frank Baldwin, and William F. Cody. There he observed the reenactment of famous Indian battles being filmed by the W. F. Cody Historical Picture Company, which planned a historical motion picture about the Indian wars, using as many living participants as could be mustered. The army had generously offered the Twelfth U.S. Cavalry to portray Indian fighters; Sioux from the Pine Ridge recreated the original Indian roles. Two of Cody's fights, Summit Springs and Warbonnet, were staged in front of cameras. General Miles acted as technical consultant in the reenactment of the fight at Wounded Knee. King did not participate in any of the filming, but he was credited with writing the film's scenario. That so many actual participants, both Indian and white, could get together was remarkable. Unfortunately, only short clips of this epic survive today, but those remaining pieces form a valuable visual record of people and events of enduring interest.[49]

In 1916, as the nation's attention was being drawn to events in Europe, the War Department invited retired officers to be examined for transfer to the active list. King, then 71 years old, responded promptly with a letter to the adjutant general, indicating his willingness to undergo the necessary examinations. The War Department did not encourage his application, but six days after the United States declared war on Germany on April 6, 1917, King formally tendered his services, offering to go overseas if required or to remain active in training work at home: "I shall accept the service, whatever it be, with all fidelity." The War Department's response was quick and appreciative: "The best service he can render in this emergency will be in Milwaukee where he can be in constant consultation with the Governor and Adjutant General of that State in connection with the increase, instruction and whipping into shape of the forces that may be called from [Wisconsin] to meet the present emergency."[50]

General King's services with the national guard were continuous throughout the war and until the time of his death in 1933. By the mid-1920s, in all deference to a man in his eighties, his duties were more ceremonial than functionary, yet he regularly attended the guard's training maneuvers each summer and served as aide-de-camp to the state's chief executives until the last. In 1931, Governor Philip F. LaFollette honored King with a special citation presented at summer camp. It recognized his 70 years of service, his participation in five wars, and his value as a symbol and inspiration to the state. LaFollette concluded by awarding King the title of "Grand Old Man of the Wisconsin National Guard."[51]

Other activities, too, filled King's last years. He was a voluminous correspondent, working late into the night answering letters from army friends, inquiries on historical matters, and requests from newspapers and West Point for, of all things, obituaries of old army comrades. He continued his duties at Delafield until 1931; one sentimental newspaperman observed King's relentless response to duty: "A never to be forgotten picture is one of the general in his olive drab overcoat, trudging off alone through the snow, bound for St. John's."[52] Although the last of his books was published in 1914, he still produced an occasional short story. And in 1929 his old friend General William Carey Brown convinced him to redraw the War Department map he had first prepared for General Crook in 1876, showing the campaigns and battles against the Sioux and Cheyennes. King added excerpts from his 1876 diary to one of the map's margins before it was reproduced in 1930.

On March 15, 1933, General King stumbled on a rug in his apartment and broke his shoulder. Two days later, on St. Patrick's Day, he died from shock attributed to the injury. He was 89. King was buried with full military honors in Milwaukee on March 20 with Wisconsin's governor in attendance, as well as high-ranking representatives from the army and navy, the Wisconsin National Guard, and St. John's Military Academy.

To Charles King goes the lasting recognition that his was a length of service that has never been equaled. Moreover, to King goes the recognition that he helped fashion America's image of the Old Army and its role, particularly in the American West. He was a keenly literate, observant, and articulate gentleman, who in a certain sense, as one historian perceptively noted, "went to war with a sword in one hand and a pen in the other."[53]

Notes

1. W. C. Brown, "Charles King," *Sixty-Fourth Annual Report of the Association of Graduates of the United States Military Academy at West Point, New York, June 12, 1933* (Newburgh, N.Y.: Moore, 1933), 64–67.

2. Philip Reade, "Captain Charles King," *Lippincott's Monthly Magazine* 42 (De-

cember 1888): 856; Charles King, *Memories of a Busy Life* (Madison: State Historical Society of Wisconsin, 1922), 13–14.

3. King, *Memories*, 11–13; Charles King to W. C. Brown, April 14, 1928, April 24, 1926, William Carey Brown Collection, University of Colorado, Boulder.

4. King, *Memories*, 16–20.

5. Richard H. Savage, "Orsemus B. Boyd," in *Association of the Graduates of the United States Military Academy, Annual Reunion, June 10, 1886* (East Saginaw, Mich.: Evening News, 1886), 46–49; Mrs. Orsemus B. Boyd, *Cavalry Life in Tent and Field* (Lincoln: University of Nebraska Press, 1982), 8–20.

6. King to Brown, January 28, 1885, Brown Collection; King, *Memories*, 21.

7. Reade, "Captain Charles King," 857; King, *Memories*, 22–23.

8. King, *Memories*, 23, 26.

9. George F. Price, *Across the Continent with the Fifth Cavalry* (New York: Antiquarian Press, 1959), 658–61; Charles King Appointment, Commission, Personal File, July 2, 1890, June 12, 1894, Records of the Adjutant General's Office, Record Group 94, National Archives (hereafter cited as King ACP File); King to Brown, January 29, 1925, Brown Collection.

10. Paul L. Hedren, "Captain Charles King at Sunset Pass," *Journal of Arizona History* 17 (Autumn 1976): 253–59; King ACP File, Exhibit 2, October 18, 1878.

11. Charles King, *Campaigning with Crook and Stories of Army Life* (New York: Harper, 1890), 3–9; William F. Cody, *The Life of Hon. William F. Cody* (Lincoln: University of Nebraska Press, 1978), 340.

12. Paul L. Hedren, *First Scalp for Custer: The Skirmish at Warbonnet Creek, Nebraska, July 17, 1876* (Glendale, Calif.: Arthur H. Clark, 1980), 40–62.

13. Ibid., 63–68; King to the Army War College, February 18, 1929, King Papers, U.S. Army Military History Institute, Carlisle Barracks, Pennsylvania.

14. King, *Campaigning with Crook*, 141. Julius W. Mason and Albert W. Woodson were Fifth Cavalry officers.

15. King to Army War College, February 18, 1929, King Papers; King to Brown, April 15, 1925, Brown Collection.

16. King ACP Files, Exhibit 2, October 18, 1878.

17. Price, *Across the Continent with the Fifth Cavalry*, 167–68; King, *Memories*, 29.

18. King to Brown, March 26, 1930, Brown Collection.

19. King ACP File, Exhibit 11, June 7, 1878.

20. Ibid., and Proceedings of the Retirement Board, November 11, 1878.

21. King ACP File, April 21, 1878, and January 15, 1897; King, *Memories*, 30–31.

22. "Human Documents," *McClure's Magazine* 3 (July 1894): 128.

23. Charles King, "Thirty Years of Pencraft, What It Came To and What It Cost," *Historical Messenger of the Milwaukee County Historical Society* 29 (Spring 1973): 28.

24. Harry H. Anderson, "Some Footnotes to Charles King's 'Campaigning with Crook,'" *Historical Messenger of the Milwaukee County Historical Society* 29 (Spring 1973): 10–16.

25. King, "Thirty Years of Pencraft," 28–30; *The Centennial of the United States Military Academy at West Point, New York*, 2 vols. (Washington: Government Printing Office, 1904), 2:290.

26. Don Russell, Introduction to Charles King, *Campaigning with Crook* (Norman: University of Oklahoma Press, 1964), xi.

27. Charles King, "Custer's Last Battle," *Harper's New Monthly Magazine* 81 (August 1890): 378–87; Charles King, "In Vindication of General Rufus King," *Century Magazine* 31 (April 1886): 935; Charles King, "Summit Springs," Denver *Post*, March 9, 1914; Charles King, "The Leavenworth School," *Harper's New Monthly Magazine* 76 (April 1888): 777–92; Charles King, "The Story of a March," *Journal of the United States Cavalry Association* 3 (June 1890): 121–29.

28. Paul L. Hedren, "Eben Swift's Army Service on the Plains, 1876–1879," *Annals of Wyoming* 50 (Spring 1978): 145–46. There exist several bibliographies of King's varied works. A useful book reference is Charles E. Dornbusch, *Charles King, American Army Novelist* (Cornwallville, N.Y.: Hope Farm Press, 1963), which lists all of King's titles and many variant editions. Soon to replace this is a comprehensive King book catalogue now being researched by Louis A. Hieb, University of Arizona. Paul L. Hedren, *King on Custer: An Annotated Bibliography* (College Station, Tex.: Brazos Corral of the Westerners, 1982), lists 30 items. Hedren has also compiled in typescript a "Preliminary Bibliography of Books and Other Materials with Contributions by General Charles King, but Not Outrightly Carrying a King By-Line" (Brigham City, Utah, 1982).

29. Review of *Foes in Ambush* in *Athenaeum*, March 3, 1894, p. 276.

30. *Current Literature*, August 1900, p. 150.

31. *Journal of the U.S. Cavalry Association* 9 (March 1898): 245.

32. *Army and Navy Journal*, March 25, 1893, p. 515.

33. Ibid., December 12, 1896, p. 255.

34. S. J. Sackett, "Captain Charles King, U.S.A.," *Midwest Quarterly* 3 (October 1961): 71–80.

35. Gordon Chappell, "Use of Fiction as a Historical Source," *Cultural Resources Management Bulletin* 2 (June 1979): 3–4; Oliver Knight, *Life and Manners in the Frontier Army* (Norman: University of Oklahoma Press, 1978); Harry H. Anderson, "Home and Family as Sources of Charles King's Fiction," *Historical Messenger of the Milwaukee County Historical Society* 31 (Summer 1975): 50–68.

36. Don Russell, "Captain Charles King, Chronicler of the Frontier," *Westerners* (Chicago) *Brand Book* 9 (March 1952): 1.

37. King, *Memories*, 30–38.

38. Ibid., 41–44; King ACP File, January 15, 1897; Jerry M. Cooper, "The Wisconsin National Guard in the Milwaukee Riots of 1886," *Wisconsin Magazine of History* 55 (Autumn 1971): 32.

39. *Old Boy's Alumni Association Newsletter* (Delafield, Wis.: St. John's Military Academy, n.d.), 1–2.

40. *Report of the Board of Visitors to the United States Military Academy, Made to the Secretary of War, for the Year 1889* (Washington, D.C.: Government Printing Office, 1889).

41. King ACP File, January 15, 1897; King, *Memories*, 49.

42. King ACP File, January 15, 1897; *Army and Navy Journal*, December 12, 1896, p. 258.

43. Graham A. Cosmos, *An Army for Empire: The United States Army in the Span-

ish-American War (Columbia: University of Missouri Press, 1971), 148.

44. King ACP File, May 28, 1898.

45. Maurice Matloff, ed., *American Military History* (Washington, D.C.: Office of the Chief of Military History, 1969), 335–37; David F. Trask, *The War with Spain in 1898* (New York: Macmillan, 1981), 369–422.

46. King, *Memories,* 61, 64, 72–77; Matloff, *American Military History,* 337.

47. King, *Memories,* 77–78, 82, 84.

48. Ibid., 78, 80–81; King ACP File, Special Orders no. 129, June 3, 1899.

49. Harry H. Anderson, "General Charles King and Buffalo Bill's Silent Western Movies," *Historical Messenger of the Milwaukee County Historical Society* 22 (September 1966): 93–98; Kevin Brownlow, *The War, The West, and the Wilderness* (New York: Knopf, 1979), 224–29. The Buffalo Bill Historical Center in Cody, Wyoming, preserves a collection of clips from this film.

50. King ACP File, January 20, 1916, April 12, 15, 1917.

51. Citation dated July 19, 1931, General Charles King File, Office of the Adjutant General, State of Wisconsin, Madison.

52. Unidentified newspaper clipping, Dr. H. J. McGinnis Notebooks, Waupaca, Wisconsin.

53. James T. King, review of *Campaigning with Crook* by Charles King, *Wisconsin Magazine of History* 47 (Summer 1964): 352.

The Contributors

Robert C. Carriker is a professor of history at Gonzaga University, Spokane, Washington. His publications include *Fort Supply, Indian Territory: Frontier Outpost on the Plains* (1970), *Kalispel People* (1973), and an edition, *An Army Wife on the Frontier: The Memoirs of Alice Baldwin,* (1975). Among his numerous articles are two on the scouting detachment in the Red River War led by Frank D. Baldwin.

Richmond L. Clow received his doctorate in history from the University of New Mexico in 1977 and now teaches in the Native American Studies Program at the University of Montana, Missoula. He has published articles on the history of the Sioux Indians, and a monograph on gold milling technologies in the Black Hills of South Dakota.

Bruce J. Dinges received his doctorate in 1978 at Rice University, where he worked with Frank E. Vandiver. He has published articles on the military history of the frontier and on the Civil War. He is editor of the *Journal of Arizona History* and director of publications for the Arizona Historical Society.

Brian W. Dippie is a professor of history at the University of Victoria, British Columbia. Among his publications are *Custer's Last Stand: The Anatomy of an American Myth* (1976), *Nomad: George A. Custer in Turf, Field and Farm,* an edition (1980), *Remington and Russell* (1982), and *The Vanishing American: White Attitudes and U.S. Indian Policy* (1982).

Arrell Morgan Gibson is George Lynn Cross Research Professor at the University of Oklahoma and the author of 23 books and 150 articles on frontier and Indian history. His latest books are *The American Indian: Prehistory to the Present* (1980) and *The Santa Fe and Taos Colonies: Age of the Muses, 1900– 1942* (1983).

Jerome A. Greene is a research historian with the National Park Service. Among his many publications dealing with the military frontier are *Evidence and the Custer Enigma* (1973) and *Slim Buttes, 1876: An Episode of the Great Sioux War* (1982). He is currently writing an account of Nelson Miles's 1877 campaign during the Great Sioux War.

Paul L. Hedren is National Park Service superintendent of the Fort Union Trading Post National Historic Site, North Dakota. He is the author of numerous articles and two books, *First Scalp for Custer: The Skirmish at Warbonnet Creek, Nebraska, July 17, 1876* (1980) and *With Crook in the Black Hills: Stanley J. Morrow's 1876 Photographic Legacy* (1985), and has recently completed a history of Fort Laramie during the era of the Great Sioux War.

Paul Andrew Hutton is an associate professor of history at the University of New Mexico and editor of the *New Mexico Historical Review*. He has published several articles in both scholarly and popular magazines, as well as two books, *Phil Sheridan and His Army* (1985) and *Ten Days on the Plains,* an edition (1985). He is currently writing on the Alamo as a symbol in American history.

Marvin E. Kroeker received his doctorate from the University of Oklahoma and is a professor of history at East Central State University, Ada, Oklahoma. He is the author of several articles concerning the military frontier, as well as *Great Plains Command: William B. Hazen in the Frontier West* (1976).

Roger L. Nichols is a professor of history at the University of Arizona. His many publications on Indian and frontier military topics include *General Henry Atkinson* (1965), *Stephen Long and American Scientific Exploration* (1980), and *The American Indian: Past and Present* (1981).

J'Nell L. Pate is a professor of history and government, Tarrant County Junior College, Fort Worth. She has written numerous articles on the Texas–Oklahoma military frontier and was a contributor to *Indian Leaders: Oklahoma's First Statesmen* (1979). She has a book forthcoming on the Fort Worth stockyards.

Joseph C. Porter is curator of Western American History and Ethnology at the Joslyn Art Museum, Omaha. He received his doctorate in history from the University of Texas in 1980 and is the author of several articles and a book, *Paper Medicine Man: John Gregory Bourke and His American West* (1986).

Jerome O. Steffen is an associate professor of history at the University of Oklahoma. His books include *William Clark: Jeffersonian Man on the Frontier* (1977) and *Comparative Frontiers: A Proposal for Studying the American West* (1980).

Robert M. Utley, former chief historian of the National Park Service, is the dean of frontier military historians. Among his numerous publications are *The Last Days of the Sioux Nation* (1963), *Frontiersmen in Blue: The United States Army and the Indian, 1848–1865* (1967), *Frontier Regulars: The United States Army and the Indian, 1866–1891* (1973), and *The Indian Frontier of the American West, 1846–1890* (1984). He is currently writing a history of New Mexico's Lincoln County War.

Index